American Vampire

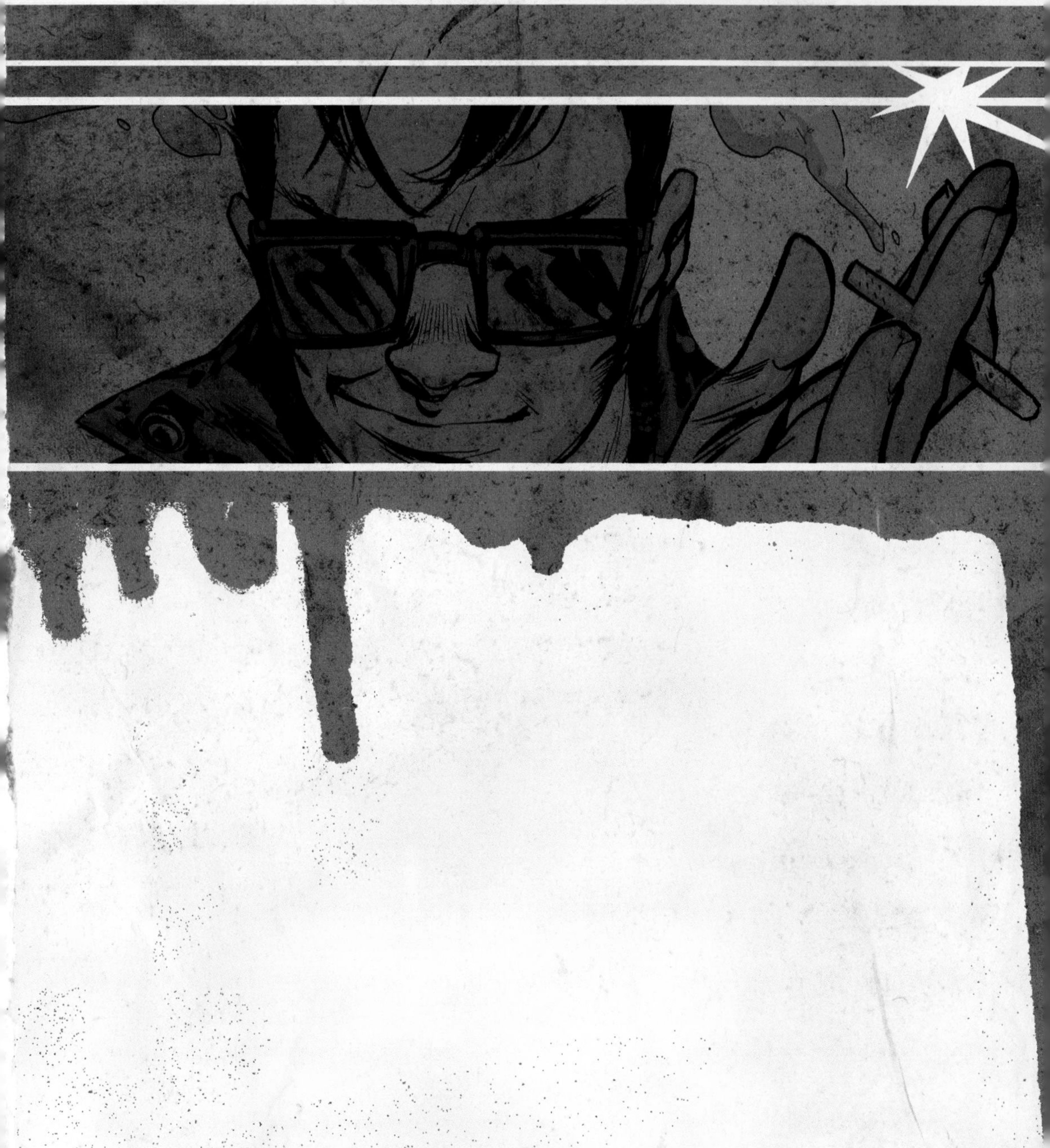

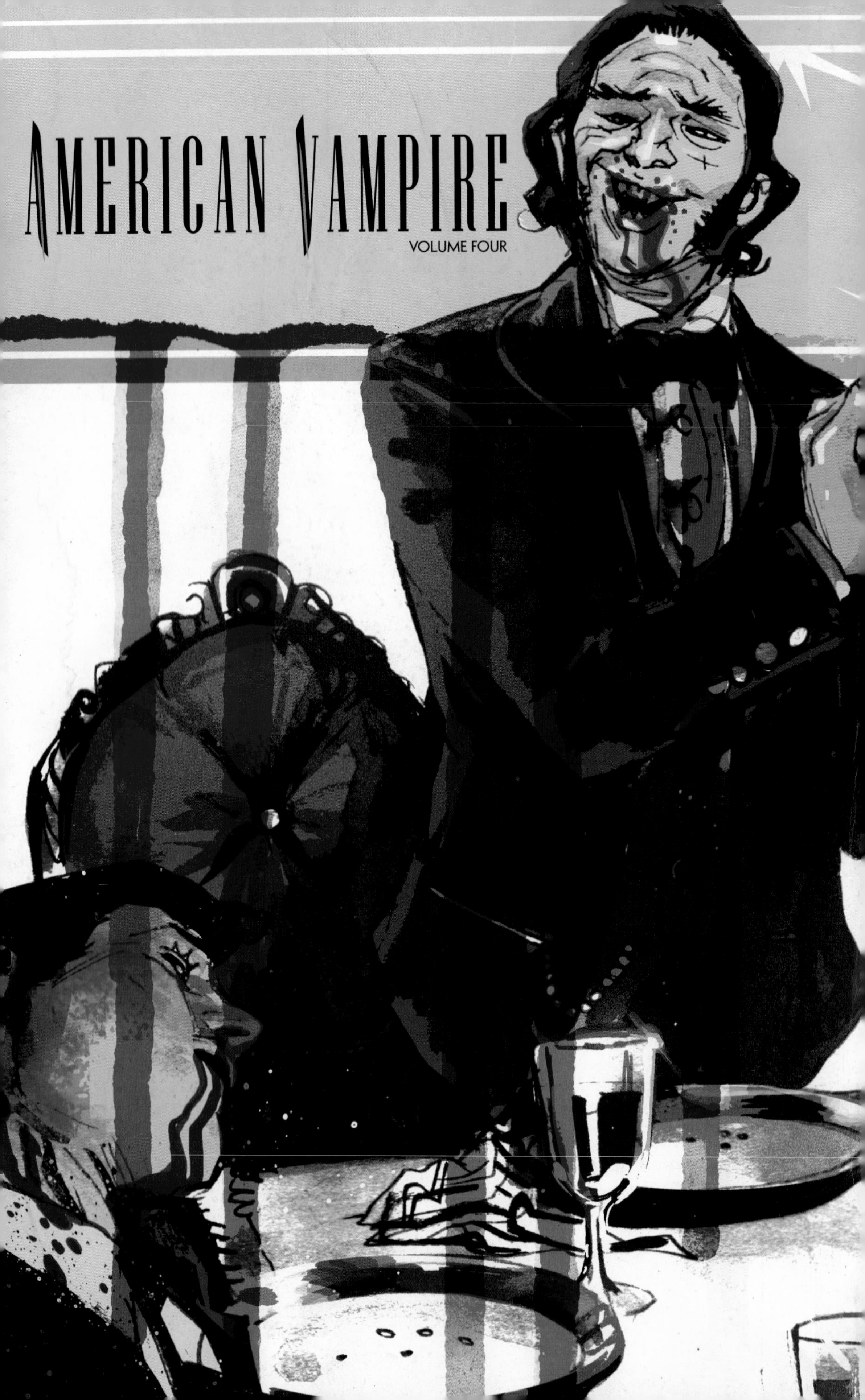
AMERICAN VAMPIRE
VOLUME FOUR

Scott Snyder Writer

Rafael Albuquerque Jordi Bernet

Roger Cruz Riccardo Burchielli Artists Dave McCaig Colorist

Jared K. Fletcher Pat Brosseau Letterers Rafael Albuquerque Cover Artist

American Vampire created by Scott Snyder and Rafael Albuquerque

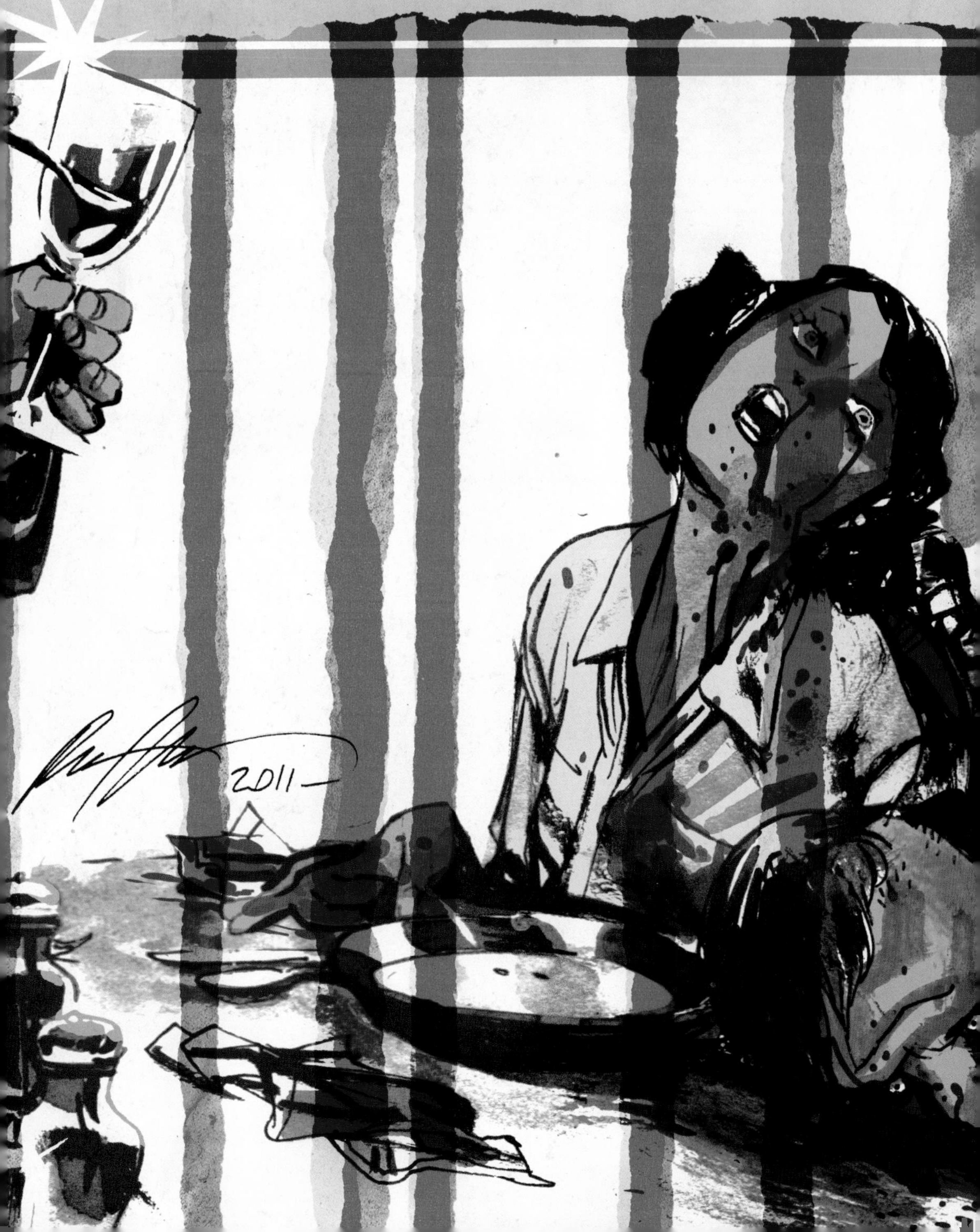
2011

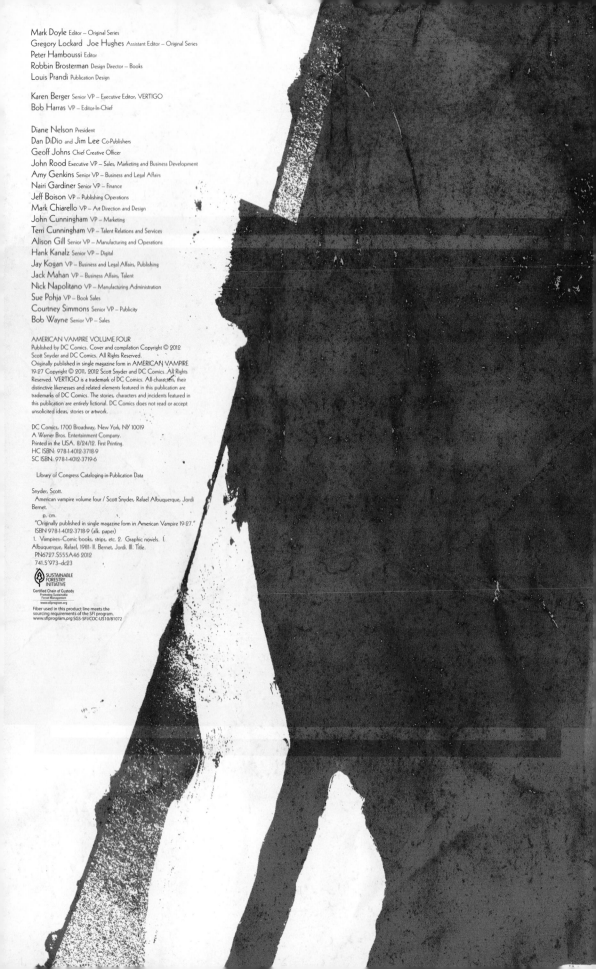

Mark Doyle Editor – Original Series
Gregory Lockard Joe Hughes Assistant Editor – Original Series
Peter Hamboussi Editor
Robbin Brosterman Design Director – Books
Louis Prandi Publication Design

Karen Berger Senior VP – Executive Editor, VERTIGO
Bob Harras VP – Editor-In-Chief

Diane Nelson President
Dan DiDio and Jim Lee Co-Publishers
Geoff Johns Chief Creative Officer
John Rood Executive VP – Sales, Marketing and Business Development
Amy Genkins Senior VP – Business and Legal Affairs
Nairi Gardiner Senior VP – Finance
Jeff Boison VP – Publishing Operations
Mark Chiarello VP – Art Direction and Design
John Cunningham VP – Marketing
Terri Cunningham VP – Talent Relations and Services
Alison Gill Senior VP – Manufacturing and Operations
Hank Kanalz Senior VP – Digital
Jay Kogan VP – Business and Legal Affairs, Publishing
Jack Mahan VP – Business Affairs, Talent
Nick Napolitano VP – Manufacturing Administration
Sue Pohja VP – Book Sales
Courtney Simmons Senior VP – Publicity
Bob Wayne Senior VP – Sales

DC Comics, 1700 Broadway, New York, NY 10019
A Warner Bros. Entertainment Company.
Printed in the USA. 8/24/12. First Printing.
HC ISBN: 978-1-4012-3718-9
SC ISBN: 978-1-4012-3719-6

Library of Congress Cataloging-in-Publication Data

Snyder, Scott.
American vampire volume four / Scott Snyder, Rafael Albuquerque, Jordi Bernet.
p. cm.
"Originally published in single magazine form in American Vampire 19-27."
ISBN 978-1-4012-3718-9 (alk. paper)
1. Vampires--Comic books, strips, etc. 2. Graphic novels. I. Albuquerque, Rafael, 1981- II. Bernet, Jordi. III. Title.
PN6727.S555A46 2012
741.5'973--dc23

SUSTAINABLE FORESTRY INITIATIVE
Certified Chain of Custody
Promoting Sustainable Forest Management
www.sfiprogram.org
Fiber used in this product line meets the sourcing requirements of the SFI program.
www.sfiprogram.org SGS-SFI/COC-US10/81072

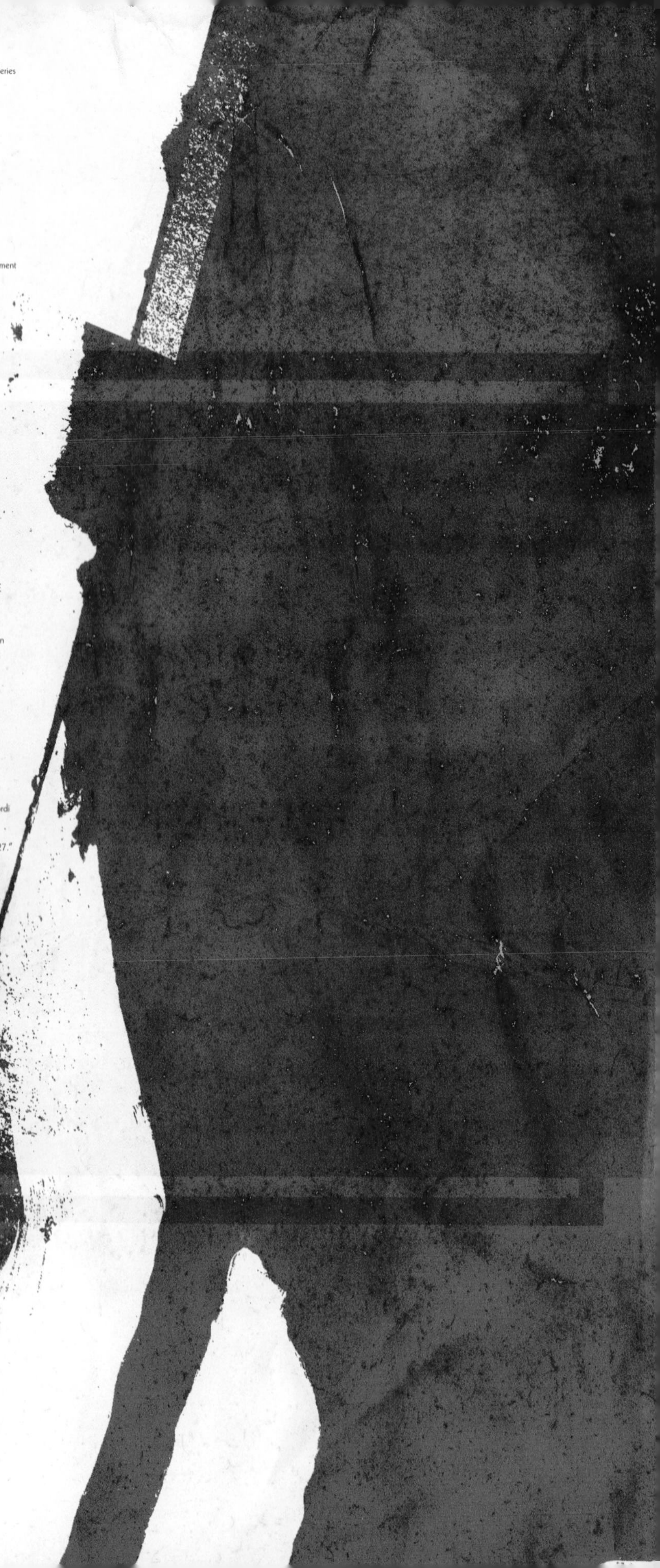

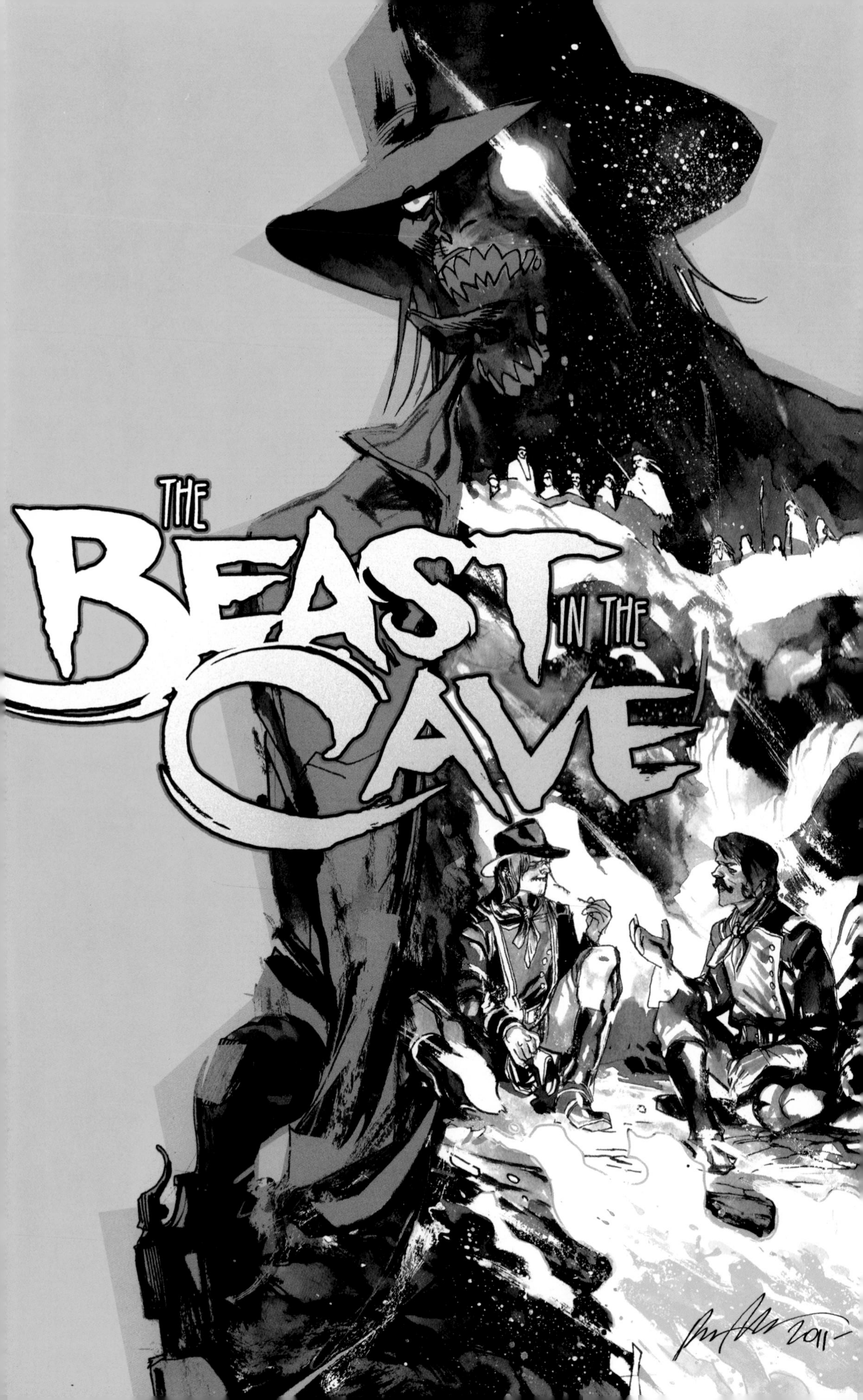
THE
BEAST
IN THE
CAVE
2011

The Beast in the Cave

Jordi Bernet
Artist

Rafael Albuquerque
Covers

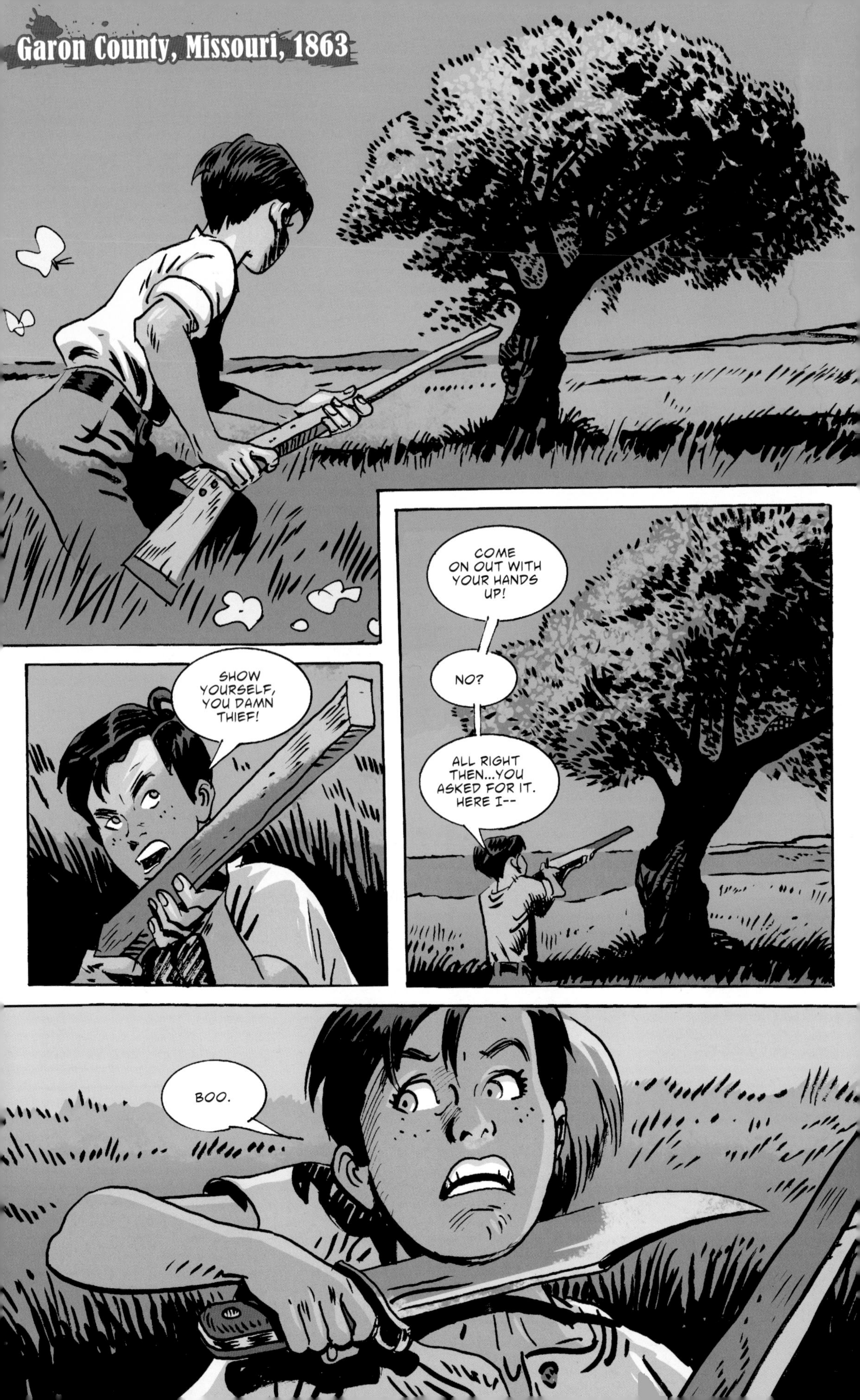
Garon County, Missouri, 1863
SHOW YOURSELF, YOU DAMN THIEF!
COME ON OUT WITH YOUR HANDS UP!
NO?
ALL RIGHT THEN...YOU ASKED FOR IT. HERE I--
BOO.

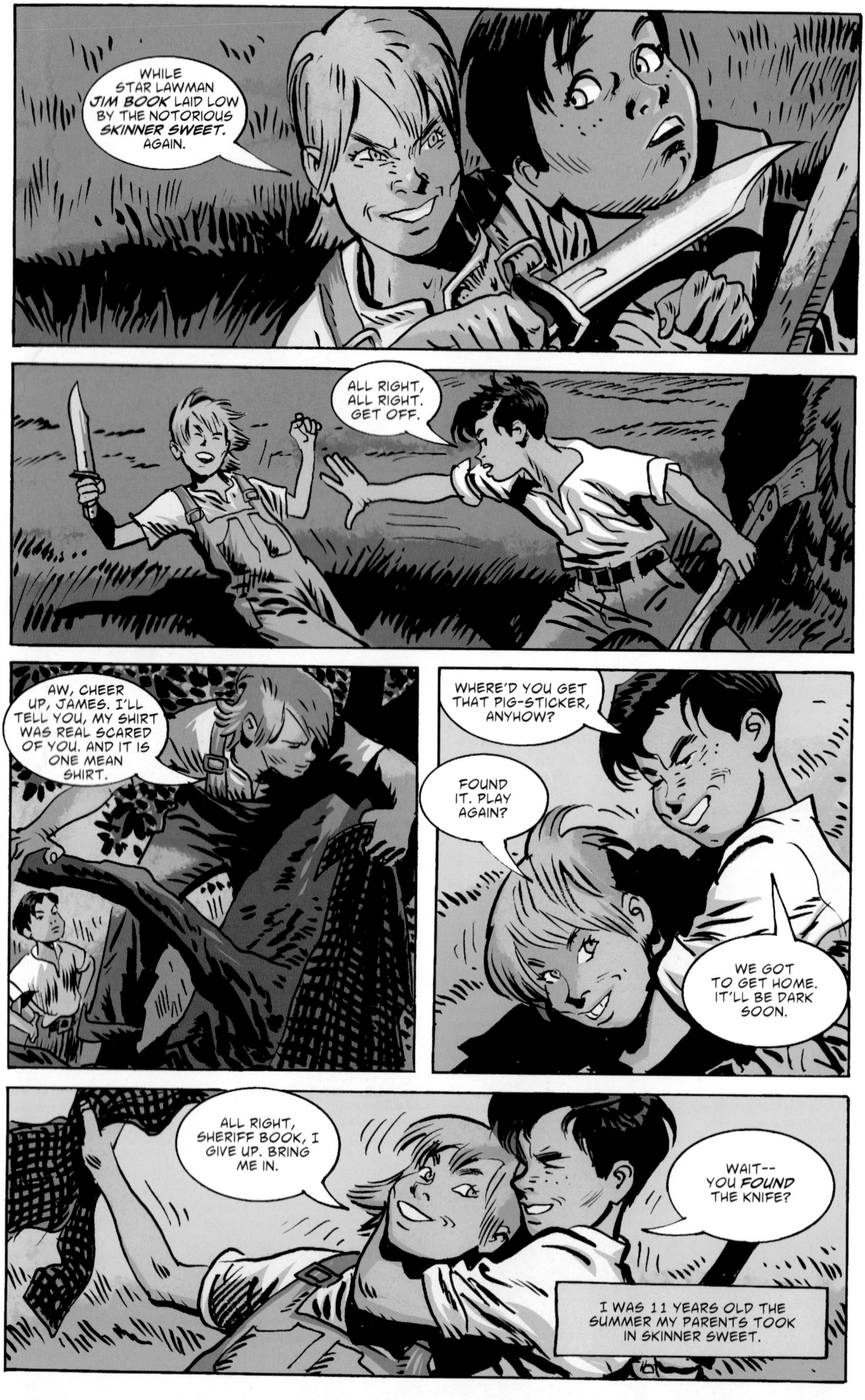

WHILE STAR LAWMAN JIM BOOK LAID LOW BY THE NOTORIOUS SKINNER SWEET. AGAIN.
ALL RIGHT, ALL RIGHT. GET OFF.
AW, CHEER UP, JAMES. I'LL TELL YOU, MY SHIRT WAS REAL SCARED OF YOU. AND IT IS ONE MEAN SHIRT.
WHERE'D YOU GET THAT PIG-STICKER, ANYHOW?
FOUND IT. PLAY AGAIN?
WE GOT TO GET HOME. IT'LL BE DARK SOON.
ALL RIGHT, SHERIFF BOOK, I GIVE UP. BRING ME IN.
WAIT-- YOU FOUND THE KNIFE?
I WAS 11 YEARS OLD THE SUMMER MY PARENTS TOOK IN SKINNER SWEET.

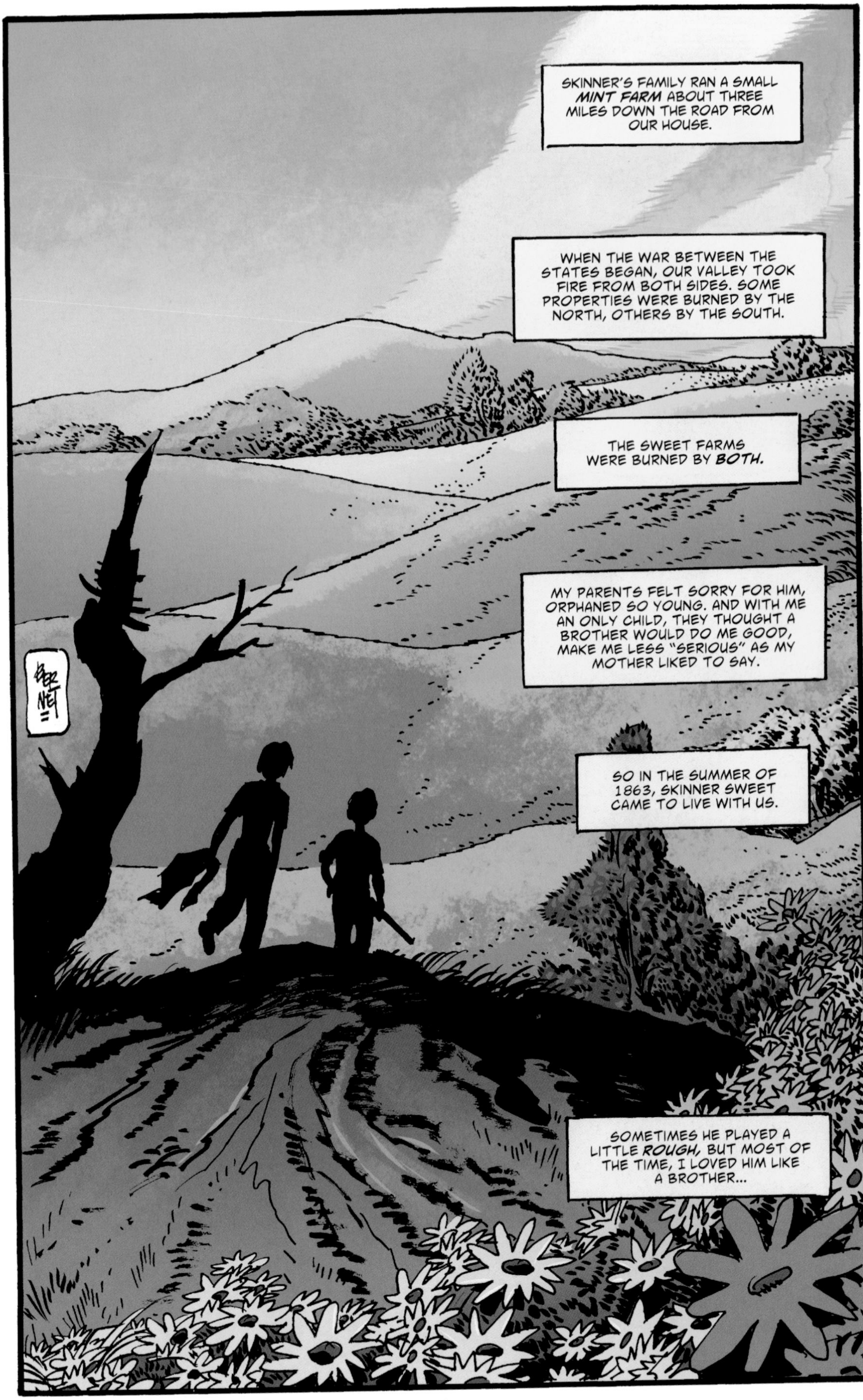
SKINNER'S FAMILY RAN A SMALL *MINT FARM* ABOUT THREE MILES DOWN THE ROAD FROM OUR HOUSE.
WHEN THE WAR BETWEEN THE STATES BEGAN, OUR VALLEY TOOK FIRE FROM BOTH SIDES. SOME PROPERTIES WERE BURNED BY THE NORTH, OTHERS BY THE SOUTH.
THE SWEET FARMS WERE BURNED BY *BOTH.*
MY PARENTS FELT SORRY FOR HIM, ORPHANED SO YOUNG. AND WITH ME AN ONLY CHILD, THEY THOUGHT A BROTHER WOULD DO ME GOOD, MAKE ME LESS "SERIOUS" AS MY MOTHER LIKED TO SAY.
SO IN THE SUMMER OF 1863, SKINNER SWEET CAME TO LIVE WITH US.
SOMETIMES HE PLAYED A LITTLE *ROUGH,* BUT MOST OF THE TIME, I LOVED HIM LIKE A BROTHER...

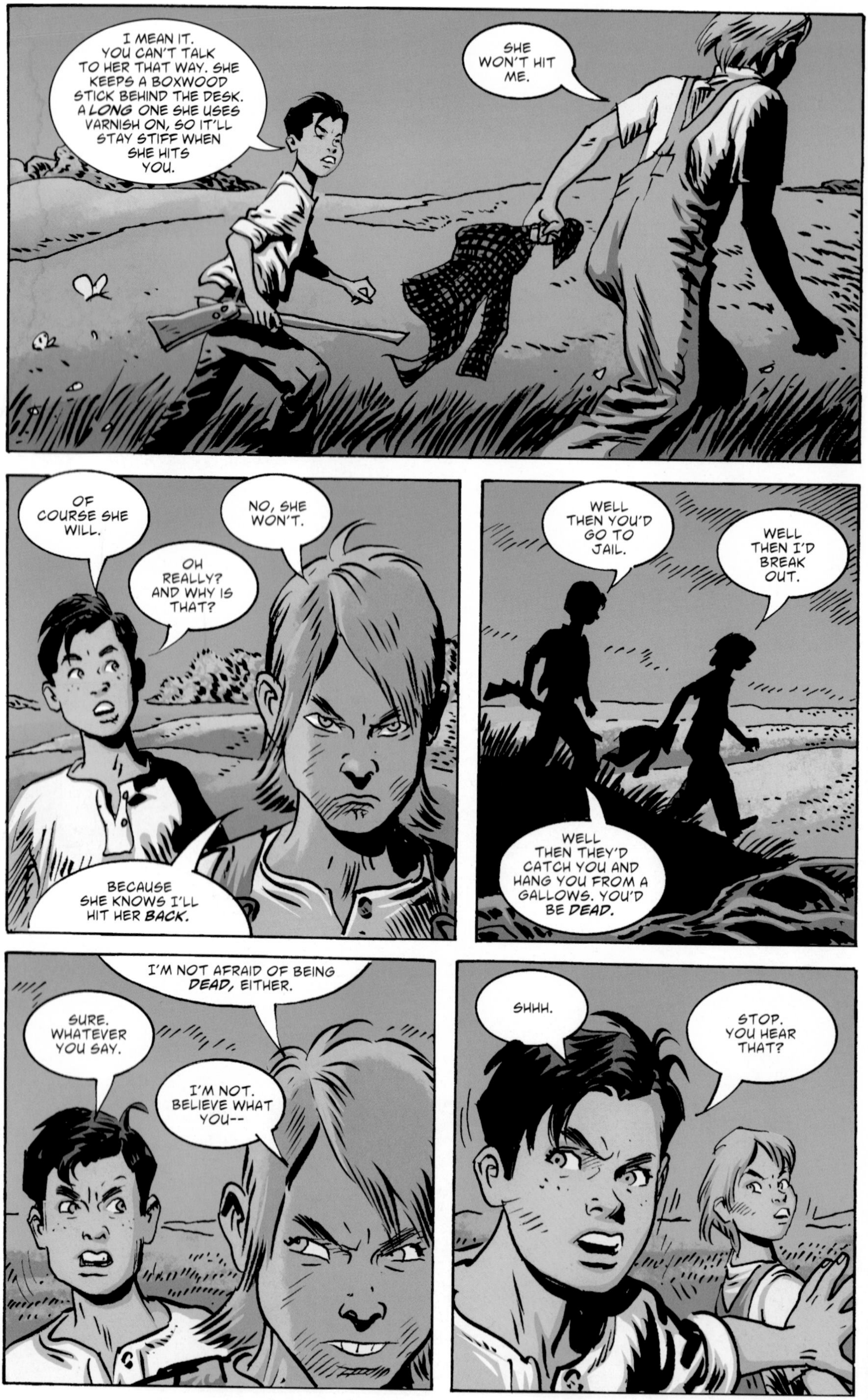
I MEAN IT. YOU CAN'T TALK TO HER THAT WAY. SHE KEEPS A BOXWOOD STICK BEHIND THE DESK. A *LONG* ONE SHE USES VARNISH ON, SO IT'LL STAY STIFF WHEN SHE HITS YOU.
SHE WON'T HIT ME.
OF COURSE SHE WILL.
NO, SHE WON'T.
OH REALLY? AND WHY IS THAT?
BECAUSE SHE KNOWS I'LL HIT HER *BACK.*
WELL THEN YOU'D GO TO JAIL.
WELL THEN I'D BREAK OUT.
WELL THEN THEY'D CATCH YOU AND HANG YOU FROM A GALLOWS. YOU'D BE *DEAD.*
I'M NOT AFRAID OF BEING *DEAD,* EITHER.
SURE. WHATEVER YOU SAY.
I'M NOT. BELIEVE WHAT YOU--
SHHH.
STOP. YOU HEAR THAT?

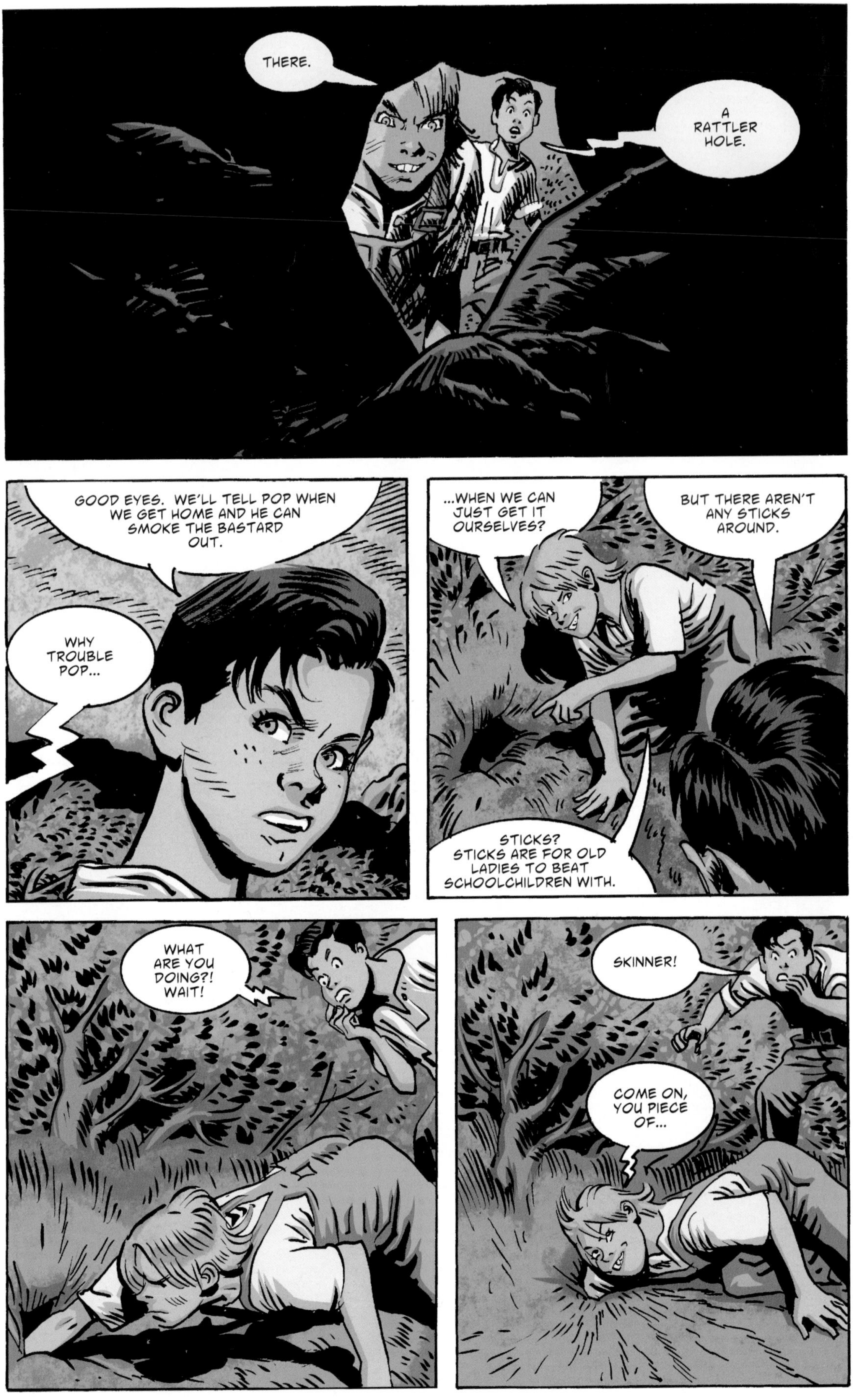
THERE.
A RATTLER HOLE.
GOOD EYES. WE'LL TELL POP WHEN WE GET HOME AND HE CAN SMOKE THE BASTARD OUT.
WHY TROUBLE POP...
...WHEN WE CAN JUST GET IT OURSELVES?
BUT THERE AREN'T ANY STICKS AROUND.
STICKS? STICKS ARE FOR OLD LADIES TO BEAT SCHOOLCHILDREN WITH.
WHAT ARE YOU DOING?! WAIT!
SKINNER!
COME ON, YOU PIECE OF...

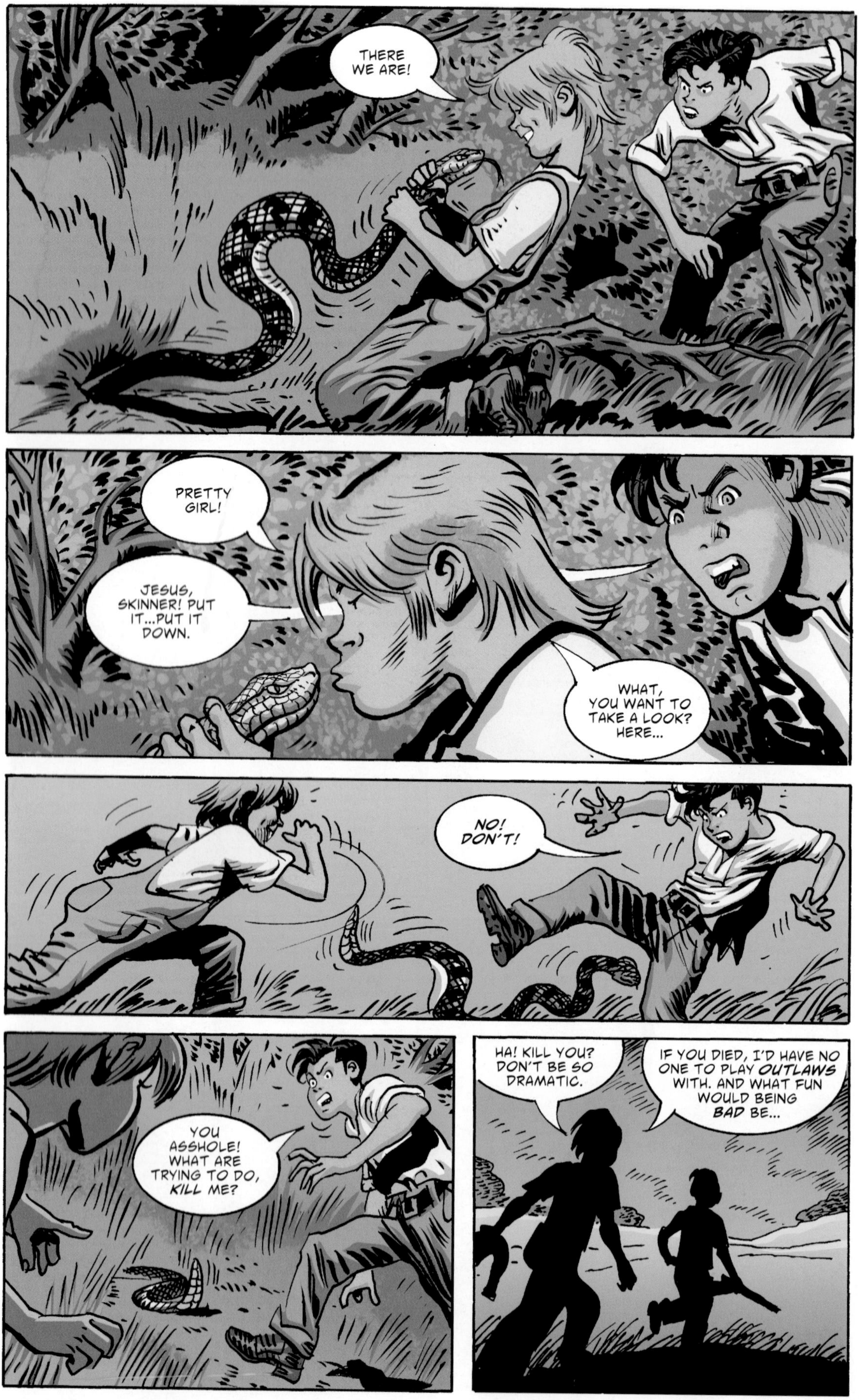
THERE WE ARE!
PRETTY GIRL!
JESUS, SKINNER! PUT IT...PUT IT DOWN.
WHAT, YOU WANT TO TAKE A LOOK? HERE...
NO! DON'T!
YOU ASSHOLE! WHAT ARE TRYING TO DO, KILL ME?
HA! KILL YOU? DON'T BE SO DRAMATIC.
IF YOU DIED, I'D HAVE NO ONE TO PLAY OUTLAWS WITH. AND WHAT FUN WOULD BEING BAD BE...

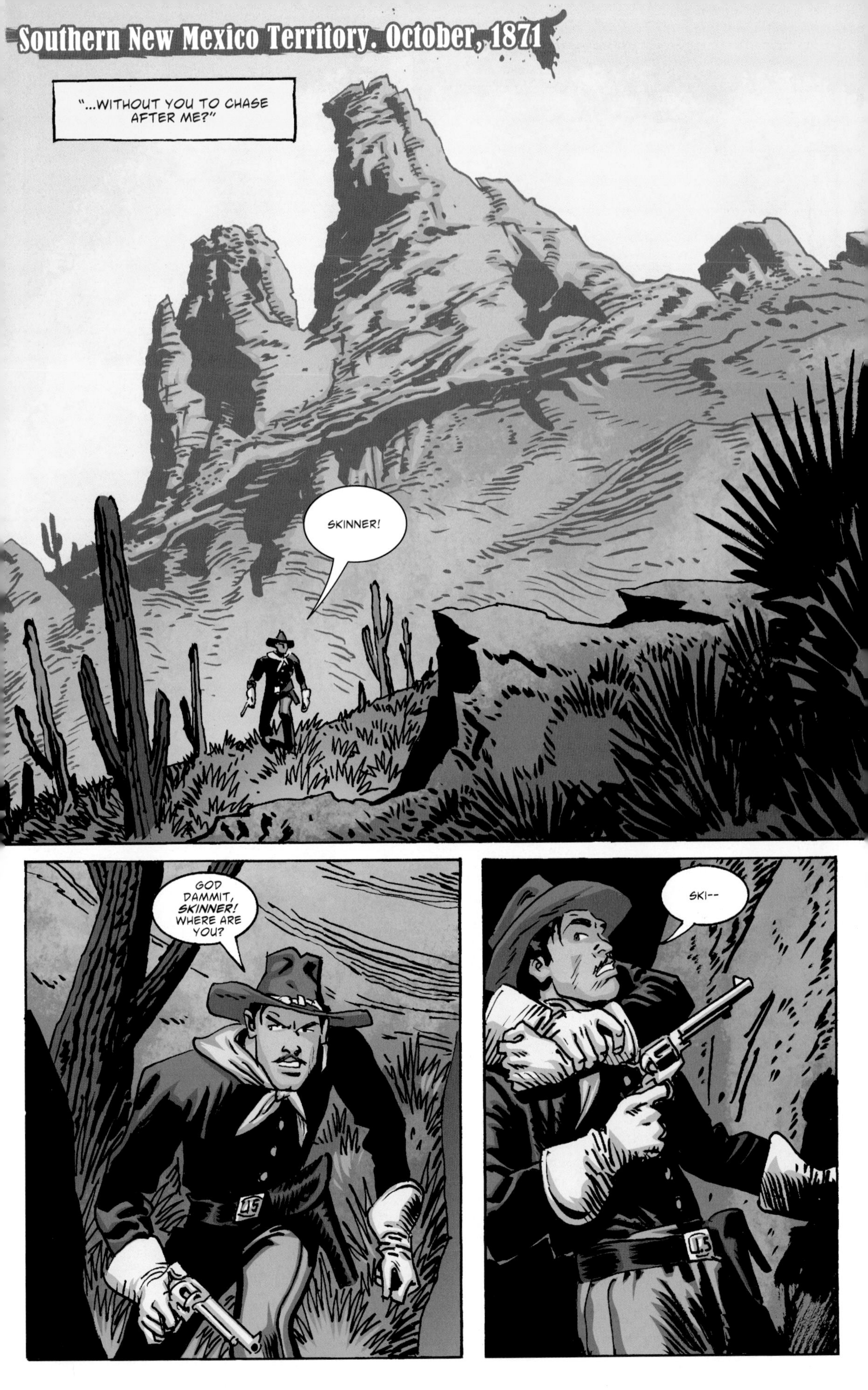
Southern New Mexico Territory. October, 1871
"...WITHOUT YOU TO CHASE AFTER ME?"
SKINNER!
GOD DAMMIT, SKINNER! WHERE ARE YOU?
SKI--

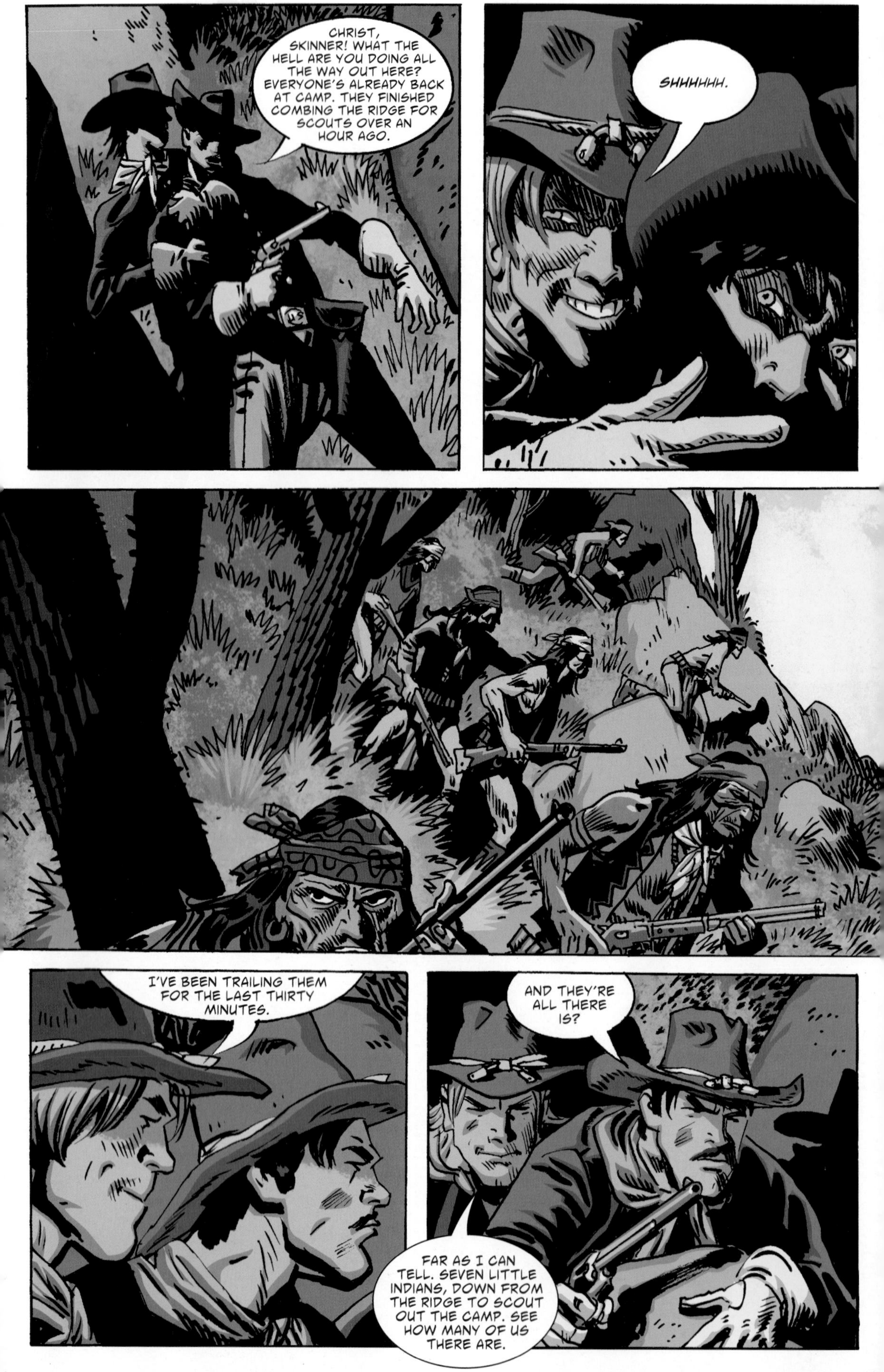
CHRIST, SKINNER! WHAT THE HELL ARE YOU DOING ALL THE WAY OUT HERE? EVERYONE'S ALREADY BACK AT CAMP. THEY FINISHED COMBING THE RIDGE FOR SCOUTS OVER AN HOUR AGO.
SHHHHHH.
I'VE BEEN TRAILING THEM FOR THE LAST THIRTY MINUTES.
AND THEY'RE ALL THERE IS?
FAR AS I CAN TELL. SEVEN LITTLE INDIANS, DOWN FROM THE RIDGE TO SCOUT OUT THE CAMP. SEE HOW MANY OF US THERE ARE.

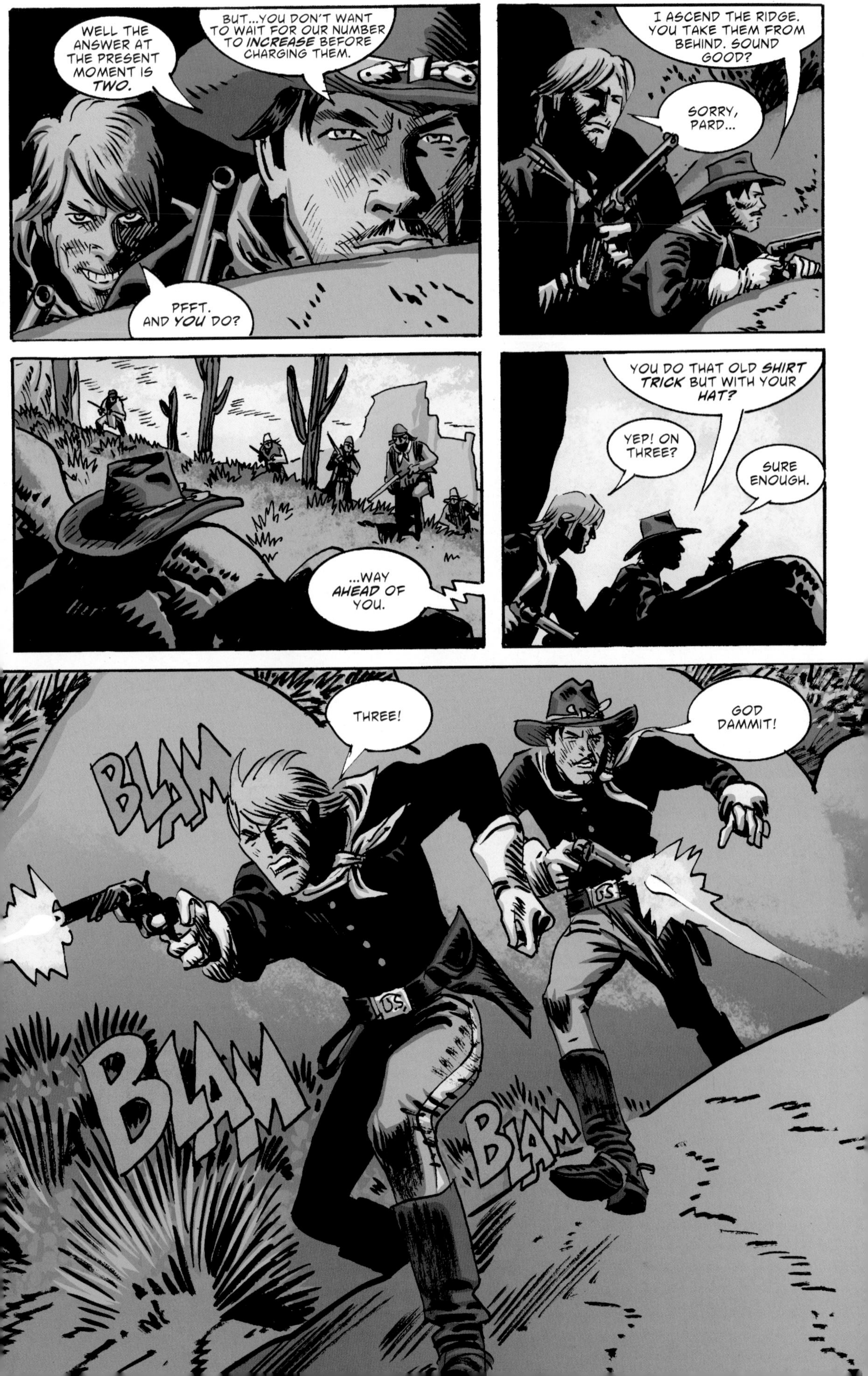
WELL THE ANSWER AT THE PRESENT MOMENT IS TWO.
BUT...YOU DON'T WANT TO WAIT FOR OUR NUMBER TO INCREASE BEFORE CHARGING THEM.
PFFT. AND YOU DO?
I ASCEND THE RIDGE. YOU TAKE THEM FROM BEHIND. SOUND GOOD?
SORRY, PARD...
...WAY AHEAD OF YOU.
YOU DO THAT OLD SHIRT TRICK BUT WITH YOUR HAT?
YEP! ON THREE?
SURE ENOUGH.
THREE!
GOD DAMMIT!
BLAM
BLAM
BLAM

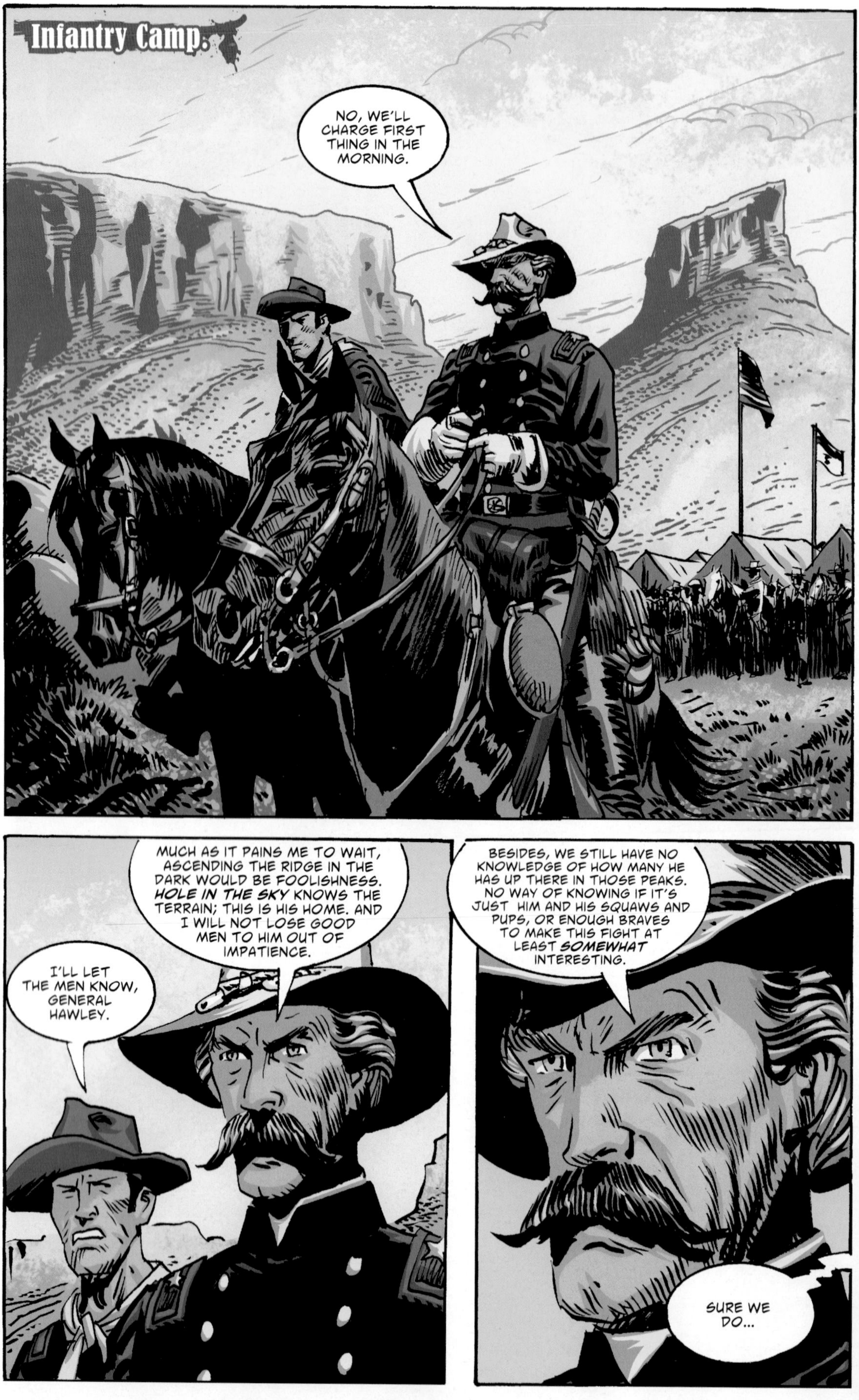
Infantry Camp.
NO, WE'LL CHARGE FIRST THING IN THE MORNING.
MUCH AS IT PAINS ME TO WAIT, ASCENDING THE RIDGE IN THE DARK WOULD BE FOOLISHNESS. HOLE IN THE SKY KNOWS THE TERRAIN; THIS IS HIS HOME. AND I WILL NOT LOSE GOOD MEN TO HIM OUT OF IMPATIENCE.
I'LL LET THE MEN KNOW, GENERAL HAWLEY.
BESIDES, WE STILL HAVE NO KNOWLEDGE OF HOW MANY HE HAS UP THERE IN THOSE PEAKS. NO WAY OF KNOWING IF IT'S JUST HIM AND HIS SQUAWS AND PUPS, OR ENOUGH BRAVES TO MAKE THIS FIGHT AT LEAST SOMEWHAT INTERESTING.
SURE WE DO...

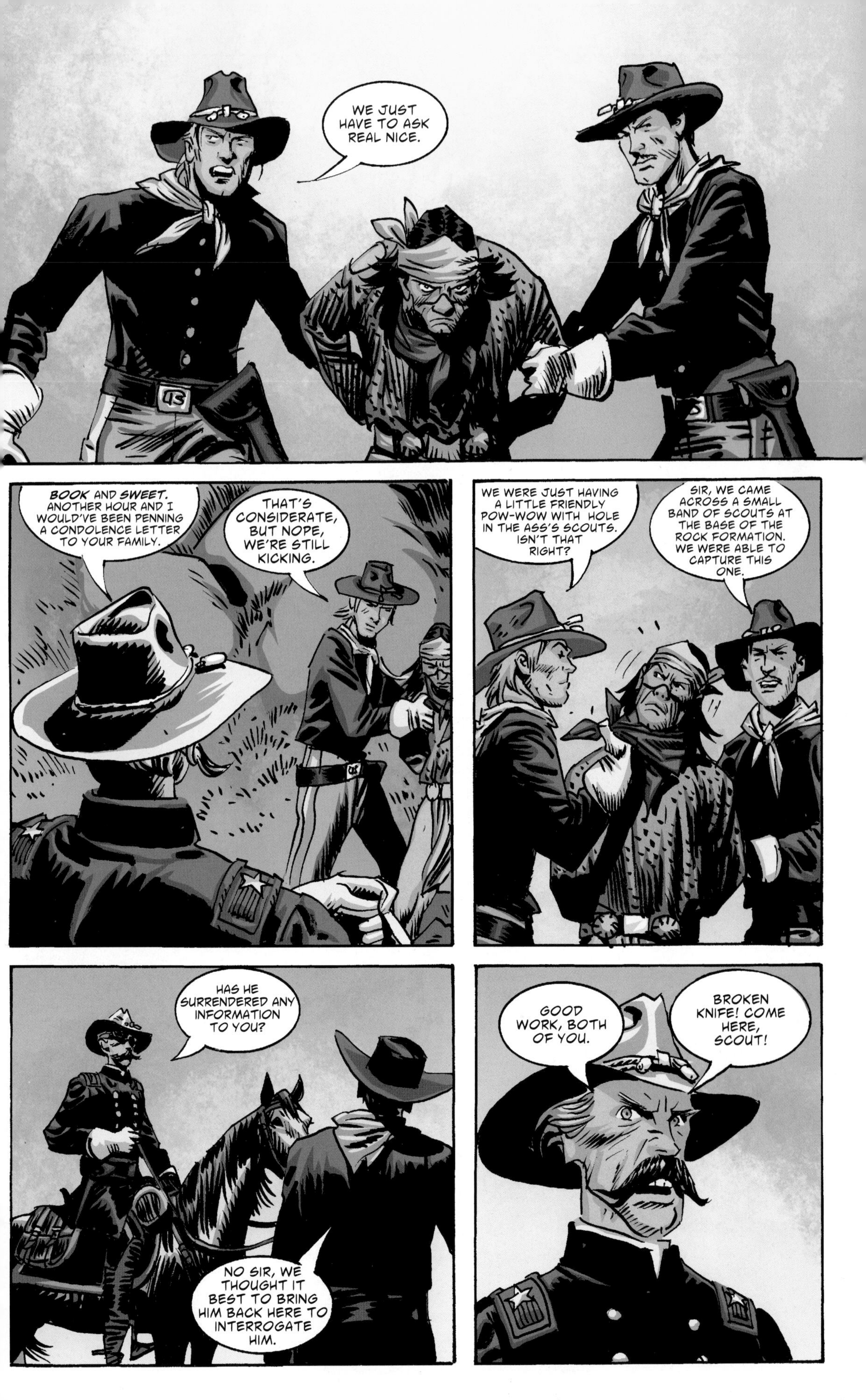
WE JUST HAVE TO ASK REAL NICE.
BOOK AND SWEET. ANOTHER HOUR AND I WOULD'VE BEEN PENNING A CONDOLENCE LETTER TO YOUR FAMILY.
THAT'S CONSIDERATE, BUT NOPE, WE'RE STILL KICKING.
WE WERE JUST HAVING A LITTLE FRIENDLY POW-WOW WITH HOLE IN THE ASS'S SCOUTS. ISN'T THAT RIGHT?
SIR, WE CAME ACROSS A SMALL BAND OF SCOUTS AT THE BASE OF THE ROCK FORMATION. WE WERE ABLE TO CAPTURE THIS ONE.
HAS HE SURRENDERED ANY INFORMATION TO YOU?
NO SIR, WE THOUGHT IT BEST TO BRING HIM BACK HERE TO INTERROGATE HIM.
GOOD WORK, BOTH OF YOU.
BROKEN KNIFE! COME HERE, SCOUT!

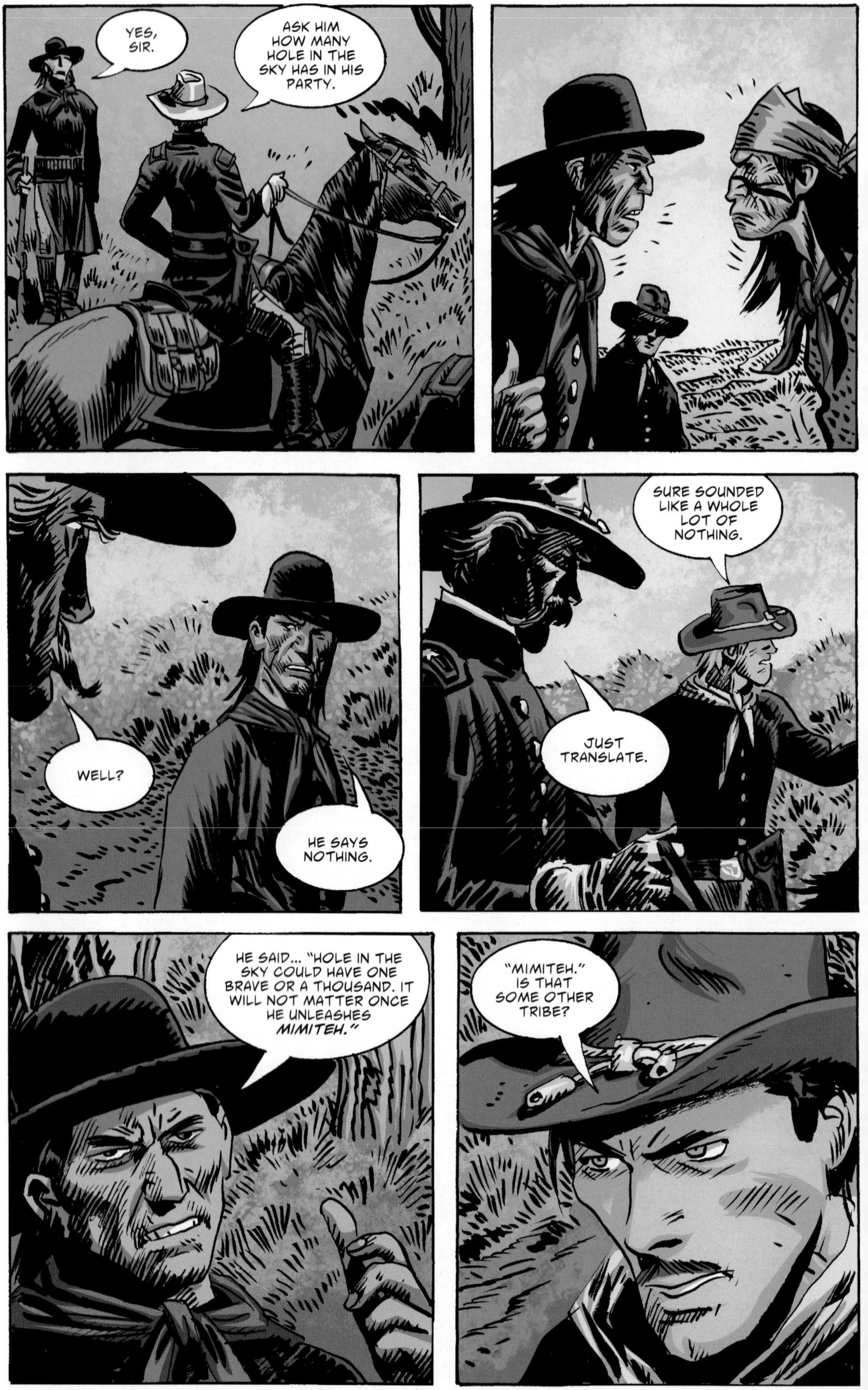
YES, SIR.
ASK HIM HOW MANY HOLE IN THE SKY HAS IN HIS PARTY.
WELL?
HE SAYS NOTHING.
SURE SOUNDED LIKE A WHOLE LOT OF NOTHING.
JUST TRANSLATE.
HE SAID... "HOLE IN THE SKY COULD HAVE ONE BRAVE OR A THOUSAND. IT WILL NOT MATTER ONCE HE UNLEASHES *MIMITEH.*"
"MIMITEH." IS THAT SOME OTHER TRIBE?

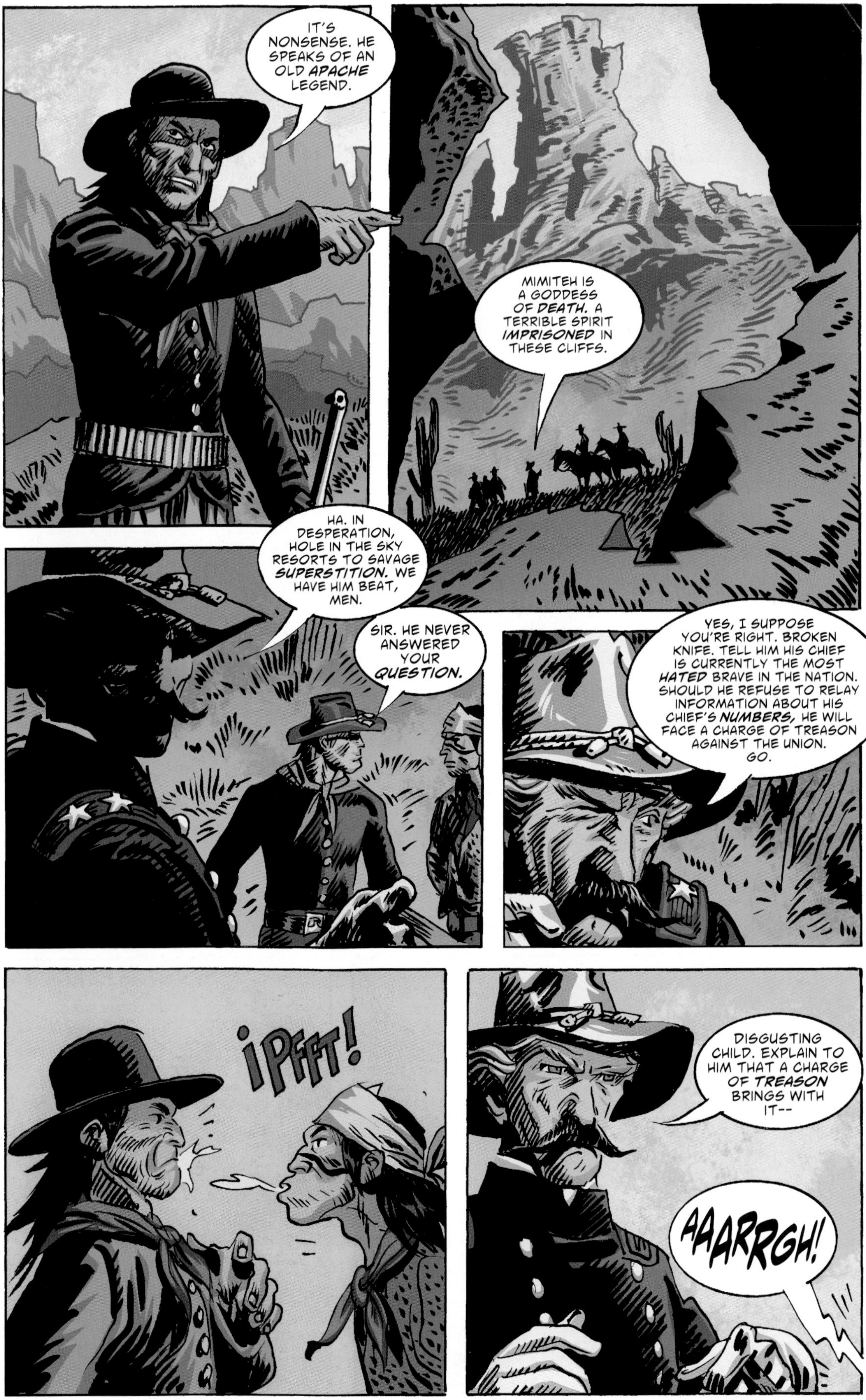
IT'S NONSENSE. HE SPEAKS OF AN OLD APACHE LEGEND.
MIMITEH IS A GODDESS OF DEATH. A TERRIBLE SPIRIT IMPRISONED IN THESE CLIFFS.
HA. IN DESPERATION, HOLE IN THE SKY RESORTS TO SAVAGE SUPERSTITION. WE HAVE HIM BEAT, MEN.
SIR. HE NEVER ANSWERED YOUR QUESTION.
YES, I SUPPOSE YOU'RE RIGHT. BROKEN KNIFE. TELL HIM HIS CHIEF IS CURRENTLY THE MOST HATED BRAVE IN THE NATION. SHOULD HE REFUSE TO RELAY INFORMATION ABOUT HIS CHIEF'S NUMBERS, HE WILL FACE A CHARGE OF TREASON AGAINST THE UNION. GO.
¡PFFT!
DISGUSTING CHILD. EXPLAIN TO HIM THAT A CHARGE OF TREASON BRINGS WITH IT--
AAARRGH!

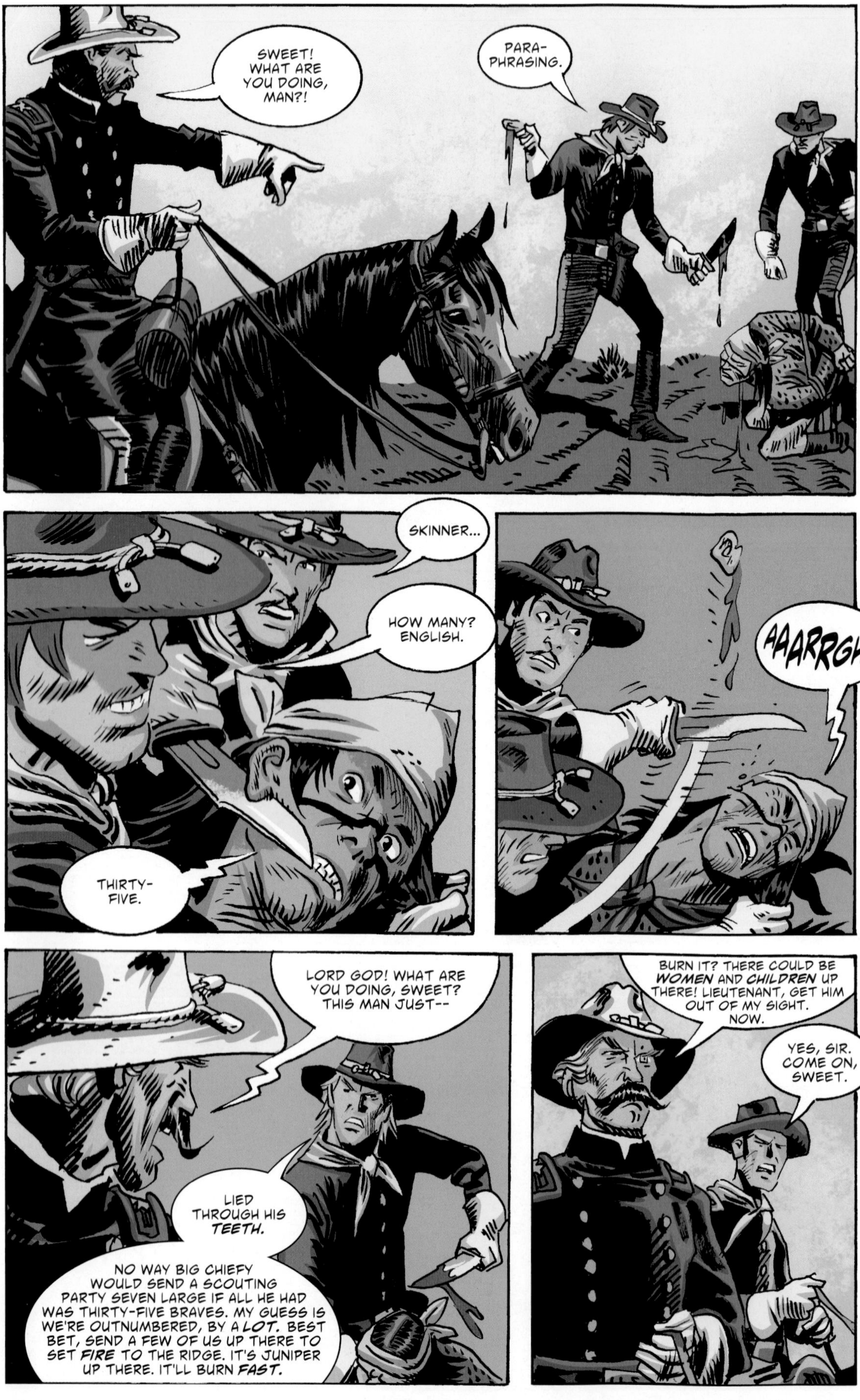
SWEET! WHAT ARE YOU DOING, MAN?!
PARA-PHRASING.
SKINNER...
HOW MANY? ENGLISH.
THIRTY-FIVE.
AAARRGH!
LORD GOD! WHAT ARE YOU DOING, SWEET? THIS MAN JUST--
LIED THROUGH HIS TEETH.
NO WAY BIG CHIEFY WOULD SEND A SCOUTING PARTY SEVEN LARGE IF ALL HE HAD WAS THIRTY-FIVE BRAVES. MY GUESS IS WE'RE OUTNUMBERED, BY A LOT. BEST BET, SEND A FEW OF US UP THERE TO SET FIRE TO THE RIDGE. IT'S JUNIPER UP THERE. IT'LL BURN FAST.
BURN IT? THERE COULD BE WOMEN AND CHILDREN UP THERE! LIEUTENANT, GET HIM OUT OF MY SIGHT. NOW.
YES, SIR. COME ON, SWEET.

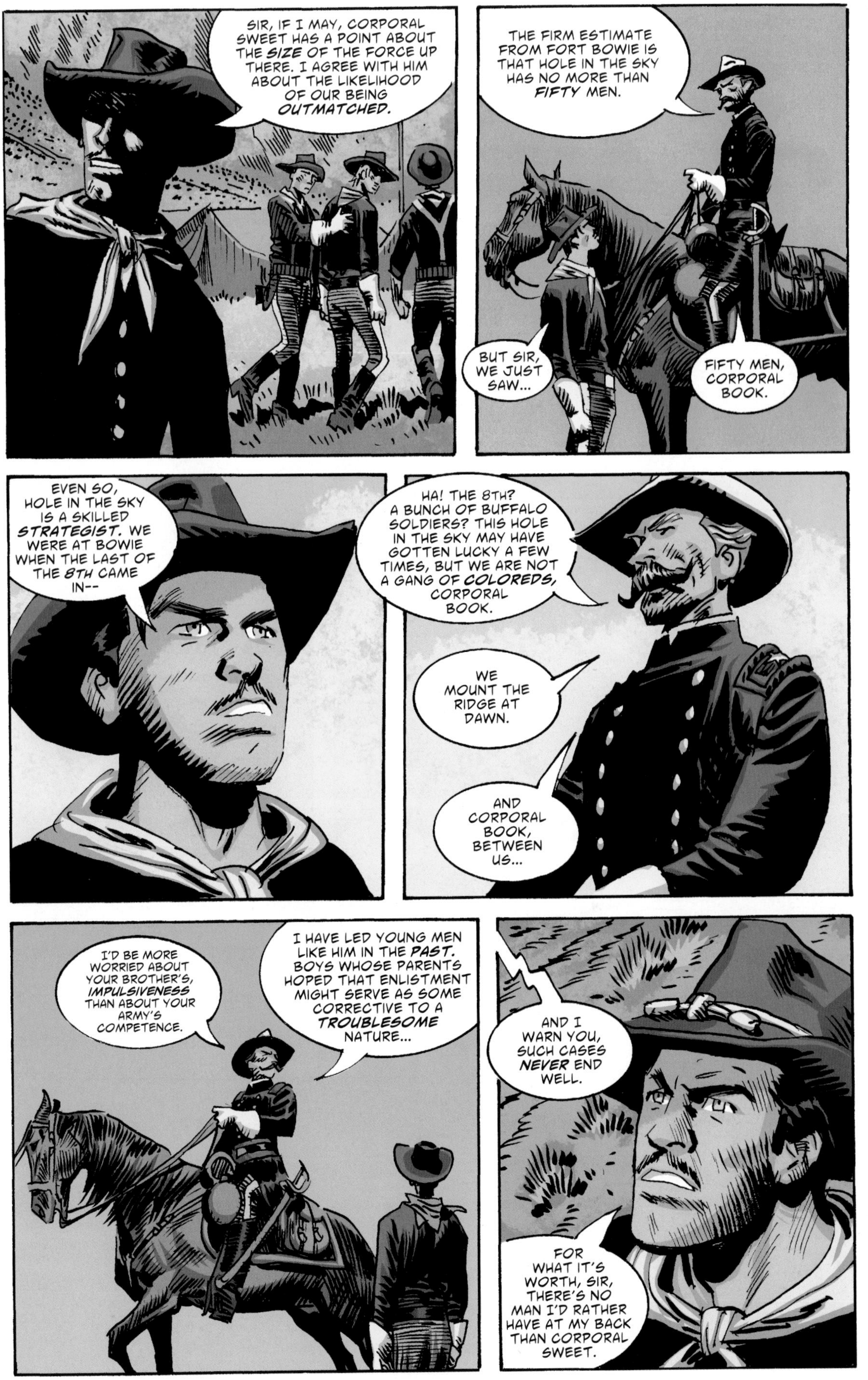
SIR, IF I MAY, CORPORAL SWEET HAS A POINT ABOUT THE *SIZE* OF THE FORCE UP THERE. I AGREE WITH HIM ABOUT THE LIKELIHOOD OF OUR BEING *OUTMATCHED.*
THE FIRM ESTIMATE FROM FORT BOWIE IS THAT HOLE IN THE SKY HAS NO MORE THAN *FIFTY* MEN.
BUT SIR, WE JUST SAW...
FIFTY MEN, CORPORAL BOOK.
EVEN SO, HOLE IN THE SKY IS A SKILLED *STRATEGIST.* WE WERE AT BOWIE WHEN THE LAST OF THE *8TH* CAME IN--
HA! THE 8TH? A BUNCH OF BUFFALO SOLDIERS? THIS HOLE IN THE SKY MAY HAVE GOTTEN LUCKY A FEW TIMES, BUT WE ARE NOT A GANG OF *COLOREDS,* CORPORAL BOOK.
WE MOUNT THE RIDGE AT DAWN.
AND CORPORAL BOOK, BETWEEN US...
I'D BE MORE WORRIED ABOUT YOUR BROTHER'S, *IMPULSIVENESS* THAN ABOUT YOUR ARMY'S COMPETENCE.
I HAVE LED YOUNG MEN LIKE HIM IN THE *PAST.* BOYS WHOSE PARENTS HOPED THAT ENLISTMENT MIGHT SERVE AS SOME CORRECTIVE TO A *TROUBLESOME* NATURE...
AND I WARN YOU, SUCH CASES *NEVER* END WELL.
FOR WHAT IT'S WORTH, SIR, THERE'S NO MAN I'D RATHER HAVE AT MY BACK THAN CORPORAL SWEET.

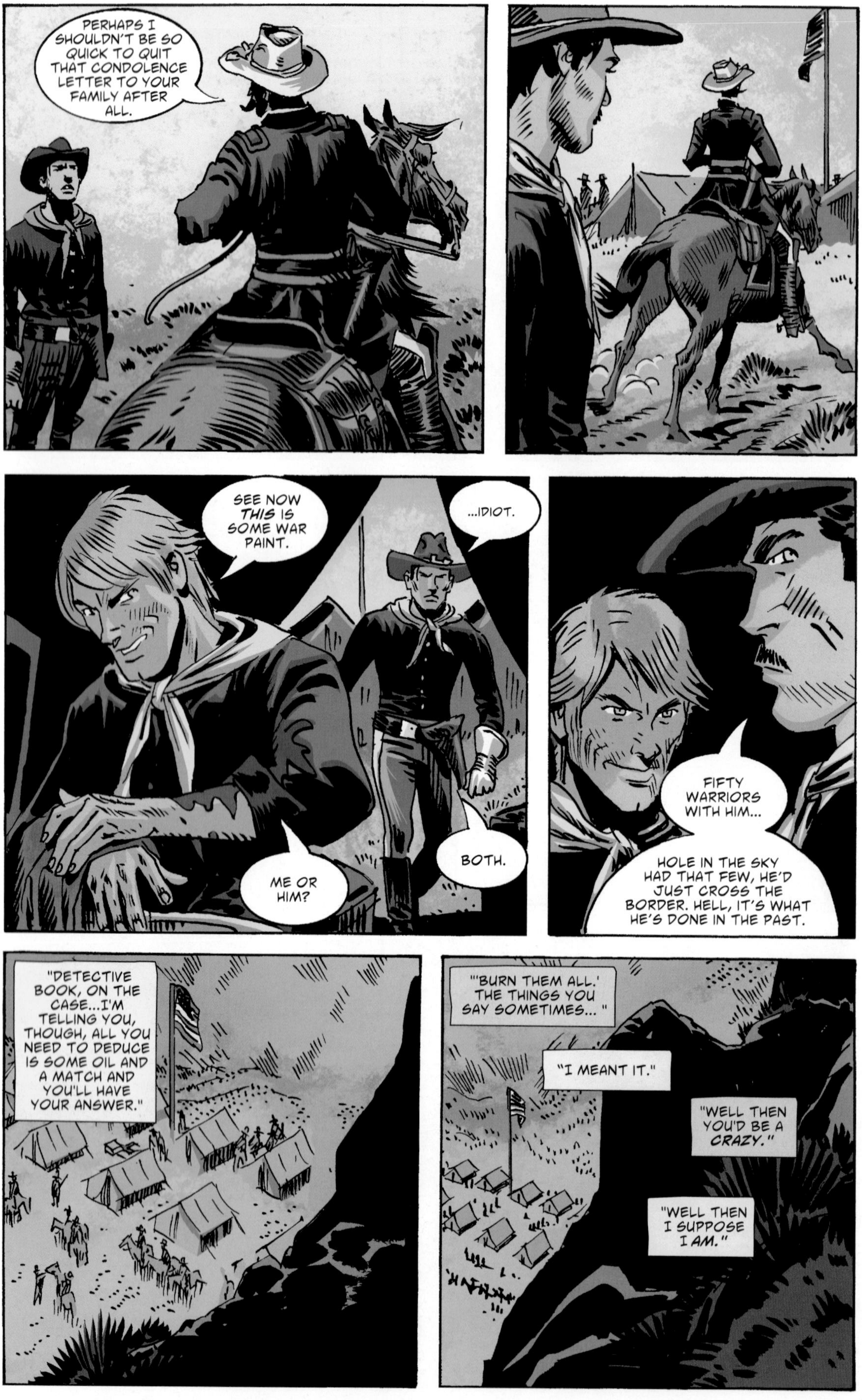
PERHAPS I SHOULDN'T BE SO QUICK TO QUIT THAT CONDOLENCE LETTER TO YOUR FAMILY AFTER ALL.
SEE NOW *THIS* IS SOME WAR PAINT.
...IDIOT.
ME OR HIM?
BOTH.
FIFTY WARRIORS WITH HIM...
HOLE IN THE SKY HAD THAT FEW, HE'D JUST CROSS THE BORDER. HELL, IT'S WHAT HE'S DONE IN THE PAST.
"DETECTIVE BOOK, ON THE CASE...I'M TELLING YOU, THOUGH, ALL YOU NEED TO DEDUCE IS SOME OIL AND A MATCH AND YOU'LL HAVE YOUR ANSWER."
"'BURN THEM ALL.' THE THINGS YOU SAY SOMETIMES... "
"I MEANT IT."
"WELL THEN YOU'D BE A *CRAZY.*"
"WELL THEN I SUPPOSE I *AM.*"

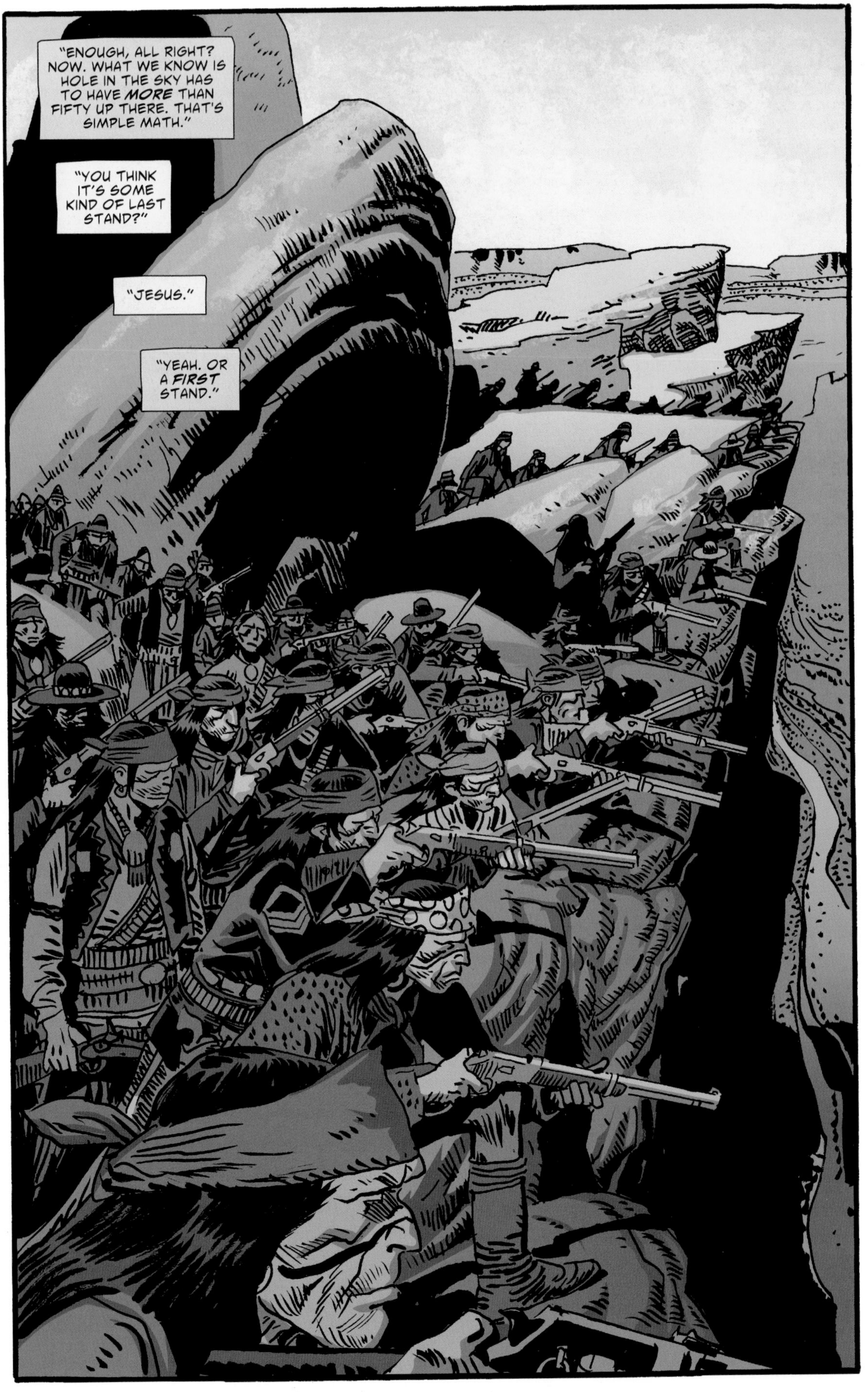
"ENOUGH, ALL RIGHT? NOW. WHAT WE KNOW IS HOLE IN THE SKY HAS TO HAVE MORE THAN FIFTY UP THERE. THAT'S SIMPLE MATH."
"YOU THINK IT'S SOME KIND OF LAST STAND?"
"JESUS."
"YEAH. OR A FIRST STAND."

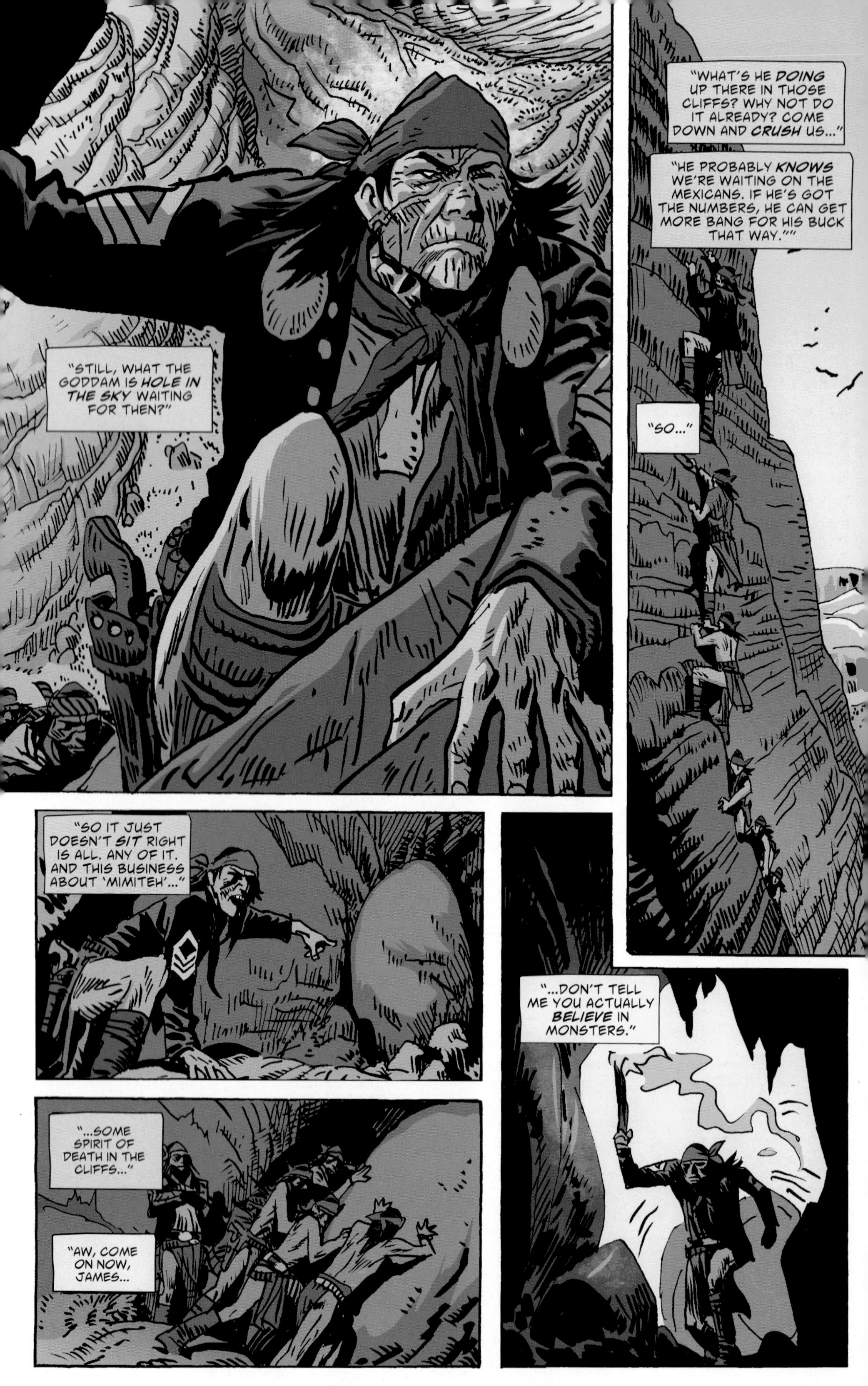
"STILL, WHAT THE GODDAM IS HOLE IN THE SKY WAITING FOR THEN?"
"WHAT'S HE DOING UP THERE IN THOSE CLIFFS? WHY NOT DO IT ALREADY? COME DOWN AND CRUSH US..."
"HE PROBABLY KNOWS WE'RE WAITING ON THE MEXICANS. IF HE'S GOT THE NUMBERS, HE CAN GET MORE BANG FOR HIS BUCK THAT WAY.""
"SO..."
"SO IT JUST DOESN'T SIT RIGHT IS ALL. ANY OF IT. AND THIS BUSINESS ABOUT 'MIMITEH'..."
"...SOME SPIRIT OF DEATH IN THE CLIFFS..."
"AW, COME ON NOW, JAMES...
"...DON'T TELL ME YOU ACTUALLY BELIEVE IN MONSTERS."

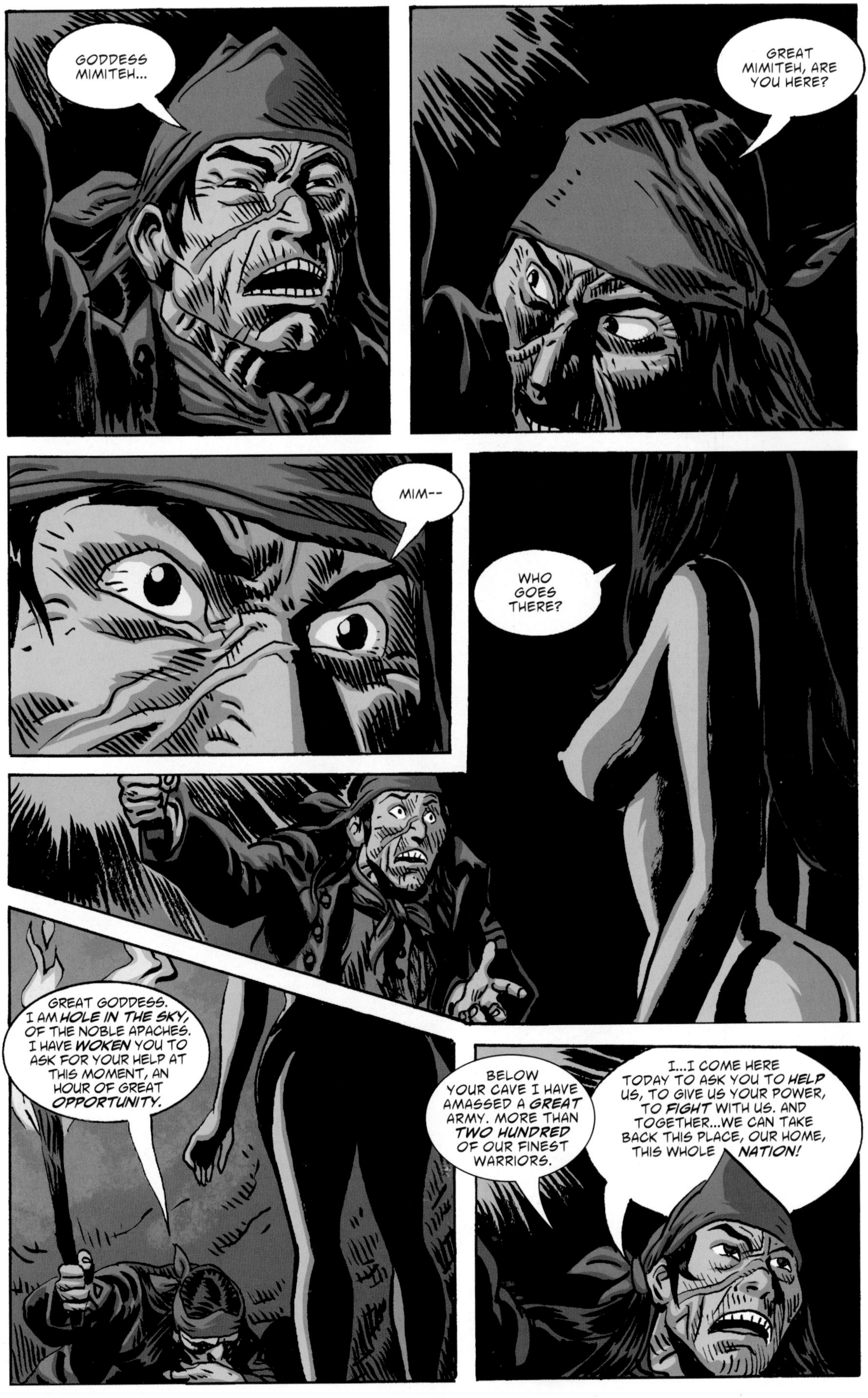
GODDESS MIMITEH...
GREAT MIMITEH, ARE YOU HERE?
MIM--
WHO GOES THERE?
GREAT GODDESS. I AM **HOLE IN THE SKY**, OF THE NOBLE APACHES. I HAVE **WOKEN** YOU TO ASK FOR YOUR HELP AT THIS MOMENT, AN HOUR OF GREAT **OPPORTUNITY**.
BELOW YOUR CAVE I HAVE AMASSED A **GREAT** ARMY. MORE THAN **TWO HUNDRED** OF OUR FINEST WARRIORS.
I...I COME HERE TODAY TO ASK YOU TO **HELP** US, TO GIVE US YOUR POWER, TO **FIGHT** WITH US. AND TOGETHER...WE CAN TAKE BACK THIS PLACE, OUR HOME, THIS WHOLE **NATION!**

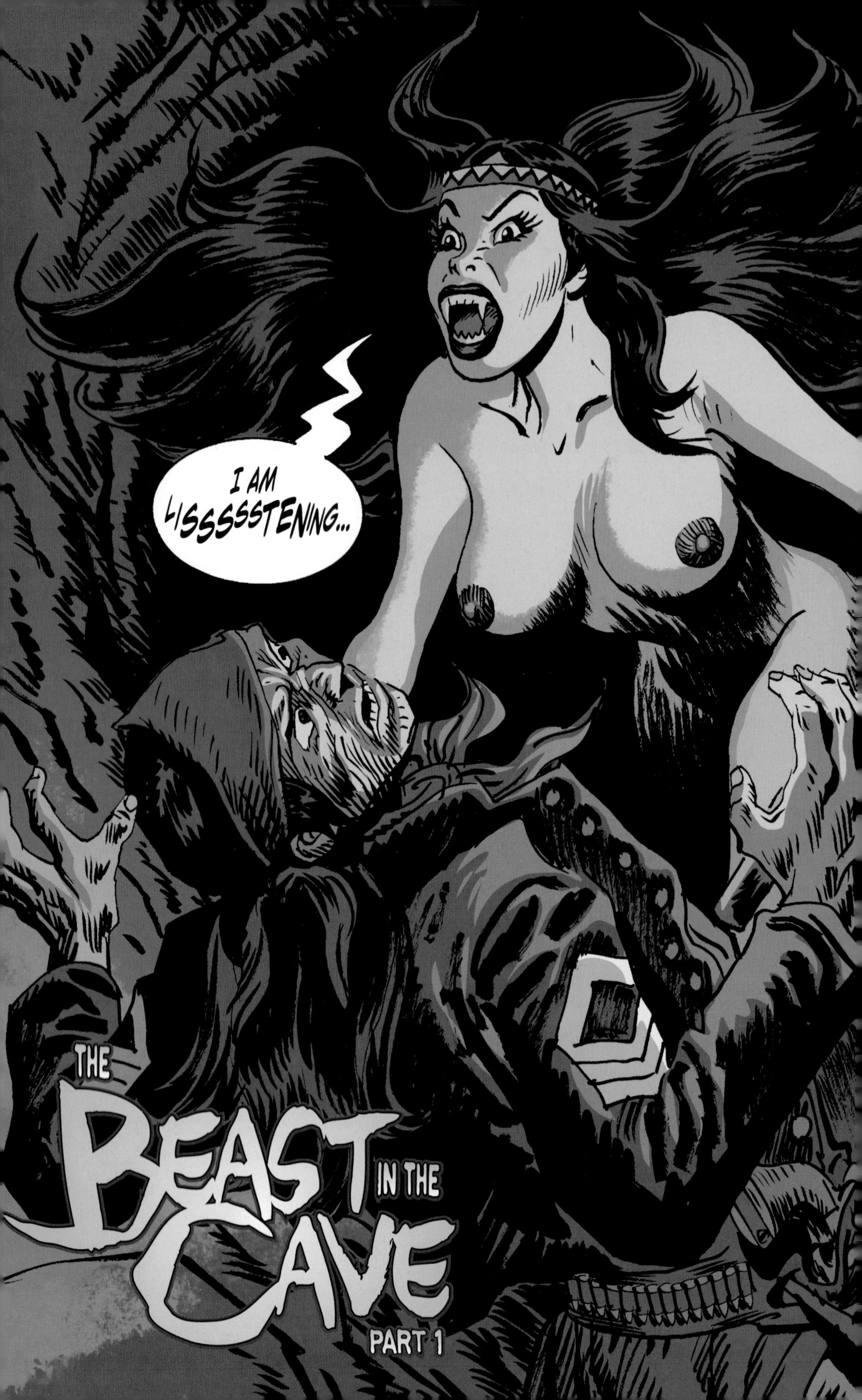
I AM LISSSSSTENING...
THE BEAST IN THE CAVE
PART 1

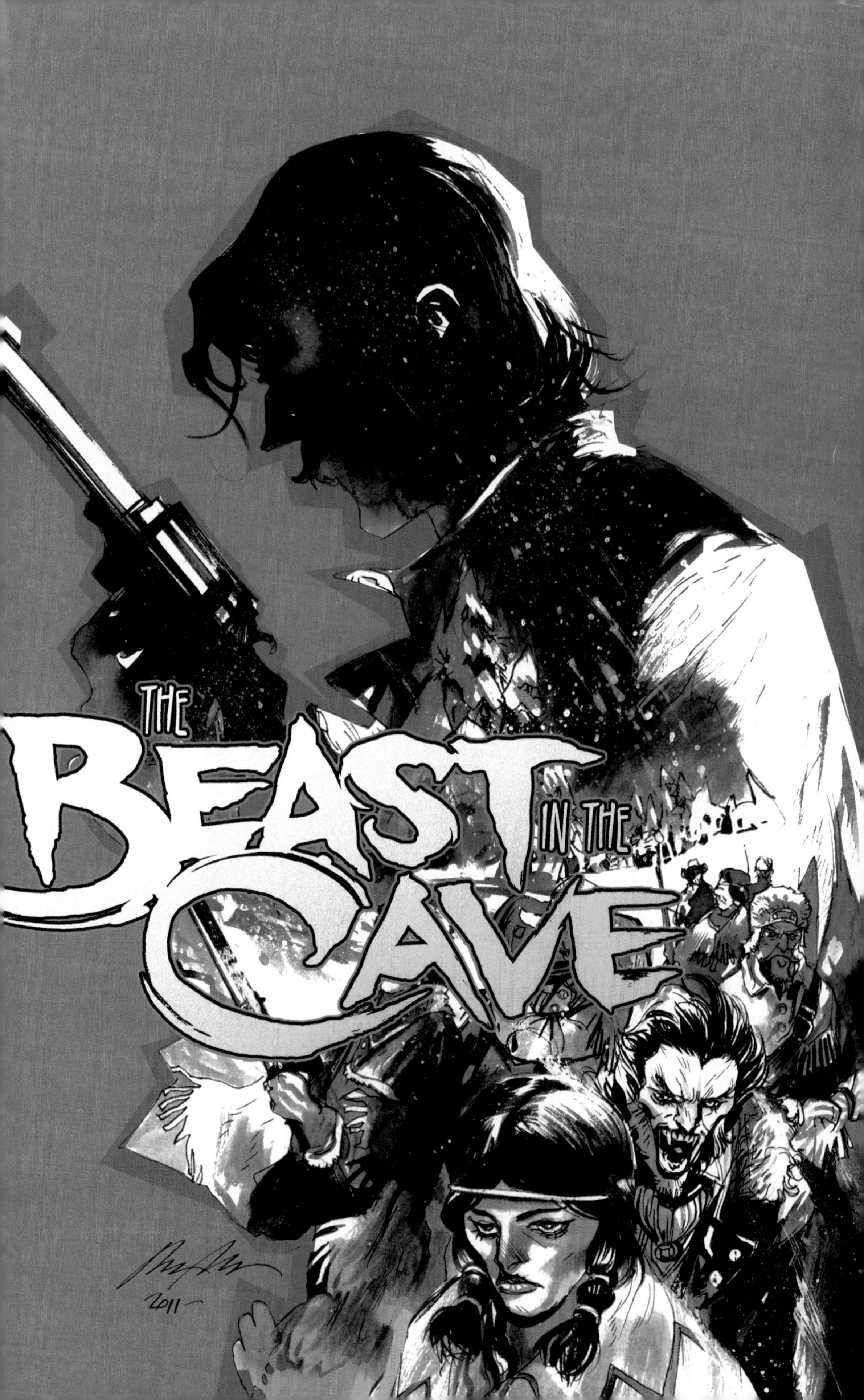
THE BEAST IN THE CAVE
2011

Louisiana Territory, Winter, 1793.

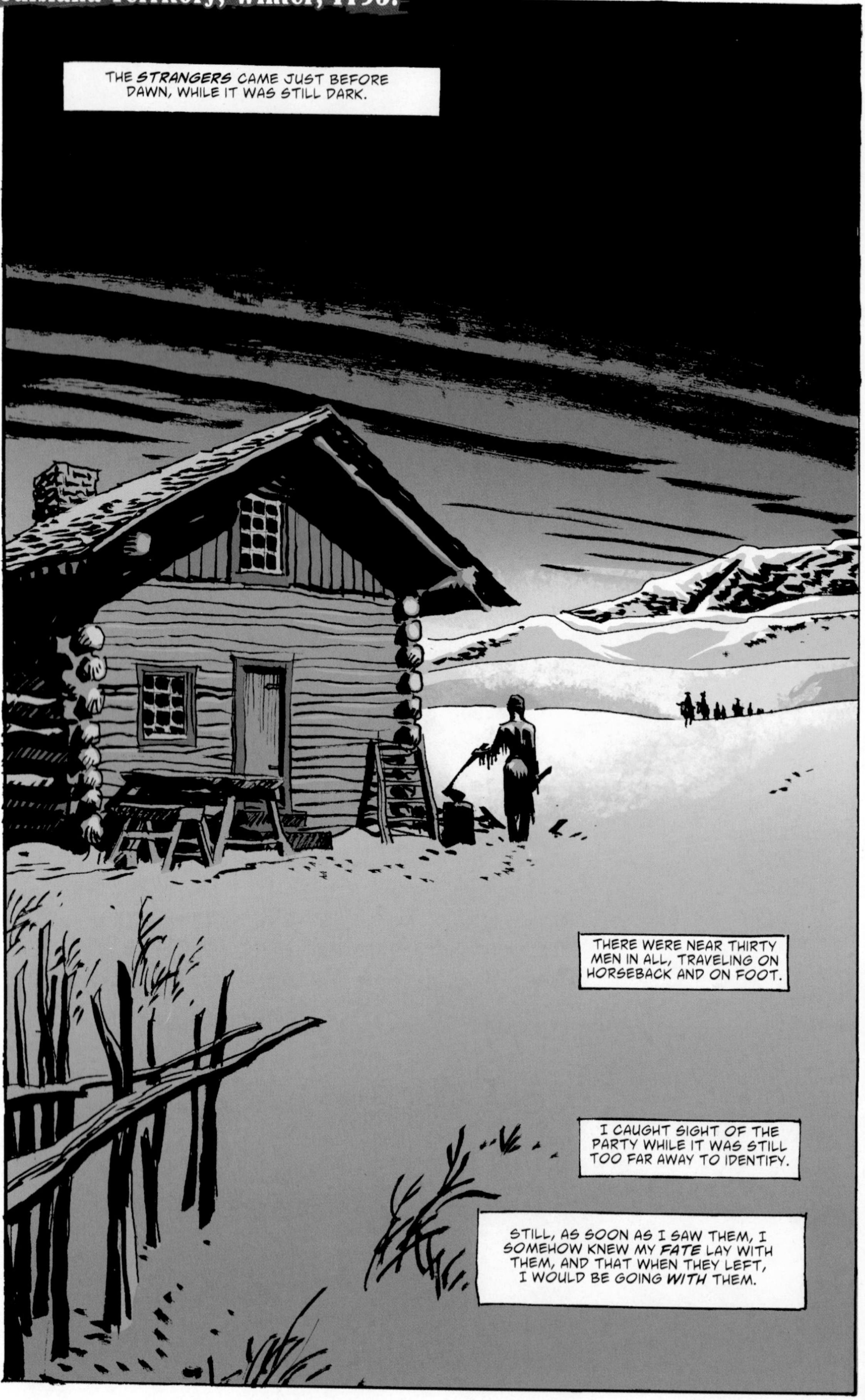
THE STRANGERS CAME JUST BEFORE DAWN, WHILE IT WAS STILL DARK.
THERE WERE NEAR THIRTY MEN IN ALL, TRAVELING ON HORSEBACK AND ON FOOT.
I CAUGHT SIGHT OF THE PARTY WHILE IT WAS STILL TOO FAR AWAY TO IDENTIFY.
STILL, AS SOON AS I SAW THEM, I SOMEHOW KNEW MY FATE LAY WITH THEM, AND THAT WHEN THEY LEFT, I WOULD BE GOING WITH THEM.

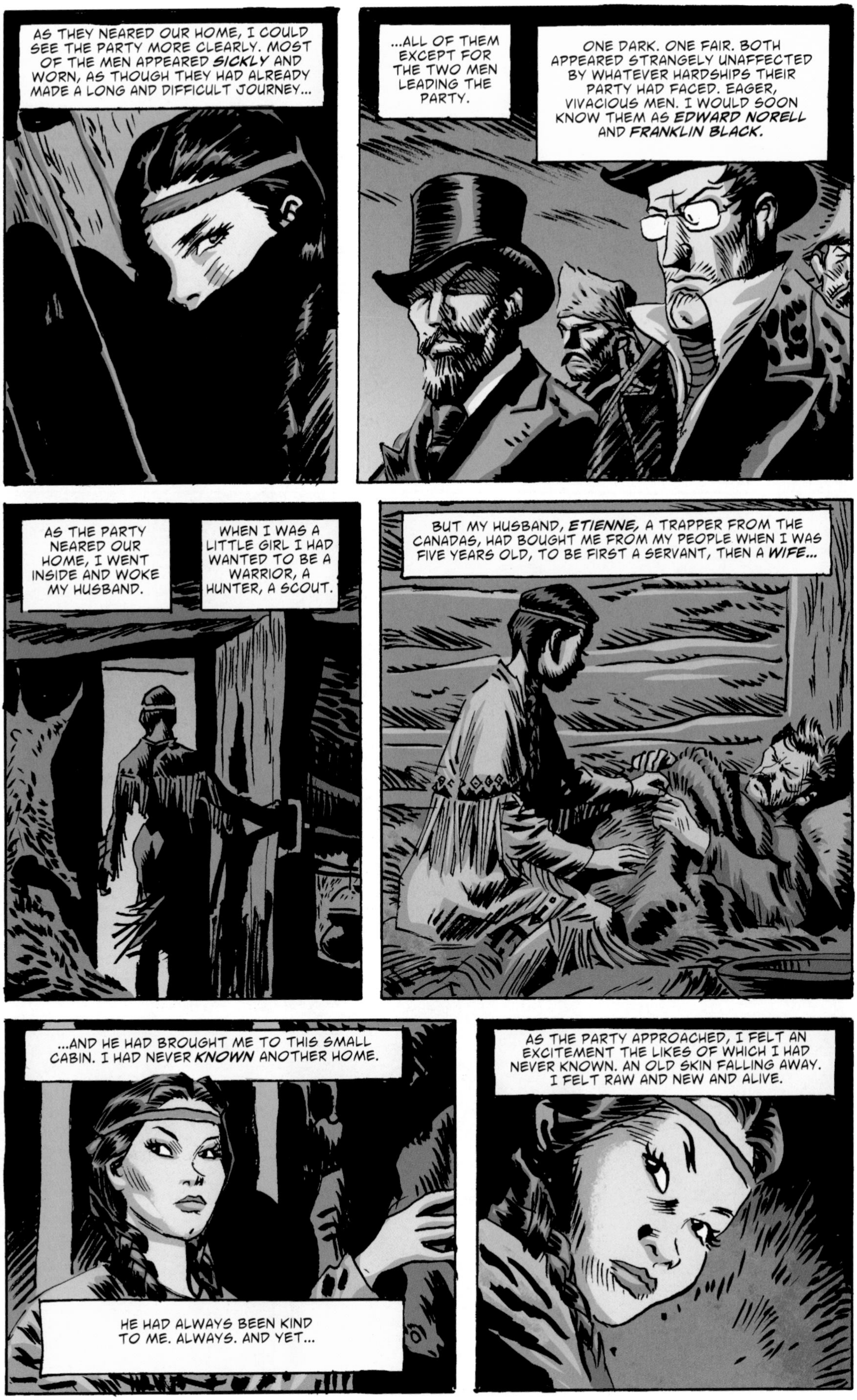
AS THEY NEARED OUR HOME, I COULD SEE THE PARTY MORE CLEARLY. MOST OF THE MEN APPEARED *SICKLY* AND WORN, AS THOUGH THEY HAD ALREADY MADE A LONG AND DIFFICULT JOURNEY...
...ALL OF THEM EXCEPT FOR THE TWO MEN LEADING THE PARTY.
ONE DARK. ONE FAIR. BOTH APPEARED STRANGELY UNAFFECTED BY WHATEVER HARDSHIPS THEIR PARTY HAD FACED. EAGER, VIVACIOUS MEN. I WOULD SOON KNOW THEM AS ***EDWARD NORELL*** AND ***FRANKLIN BLACK.***
AS THE PARTY NEARED OUR HOME, I WENT INSIDE AND WOKE MY HUSBAND.
WHEN I WAS A LITTLE GIRL I HAD WANTED TO BE A WARRIOR, A HUNTER, A SCOUT.
BUT MY HUSBAND, *ETIENNE,* A TRAPPER FROM THE CANADAS, HAD BOUGHT ME FROM MY PEOPLE WHEN I WAS FIVE YEARS OLD, TO BE FIRST A SERVANT, THEN A *WIFE...*
...AND HE HAD BROUGHT ME TO THIS SMALL CABIN. I HAD NEVER *KNOWN* ANOTHER HOME.
HE HAD ALWAYS BEEN KIND TO ME. ALWAYS. AND YET...
AS THE PARTY APPROACHED, I FELT AN EXCITEMENT THE LIKES OF WHICH I HAD NEVER KNOWN. AN OLD SKIN FALLING AWAY. I FELT RAW AND NEW AND ALIVE.

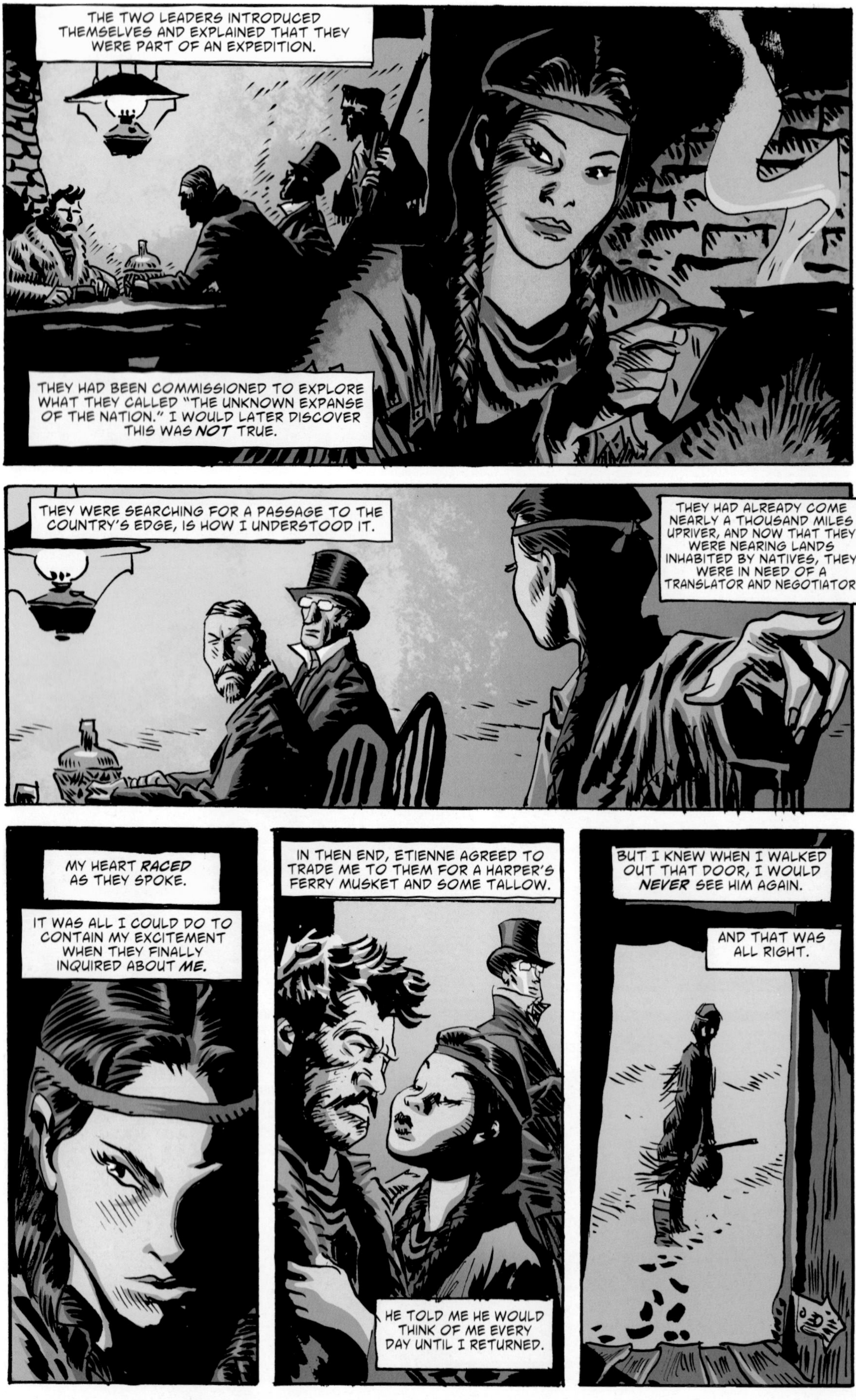
THE TWO LEADERS INTRODUCED THEMSELVES AND EXPLAINED THAT THEY WERE PART OF AN EXPEDITION.
THEY HAD BEEN COMMISSIONED TO EXPLORE WHAT THEY CALLED "THE UNKNOWN EXPANSE OF THE NATION." I WOULD LATER DISCOVER THIS WAS *NOT* TRUE.
THEY WERE SEARCHING FOR A PASSAGE TO THE COUNTRY'S EDGE, IS HOW I UNDERSTOOD IT.
THEY HAD ALREADY COME NEARLY A THOUSAND MILES UPRIVER, AND NOW THAT THEY WERE NEARING LANDS INHABITED BY NATIVES, THEY WERE IN NEED OF A TRANSLATOR AND NEGOTIATOR.
MY HEART *RACED* AS THEY SPOKE.
IT WAS ALL I COULD DO TO CONTAIN MY EXCITEMENT WHEN THEY FINALLY INQUIRED ABOUT *ME*.
IN THEN END, ETIENNE AGREED TO TRADE ME TO THEM FOR A HARPER'S FERRY MUSKET AND SOME TALLOW.
HE TOLD ME HE WOULD THINK OF ME EVERY DAY UNTIL I RETURNED.
BUT I KNEW WHEN I WALKED OUT THAT DOOR, I WOULD *NEVER* SEE HIM AGAIN.
AND THAT WAS ALL RIGHT.

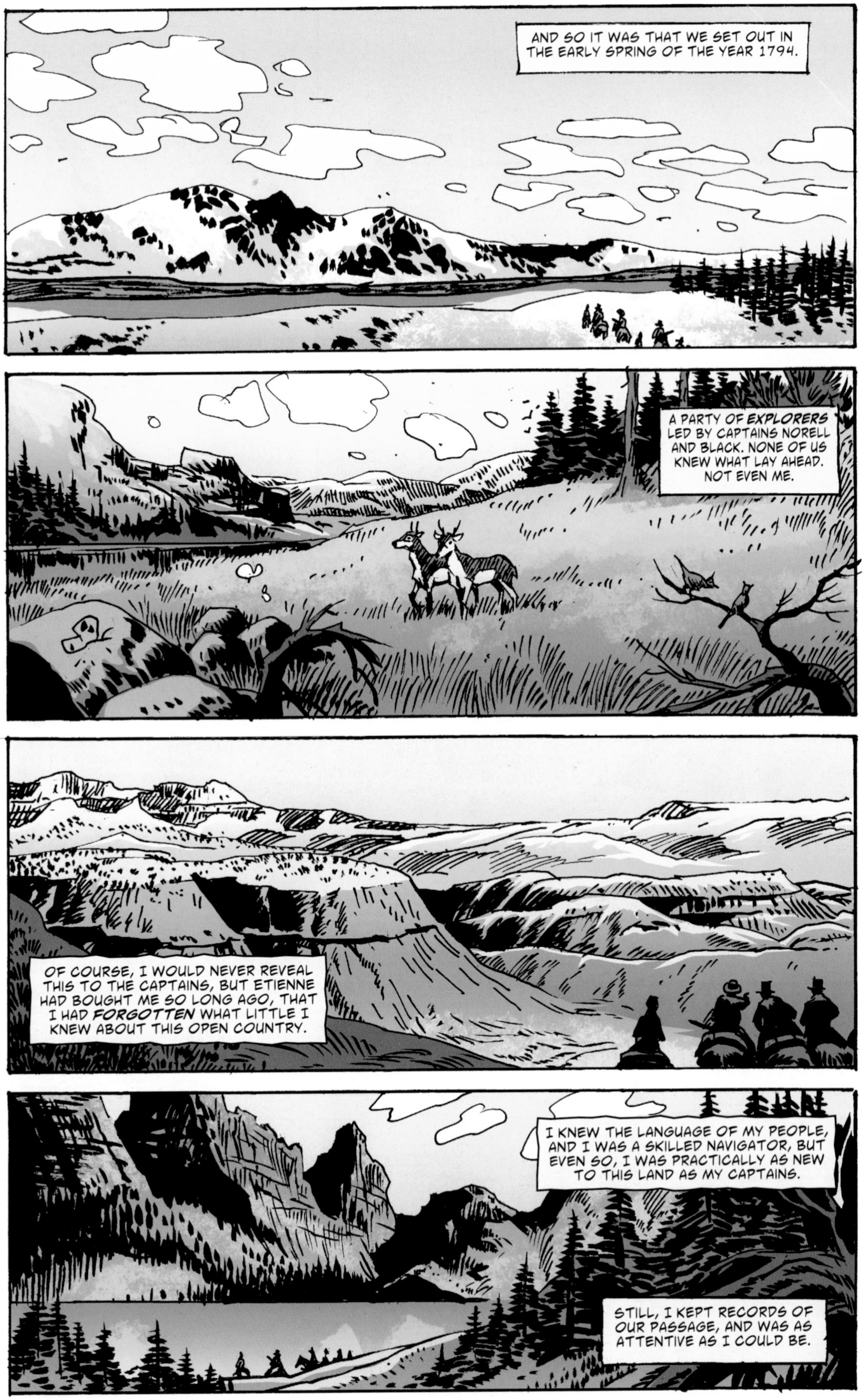
AND SO IT WAS THAT WE SET OUT IN THE EARLY SPRING OF THE YEAR 1794.
A PARTY OF EXPLORERS LED BY CAPTAINS NORELL AND BLACK. NONE OF US KNEW WHAT LAY AHEAD. NOT EVEN ME.
OF COURSE, I WOULD NEVER REVEAL THIS TO THE CAPTAINS, BUT ETIENNE HAD BOUGHT ME SO LONG AGO, THAT I HAD FORGOTTEN WHAT LITTLE I KNEW ABOUT THIS OPEN COUNTRY.
I KNEW THE LANGUAGE OF MY PEOPLE, AND I WAS A SKILLED NAVIGATOR, BUT EVEN SO, I WAS PRACTICALLY AS NEW TO THIS LAND AS MY CAPTAINS.
STILL, I KEPT RECORDS OF OUR PASSAGE, AND WAS AS ATTENTIVE AS I COULD BE.

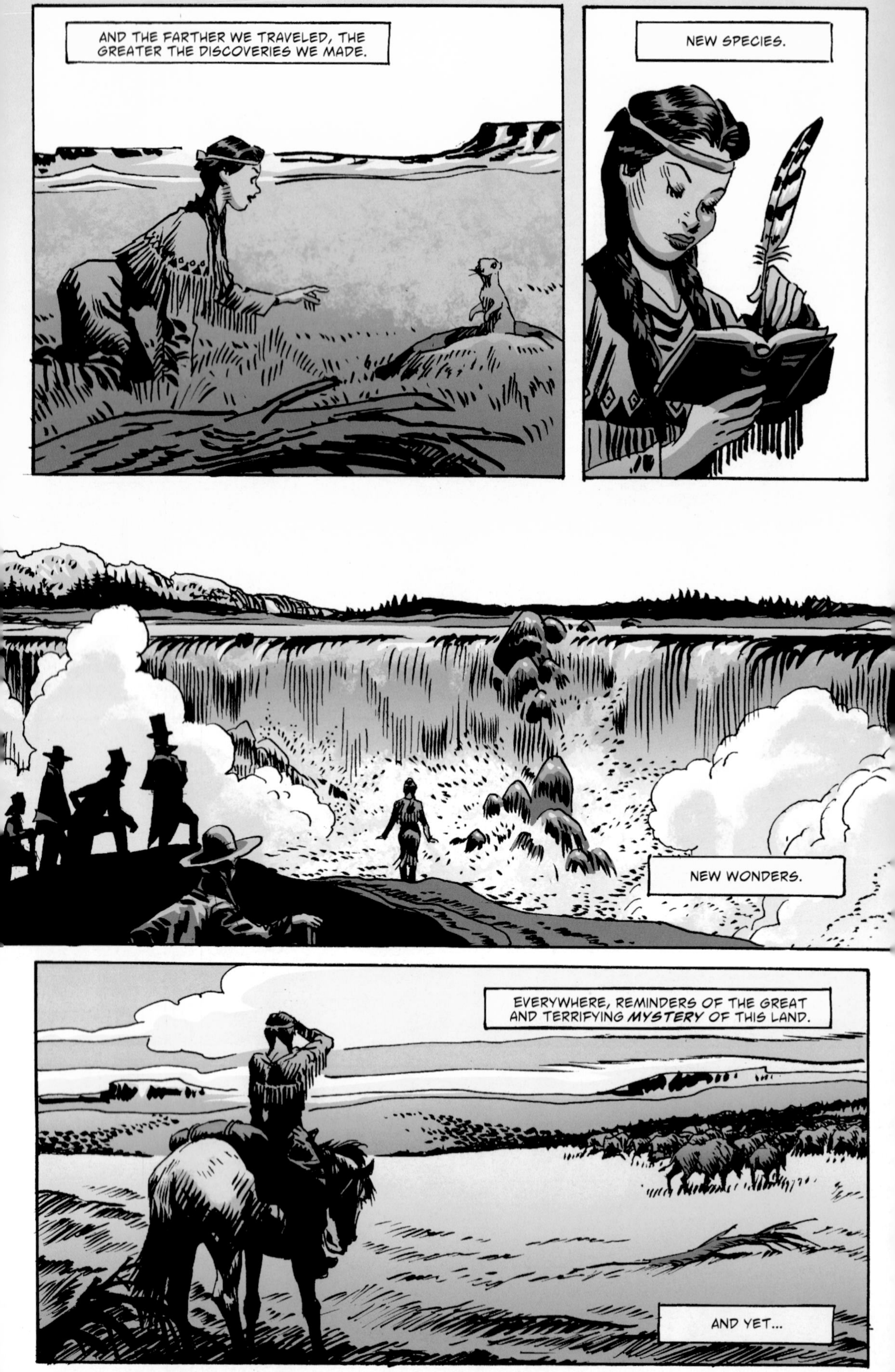
AND THE FARTHER WE TRAVELED, THE GREATER THE DISCOVERIES WE MADE.
NEW SPECIES.
NEW WONDERS.
EVERYWHERE, REMINDERS OF THE GREAT AND TERRIFYING *MYSTERY* OF THIS LAND.
AND YET...

OUR LEADERS SEEMED STRANGELY *UNINTERESTED* IN THE DISCOVERIES WE WERE MAKING.

IN FACT, THERE WAS LITTLE THAT CAUGHT THEIR ATTENTION BESIDES THE LAND'S ABUNDANT *RESOURCES,* WHICH THEY REMARKED ON FREQUENTLY...

AND *HUNTING.* THEY WOULD HUNT ALONE NEARLY EVERY EVENING, VENTURING OFF INTO THE WILDERNESS WITH ONLY THEIR MUSKETS AND KNIVES.

BUT THEY WOULD RETURN WITH GAME THAT IMPRESSED EVEN THE NATIVES IN OUR PARTY.

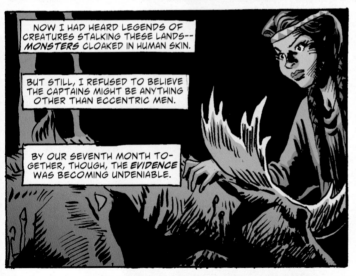

NOW I HAD HEARD LEGENDS OF CREATURES STALKING THESE LANDS-- *MONSTERS* CLOAKED IN HUMAN SKIN.

BUT STILL, I REFUSED TO BELIEVE THE CAPTAINS MIGHT BE ANYTHING OTHER THAN ECCENTRIC MEN.

BY OUR SEVENTH MONTH TO-GETHER, THOUGH, THE *EVIDENCE* WAS BECOMING UNDENIABLE.

AND I FEARED THAT IF I DIDN'T LEAVE THE EXPEDITION SOON, MY LIFE WOULD BE IN DANGER.

AND YET EVEN SO, I *HAD* TO KNOW.

SO ONE NIGHT, I FOLLOWED THEM INTO THE WOODS, ON ONE OF THEIR HUNTING EXPEDITIONS.

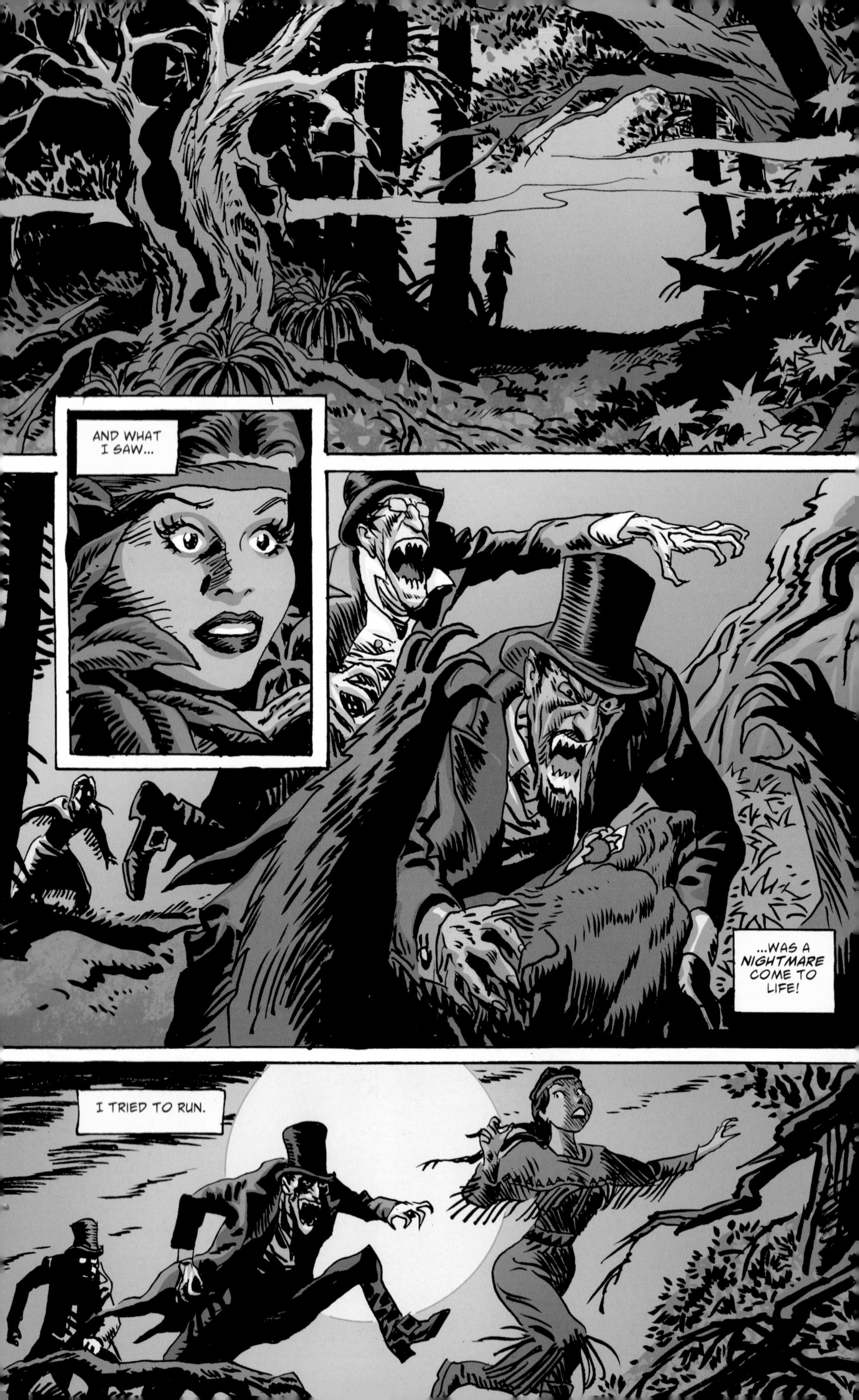
AND WHAT I SAW...
...WAS A NIGHTMARE COME TO LIFE!
I TRIED TO RUN.

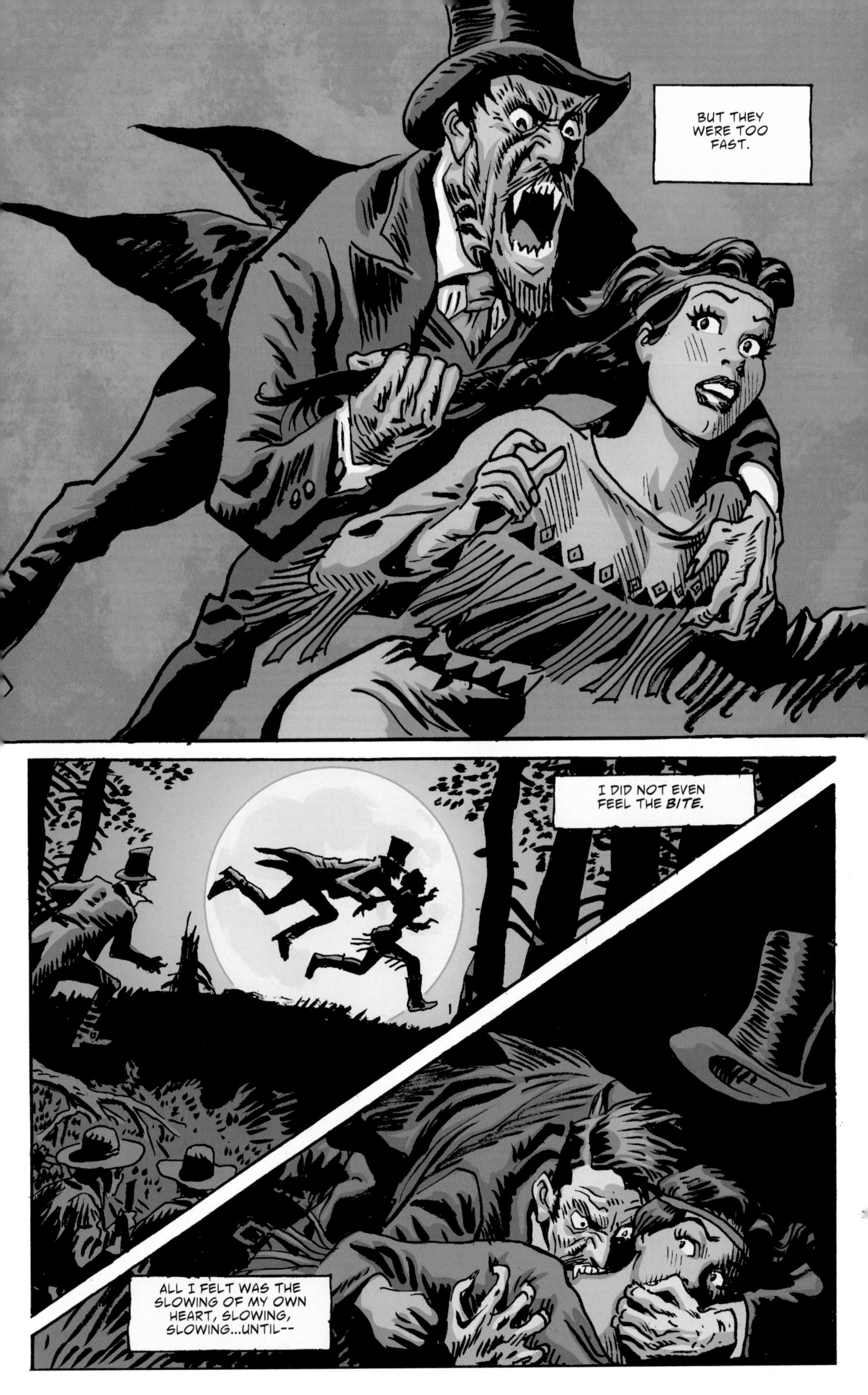
BUT THEY WERE TOO FAST.
I DID NOT EVEN FEEL THE *BITE*.
ALL I FELT WAS THE SLOWING OF MY OWN HEART, SLOWING, SLOWING...UNTIL--

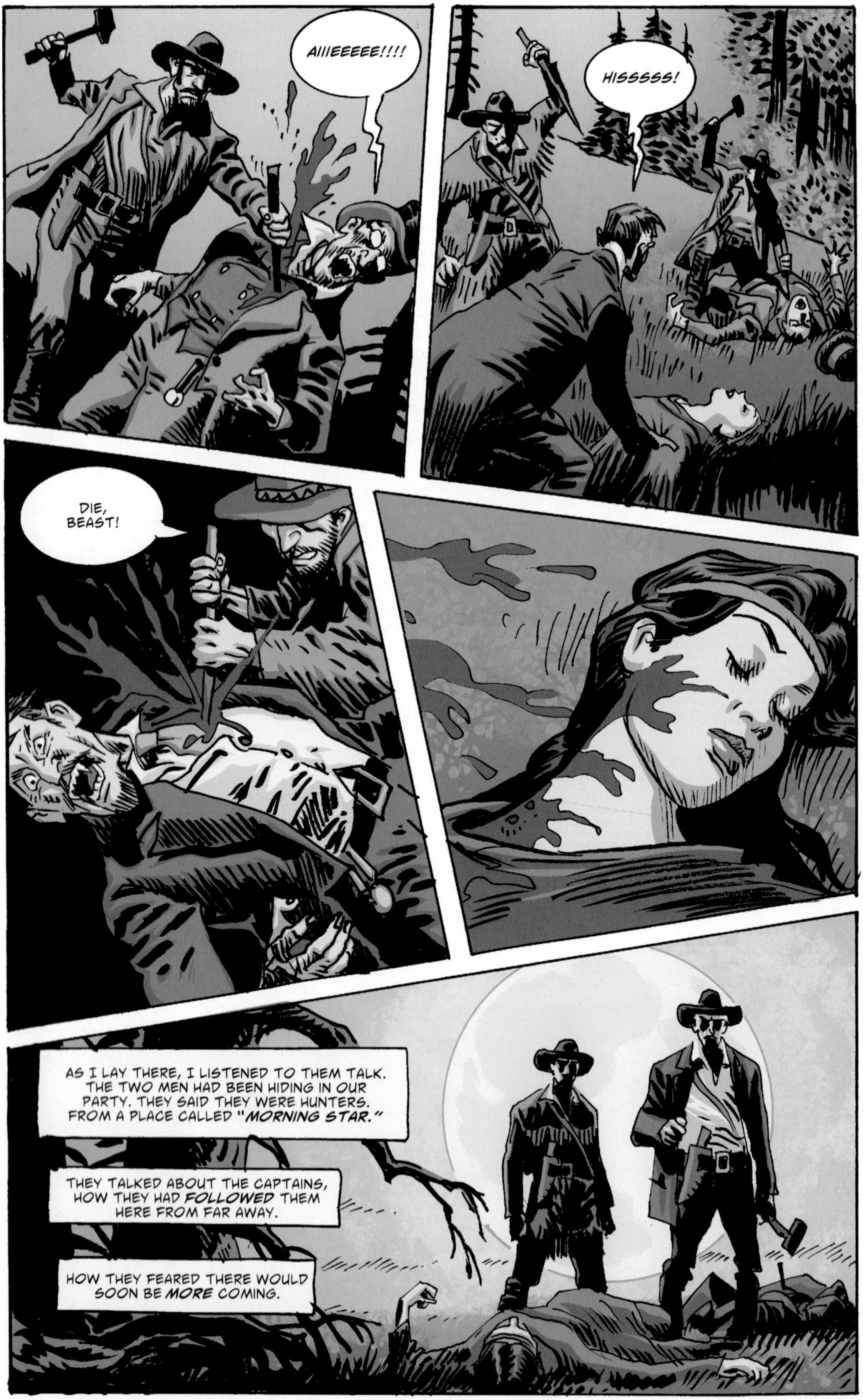
AIIIEEEEE!!!!
HISSSSS!
DIE, BEAST!
AS I LAY THERE, I LISTENED TO THEM TALK. THE TWO MEN HAD BEEN HIDING IN OUR PARTY. THEY SAID THEY WERE HUNTERS. FROM A PLACE CALLED "MORNING STAR."
THEY TALKED ABOUT THE CAPTAINS, HOW THEY HAD FOLLOWED THEM HERE FROM FAR AWAY.
HOW THEY FEARED THERE WOULD SOON BE MORE COMING.

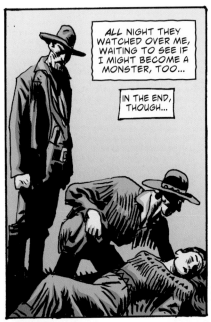

ALL NIGHT THEY WATCHED OVER ME, WAITING TO SEE IF I MIGHT BECOME A MONSTER, TOO...

IN THE END, THOUGH...

...THEY DECIDED IT WAS NOT WORTH THE RISK.

AND THEY LEFT ME THERE TO *DIE* AMONG THE CAPTAINS.

BUT, YOU SEE... I *DIDN'T* DIE.

NO. BECAUSE I WAS NOT LIKE THE CAPTAINS, NOT A MONSTER LIKE THEM.

I HAD BECOME SOMETHING *NEW*.

SOMETHING EVEN MORE TERRIBLE. A NEW KIND OF DEMON. BORN OF *THIS* LAND.

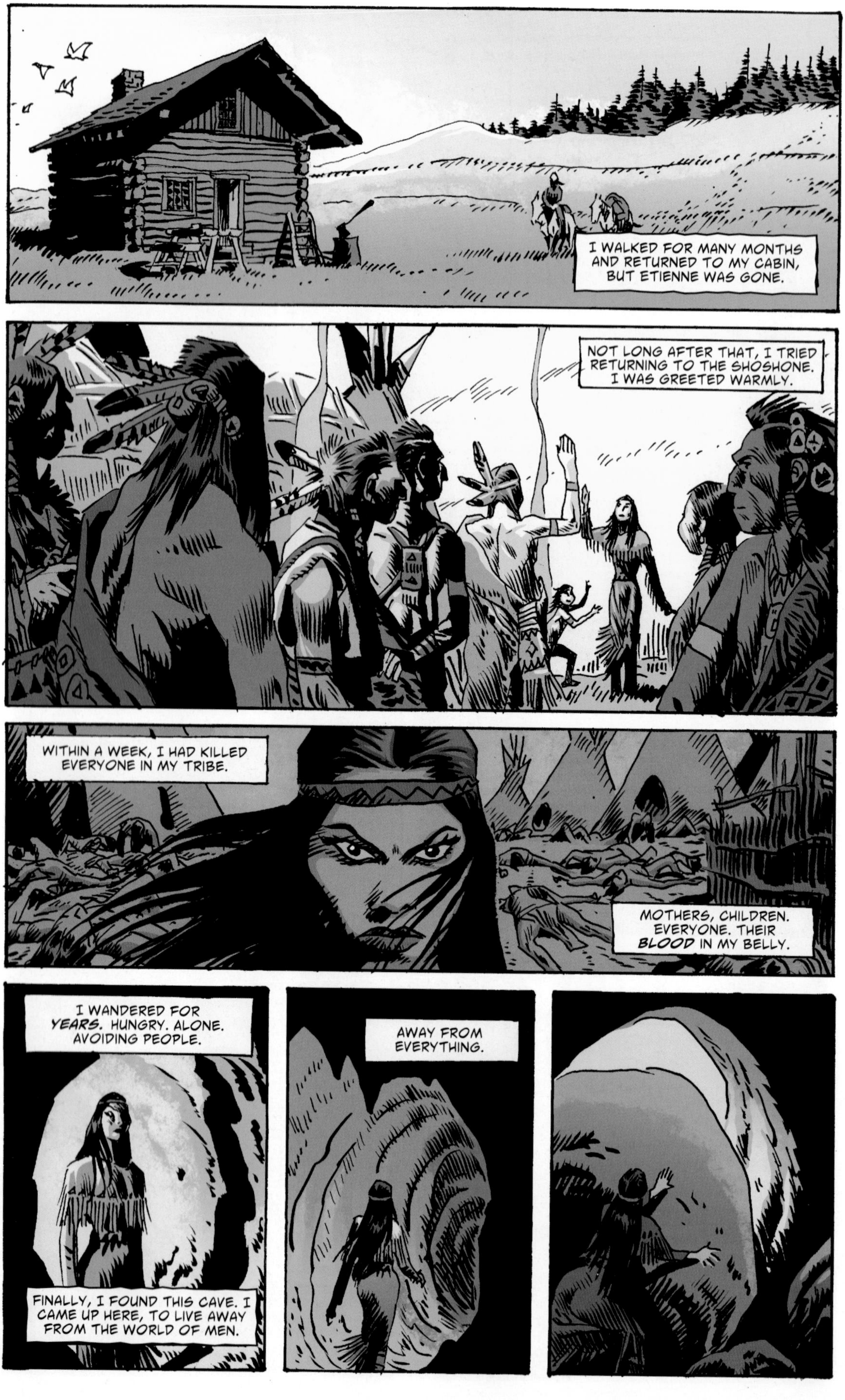
I WALKED FOR MANY MONTHS AND RETURNED TO MY CABIN, BUT ETIENNE WAS GONE.
NOT LONG AFTER THAT, I TRIED RETURNING TO THE SHOSHONE. I WAS GREETED WARMLY.
WITHIN A WEEK, I HAD KILLED EVERYONE IN MY TRIBE.
MOTHERS, CHILDREN. EVERYONE. THEIR BLOOD IN MY BELLY.
I WANDERED FOR YEARS. HUNGRY. ALONE. AVOIDING PEOPLE.
FINALLY, I FOUND THIS CAVE. I CAME UP HERE, TO LIVE AWAY FROM THE WORLD OF MEN.
AWAY FROM EVERYTHING.

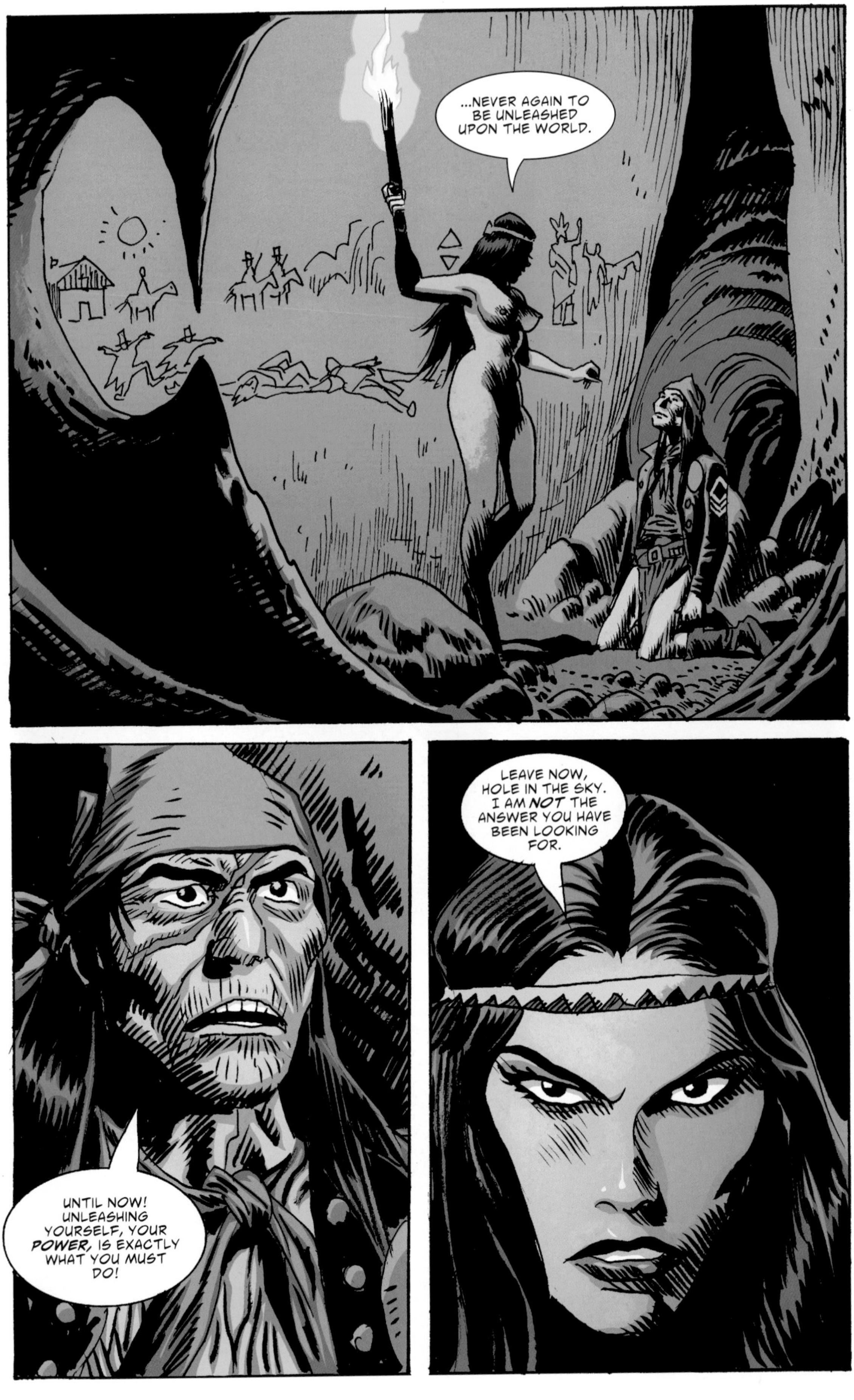
...NEVER AGAIN TO BE UNLEASHED UPON THE WORLD.
LEAVE NOW, HOLE IN THE SKY. I AM NOT THE ANSWER YOU HAVE BEEN LOOKING FOR.
UNTIL NOW! UNLEASHING YOURSELF, YOUR POWER, IS EXACTLY WHAT YOU MUST DO!

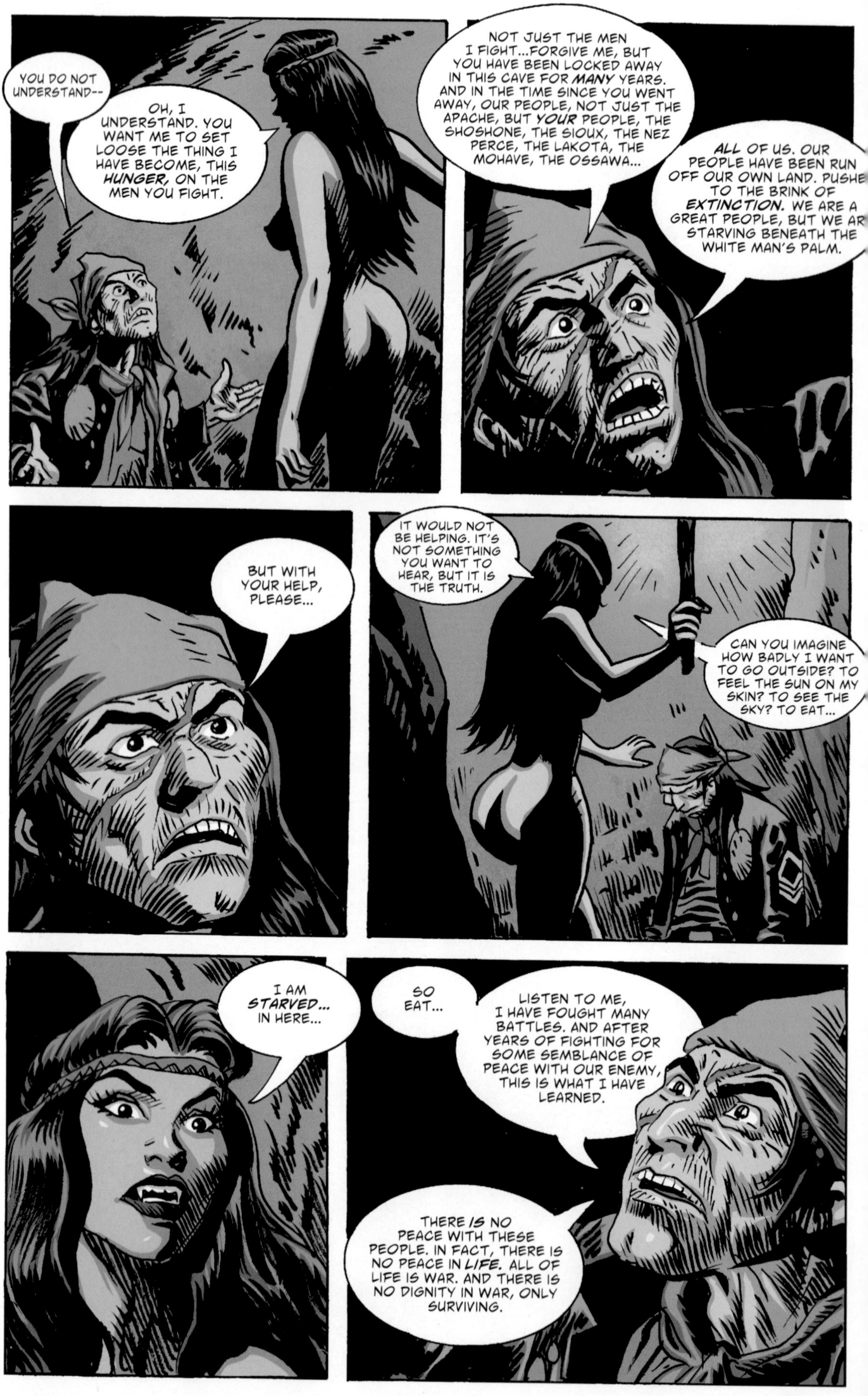
YOU DO NOT UNDERSTAND--
OH, I UNDERSTAND. YOU WANT ME TO SET LOOSE THE THING I HAVE BECOME, THIS HUNGER, ON THE MEN YOU FIGHT.
NOT JUST THE MEN I FIGHT...FORGIVE ME, BUT YOU HAVE BEEN LOCKED AWAY IN THIS CAVE FOR MANY YEARS. AND IN THE TIME SINCE YOU WENT AWAY, OUR PEOPLE, NOT JUST THE APACHE, BUT YOUR PEOPLE, THE SHOSHONE, THE SIOUX, THE NEZ PERCE, THE LAKOTA, THE MOHAVE, THE OSSAWA...
ALL OF US. OUR PEOPLE HAVE BEEN RUN OFF OUR OWN LAND. PUSHE TO THE BRINK OF EXTINCTION. WE ARE A GREAT PEOPLE, BUT WE AR STARVING BENEATH THE WHITE MAN'S PALM.
BUT WITH YOUR HELP, PLEASE...
IT WOULD NOT BE HELPING. IT'S NOT SOMETHING YOU WANT TO HEAR, BUT IT IS THE TRUTH.
CAN YOU IMAGINE HOW BADLY I WANT TO GO OUTSIDE? TO FEEL THE SUN ON MY SKIN? TO SEE THE SKY? TO EAT...
I AM STARVED... IN HERE...
SO EAT...
LISTEN TO ME, I HAVE FOUGHT MANY BATTLES. AND AFTER YEARS OF FIGHTING FOR SOME SEMBLANCE OF PEACE WITH OUR ENEMY, THIS IS WHAT I HAVE LEARNED.
THERE IS NO PEACE WITH THESE PEOPLE. IN FACT, THERE IS NO PEACE IN LIFE. ALL OF LIFE IS WAR. AND THERE IS NO DIGNITY IN WAR, ONLY SURVIVING.

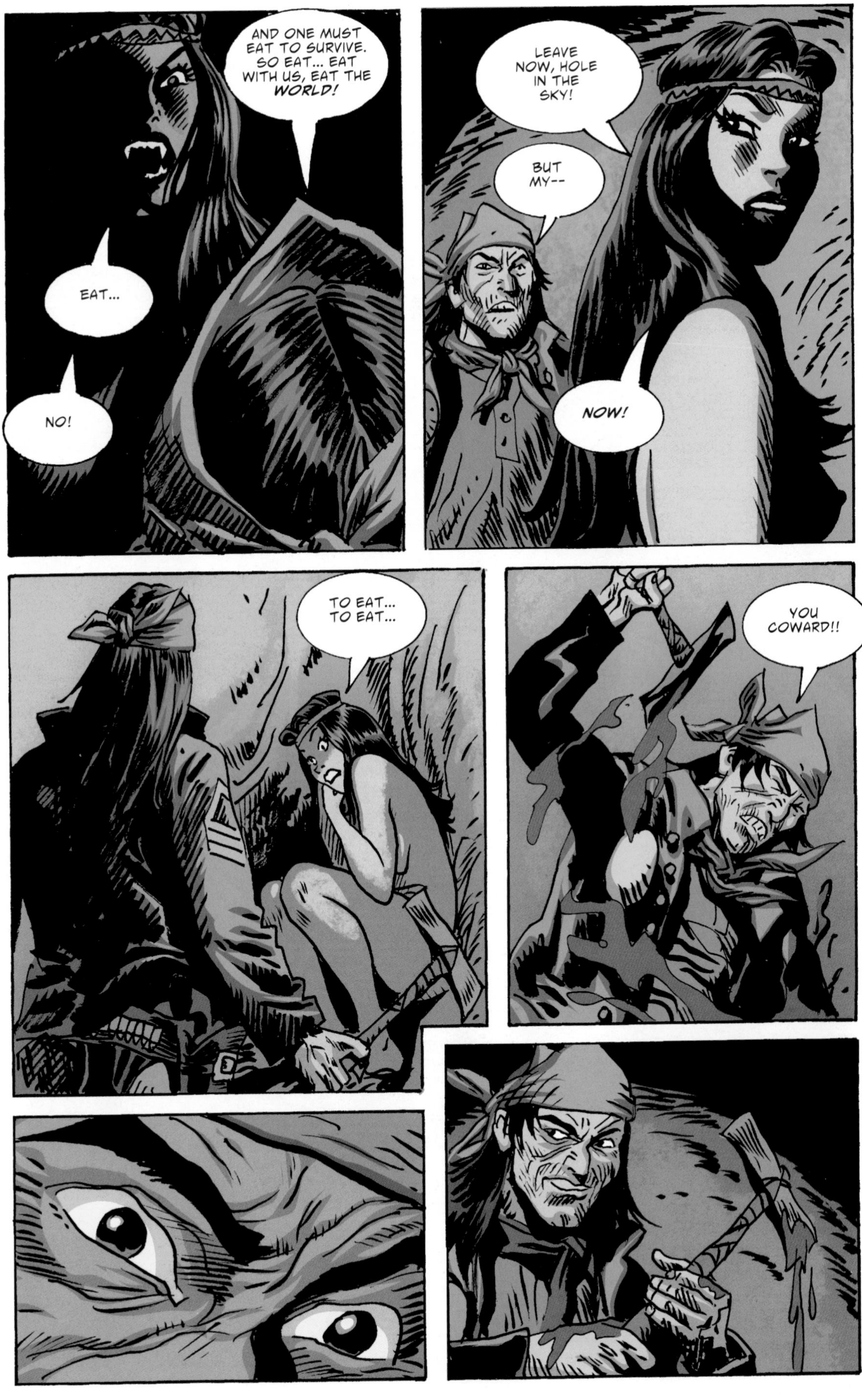
AND ONE MUST EAT TO SURVIVE. SO EAT... EAT WITH US, EAT THE *WORLD!*
EAT...
NO!
LEAVE NOW, HOLE IN THE SKY!
BUT MY--
NOW!
TO EAT... TO EAT...
YOU COWARD!!

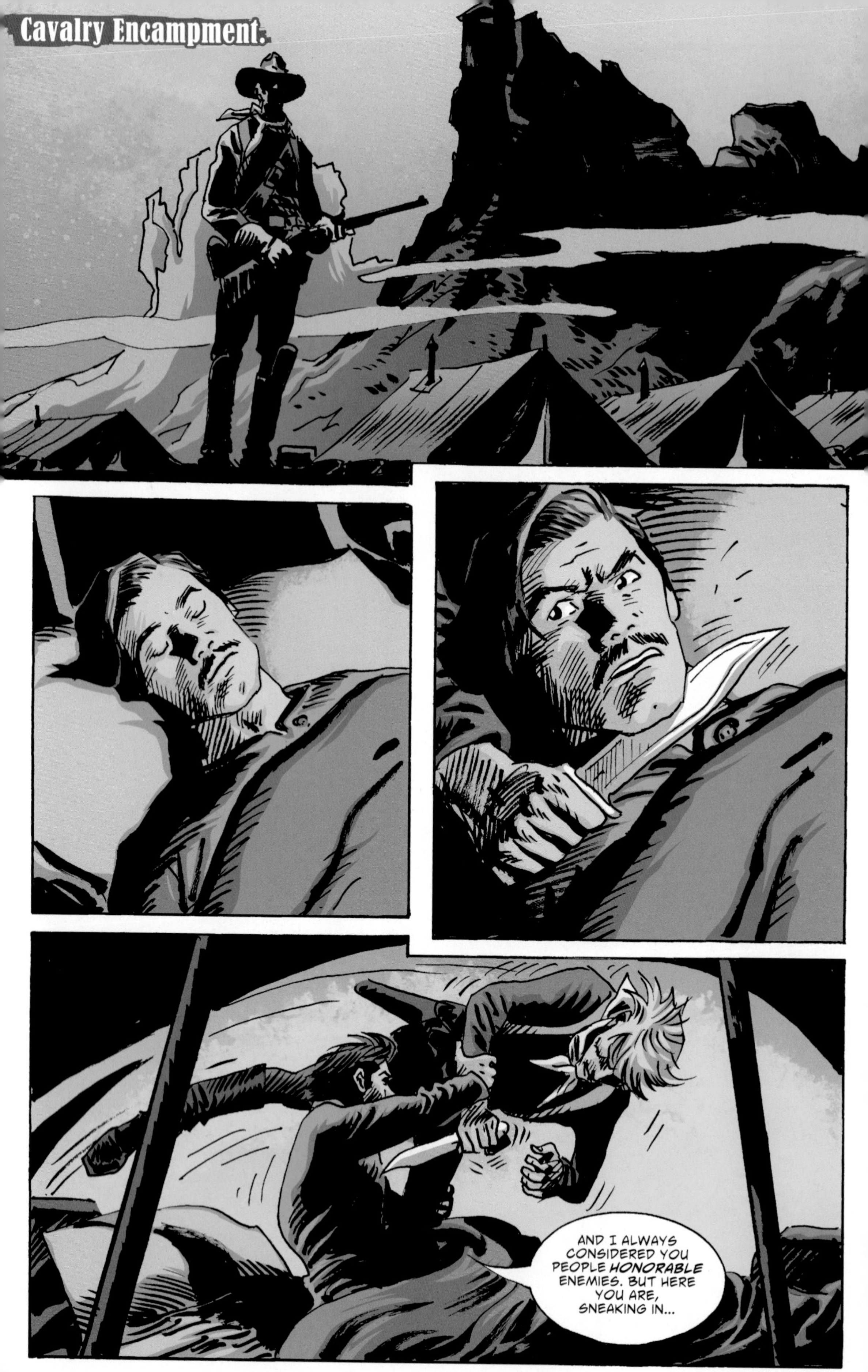
Cavalry Encampment.
AND I ALWAYS CONSIDERED YOU PEOPLE HONORABLE ENEMIES. BUT HERE YOU ARE, SNEAKING IN...

"HOW."

SKINNER?

YOU THINK THAT'S FUNNY? I COULD'VE KILLED YOU!

YOU COULD'VE TRIED...

I CAME FOR MY BROTHER, TO SHEPHERD HIM AWAY FROM THIS.

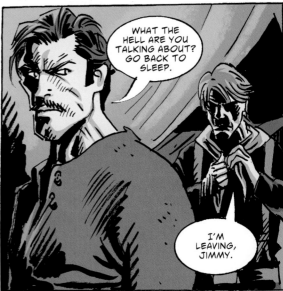

WHAT THE HELL ARE YOU TALKING ABOUT? GO BACK TO SLEEP.

I'M LEAVING, JIMMY.

THAT'S NOT FUNNY EITHER.

I'M NOT LAUGHING.

I MEANT WHAT I SAID EARLIER. YOU AND I BOTH KNOW THERE'S AT *LEAST* A HUNDRED STRONG UP THERE ON THAT RIDGE. YOU BURN THE WHOLE BUNCH, OR YOU GET *SLAUGHTERED*. AND I AIN'T ABOUT TO GET SLAUGHTERED OVER OLD HAWLEY'S STUPIDITY.

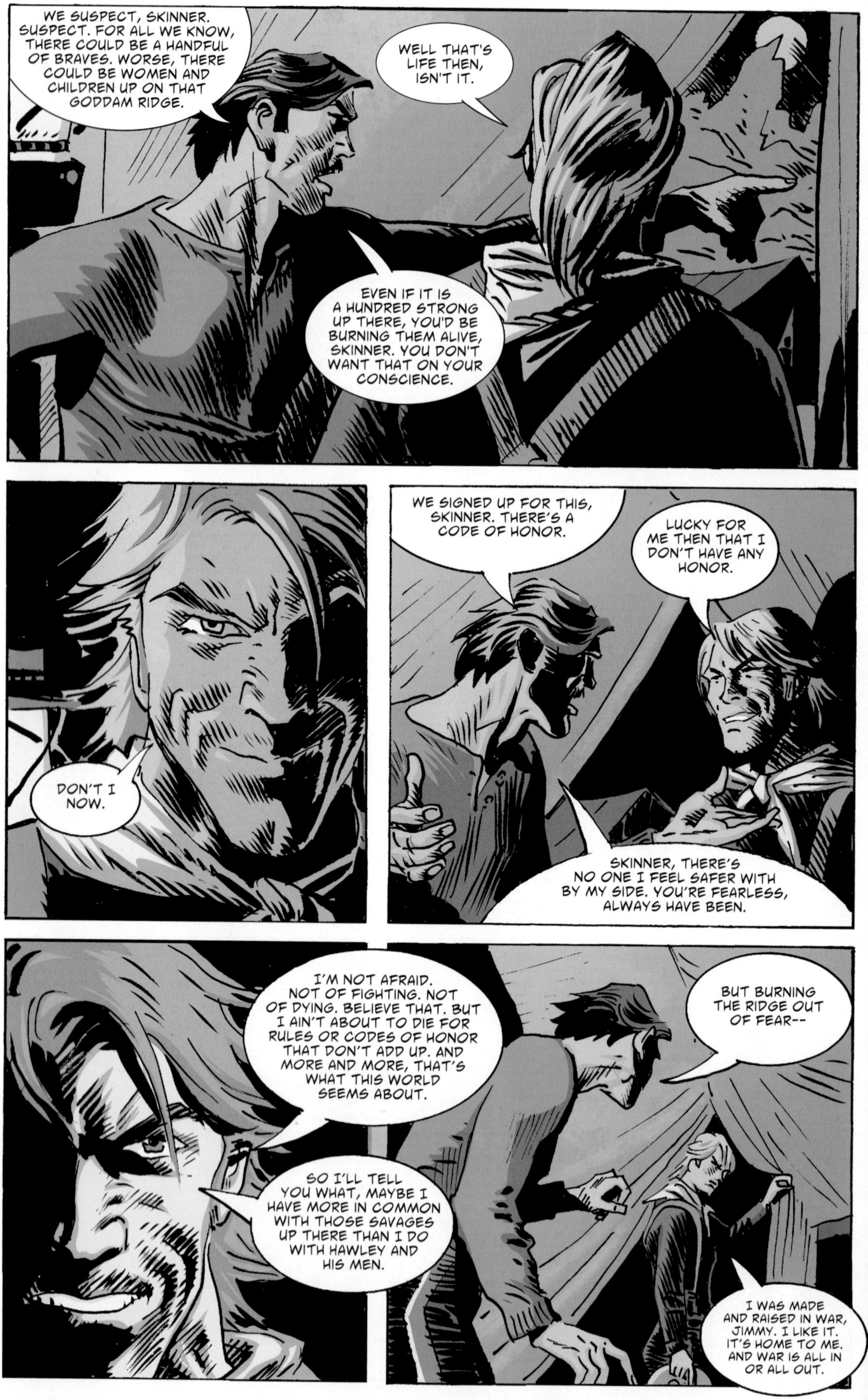
WE SUSPECT, SKINNER. SUSPECT. FOR ALL WE KNOW, THERE COULD BE A HANDFUL OF BRAVES. WORSE, THERE COULD BE WOMEN AND CHILDREN UP ON THAT GODDAM RIDGE.
WELL THAT'S LIFE THEN, ISN'T IT.
EVEN IF IT IS A HUNDRED STRONG UP THERE, YOU'D BE BURNING THEM ALIVE, SKINNER. YOU DON'T WANT THAT ON YOUR CONSCIENCE.
DON'T I NOW.
WE SIGNED UP FOR THIS, SKINNER. THERE'S A CODE OF HONOR.
LUCKY FOR ME THEN THAT I DON'T HAVE ANY HONOR.
SKINNER, THERE'S NO ONE I FEEL SAFER WITH BY MY SIDE. YOU'RE FEARLESS, ALWAYS HAVE BEEN.
I'M NOT AFRAID. NOT OF FIGHTING. NOT OF DYING. BELIEVE THAT. BUT I AIN'T ABOUT TO DIE FOR RULES OR CODES OF HONOR THAT DON'T ADD UP. AND MORE AND MORE, THAT'S WHAT THIS WORLD SEEMS ABOUT.
SO I'LL TELL YOU WHAT, MAYBE I HAVE MORE IN COMMON WITH THOSE SAVAGES UP THERE THAN I DO WITH HAWLEY AND HIS MEN.
BUT BURNING THE RIDGE OUT OF FEAR--
I WAS MADE AND RAISED IN WAR, JIMMY. I LIKE IT. IT'S HOME TO ME. AND WAR IS ALL IN OR ALL OUT.

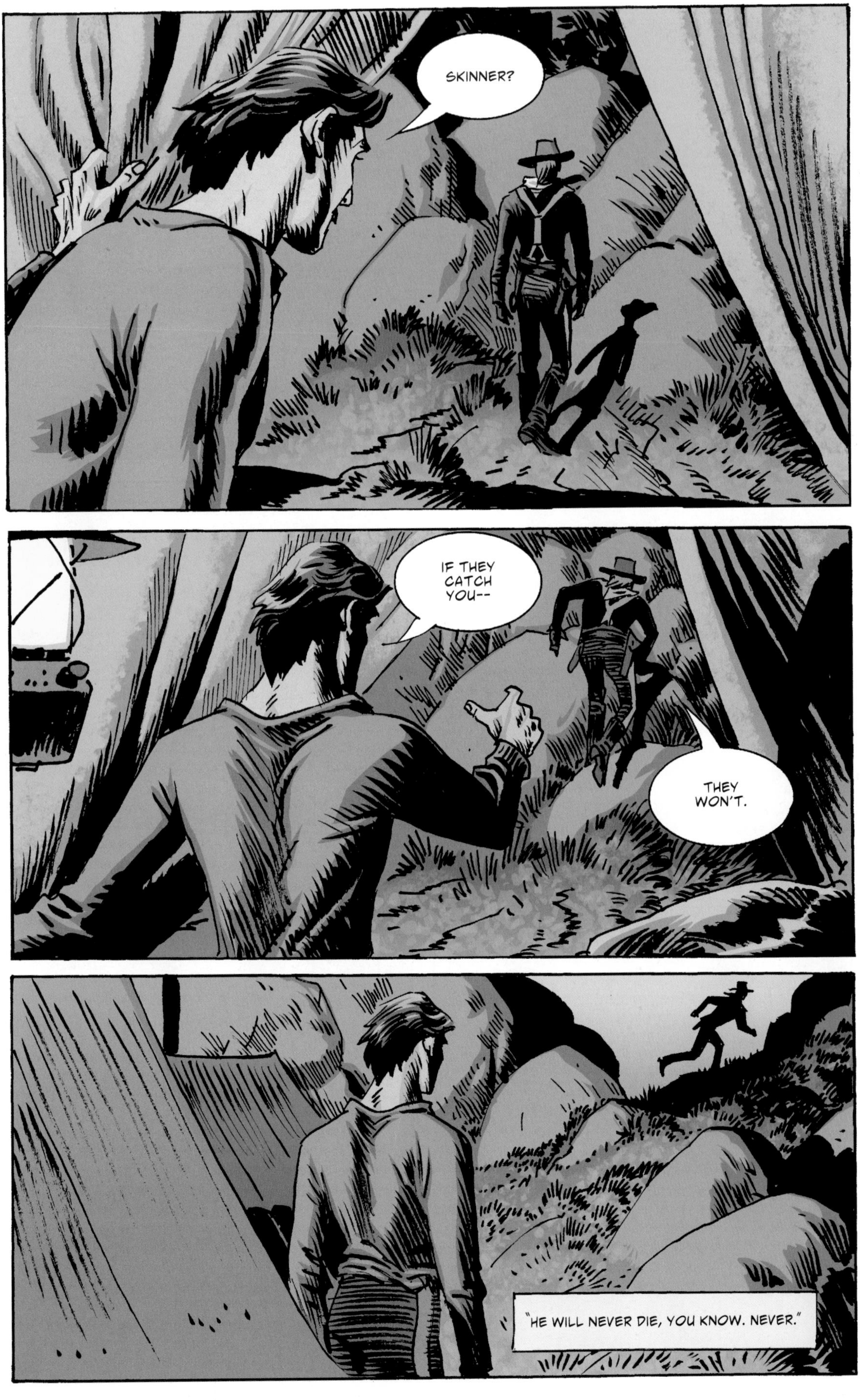
SKINNER?
IF THEY CATCH YOU--
THEY WON'T.
"HE WILL NEVER DIE, YOU KNOW. NEVER."

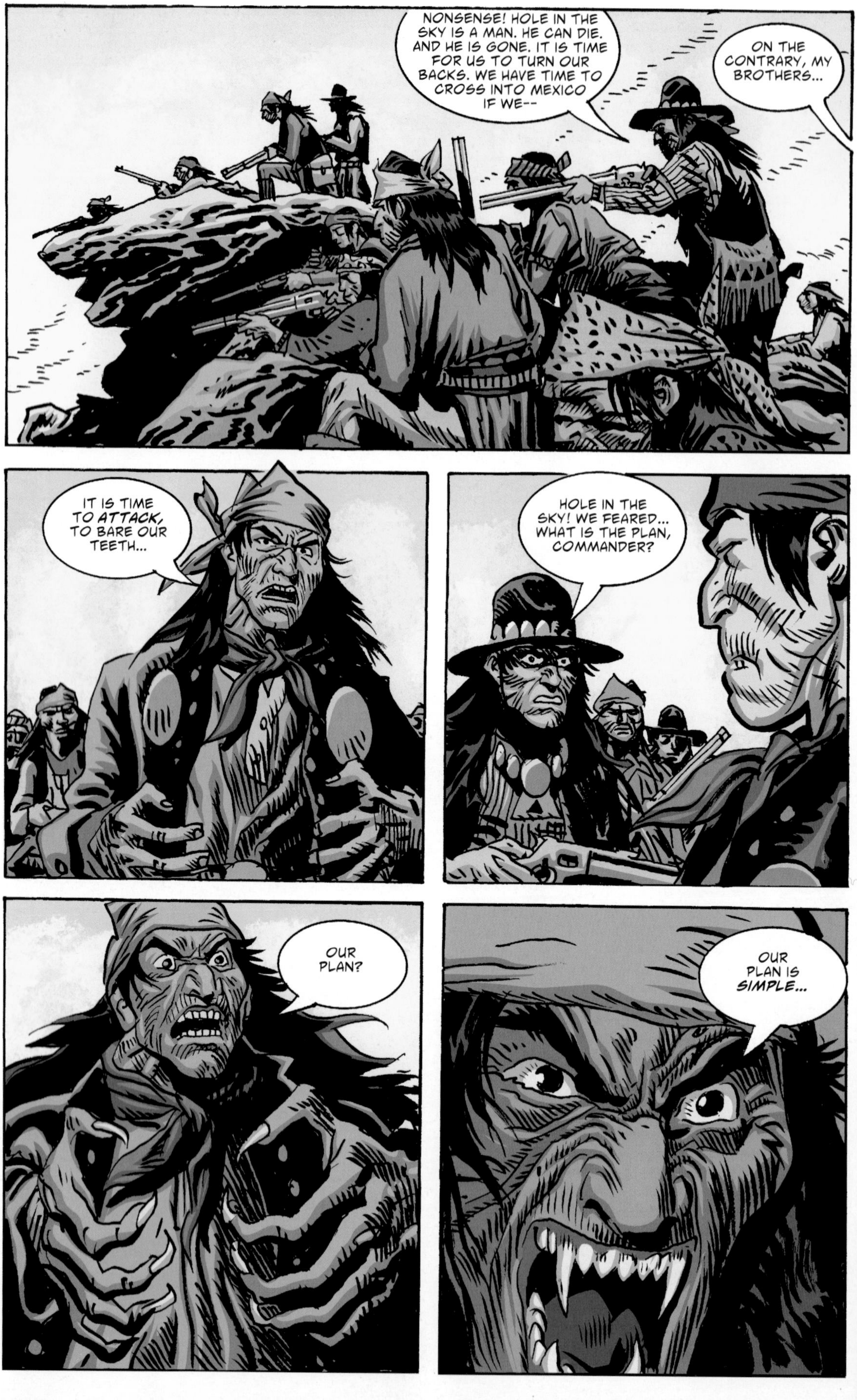
NONSENSE! HOLE IN THE SKY IS A MAN. HE CAN DIE. AND HE IS GONE. IT IS TIME FOR US TO TURN OUR BACKS. WE HAVE TIME TO CROSS INTO MEXICO IF WE--
ON THE CONTRARY, MY BROTHERS...
IT IS TIME TO *ATTACK,* TO BARE OUR TEETH...
HOLE IN THE SKY! WE FEARED... WHAT IS THE PLAN, COMMANDER?
OUR PLAN?
OUR PLAN IS *SIMPLE...*

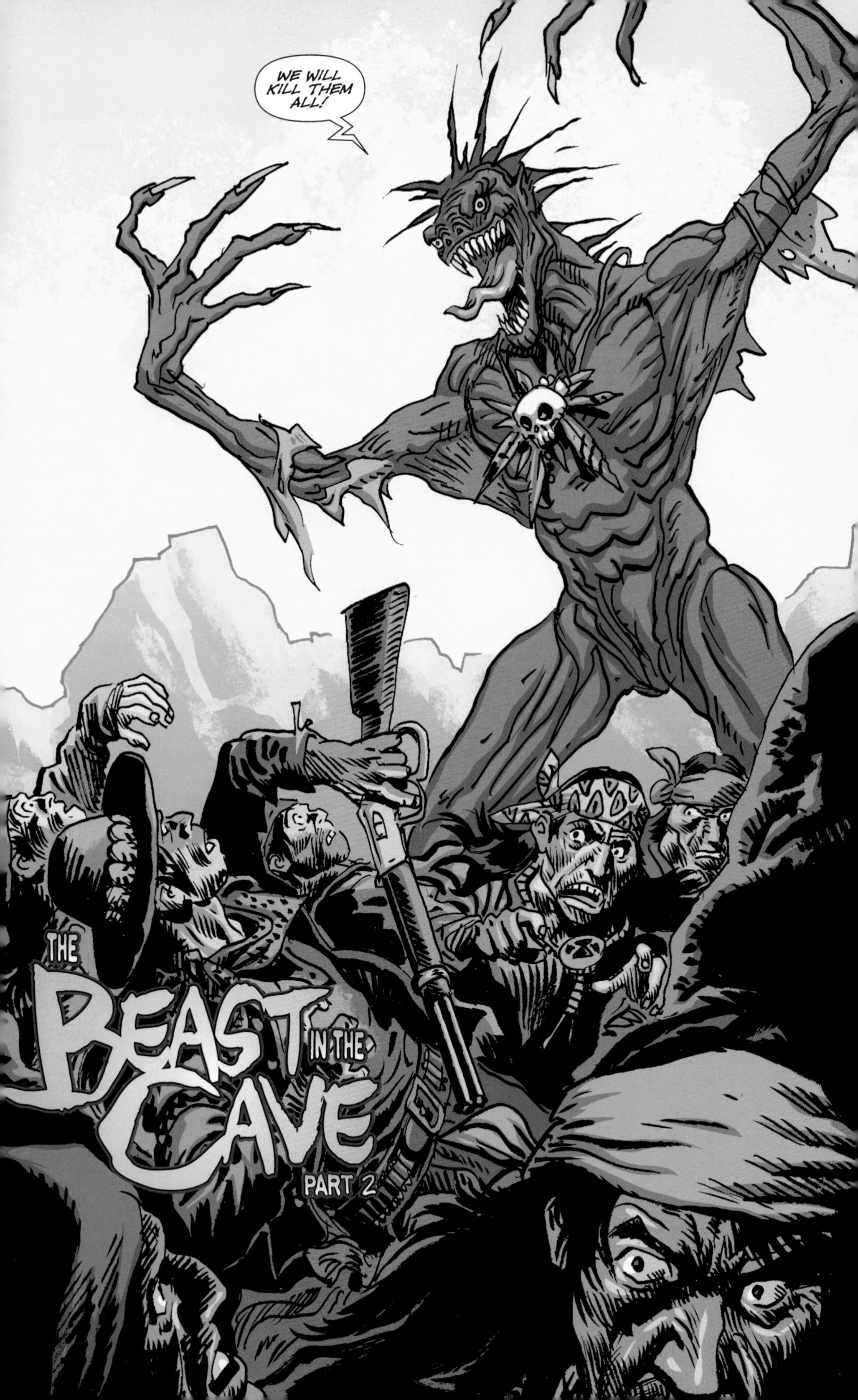
WE WILL KILL THEM ALL!
THE BEAST IN THE CAVE
PART 2

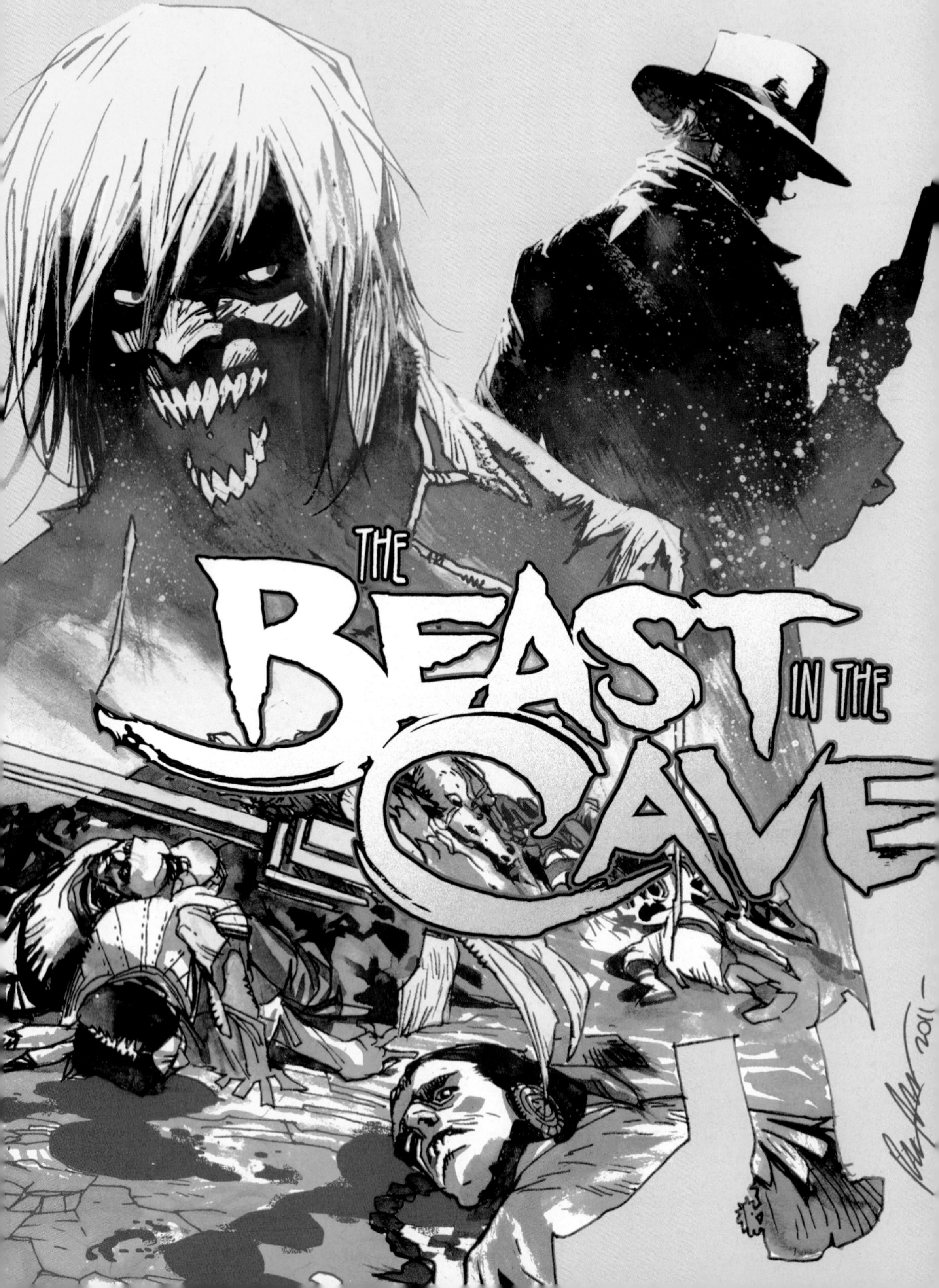
THE
BEAST
IN THE
CAVE
2011

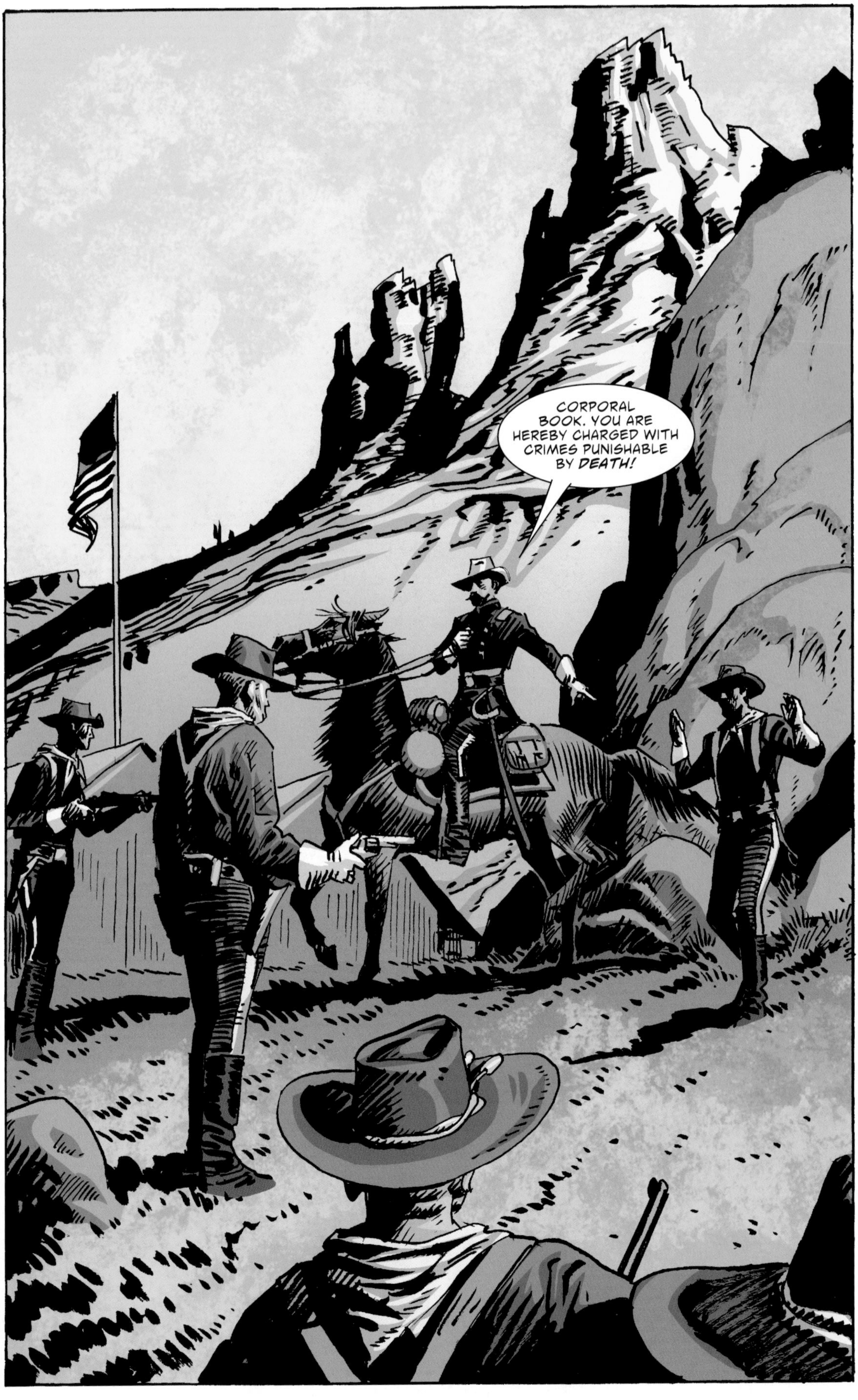
CORPORAL BOOK. YOU ARE HEREBY CHARGED WITH CRIMES PUNISHABLE BY *DEATH!*

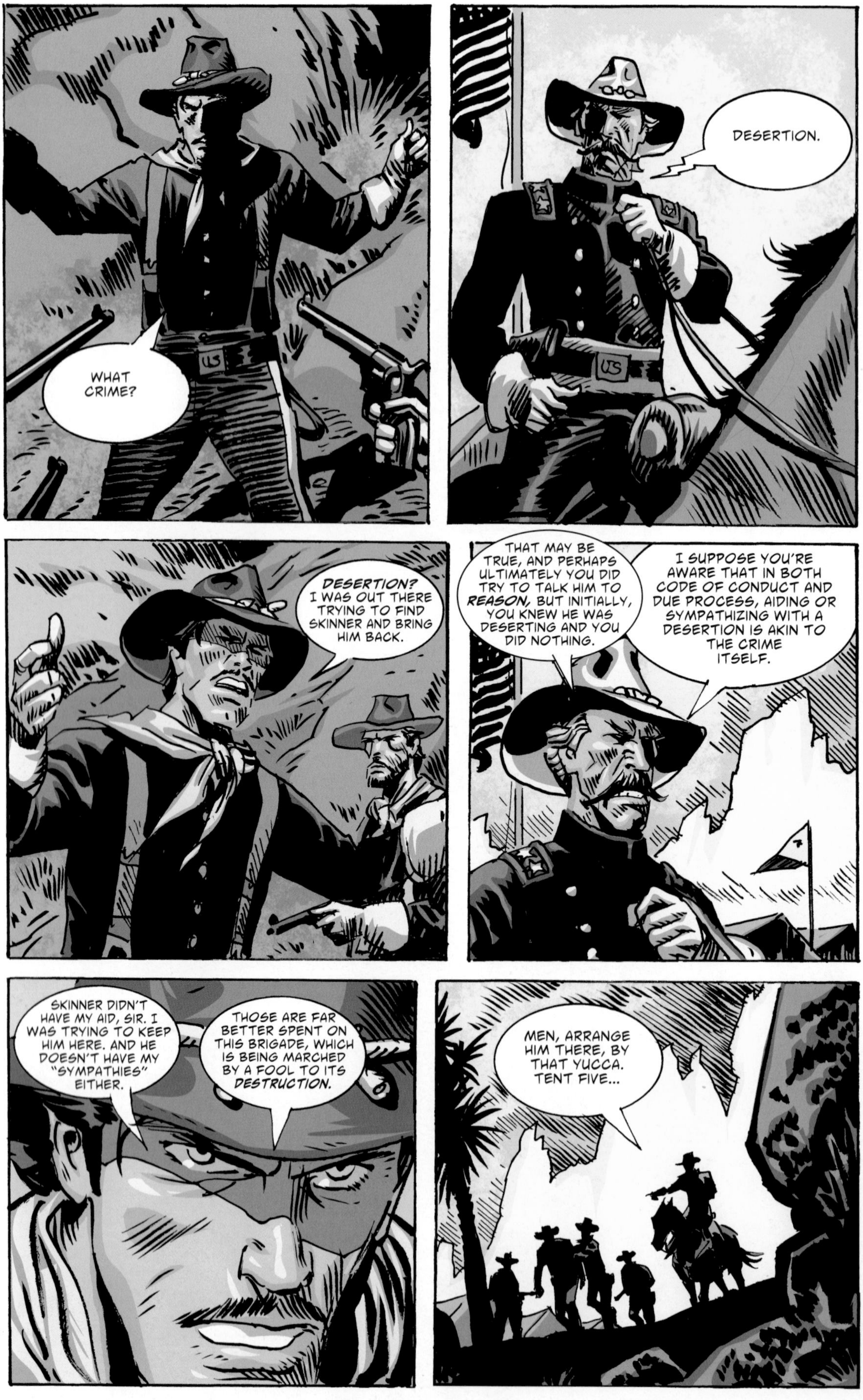
WHAT CRIME?
DESERTION.
DESERTION? I WAS OUT THERE TRYING TO FIND SKINNER AND BRING HIM BACK.
I SUPPOSE YOU'RE AWARE THAT IN BOTH CODE OF CONDUCT AND DUE PROCESS, AIDING OR SYMPATHIZING WITH A DESERTION IS AKIN TO THE CRIME ITSELF.
THAT MAY BE TRUE, AND PERHAPS ULTIMATELY YOU DID TRY TO TALK HIM TO REASON, BUT INITIALLY, YOU KNEW HE WAS DESERTING AND YOU DID NOTHING.
SKINNER DIDN'T HAVE MY AID, SIR. I WAS TRYING TO KEEP HIM HERE. AND HE DOESN'T HAVE MY "SYMPATHIES" EITHER.
THOSE ARE FAR BETTER SPENT ON THIS BRIGADE, WHICH IS BEING MARCHED BY A FOOL TO ITS DESTRUCTION.
MEN, ARRANGE HIM THERE, BY THAT YUCCA. TENT FIVE...

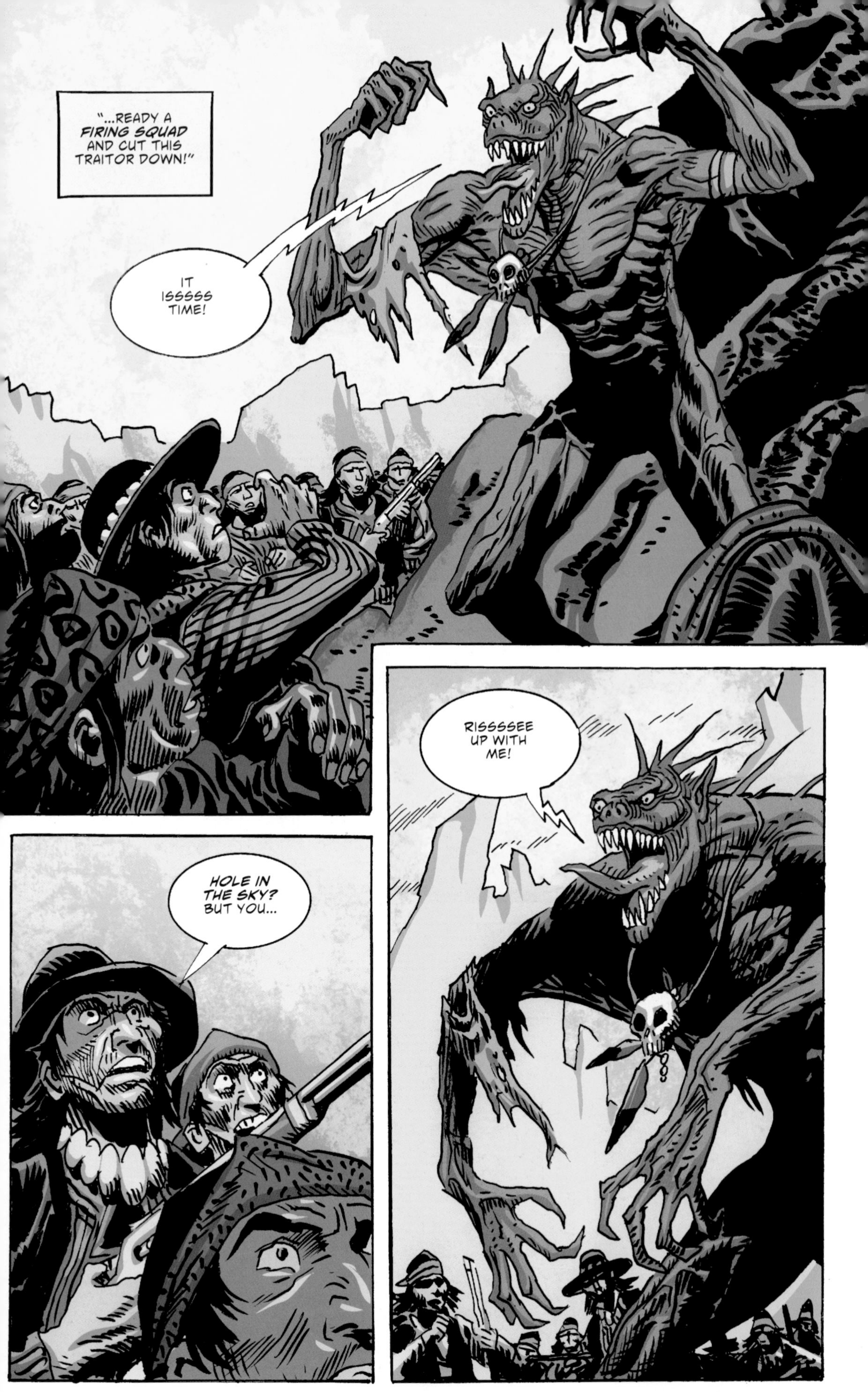
"...READY A *FIRING SQUAD* AND CUT THIS TRAITOR DOWN!"
IT ISSSSS TIME!
HOLE IN THE SKY? BUT YOU...
RISSSSEE UP WITH ME!

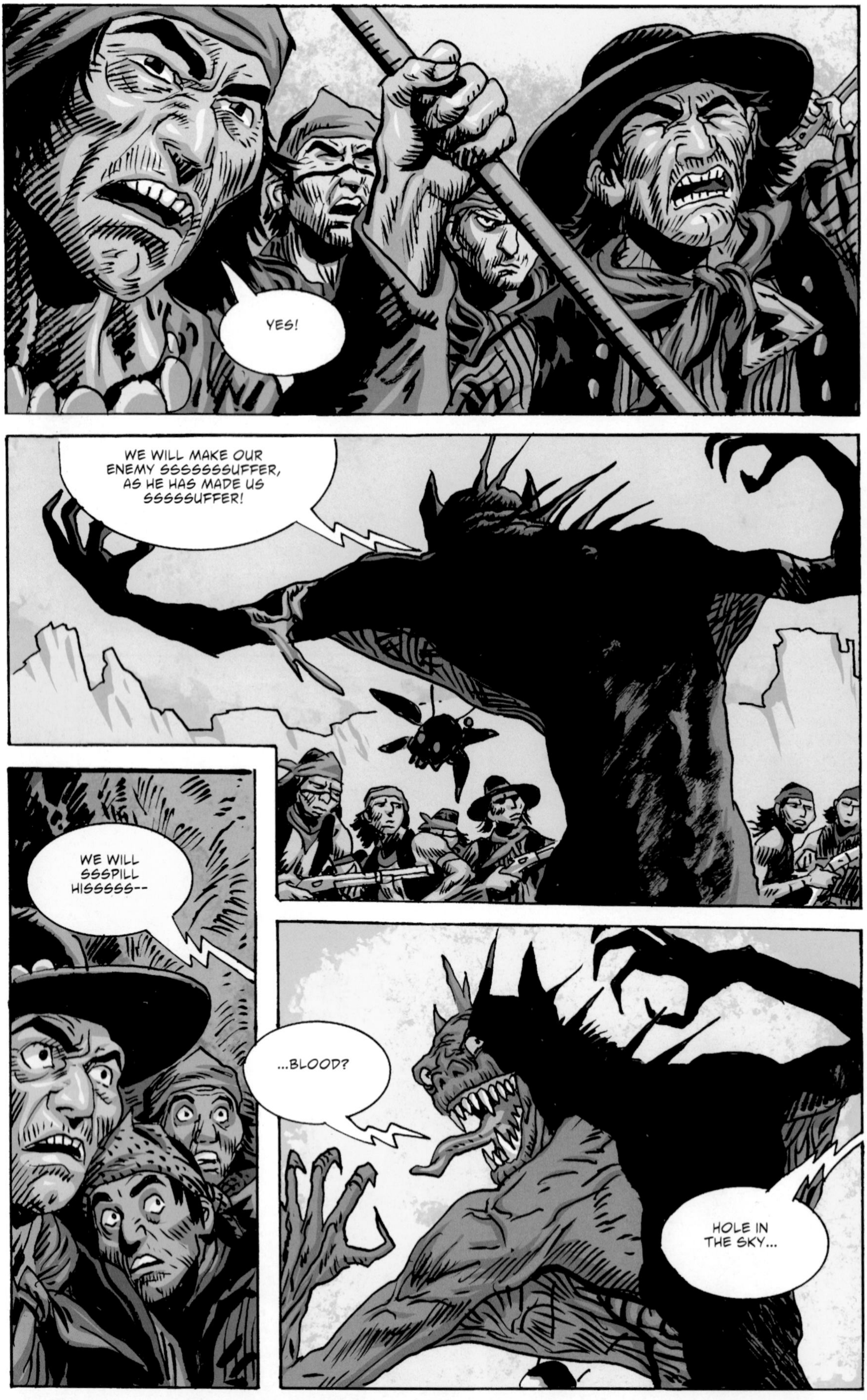
YES!
WE WILL MAKE OUR ENEMY SSSSSSSUFFER, AS HE HAS MADE US SSSSSUFFER!
WE WILL SSSPILL HISSSSS--
...BLOOD?
HOLE IN THE SKY...

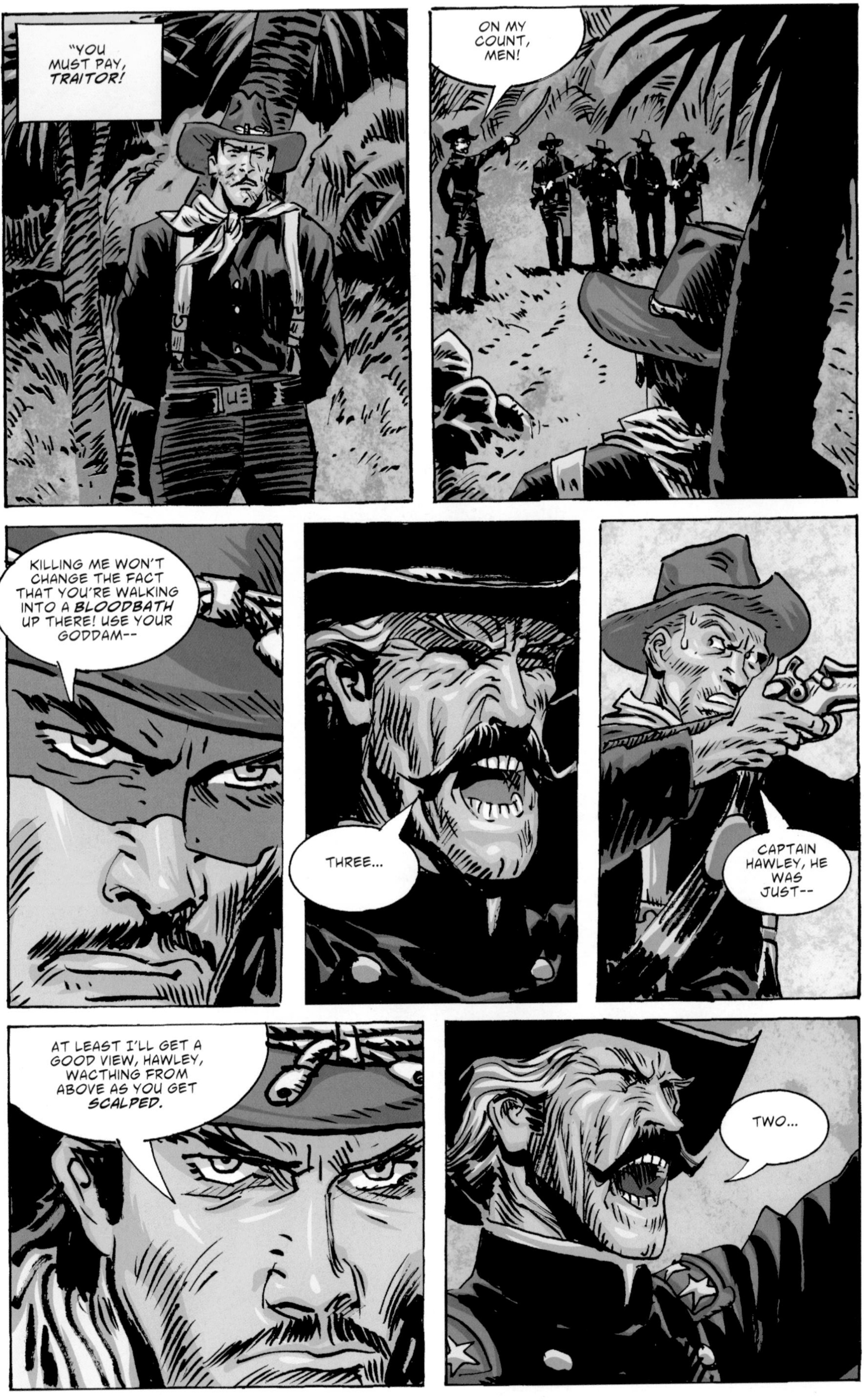
"YOU MUST PAY, TRAITOR!
ON MY COUNT, MEN!
KILLING ME WON'T CHANGE THE FACT THAT YOU'RE WALKING INTO A BLOODBATH UP THERE! USE YOUR GODDAM--
THREE...
CAPTAIN HAWLEY, HE WAS JUST--
AT LEAST I'LL GET A GOOD VIEW, HAWLEY, WACTHING FROM ABOVE AS YOU GET SCALPED.
TWO...

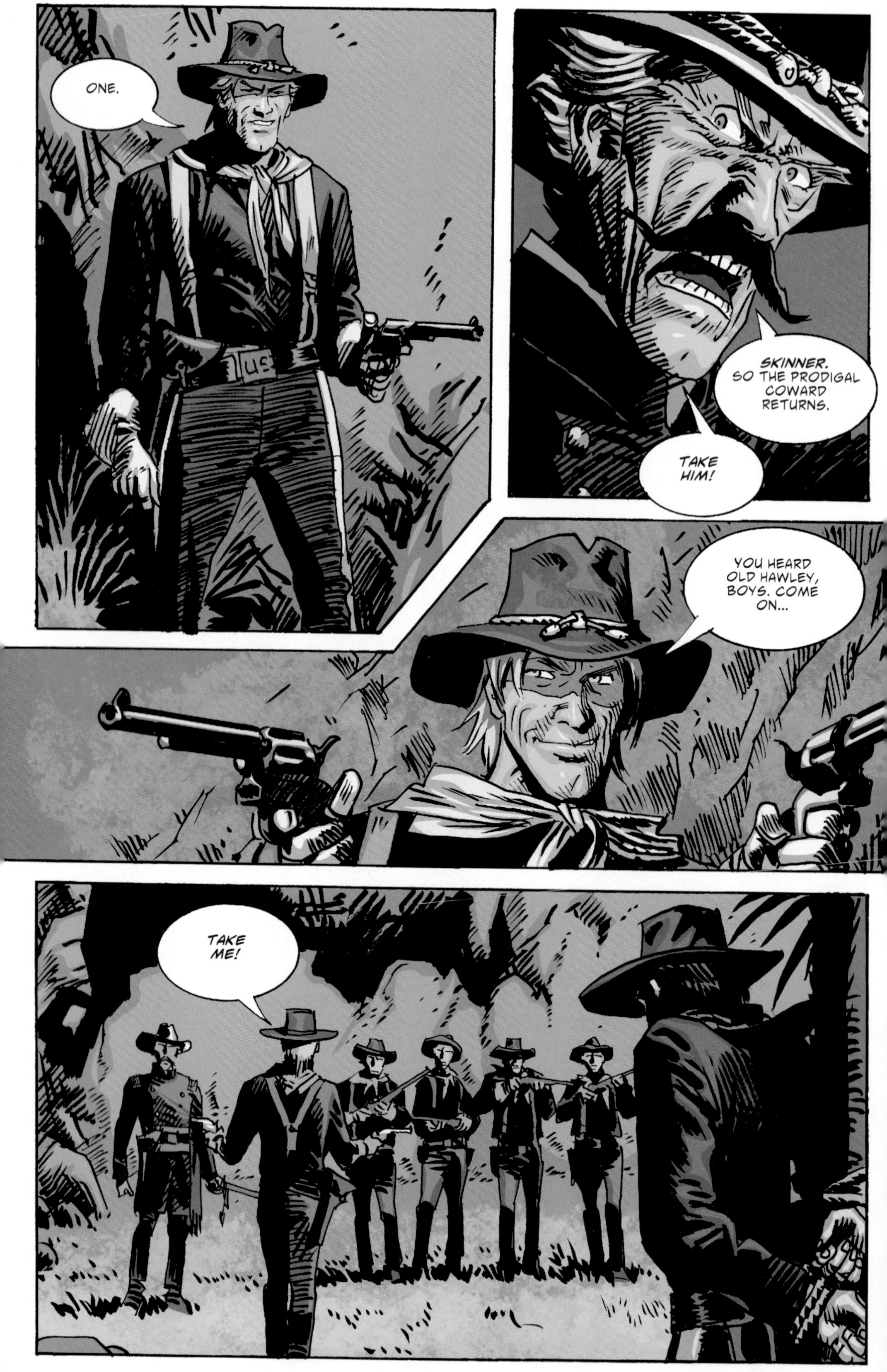
ONE.
SKINNER. SO THE PRODIGAL COWARD RETURNS.
TAKE HIM!
YOU HEARD OLD HAWLEY, BOYS. COME ON...
TAKE ME!

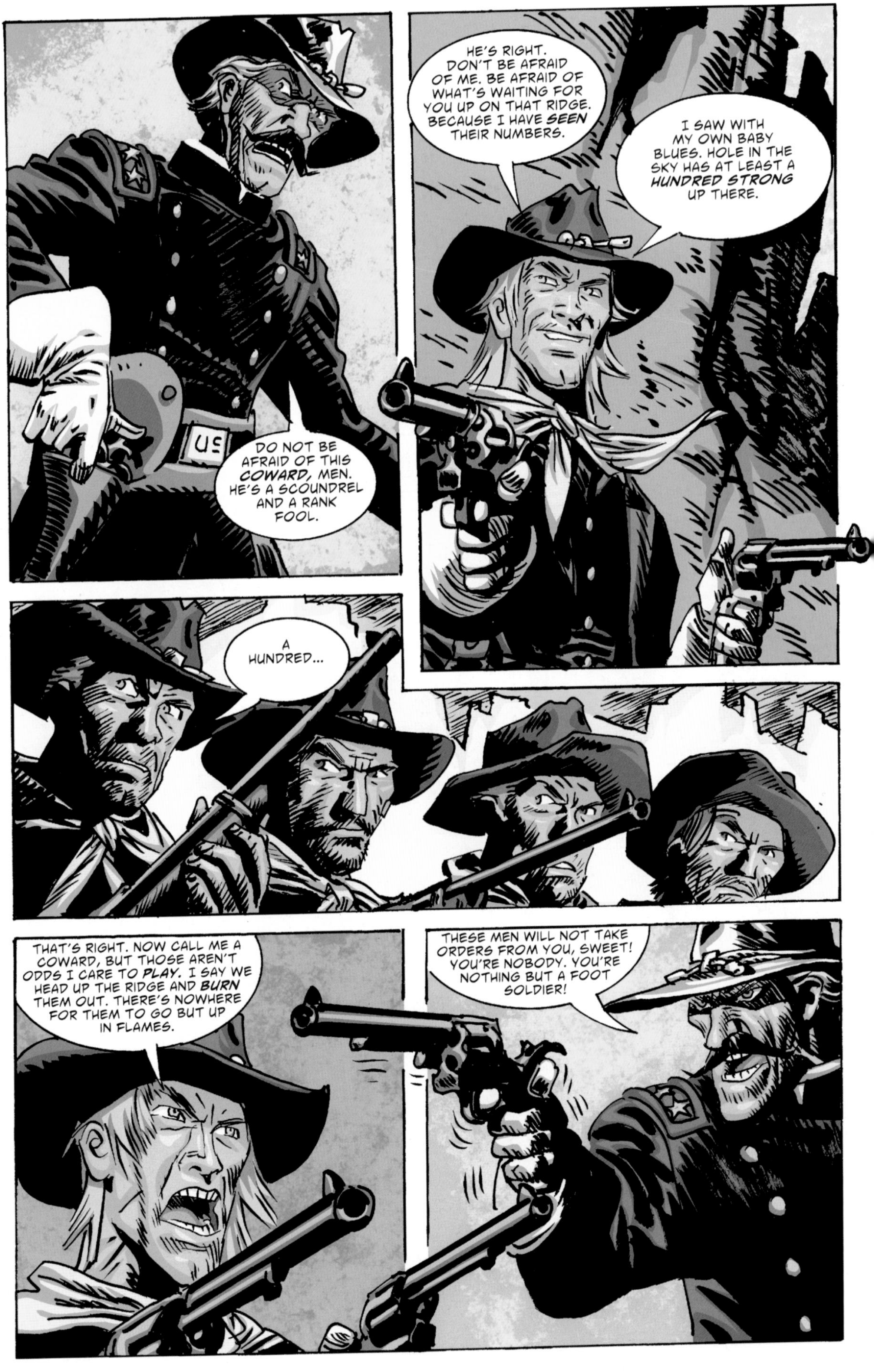
DO NOT BE AFRAID OF THIS COWARD, MEN. HE'S A SCOUNDREL AND A RANK FOOL.
HE'S RIGHT. DON'T BE AFRAID OF ME. BE AFRAID OF WHAT'S WAITING FOR YOU UP ON THAT RIDGE. BECAUSE I HAVE SEEN THEIR NUMBERS.
I SAW WITH MY OWN BABY BLUES. HOLE IN THE SKY HAS AT LEAST A HUNDRED STRONG UP THERE.
US
A HUNDRED...
THAT'S RIGHT. NOW CALL ME A COWARD, BUT THOSE AREN'T ODDS I CARE TO PLAY. I SAY WE HEAD UP THE RIDGE AND BURN THEM OUT. THERE'S NOWHERE FOR THEM TO GO BUT UP IN FLAMES.
THESE MEN WILL NOT TAKE ORDERS FROM YOU, SWEET! YOU'RE NOBODY. YOU'RE NOTHING BUT A FOOT SOLDIER!

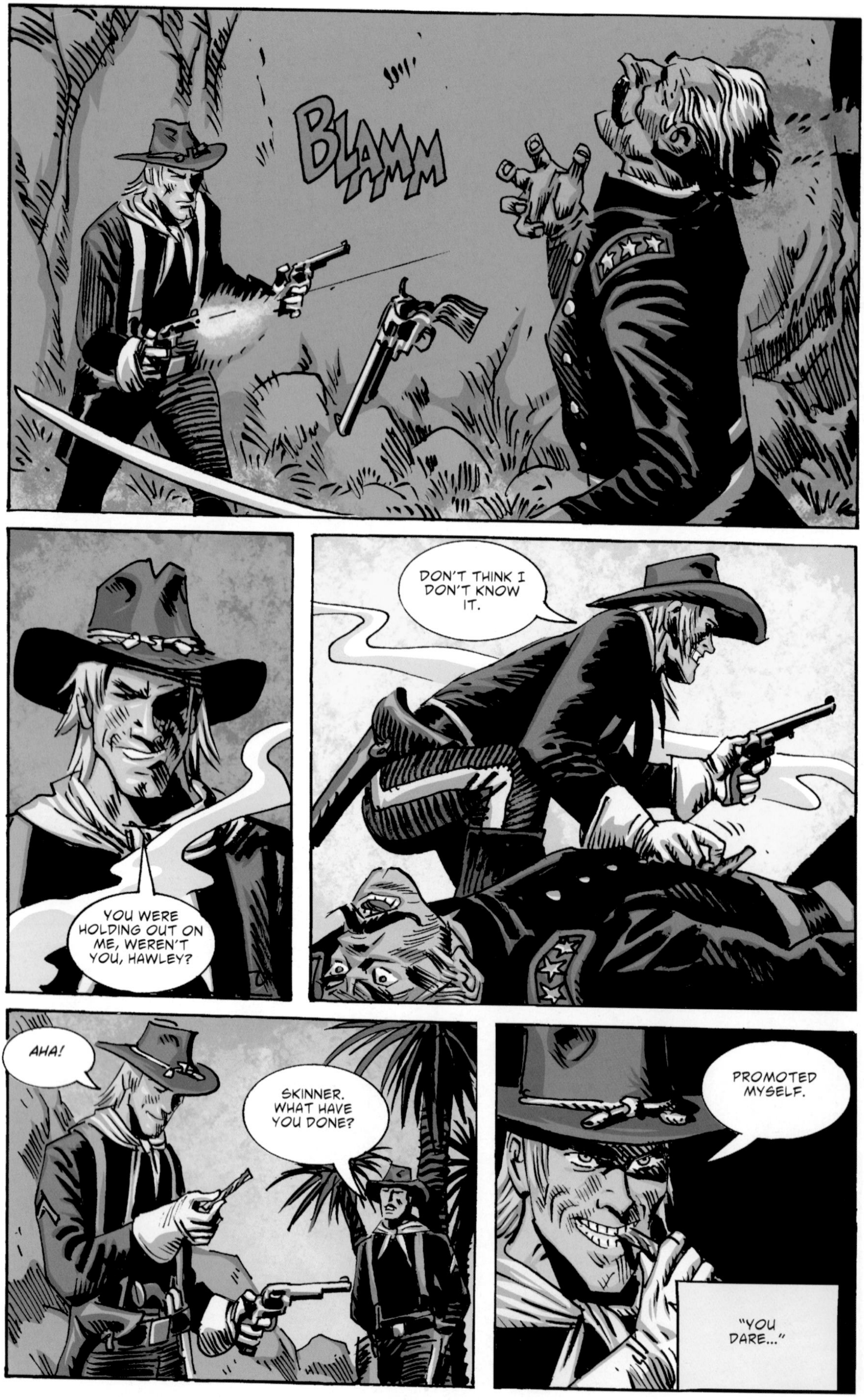
BLAMM
DON'T THINK I DON'T KNOW IT.
YOU WERE HOLDING OUT ON ME, WEREN'T YOU, HAWLEY?
AHA!
SKINNER. WHAT HAVE YOU DONE?
PROMOTED MYSELF.
"YOU DARE..."

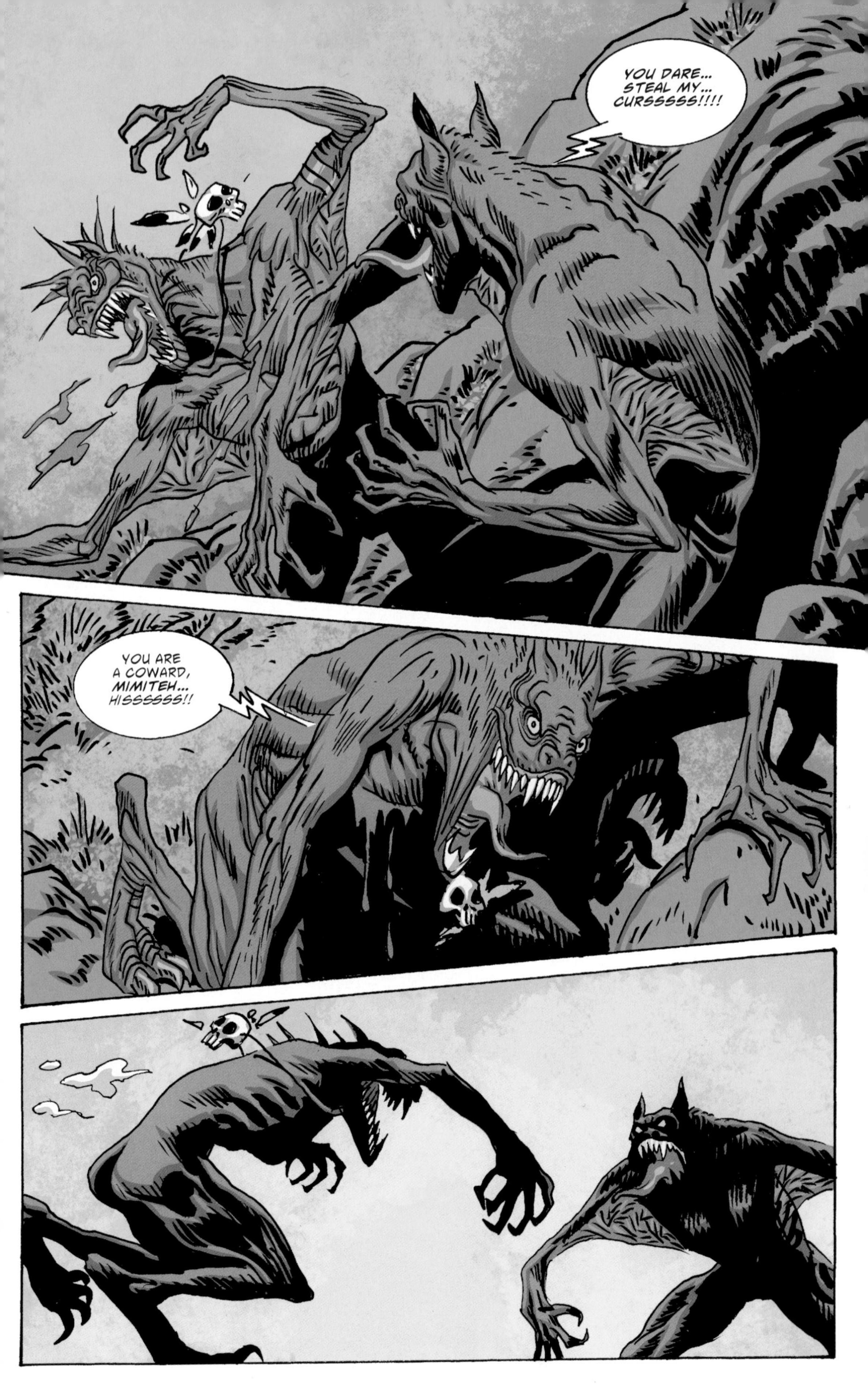
YOU DARE... STEAL MY... CURSSSSS!!!!
YOU ARE A COWARD, MIMITEH... HISSSSSS!!

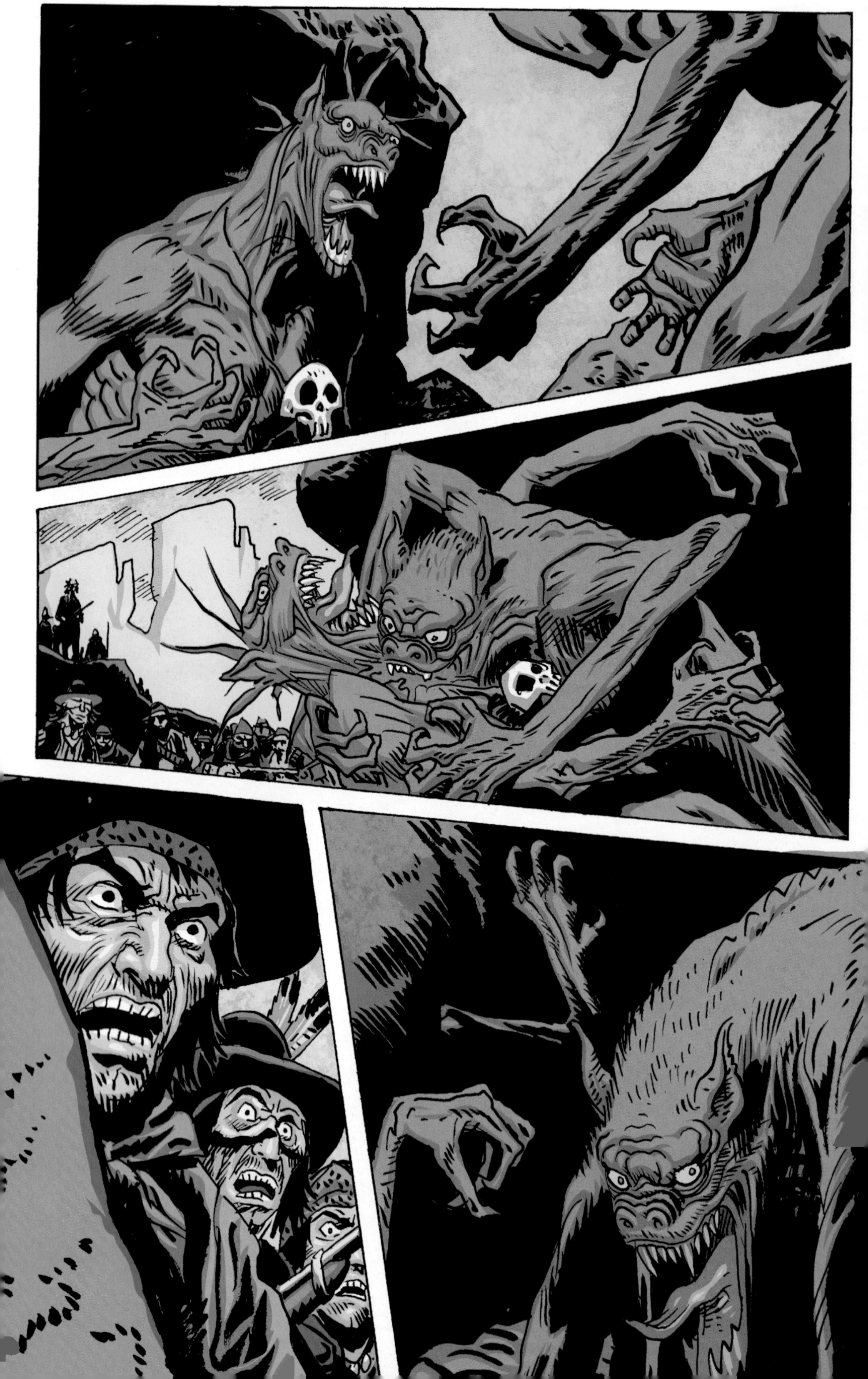

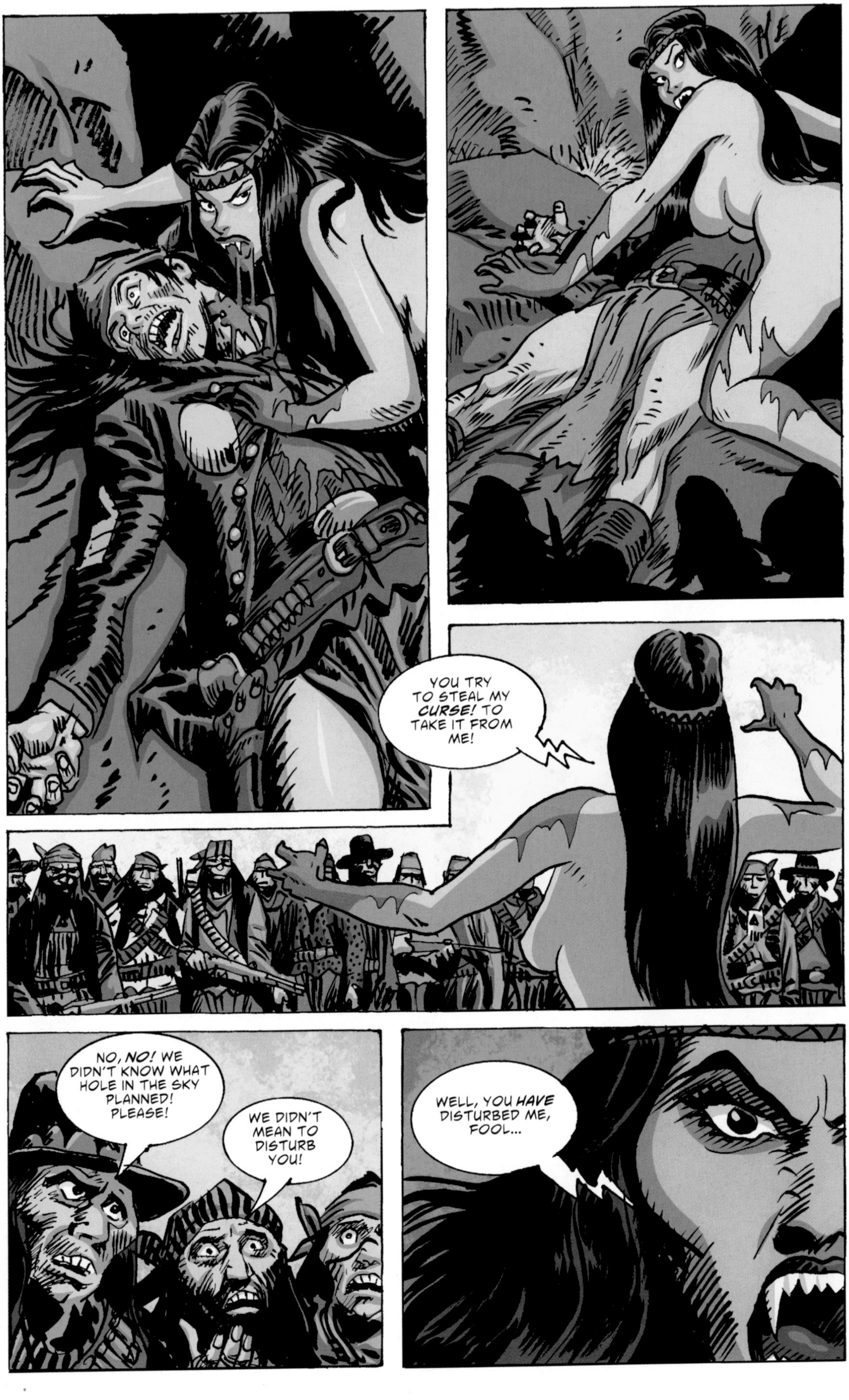
YOU TRY TO STEAL MY CURSE! TO TAKE IT FROM ME!
NO, NO! WE DIDN'T KNOW WHAT HOLE IN THE SKY PLANNED! PLEASE!
WE DIDN'T MEAN TO DISTURB YOU!
WELL, YOU HAVE DISTURBED ME, FOOL...

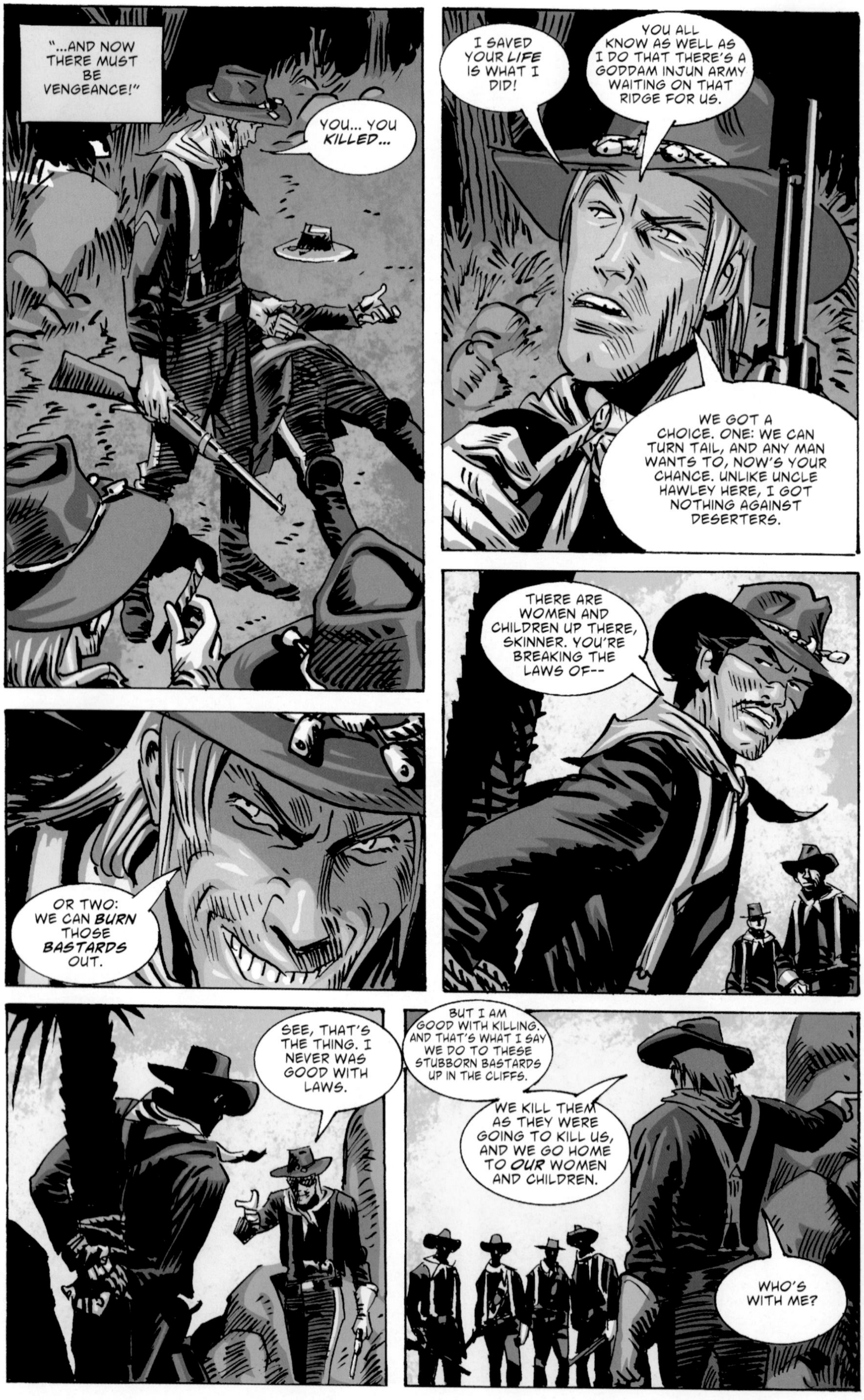

"...AND NOW THERE MUST BE VENGEANCE!"
YOU... YOU *KILLED*...
I SAVED YOUR *LIFE* IS WHAT I DID!
YOU ALL KNOW AS WELL AS I DO THAT THERE'S A GODDAM INJUN ARMY WAITING ON THAT RIDGE FOR US.
WE GOT A CHOICE. ONE: WE CAN TURN TAIL, AND ANY MAN WANTS TO, NOW'S YOUR CHANCE. UNLIKE UNCLE HAWLEY HERE, I GOT NOTHING AGAINST DESERTERS.
OR TWO: WE CAN *BURN* THOSE *BASTARDS* OUT.
THERE ARE WOMEN AND CHILDREN UP THERE, SKINNER. YOU'RE BREAKING THE LAWS OF--
SEE, THAT'S THE THING. I NEVER WAS GOOD WITH LAWS.
BUT I AM GOOD WITH KILLING. AND THAT'S WHAT I SAY WE DO TO THESE STUBBORN BASTARDS UP IN THE CLIFFS.
WE KILL THEM AS THEY WERE GOING TO KILL US, AND WE GO HOME TO *OUR* WOMEN AND CHILDREN.
WHO'S WITH ME?

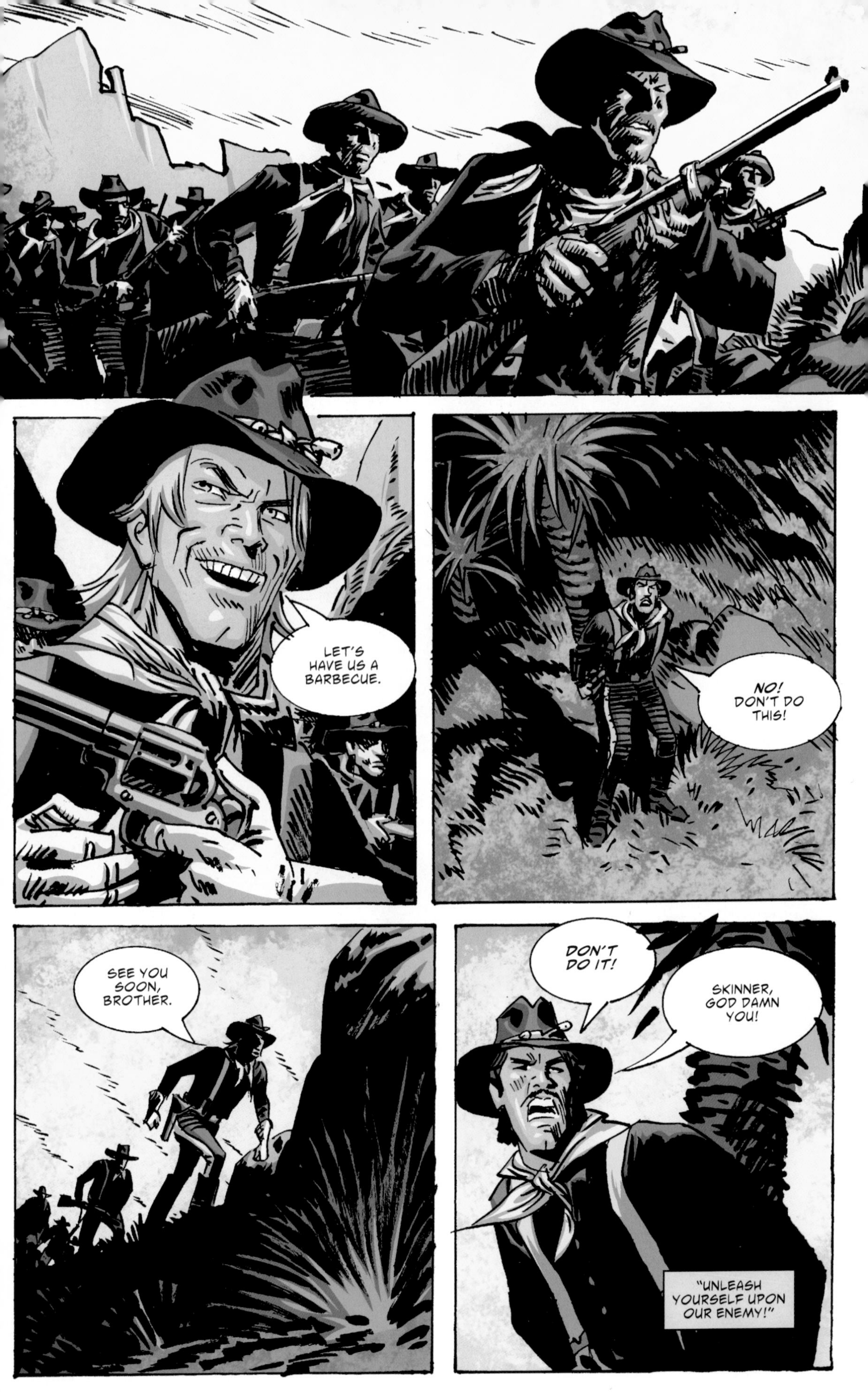
LET'S HAVE US A BARBECUE.
NO! DON'T DO THIS!
SEE YOU SOON, BROTHER.
DON'T DO IT!
SKINNER, GOD DAMN YOU!
"UNLEASH YOURSELF UPON OUR ENEMY!"

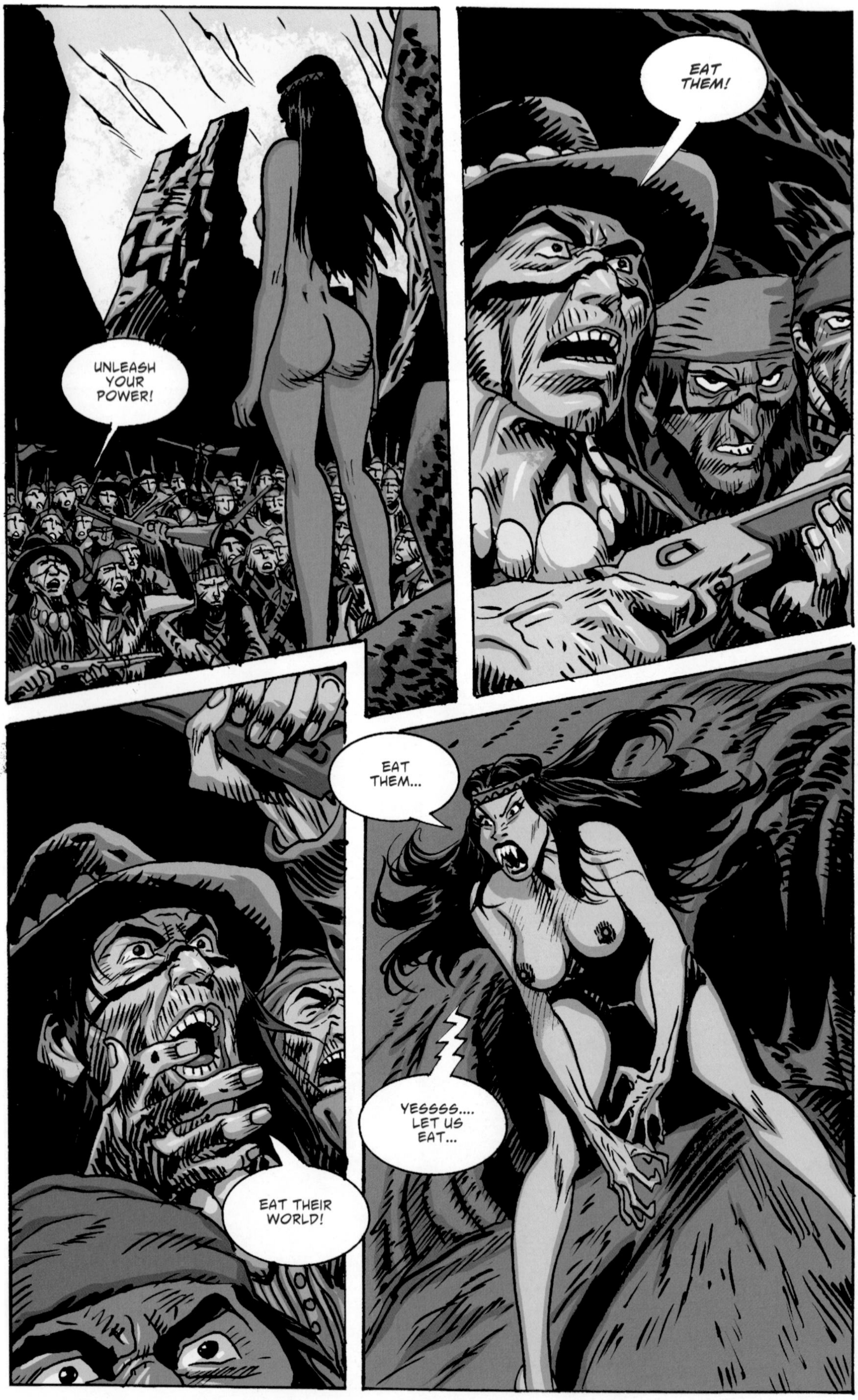
UNLEASH YOUR POWER!
EAT THEM!
EAT THEM...
YESSSS.... LET US EAT...
EAT THEIR WORLD!

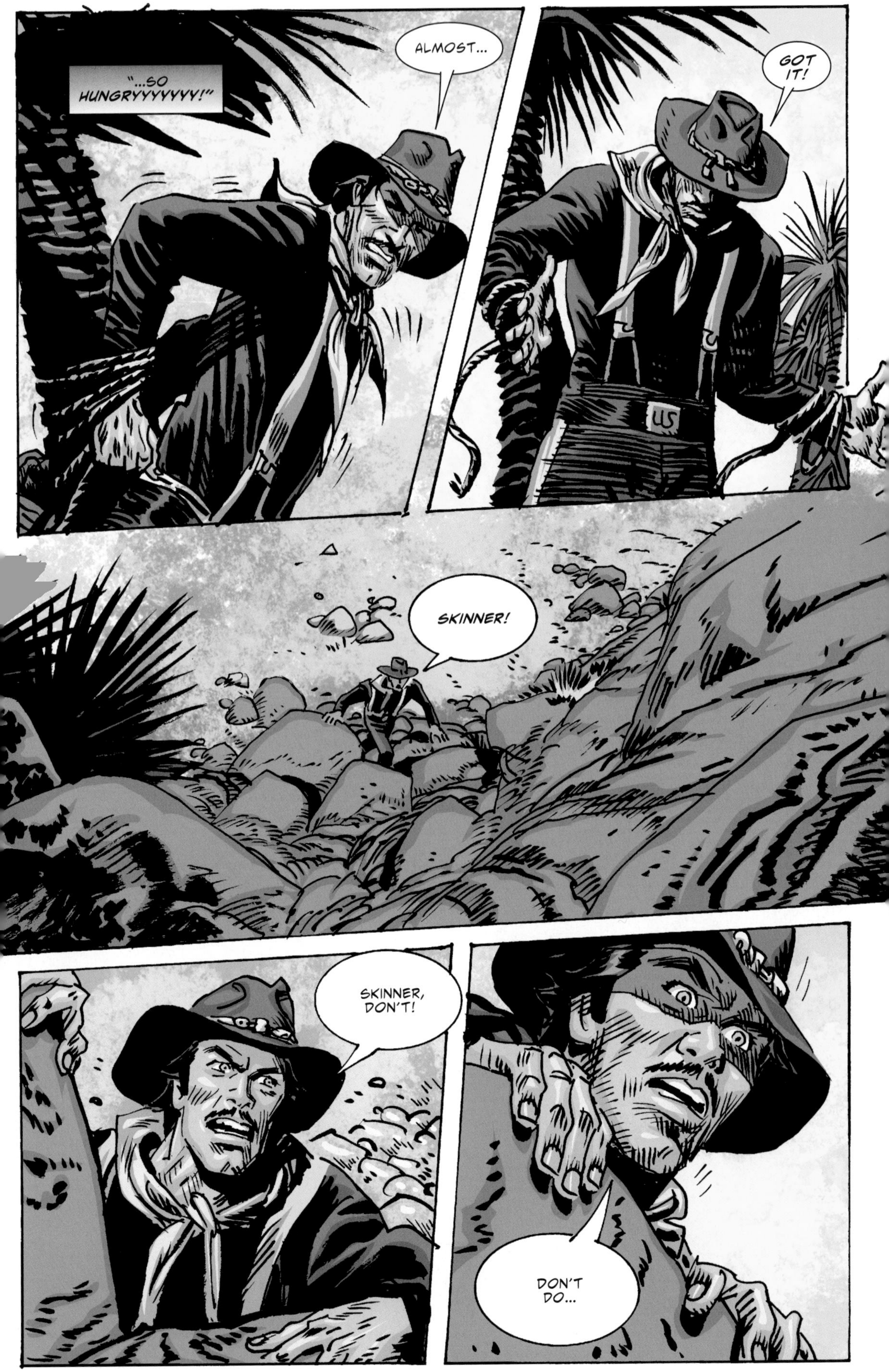
"...SO HUNGRYYYYYYY!"
ALMOST...
GOT IT!
SKINNER!
SKINNER, DON'T!
DON'T DO...

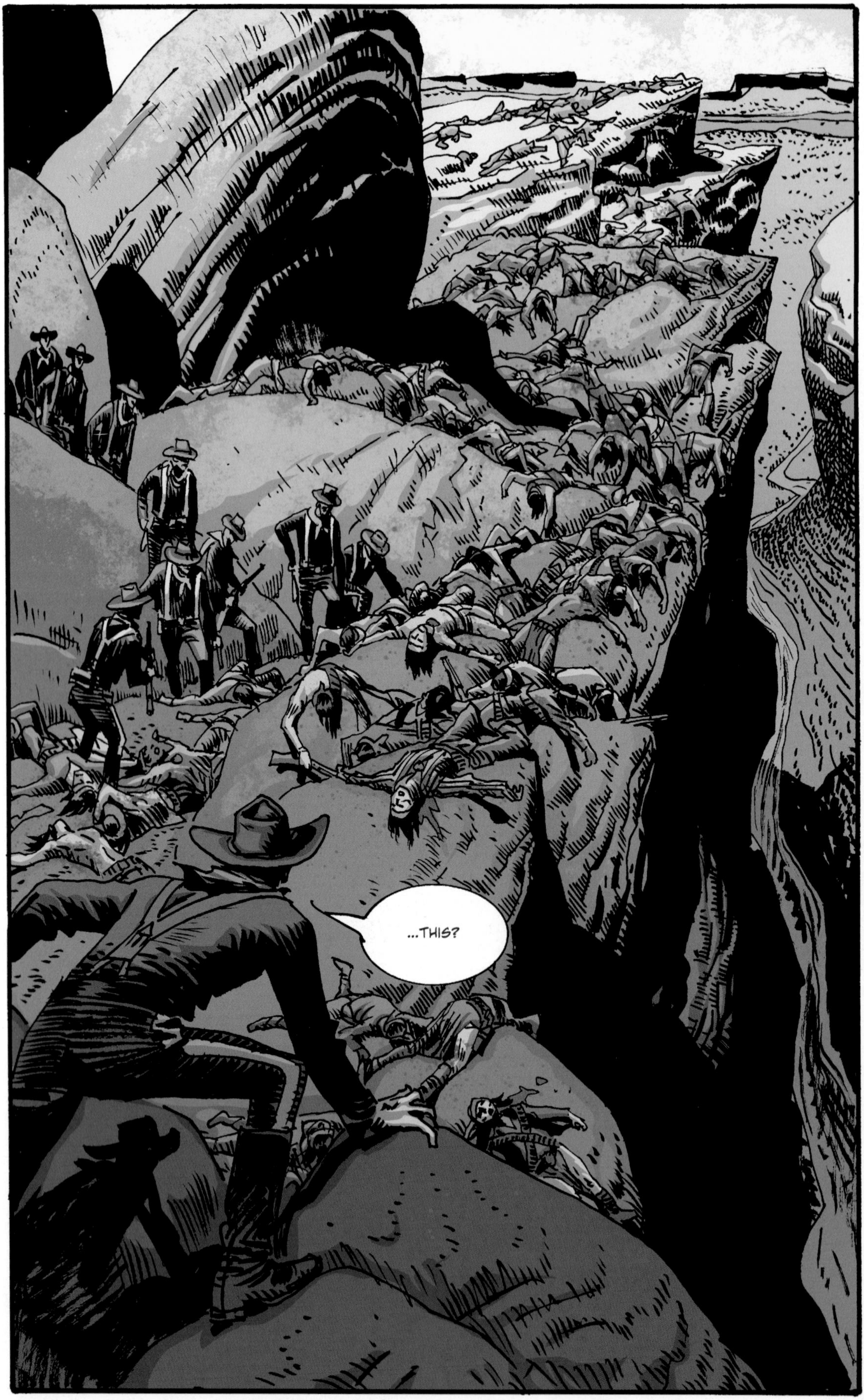
...THIS?

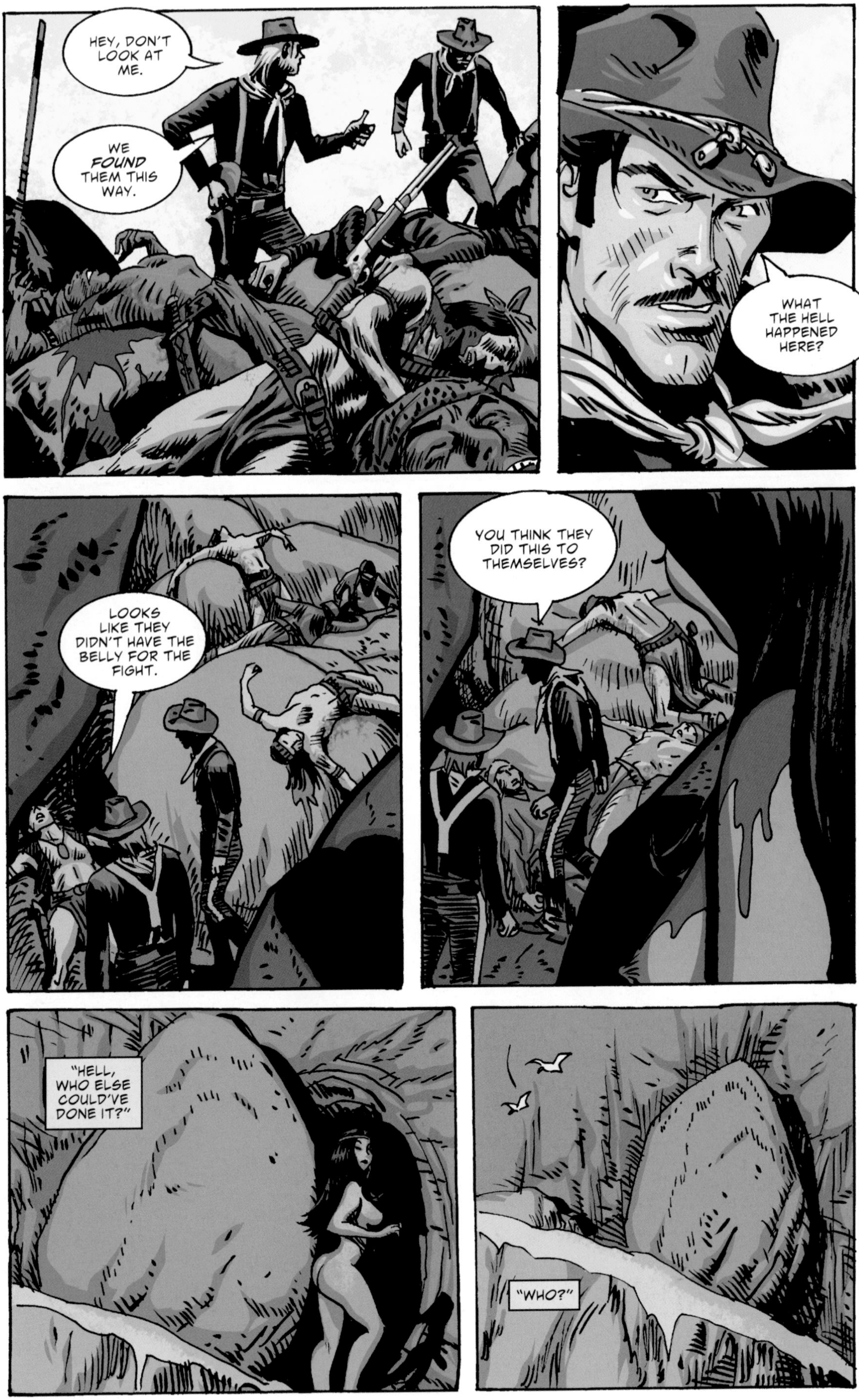
HEY, DON'T LOOK AT ME.
WE *FOUND* THEM THIS WAY.
WHAT THE HELL HAPPENED HERE?
LOOKS LIKE THEY DIDN'T HAVE THE BELLY FOR THE FIGHT.
YOU THINK THEY DID THIS TO THEMSELVES?
"HELL, WHO ELSE COULD'VE DONE IT?"
"WHO?"

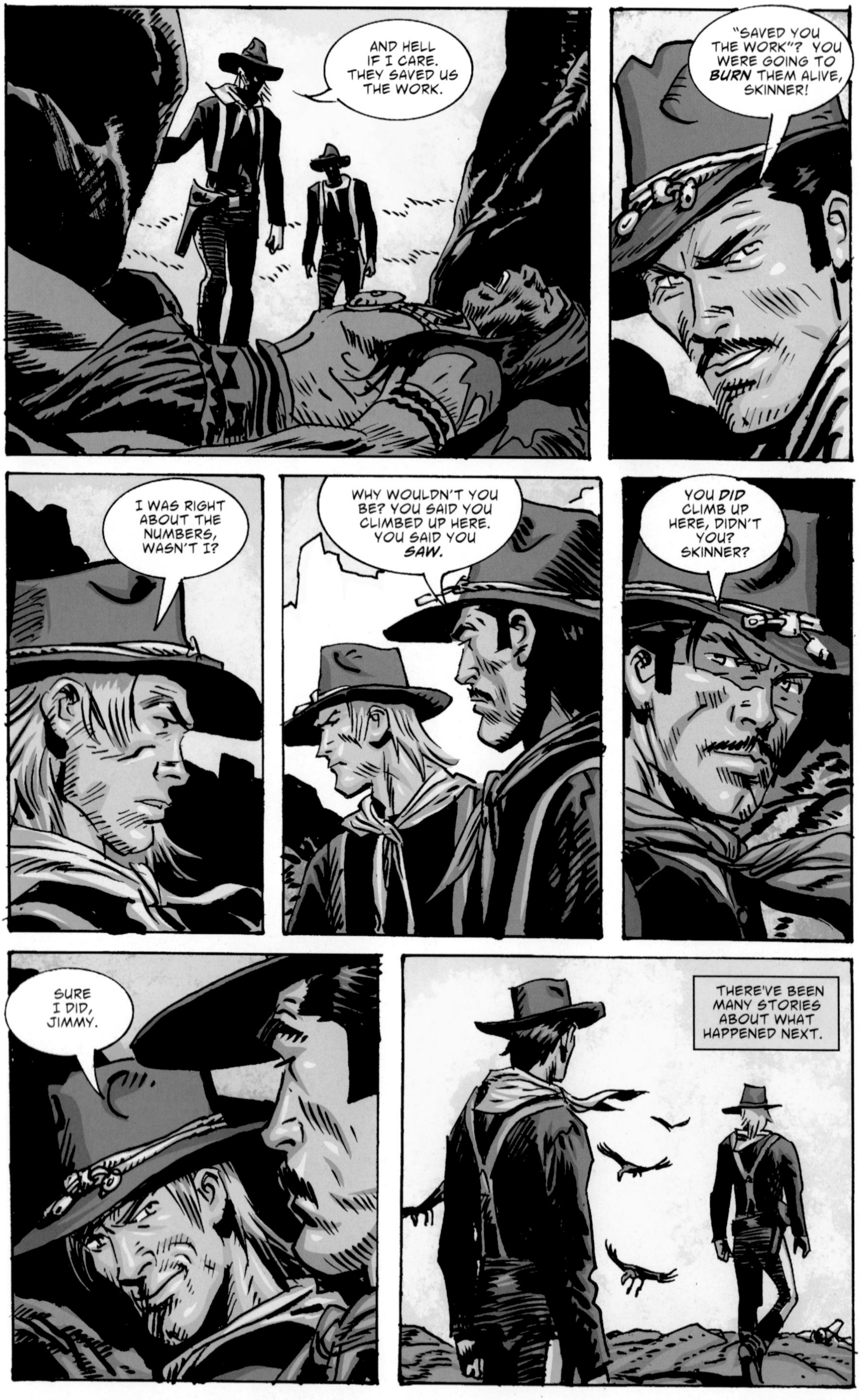
AND HELL IF I CARE. THEY SAVED US THE WORK.
"SAVED YOU THE WORK"? YOU WERE GOING TO *BURN* THEM ALIVE, SKINNER!
I WAS RIGHT ABOUT THE NUMBERS, WASN'T I?
WHY WOULDN'T YOU BE? YOU SAID YOU CLIMBED UP HERE. YOU SAID YOU *SAW.*
YOU *DID* CLIMB UP HERE, DIDN'T YOU? SKINNER?
SURE I DID, JIMMY.
THERE'VE BEEN MANY STORIES ABOUT WHAT HAPPENED NEXT.

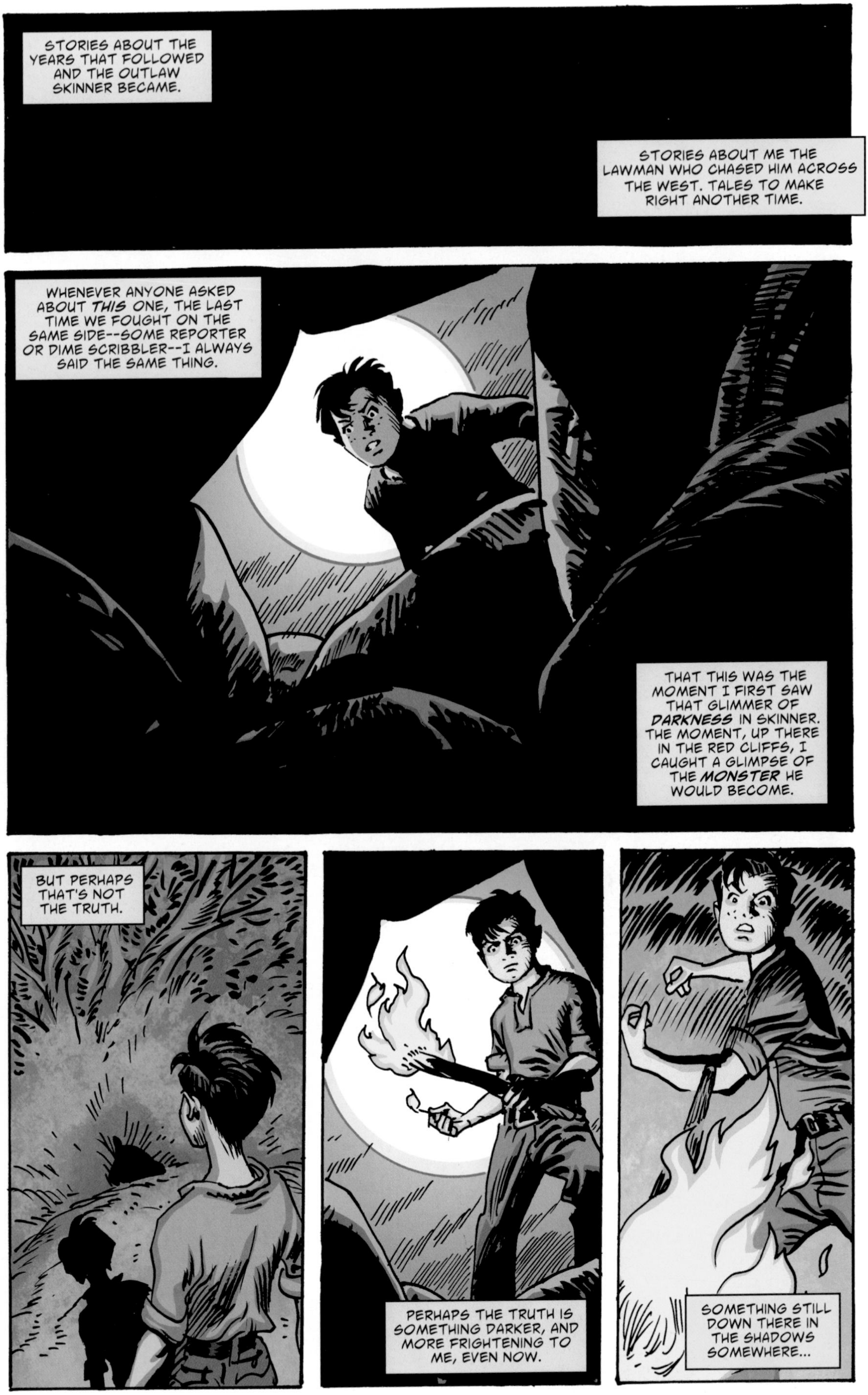
STORIES ABOUT THE YEARS THAT FOLLOWED AND THE OUTLAW SKINNER BECAME.
STORIES ABOUT ME THE LAWMAN WHO CHASED HIM ACROSS THE WEST. TALES TO MAKE RIGHT ANOTHER TIME.
WHENEVER ANYONE ASKED ABOUT *THIS* ONE, THE LAST TIME WE FOUGHT ON THE SAME SIDE--SOME REPORTER OR DIME SCRIBBLER--I ALWAYS SAID THE SAME THING.
THAT THIS WAS THE MOMENT I FIRST SAW THAT GLIMMER OF *DARKNESS* IN SKINNER. THE MOMENT, UP THERE IN THE RED CLIFFS, I CAUGHT A GLIMPSE OF THE *MONSTER* HE WOULD BECOME.
BUT PERHAPS THAT'S NOT THE TRUTH.
PERHAPS THE TRUTH IS SOMETHING DARKER, AND MORE FRIGHTENING TO ME, EVEN NOW.
SOMETHING STILL DOWN THERE IN THE SHADOWS SOMEWHERE...

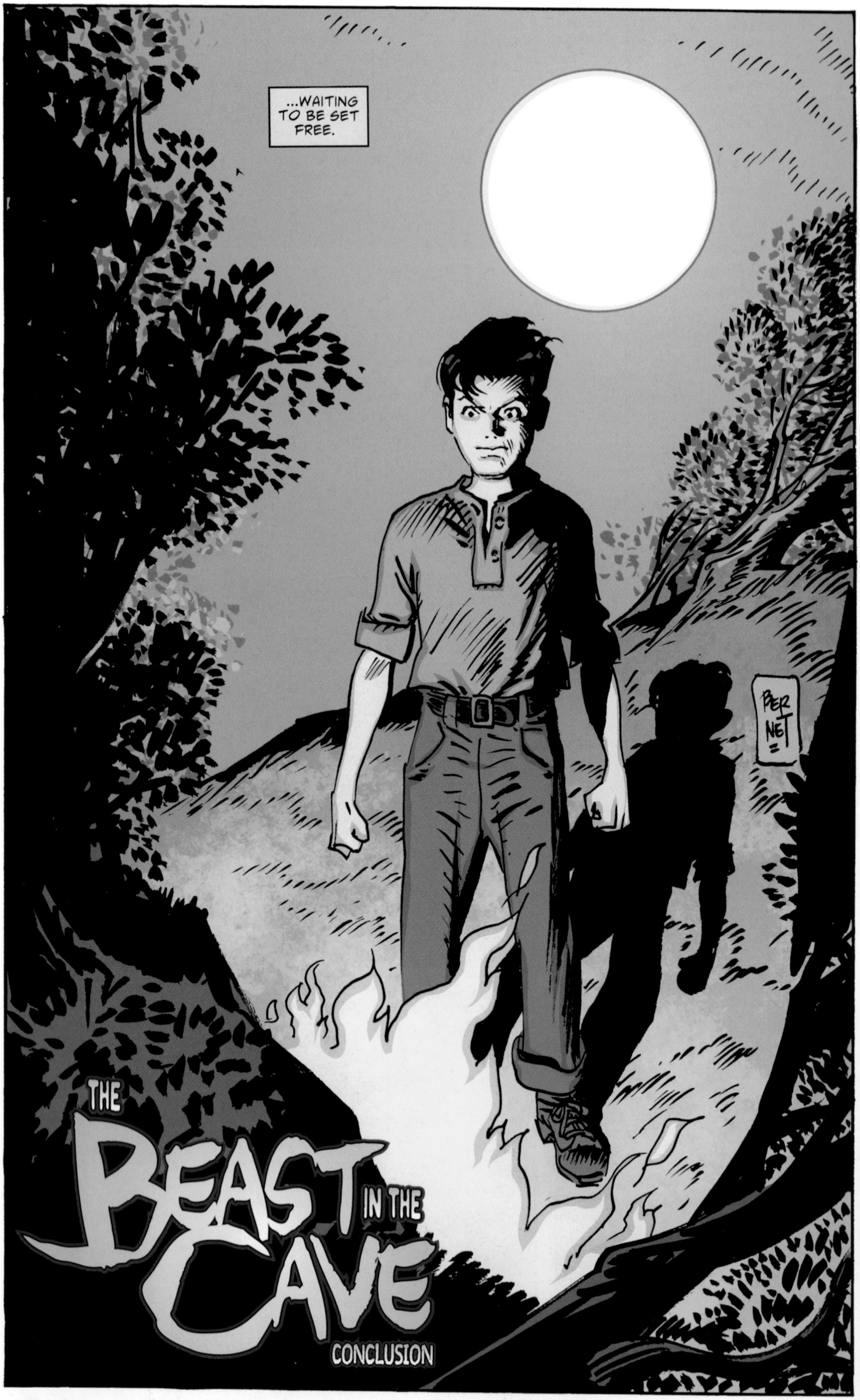

...WAITING TO BE SET FREE.
BERNET
THE BEAST IN THE CAVE
CONCLUSION

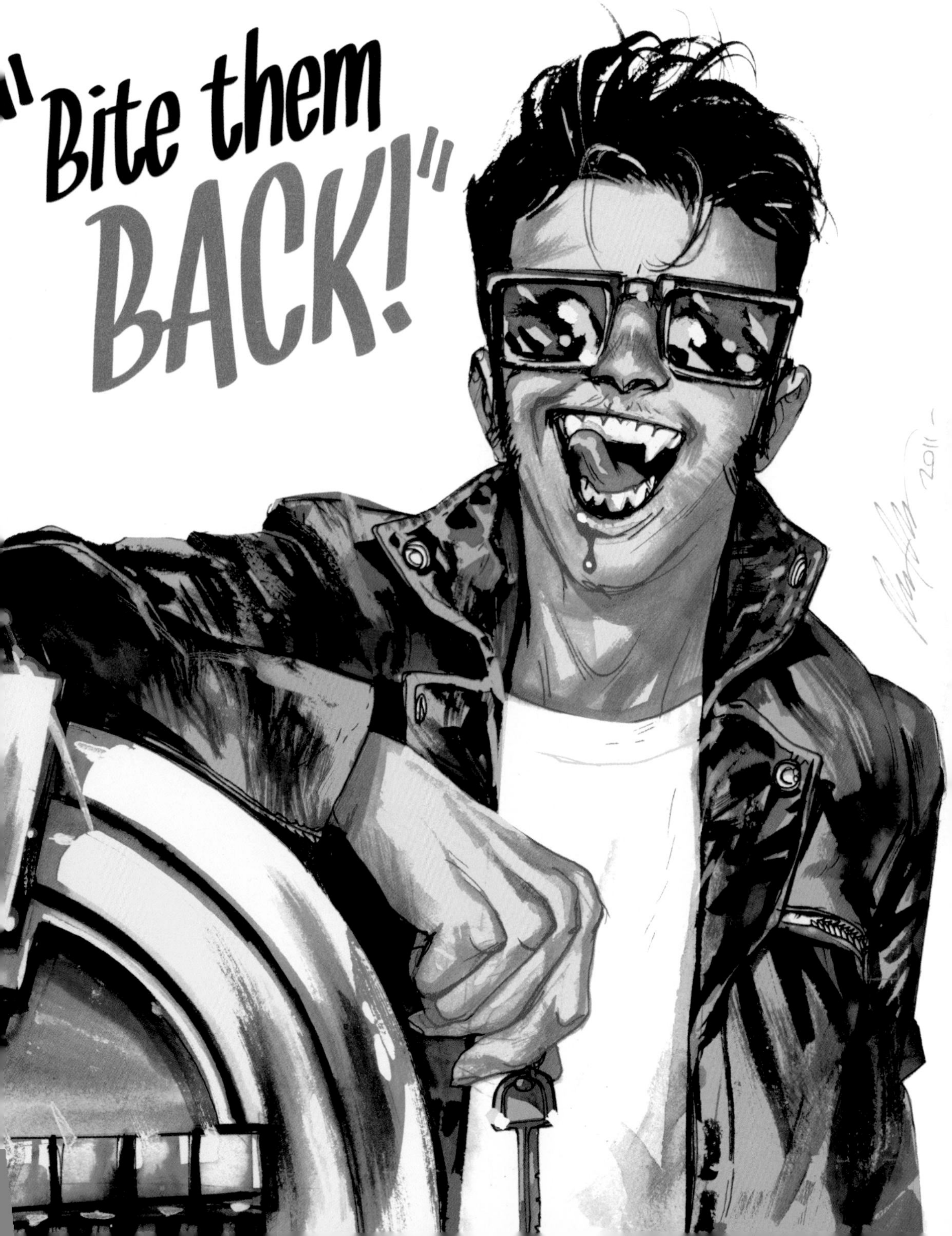
"Bite them
BACK!"

Death Race

Rafael Albuquerque
Artist and covers

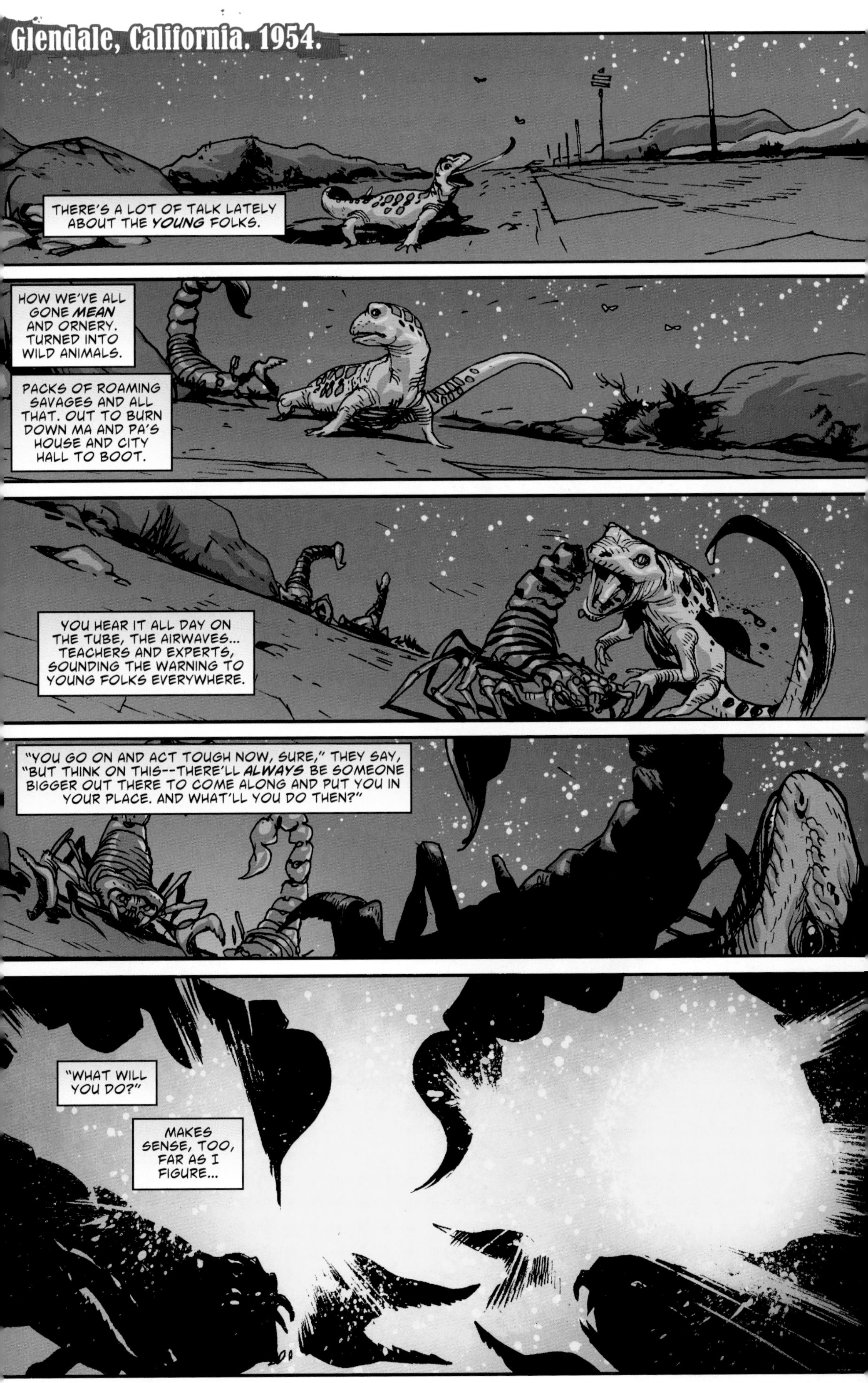
Glendale, California. 1954.
THERE'S A LOT OF TALK LATELY ABOUT THE *YOUNG* FOLKS.
HOW WE'VE ALL GONE ***MEAN*** AND ORNERY. TURNED INTO WILD ANIMALS.
PACKS OF ROAMING SAVAGES AND ALL THAT. OUT TO BURN DOWN MA AND PA'S HOUSE AND CITY HALL TO BOOT.
YOU HEAR IT ALL DAY ON THE TUBE, THE AIRWAVES... TEACHERS AND EXPERTS, SOUNDING THE WARNING TO YOUNG FOLKS EVERYWHERE.
"YOU GO ON AND ACT TOUGH NOW, SURE," THEY SAY, "BUT THINK ON THIS--THERE'LL *ALWAYS* BE SOMEONE BIGGER OUT THERE TO COME ALONG AND PUT YOU IN YOUR PLACE. AND WHAT'LL YOU DO THEN?"
"WHAT WILL YOU DO?"
MAKES SENSE, TOO, FAR AS I FIGURE...

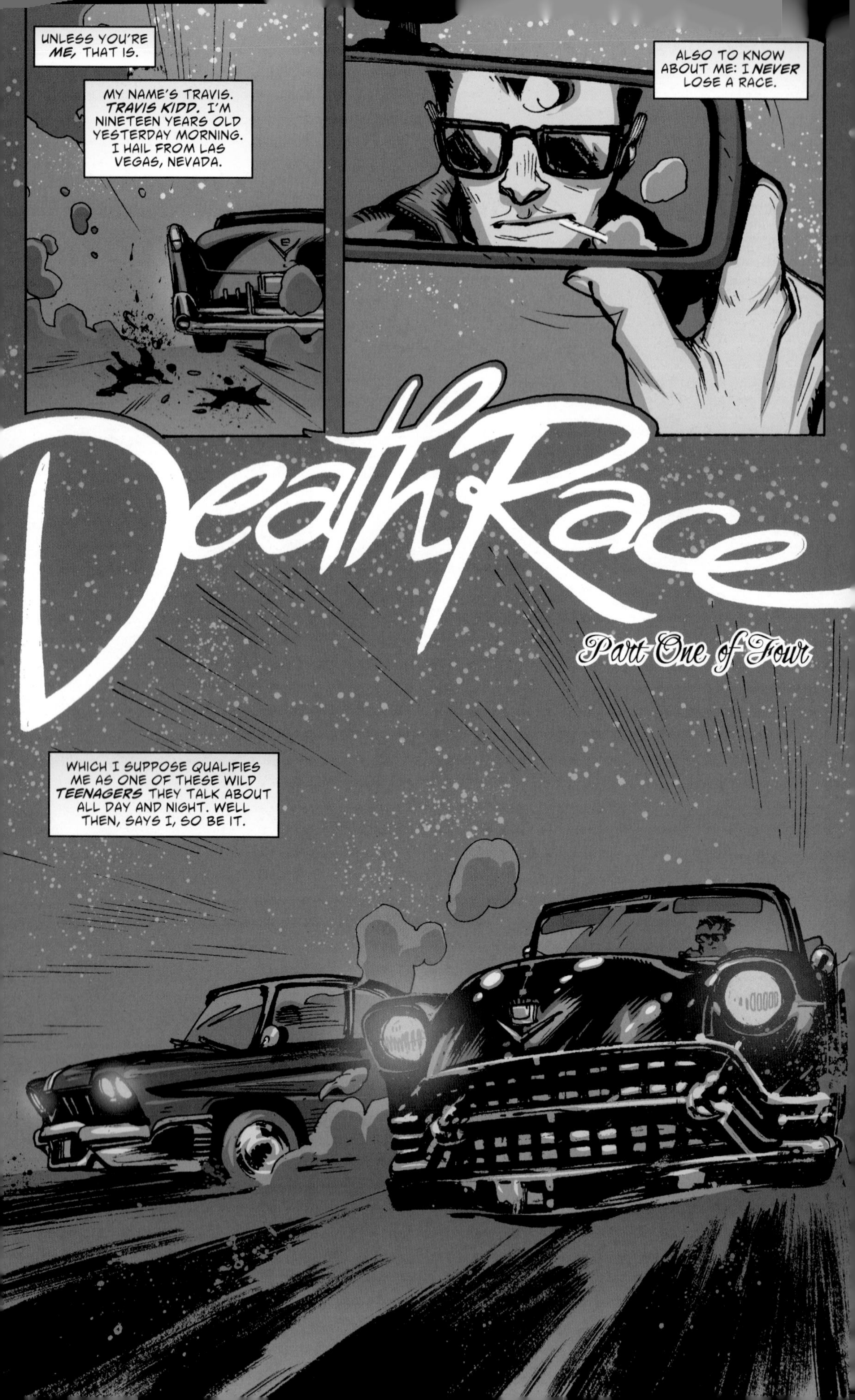
UNLESS YOU'RE ME, THAT IS.
MY NAME'S TRAVIS. TRAVIS KIDD. I'M NINETEEN YEARS OLD YESTERDAY MORNING. I HAIL FROM LAS VEGAS, NEVADA.
ALSO TO KNOW ABOUT ME: I NEVER LOSE A RACE.
Death Race
Part One of Four
WHICH I SUPPOSE QUALIFIES ME AS ONE OF THESE WILD TEENAGERS THEY TALK ABOUT ALL DAY AND NIGHT. WELL THEN, SAYS I, SO BE IT.

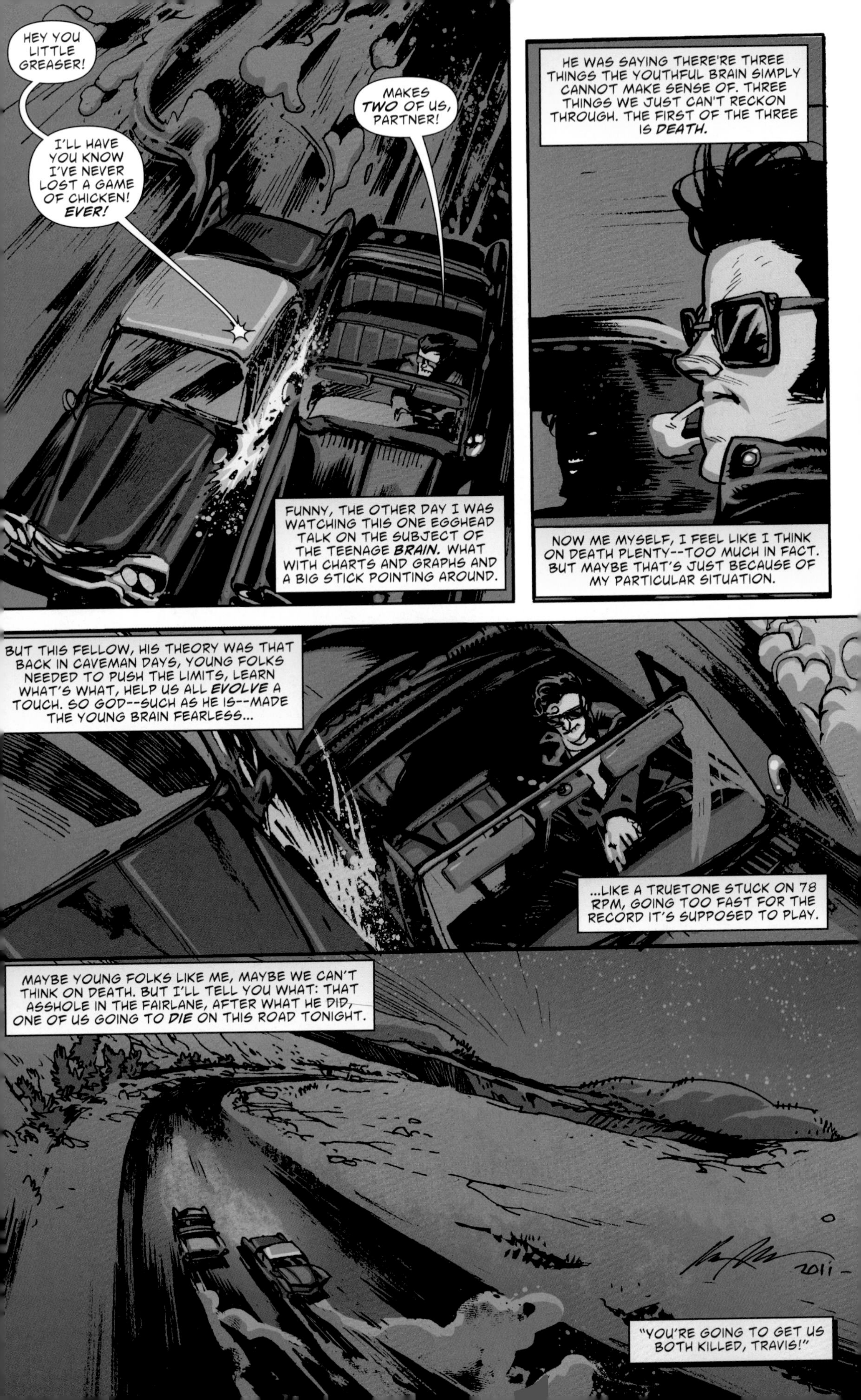

HEY YOU LITTLE GREASER!
I'LL HAVE YOU KNOW I'VE NEVER LOST A GAME OF CHICKEN! EVER!
MAKES TWO OF US, PARTNER!
FUNNY, THE OTHER DAY I WAS WATCHING THIS ONE EGGHEAD TALK ON THE SUBJECT OF THE TEENAGE BRAIN. WHAT WITH CHARTS AND GRAPHS AND A BIG STICK POINTING AROUND.
HE WAS SAYING THERE'RE THREE THINGS THE YOUTHFUL BRAIN SIMPLY CANNOT MAKE SENSE OF. THREE THINGS WE JUST CAN'T RECKON THROUGH. THE FIRST OF THE THREE IS DEATH.
NOW ME MYSELF, I FEEL LIKE I THINK ON DEATH PLENTY--TOO MUCH IN FACT. BUT MAYBE THAT'S JUST BECAUSE OF MY PARTICULAR SITUATION.
BUT THIS FELLOW, HIS THEORY WAS THAT BACK IN CAVEMAN DAYS, YOUNG FOLKS NEEDED TO PUSH THE LIMITS, LEARN WHAT'S WHAT, HELP US ALL EVOLVE A TOUCH. SO GOD--SUCH AS HE IS--MADE THE YOUNG BRAIN FEARLESS...
...LIKE A TRUETONE STUCK ON 78 RPM, GOING TOO FAST FOR THE RECORD IT'S SUPPOSED TO PLAY.
MAYBE YOUNG FOLKS LIKE ME, MAYBE WE CAN'T THINK ON DEATH. BUT I'LL TELL YOU WHAT: THAT ASSHOLE IN THE FAIRLANE, AFTER WHAT HE DID, ONE OF US GOING TO DIE ON THIS ROAD TONIGHT.
2011
"YOU'RE GOING TO GET US BOTH KILLED, TRAVIS!"

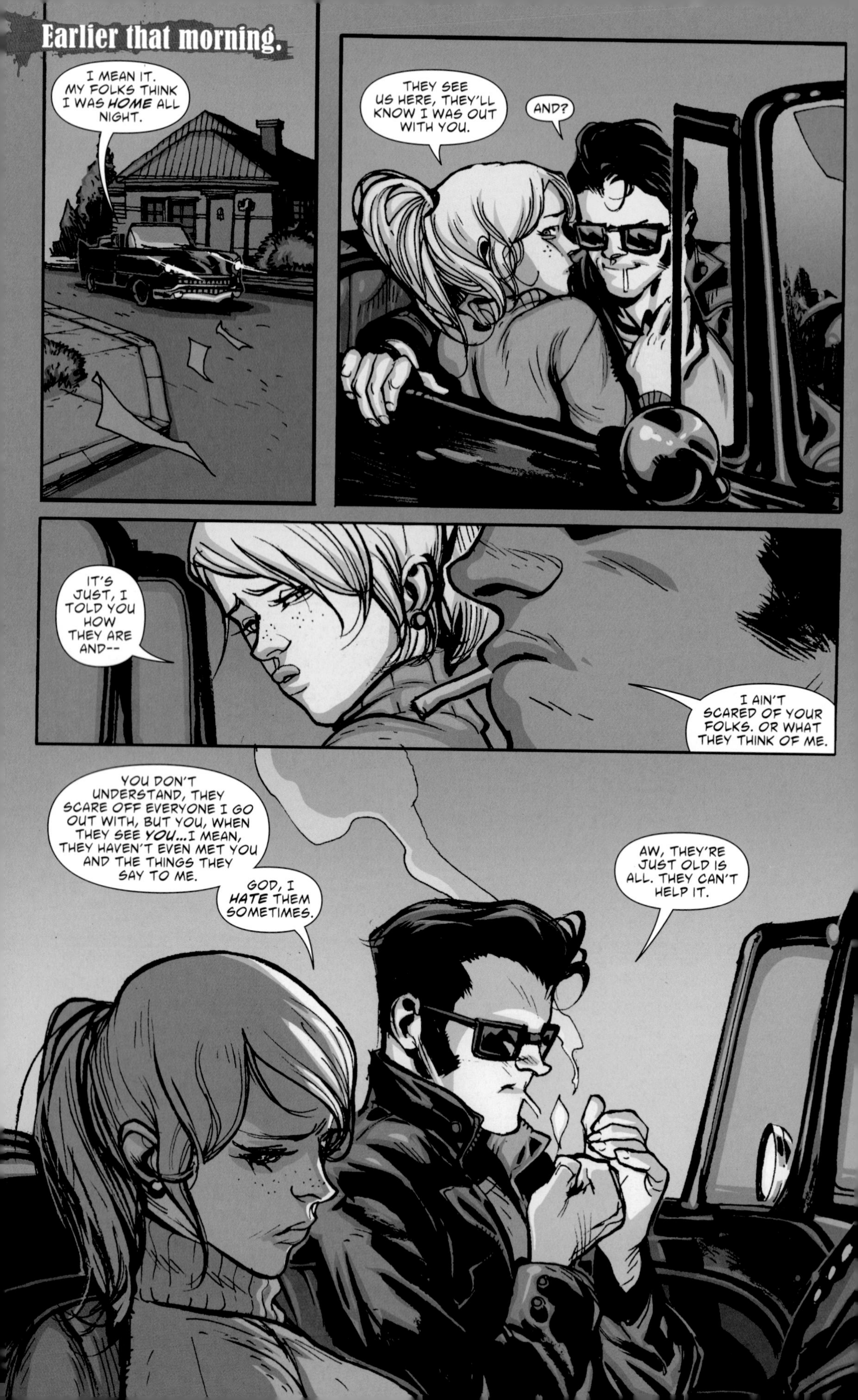
Earlier that morning.
I MEAN IT. MY FOLKS THINK I WAS HOME ALL NIGHT.
THEY SEE US HERE, THEY'LL KNOW I WAS OUT WITH YOU.
AND?
IT'S JUST, I TOLD YOU HOW THEY ARE AND--
I AIN'T SCARED OF YOUR FOLKS. OR WHAT THEY THINK OF ME.
YOU DON'T UNDERSTAND, THEY SCARE OFF EVERYONE I GO OUT WITH, BUT YOU, WHEN THEY SEE YOU...I MEAN, THEY HAVEN'T EVEN MET YOU AND THE THINGS THEY SAY TO ME.
GOD, I HATE THEM SOMETIMES.
AW, THEY'RE JUST OLD IS ALL. THEY CAN'T HELP IT.

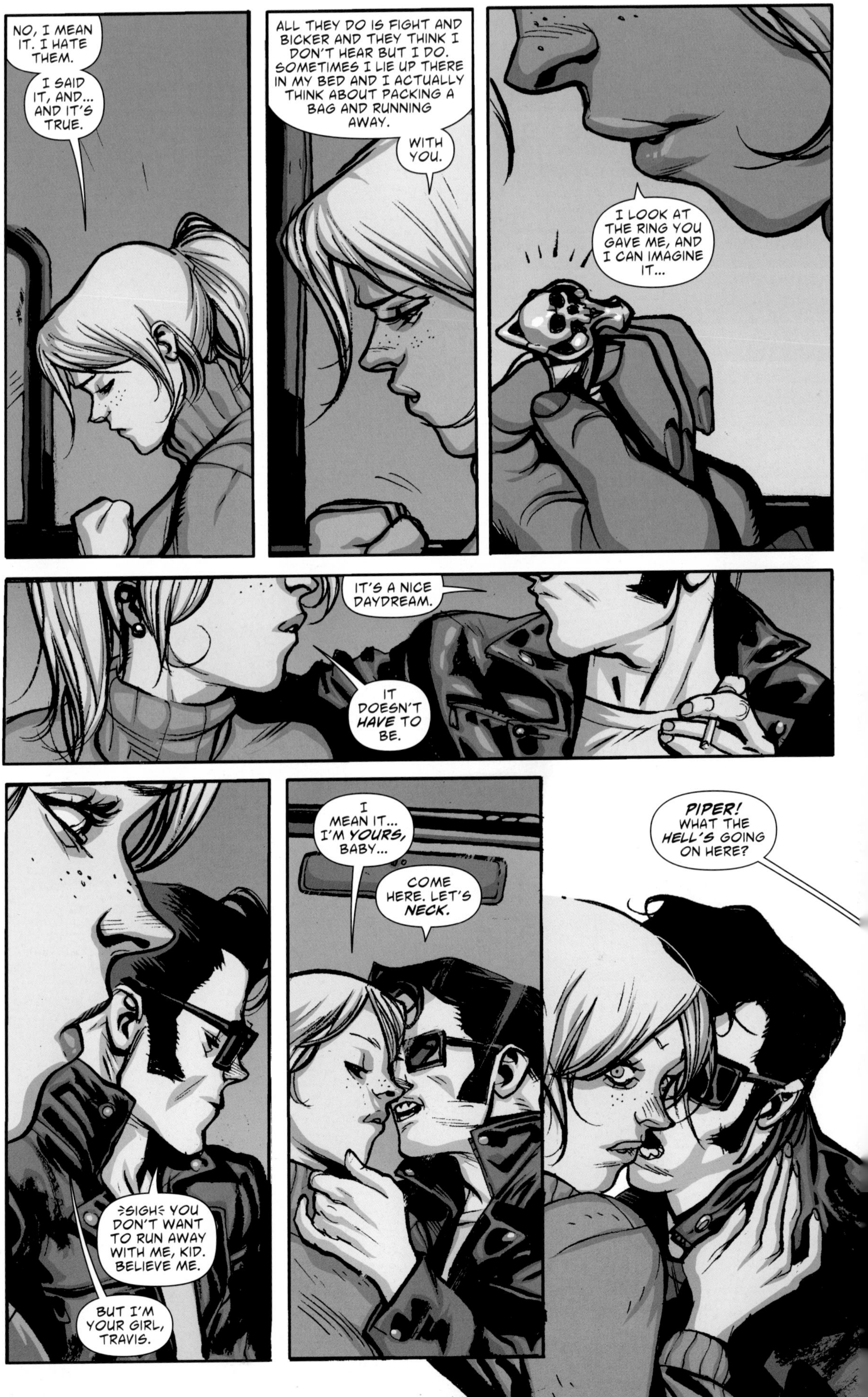
NO, I MEAN IT. I HATE THEM.
I SAID IT, AND... AND IT'S TRUE.
ALL THEY DO IS FIGHT AND BICKER AND THEY THINK I DON'T HEAR BUT I DO. SOMETIMES I LIE UP THERE IN MY BED AND I ACTUALLY THINK ABOUT PACKING A BAG AND RUNNING AWAY.
WITH YOU.
I LOOK AT THE RING YOU GAVE ME, AND I CAN IMAGINE IT...
IT'S A NICE DAYDREAM.
IT DOESN'T *HAVE* TO BE.
=SIGH= YOU DON'T WANT TO RUN AWAY WITH ME, KID. BELIEVE ME.
BUT I'M YOUR GIRL, TRAVIS.
I MEAN IT... I'M *YOURS*, BABY...
COME HERE. LET'S *NECK.*
PIPER! WHAT THE *HELL'S* GOING ON HERE?

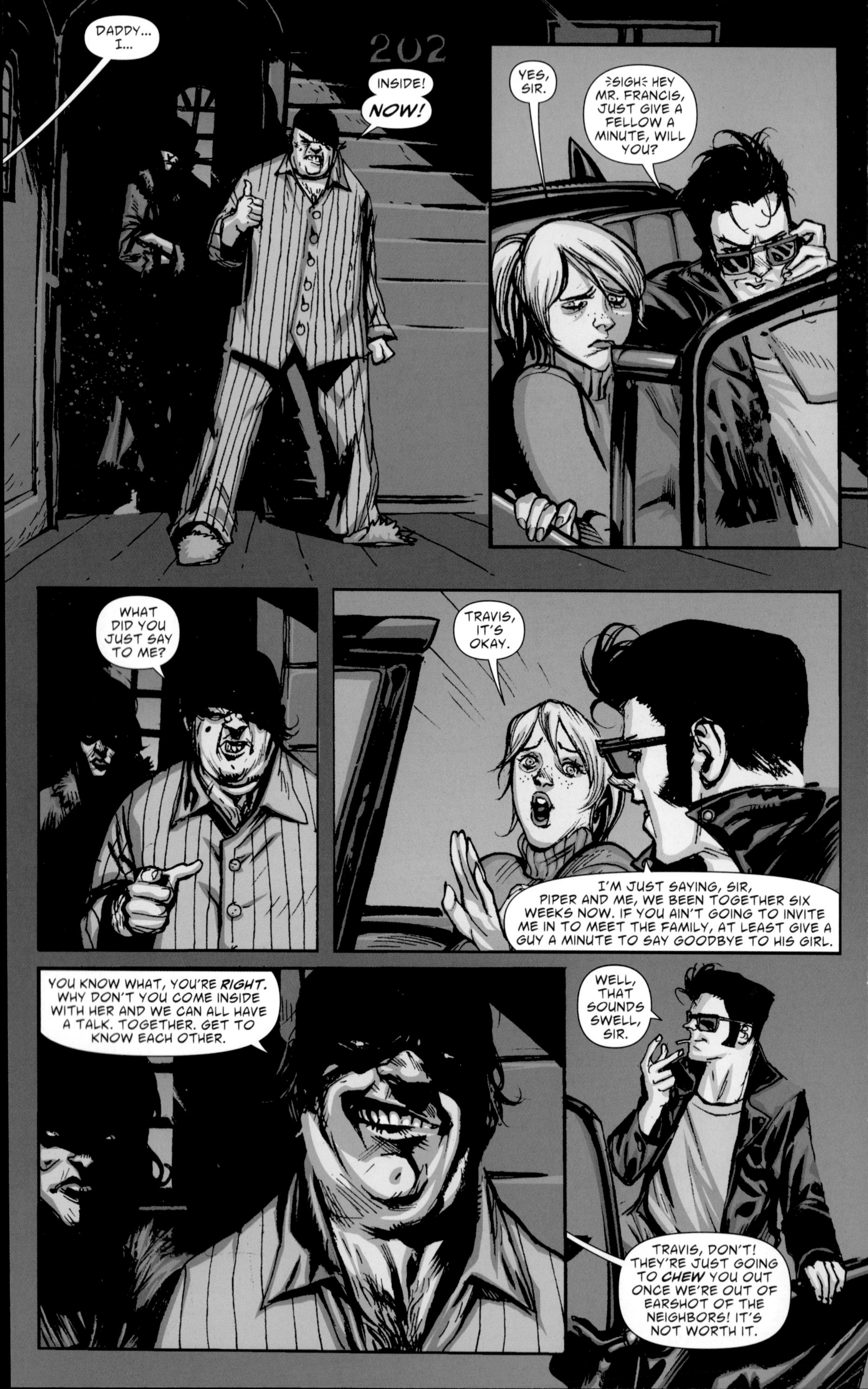
DADDY... I...
INSIDE! NOW!
YES, SIR.
=SIGH= HEY MR. FRANCIS, JUST GIVE A FELLOW A MINUTE, WILL YOU?
WHAT DID YOU JUST SAY TO ME?
TRAVIS, IT'S OKAY.
I'M JUST SAYING, SIR, PIPER AND ME, WE BEEN TOGETHER SIX WEEKS NOW. IF YOU AIN'T GOING TO INVITE ME IN TO MEET THE FAMILY, AT LEAST GIVE A GUY A MINUTE TO SAY GOODBYE TO HIS GIRL.
YOU KNOW WHAT, YOU'RE RIGHT. WHY DON'T YOU COME INSIDE WITH HER AND WE CAN ALL HAVE A TALK. TOGETHER. GET TO KNOW EACH OTHER.
WELL, THAT SOUNDS SWELL, SIR.
TRAVIS, DON'T! THEY'RE JUST GOING TO CHEW YOU OUT ONCE WE'RE OUT OF EARSHOT OF THE NEIGHBORS! IT'S NOT WORTH IT.

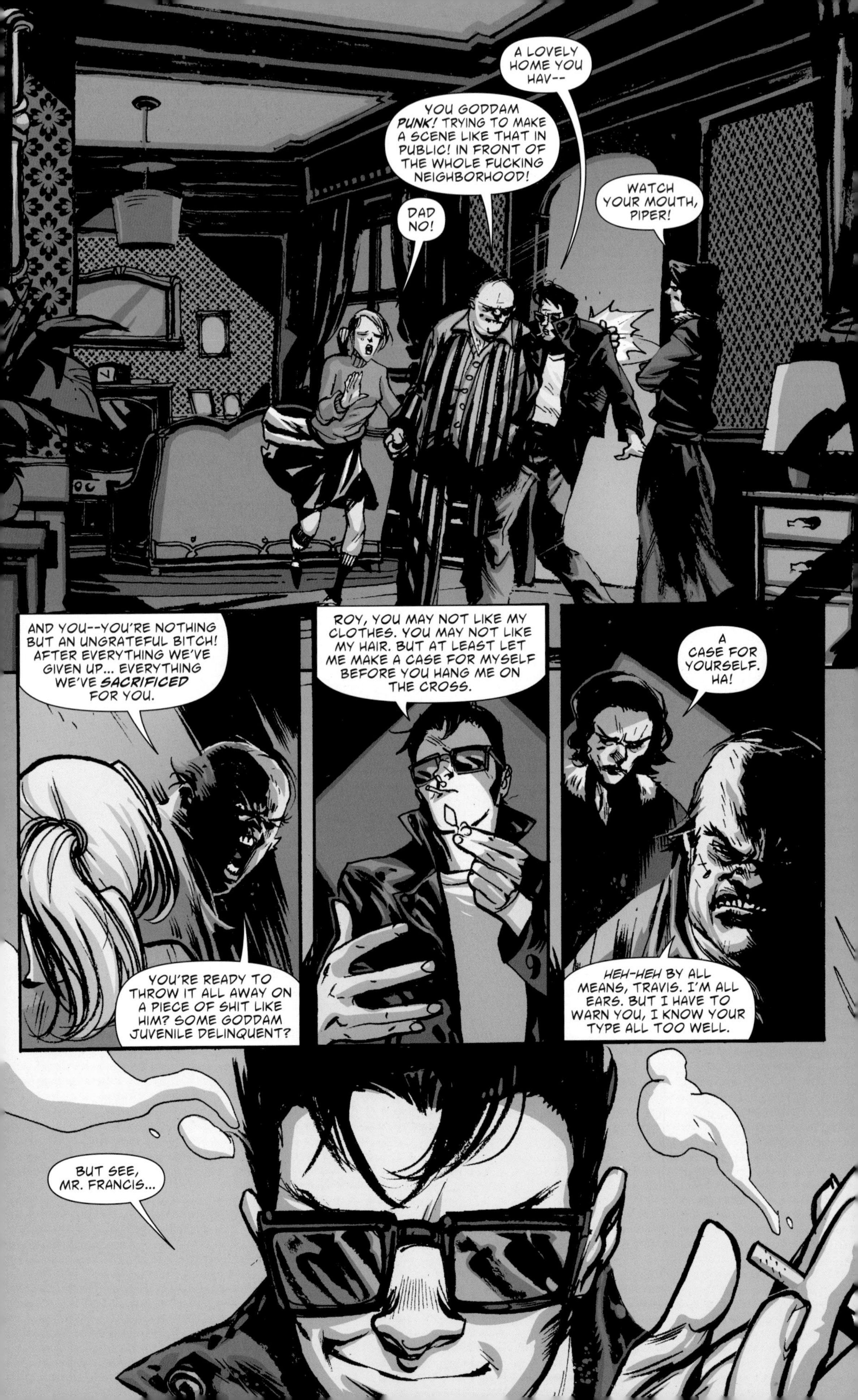

A LOVELY HOME YOU HAV--
YOU GODDAM PUNK! TRYING TO MAKE A SCENE LIKE THAT IN PUBLIC! IN FRONT OF THE WHOLE FUCKING NEIGHBORHOOD!
DAD NO!
WATCH YOUR MOUTH, PIPER!
AND YOU--YOU'RE NOTHING BUT AN UNGRATEFUL BITCH! AFTER EVERYTHING WE'VE GIVEN UP... EVERYTHING WE'VE SACRIFICED FOR YOU.
YOU'RE READY TO THROW IT ALL AWAY ON A PIECE OF SHIT LIKE HIM? SOME GODDAM JUVENILE DELINQUENT?
ROY, YOU MAY NOT LIKE MY CLOTHES. YOU MAY NOT LIKE MY HAIR. BUT AT LEAST LET ME MAKE A CASE FOR MYSELF BEFORE YOU HANG ME ON THE CROSS.
A CASE FOR YOURSELF. HA!
HEH-HEH BY ALL MEANS, TRAVIS. I'M ALL EARS. BUT I HAVE TO WARN YOU, I KNOW YOUR TYPE ALL TOO WELL.
BUT SEE, MR. FRANCIS...

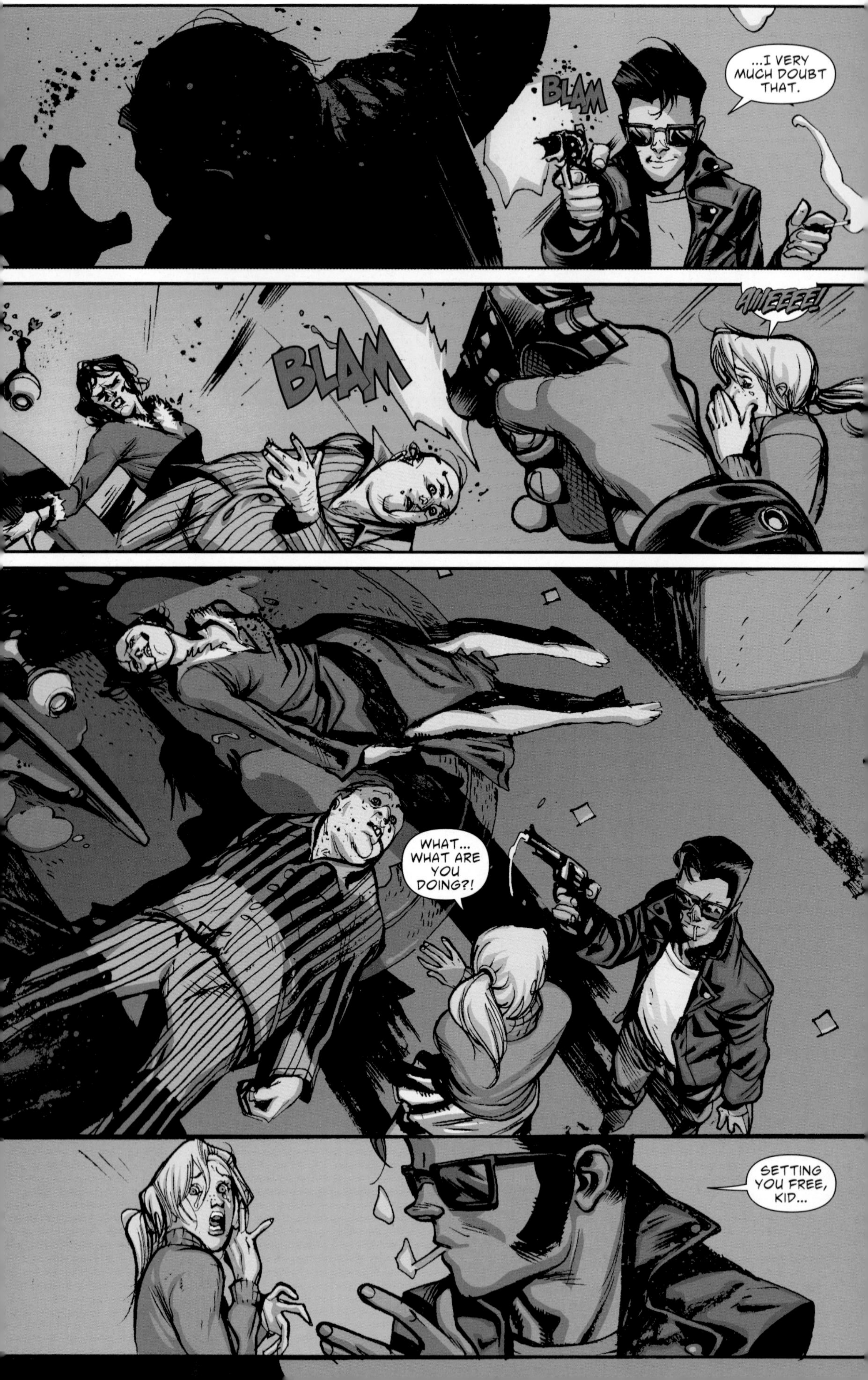
BLAM
...I VERY MUCH DOUBT THAT.
BLAM
AIIEEEEE!
WHAT... WHAT ARE YOU DOING?!
SETTING YOU FREE, KID...

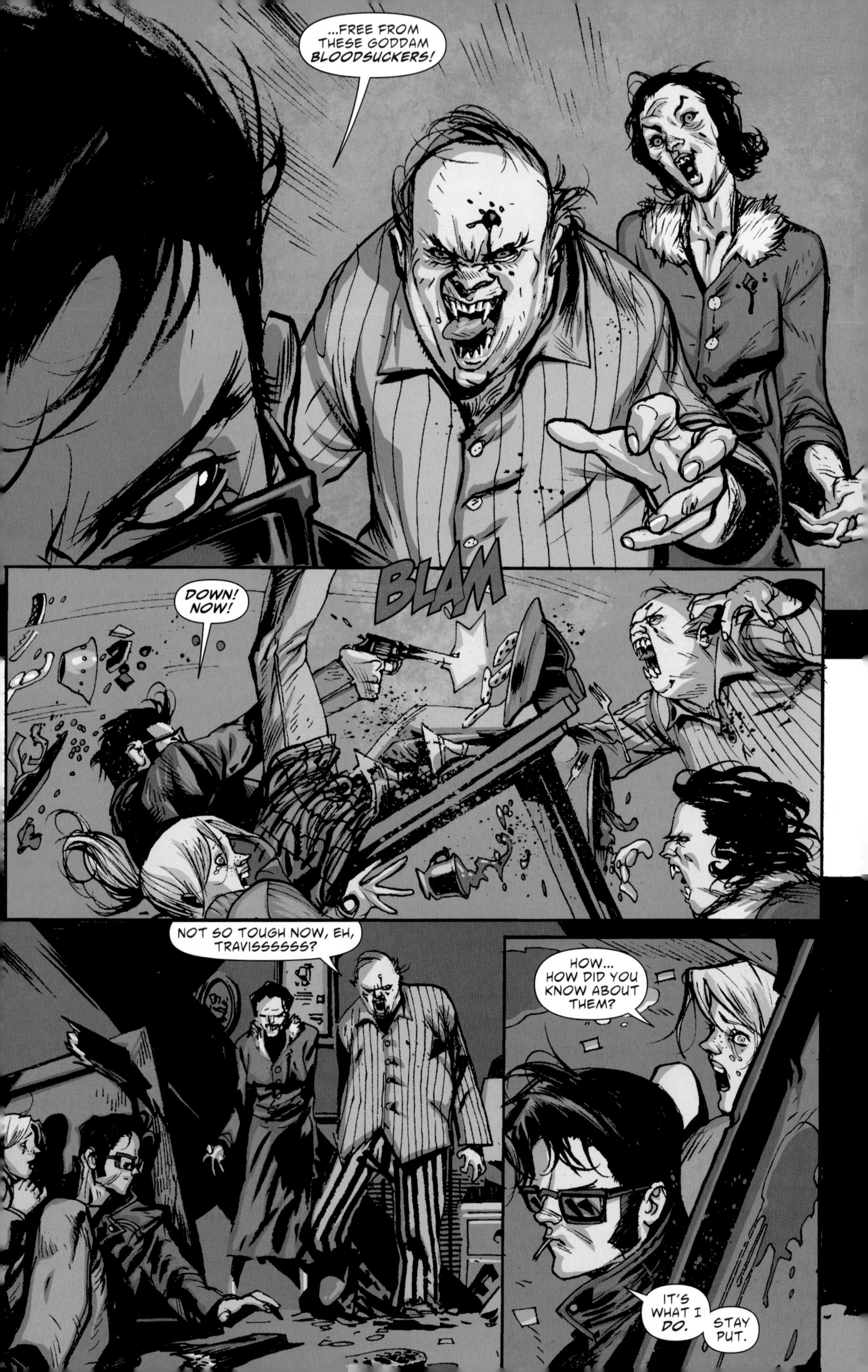

...FREE FROM THESE GODDAM BLOODSUCKERS!
BLAM
DOWN! NOW!
NOT SO TOUGH NOW, EH, TRAVISSSSSS?
HOW... HOW DID YOU KNOW ABOUT THEM?
IT'S WHAT I DO.
STAY PUT.

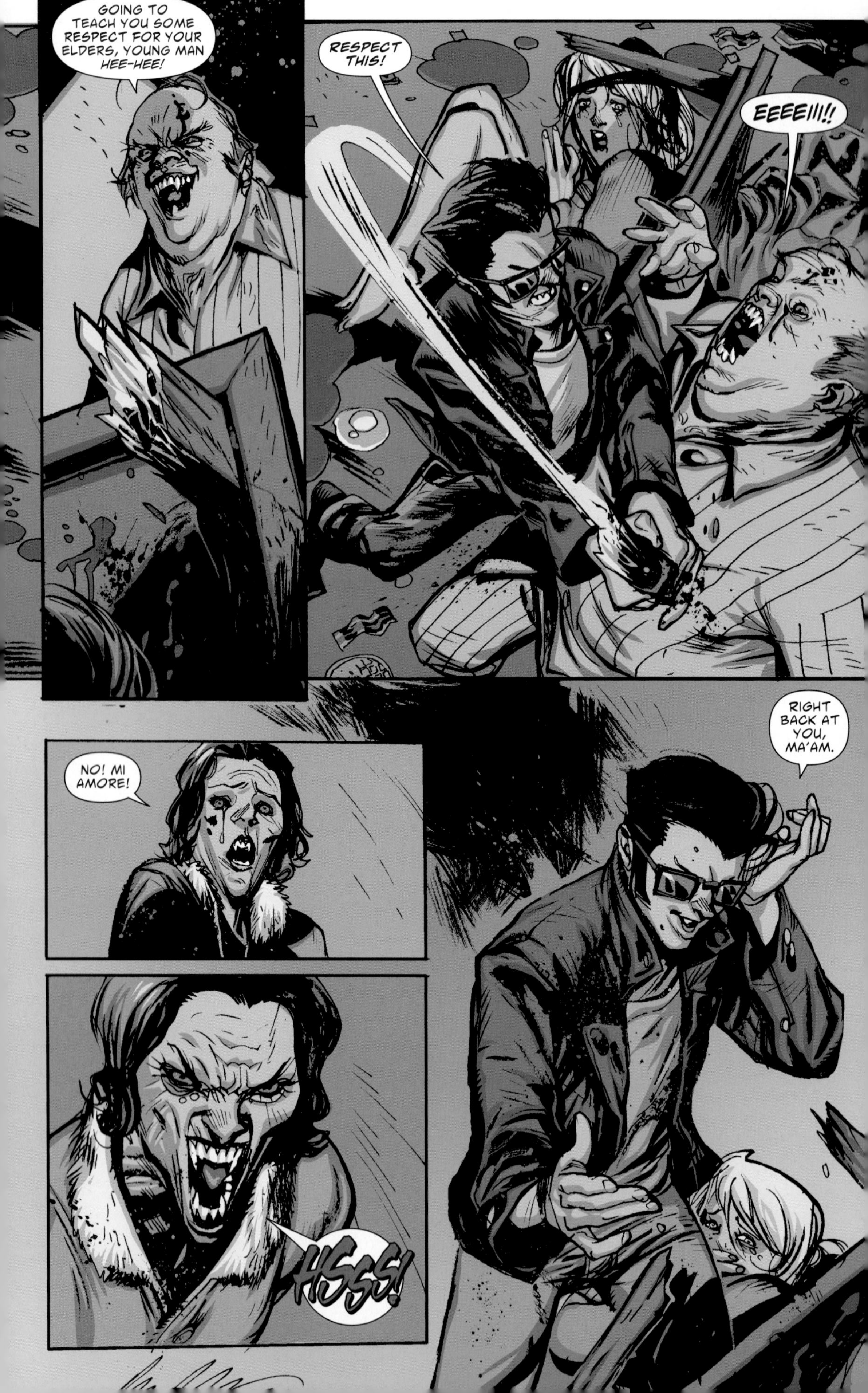
GOING TO TEACH YOU SOME RESPECT FOR YOUR ELDERS, YOUNG MAN HEE-HEE!
RESPECT THIS!
EEEE!!!!!
NO! MI AMORE!
HSSS!
RIGHT BACK AT YOU, MA'AM.

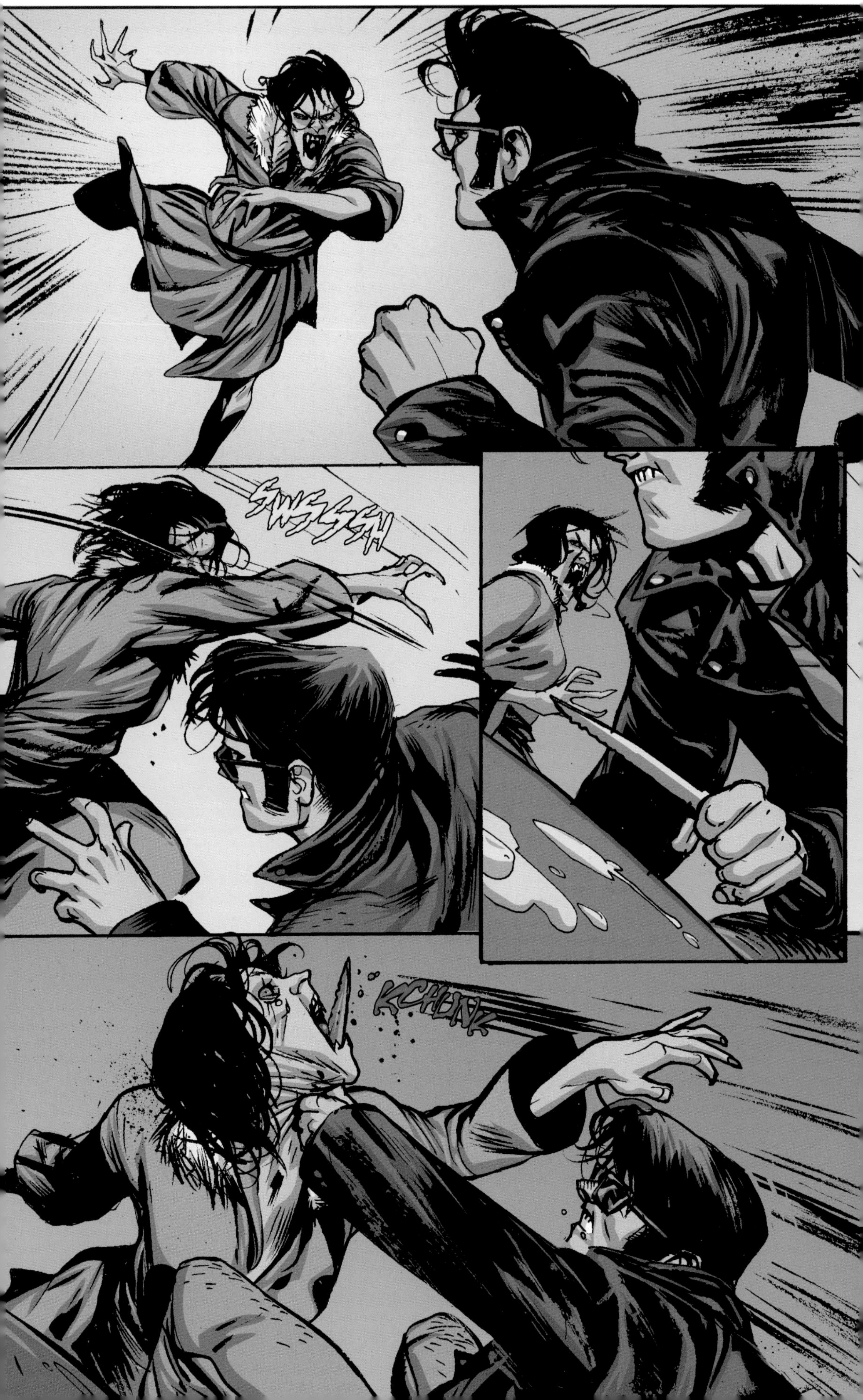
SWSSSH
KCHUNK

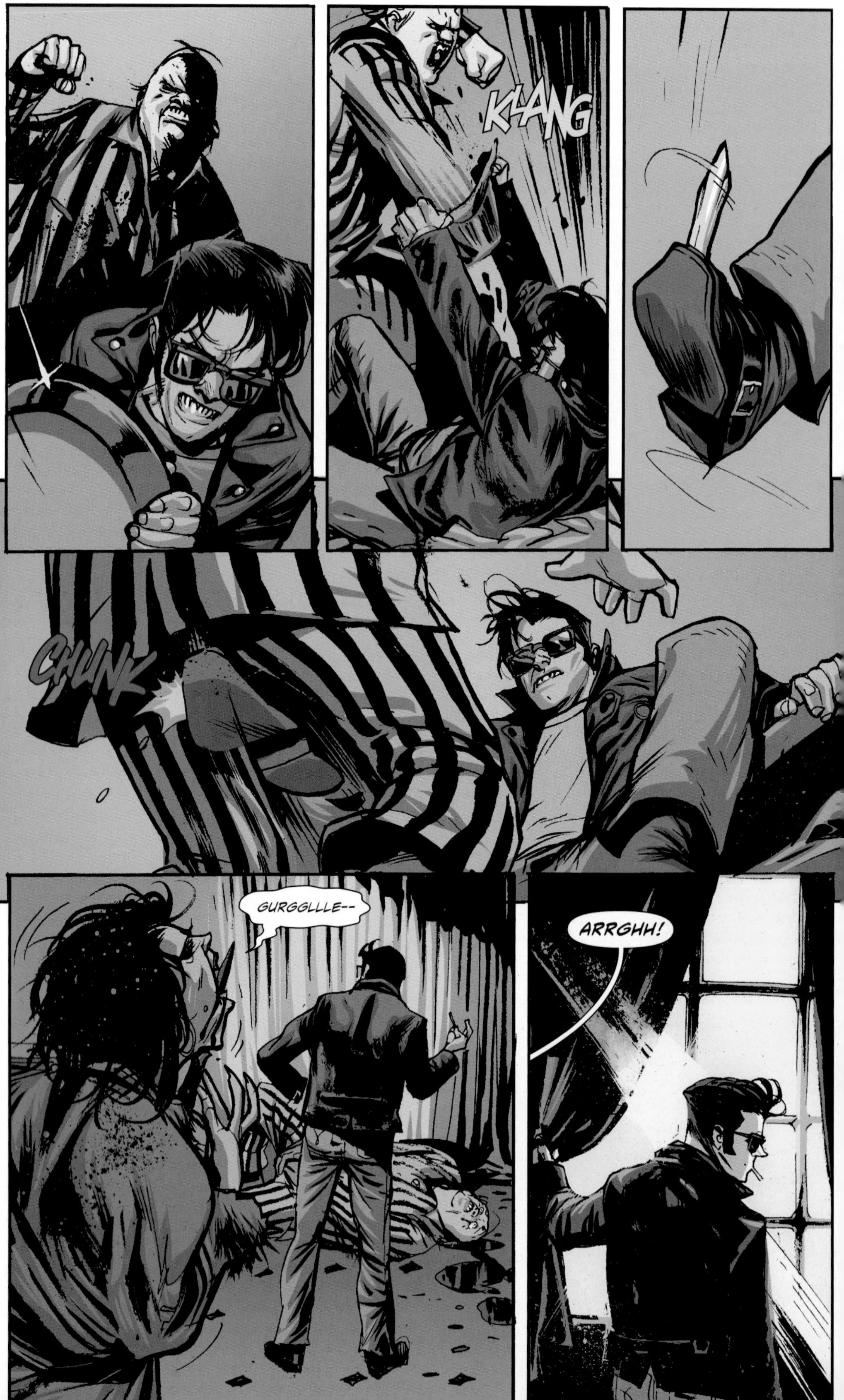
KLANG
CHUNK
GURGGLLLE--
ARRGHH!

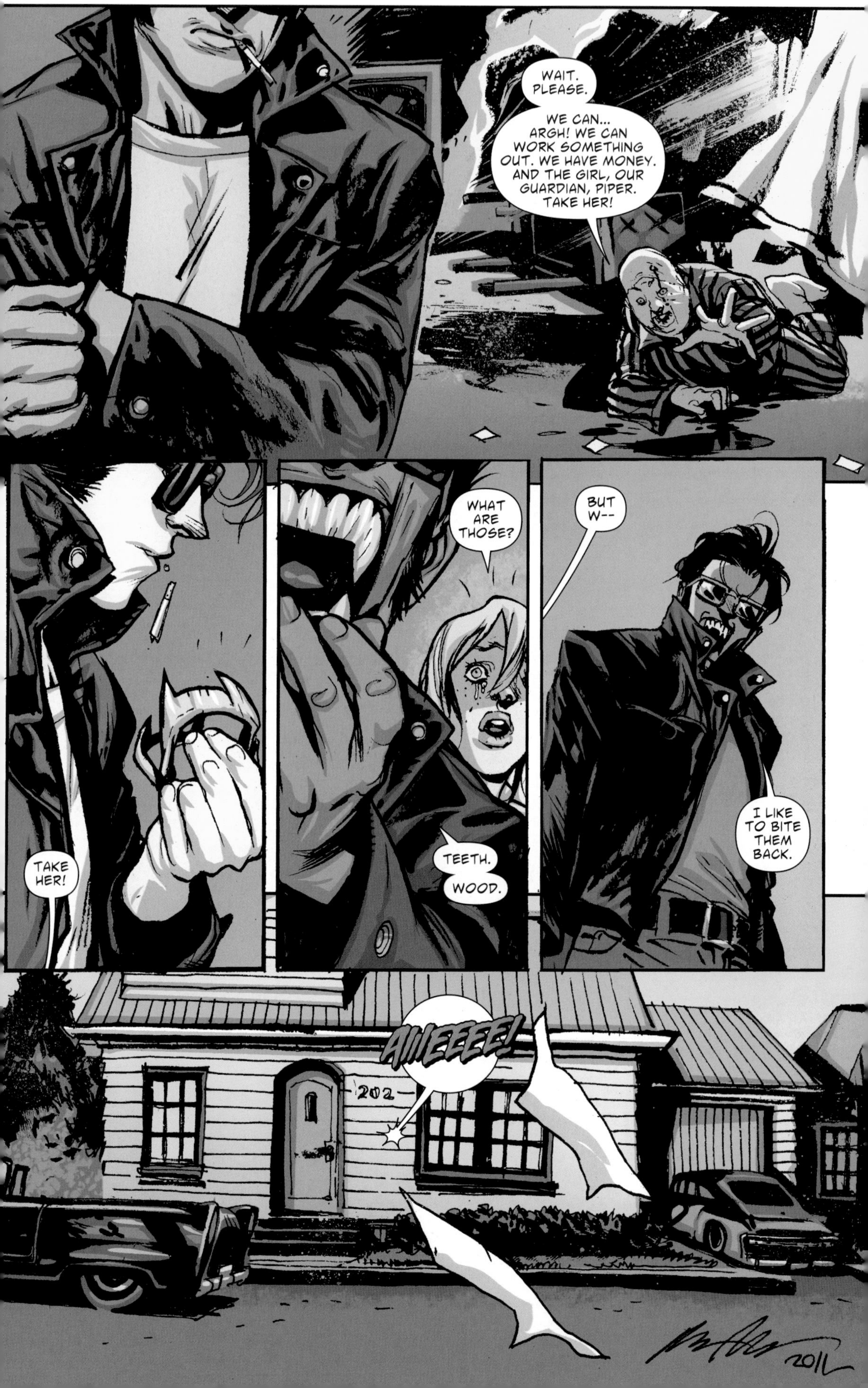
WAIT. PLEASE.
WE CAN... ARGH! WE CAN WORK SOMETHING OUT. WE HAVE MONEY. AND THE GIRL, OUR GUARDIAN, PIPER. TAKE HER!
TAKE HER!
WHAT ARE THOSE?
TEETH.
WOOD.
BUT W--
I LIKE TO BITE THEM BACK.
202
AIIIEEEEE!

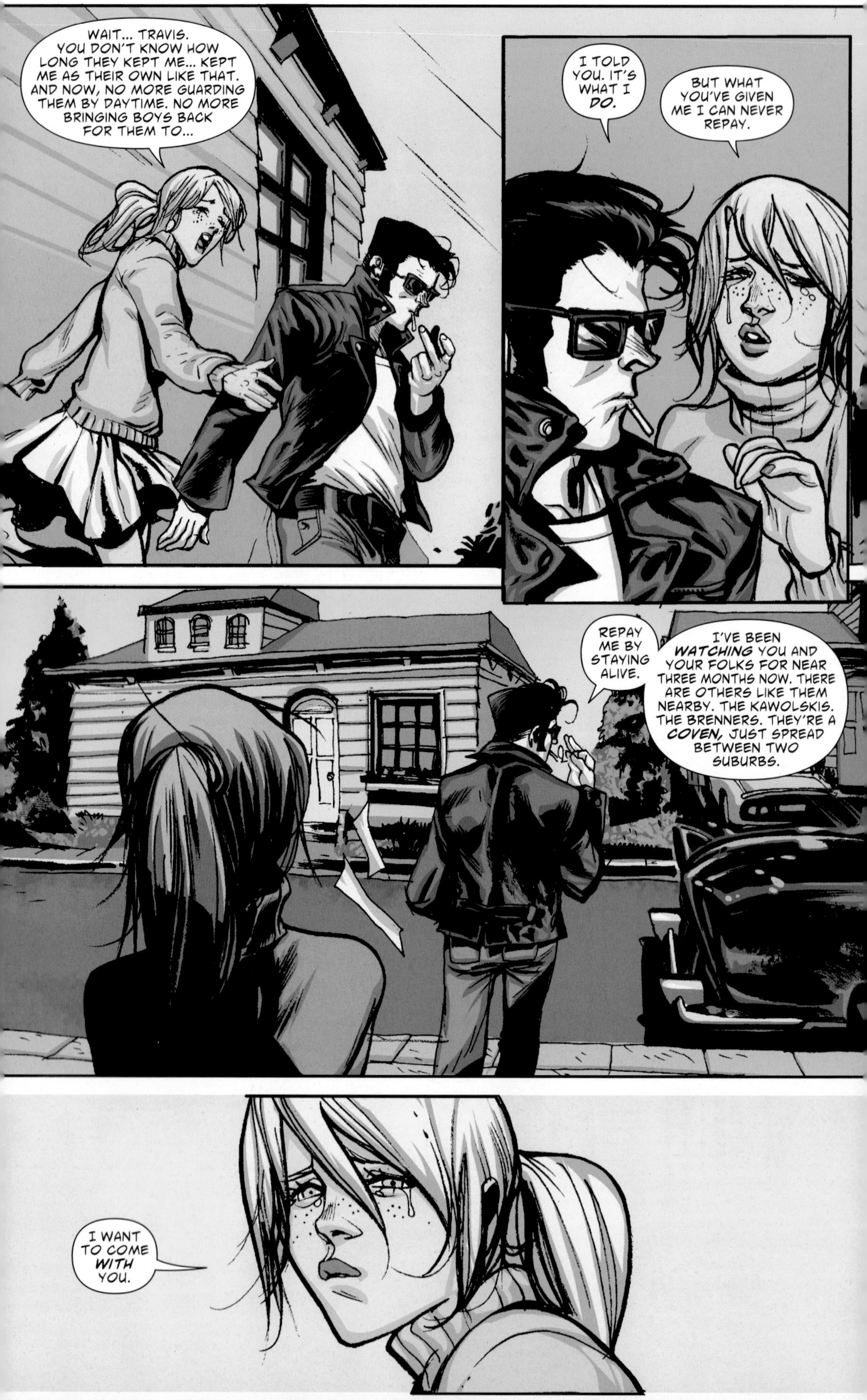
WAIT... TRAVIS. YOU DON'T KNOW HOW LONG THEY KEPT ME... KEPT ME AS THEIR OWN LIKE THAT. AND NOW, NO MORE GUARDING THEM BY DAYTIME. NO MORE BRINGING BOYS BACK FOR THEM TO...
I TOLD YOU. IT'S WHAT I *DO.*
BUT WHAT YOU'VE GIVEN ME I CAN NEVER REPAY.
REPAY ME BY STAYING ALIVE.
I'VE BEEN *WATCHING* YOU AND YOUR FOLKS FOR NEAR THREE MONTHS NOW. THERE ARE OTHERS LIKE THEM NEARBY. THE KAWOLSKIS. THE BRENNERS. THEY'RE A *COVEN,* JUST SPREAD BETWEEN TWO SUBURBS.
I WANT TO COME *WITH* YOU.

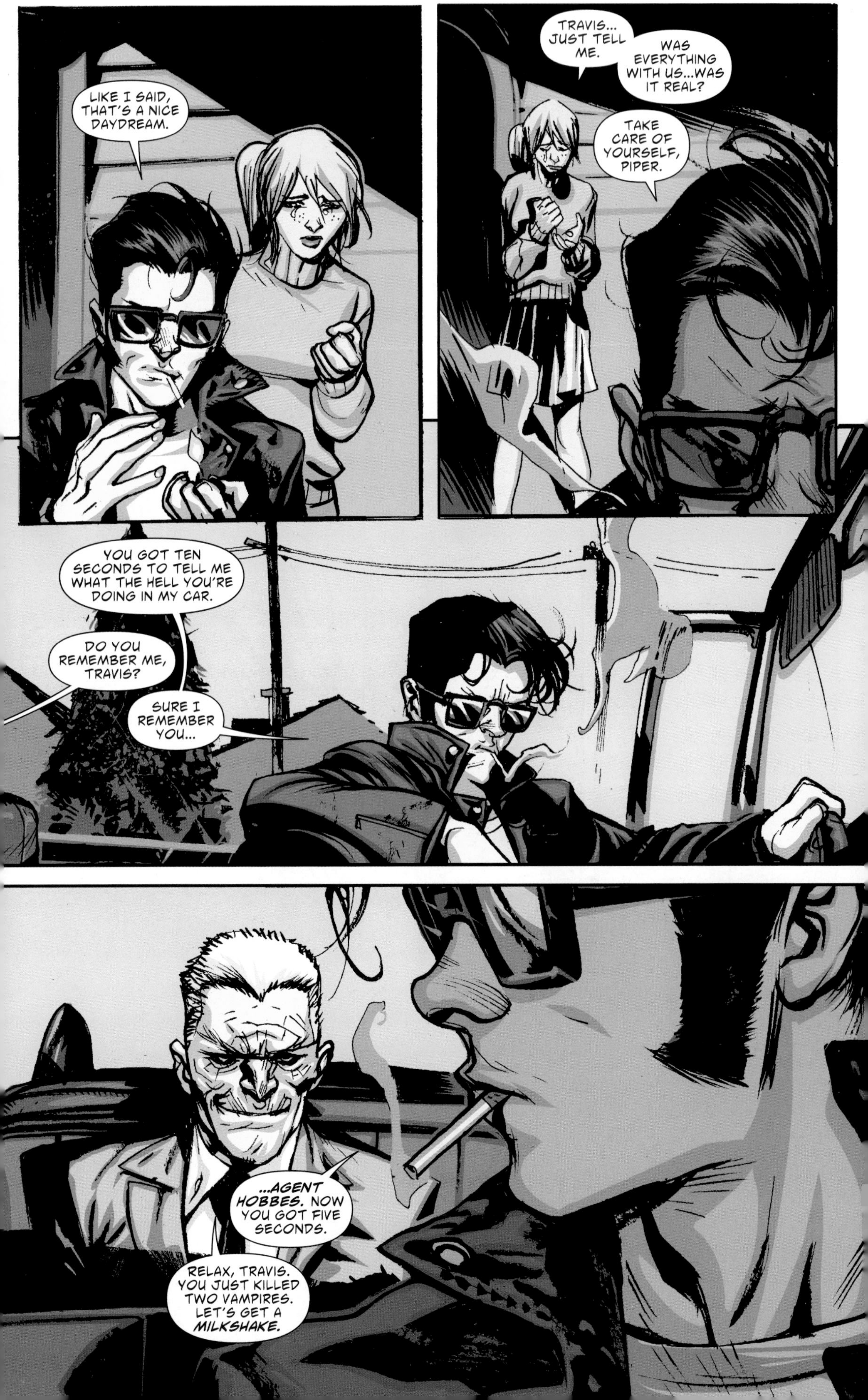
LIKE I SAID, THAT'S A NICE DAYDREAM.
TRAVIS... JUST TELL ME.
WAS EVERYTHING WITH US...WAS IT REAL?
TAKE CARE OF YOURSELF, PIPER.
YOU GOT TEN SECONDS TO TELL ME WHAT THE HELL YOU'RE DOING IN MY CAR.
DO YOU REMEMBER ME, TRAVIS?
SURE I REMEMBER YOU...
...AGENT HOBBES. NOW YOU GOT FIVE SECONDS.
RELAX, TRAVIS. YOU JUST KILLED TWO VAMPIRES. LET'S GET A MILKSHAKE.

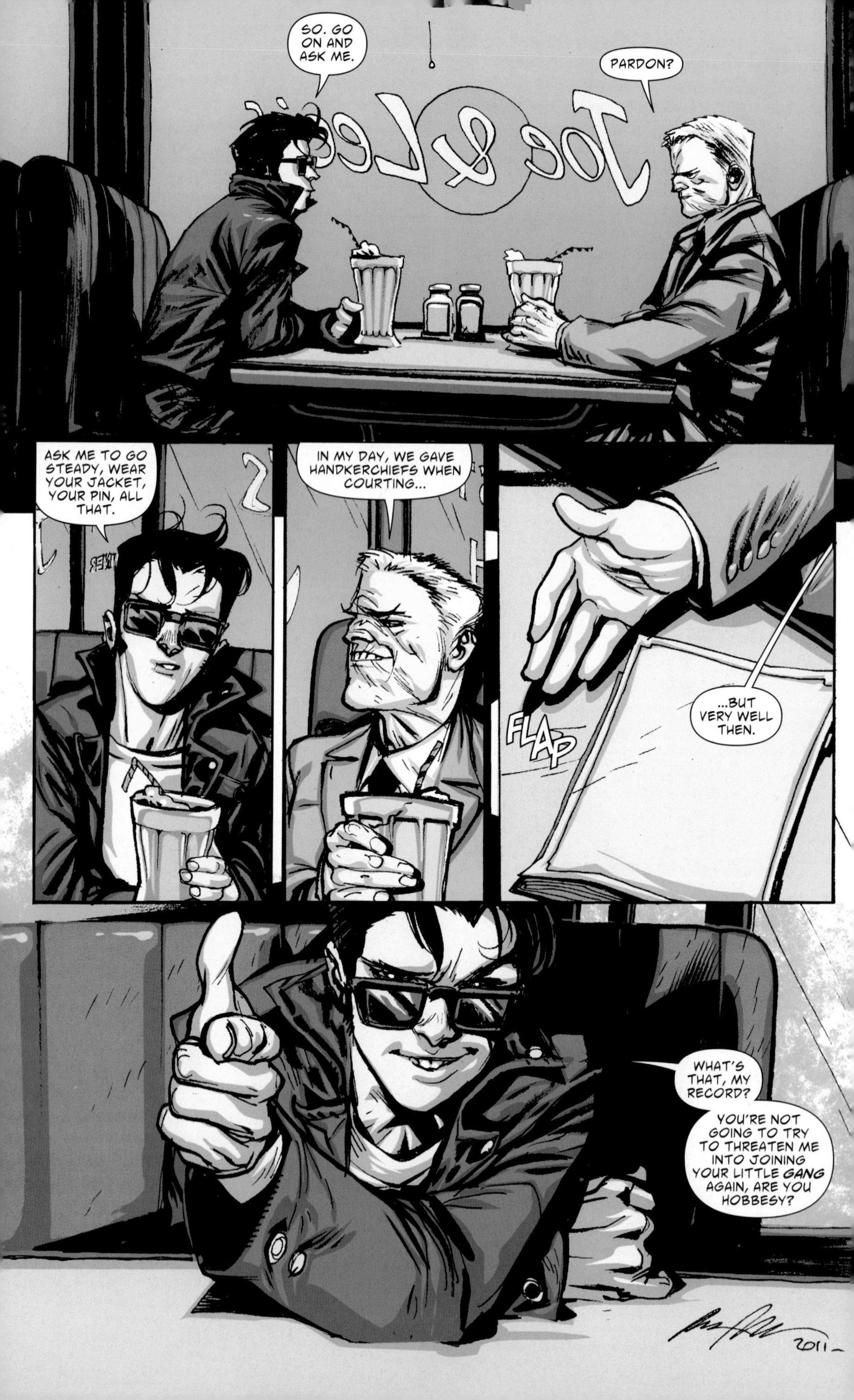
SO. GO ON AND ASK ME.
PARDON?
ASK ME TO GO STEADY, WEAR YOUR JACKET, YOUR PIN, ALL THAT.
IN MY DAY, WE GAVE HANDKERCHIEFS WHEN COURTING...
FLAP
...BUT VERY WELL THEN.
WHAT'S THAT, MY RECORD?
YOU'RE NOT GOING TO TRY TO THREATEN ME INTO JOINING YOUR LITTLE GANG AGAIN, ARE YOU HOBBESY?
2011

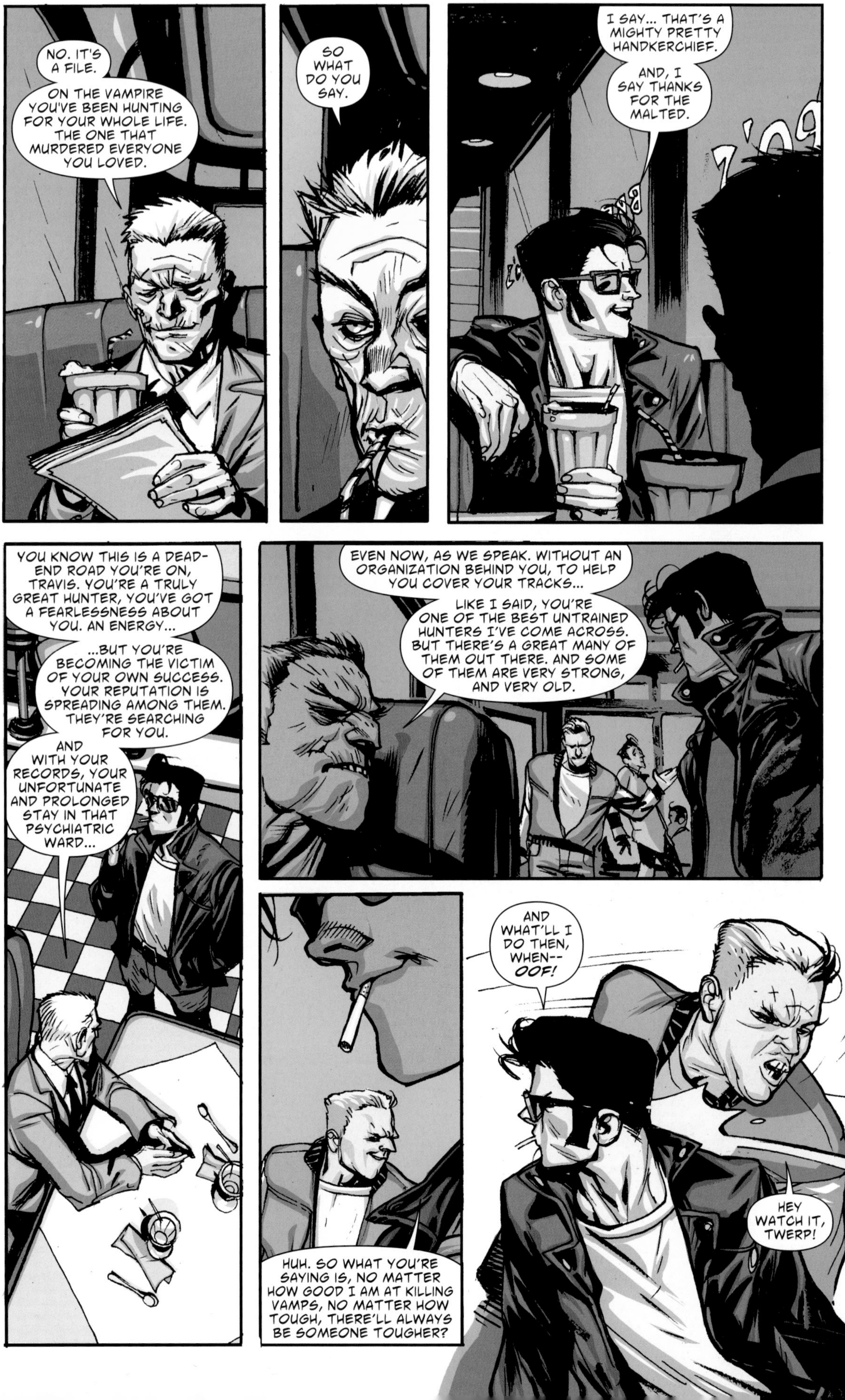
NO. IT'S A FILE.
ON THE VAMPIRE YOU'VE BEEN HUNTING FOR YOUR WHOLE LIFE. THE ONE THAT MURDERED EVERYONE YOU LOVED.
SO WHAT DO YOU SAY.
I SAY... THAT'S A MIGHTY PRETTY HANDKERCHIEF.
AND, I SAY THANKS FOR THE MALTED.
YOU KNOW THIS IS A DEAD-END ROAD YOU'RE ON, TRAVIS. YOU'RE A TRULY GREAT HUNTER, YOU'VE GOT A FEARLESSNESS ABOUT YOU. AN ENERGY...
...BUT YOU'RE BECOMING THE VICTIM OF YOUR OWN SUCCESS. YOUR REPUTATION IS SPREADING AMONG THEM. THEY'RE SEARCHING FOR YOU.
AND WITH YOUR RECORDS, YOUR UNFORTUNATE AND PROLONGED STAY IN THAT PSYCHIATRIC WARD...
EVEN NOW, AS WE SPEAK. WITHOUT AN ORGANIZATION BEHIND YOU, TO HELP YOU COVER YOUR TRACKS...
LIKE I SAID, YOU'RE ONE OF THE BEST UNTRAINED HUNTERS I'VE COME ACROSS. BUT THERE'S A GREAT MANY OF THEM OUT THERE. AND SOME OF THEM ARE VERY STRONG, AND VERY OLD.
HUH. SO WHAT YOU'RE SAYING IS, NO MATTER HOW GOOD I AM AT KILLING VAMPS, NO MATTER HOW TOUGH, THERE'LL ALWAYS BE SOMEONE TOUGHER?
AND WHAT'LL I DO THEN, WHEN-- OOF!
HEY WATCH IT, TWERP!

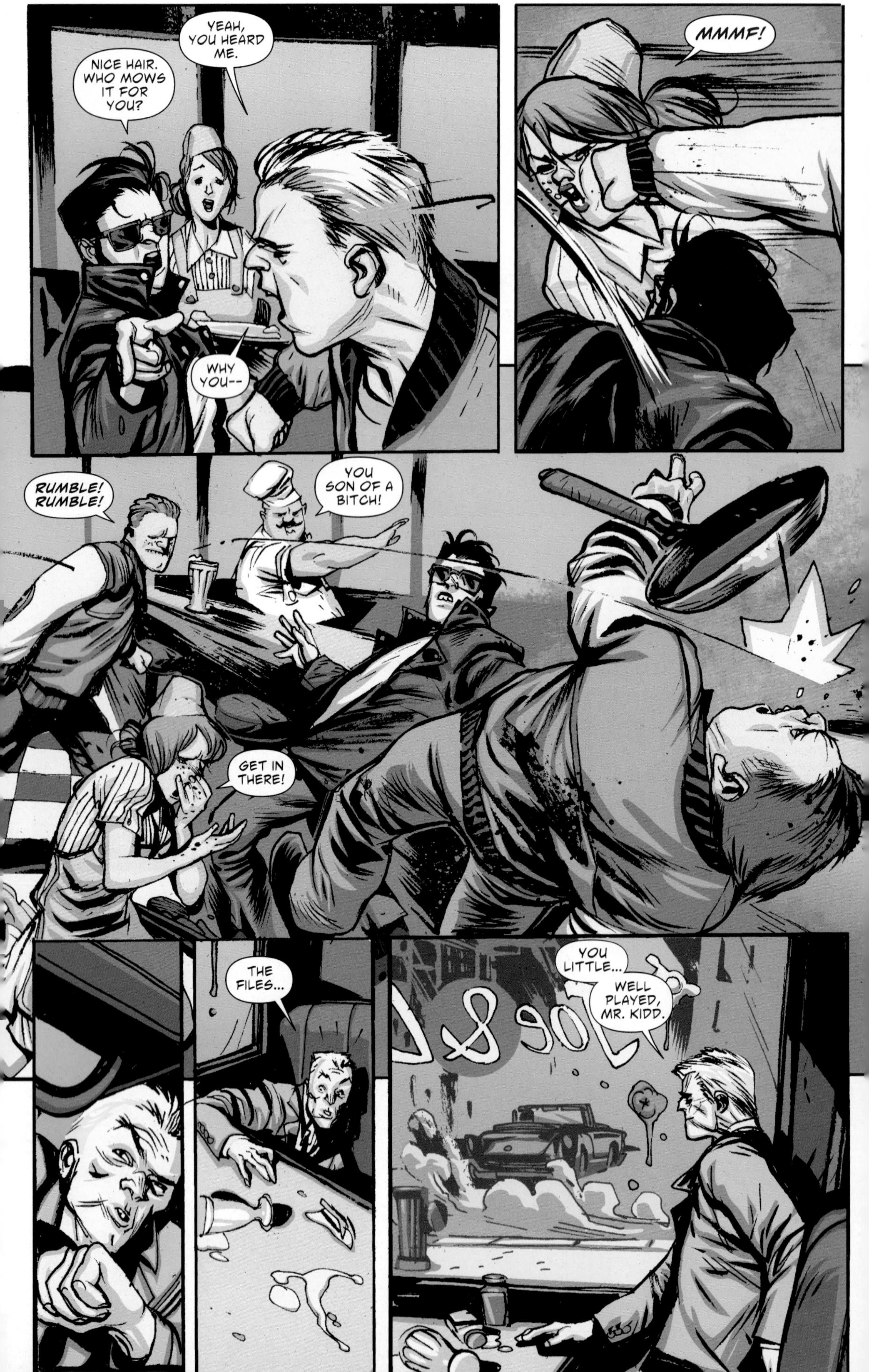
NICE HAIR. WHO MOWS IT FOR YOU?
YEAH, YOU HEARD ME.
WHY YOU--
MMMF!
RUMBLE! RUMBLE!
YOU SON OF A BITCH!
GET IN THERE!
THE FILES...
YOU LITTLE...
WELL PLAYED, MR. KIDD.

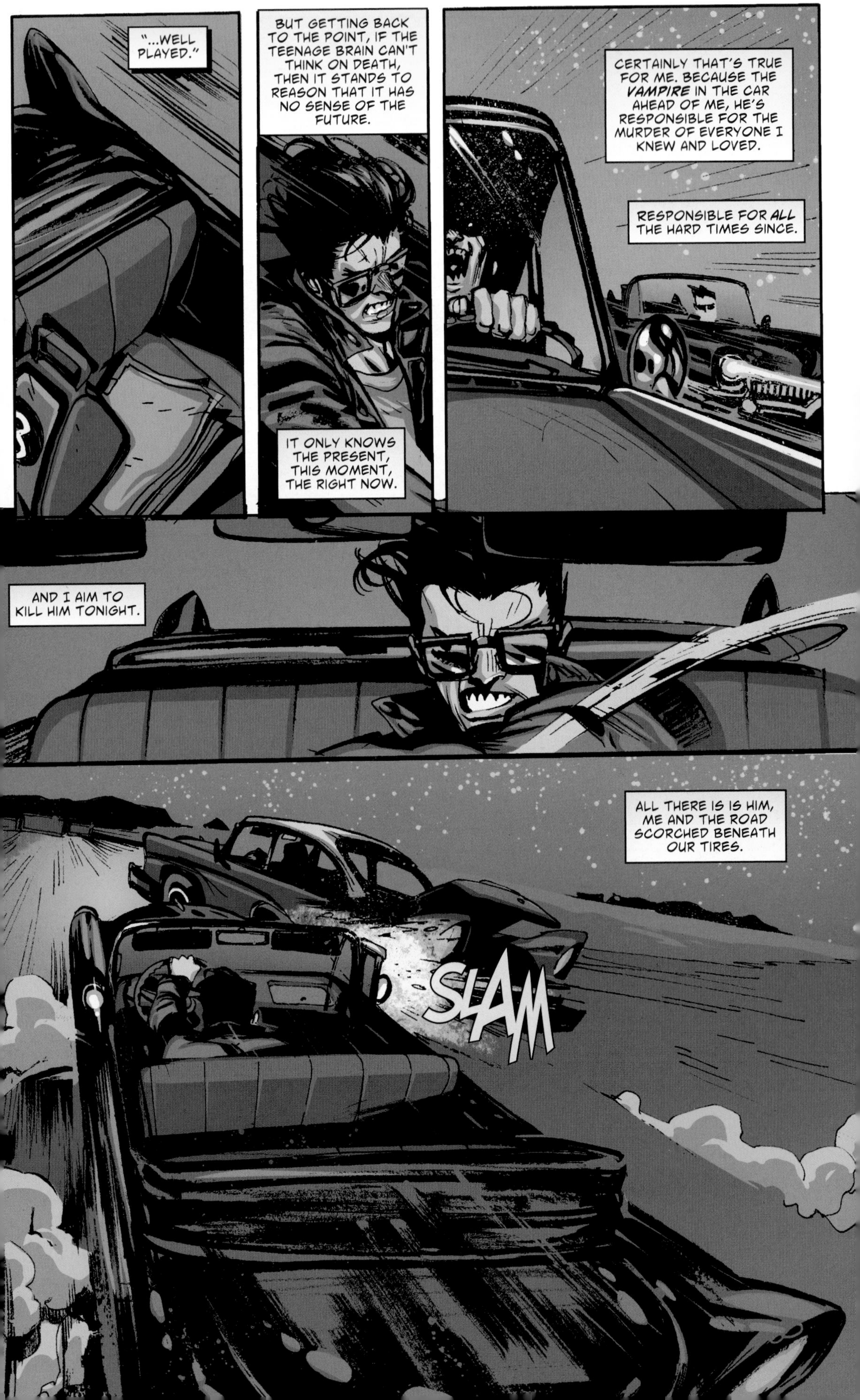
"...WELL PLAYED."
BUT GETTING BACK TO THE POINT, IF THE TEENAGE BRAIN CAN'T THINK ON DEATH, THEN IT STANDS TO REASON THAT IT HAS NO SENSE OF THE FUTURE.
IT ONLY KNOWS THE PRESENT, THIS MOMENT, THE RIGHT NOW.
CERTAINLY THAT'S TRUE FOR ME. BECAUSE THE VAMPIRE IN THE CAR AHEAD OF ME, HE'S RESPONSIBLE FOR THE MURDER OF EVERYONE I KNEW AND LOVED.
RESPONSIBLE FOR ALL THE HARD TIMES SINCE.
AND I AIM TO KILL HIM TONIGHT.
ALL THERE IS IS HIM, ME AND THE ROAD SCORCHED BENEATH OUR TIRES.
SLAM

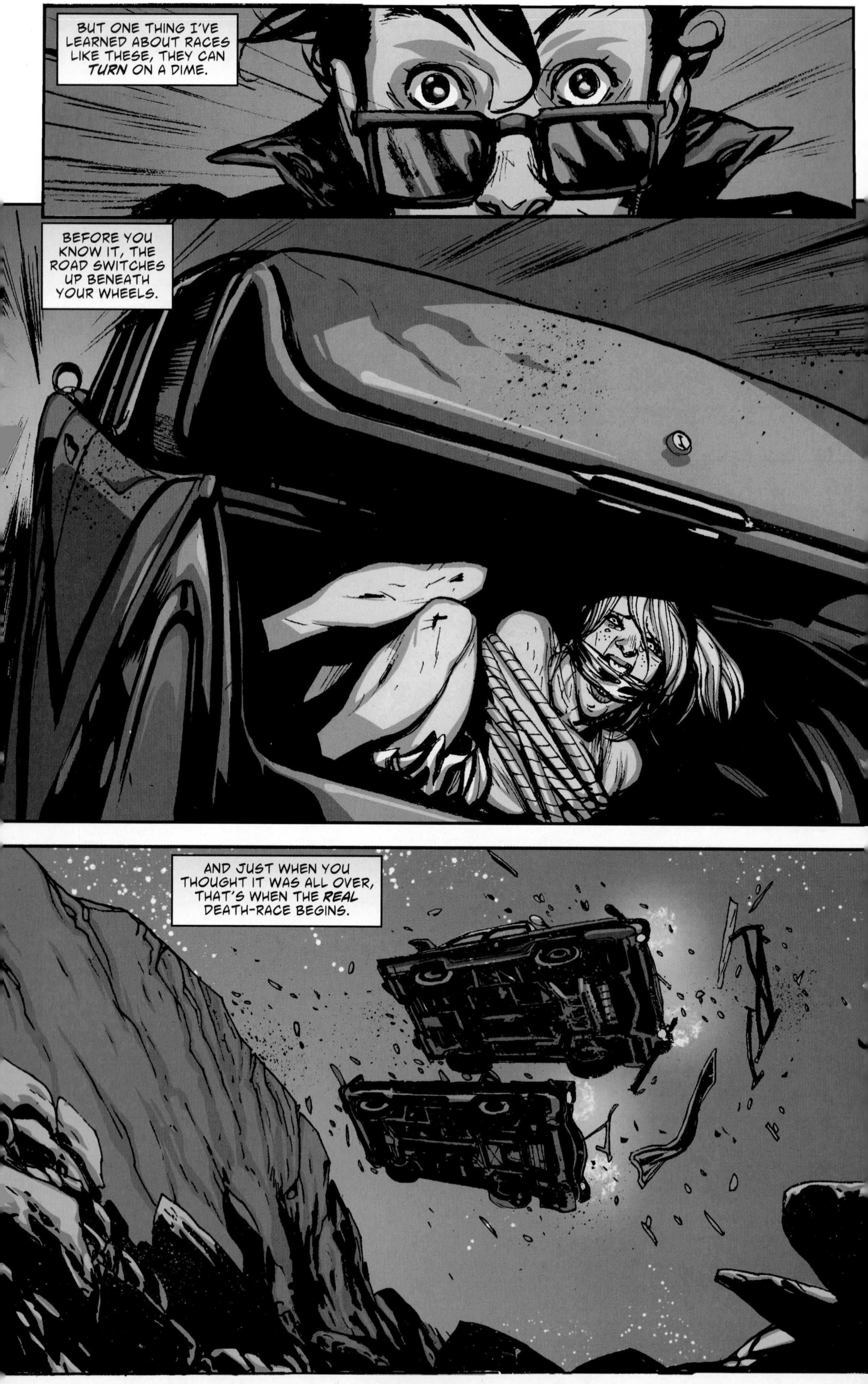
BUT ONE THING I'VE LEARNED ABOUT RACES LIKE THESE, THEY CAN *TURN* ON A DIME.
BEFORE YOU KNOW IT, THE ROAD SWITCHES UP BENEATH YOUR WHEELS.
AND JUST WHEN YOU THOUGHT IT WAS ALL OVER, THAT'S WHEN THE *REAL* DEATH-RACE BEGINS.

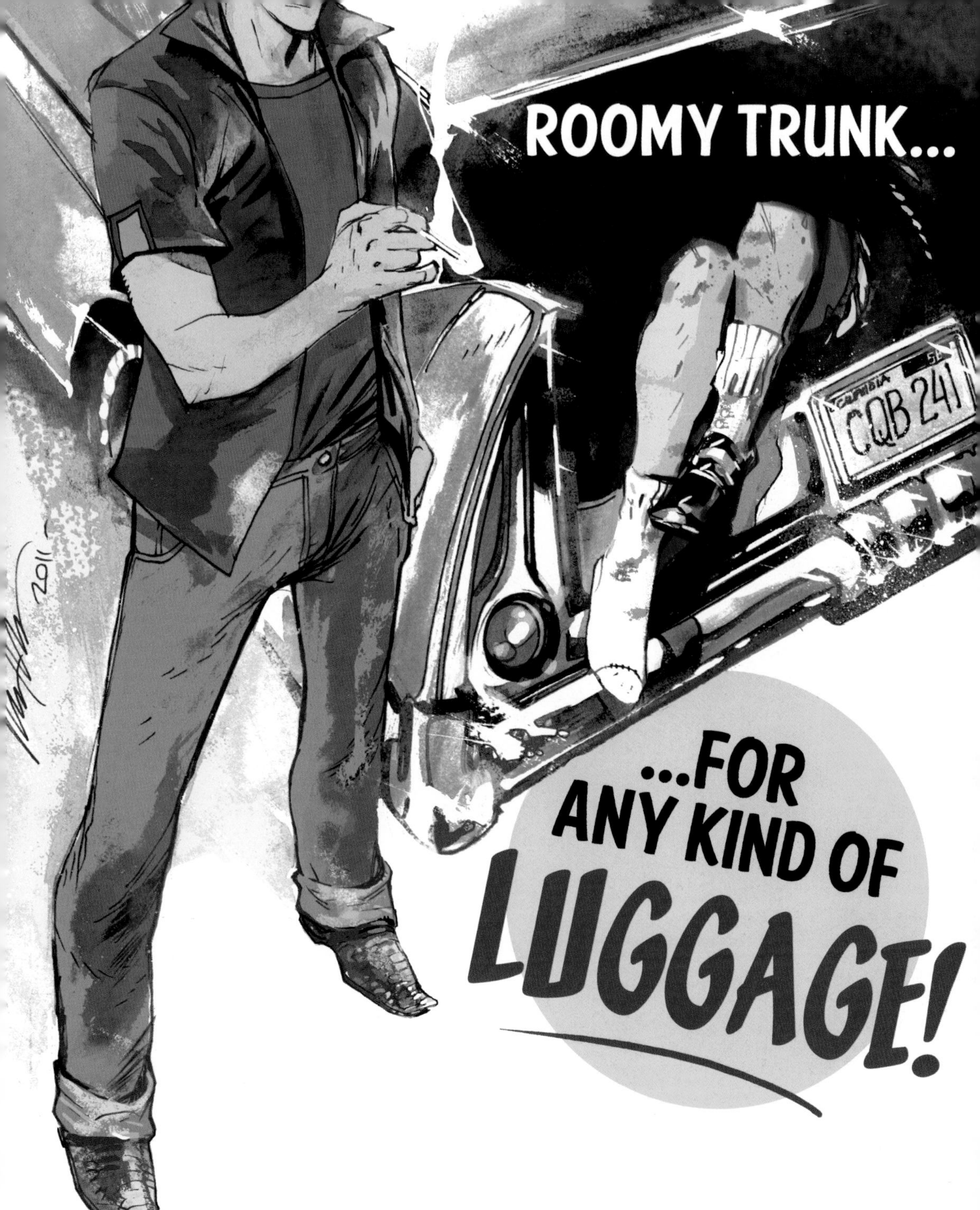
ROOMY TRUNK...
CQB 241
...FOR ANY KIND OF LUGGAGE!

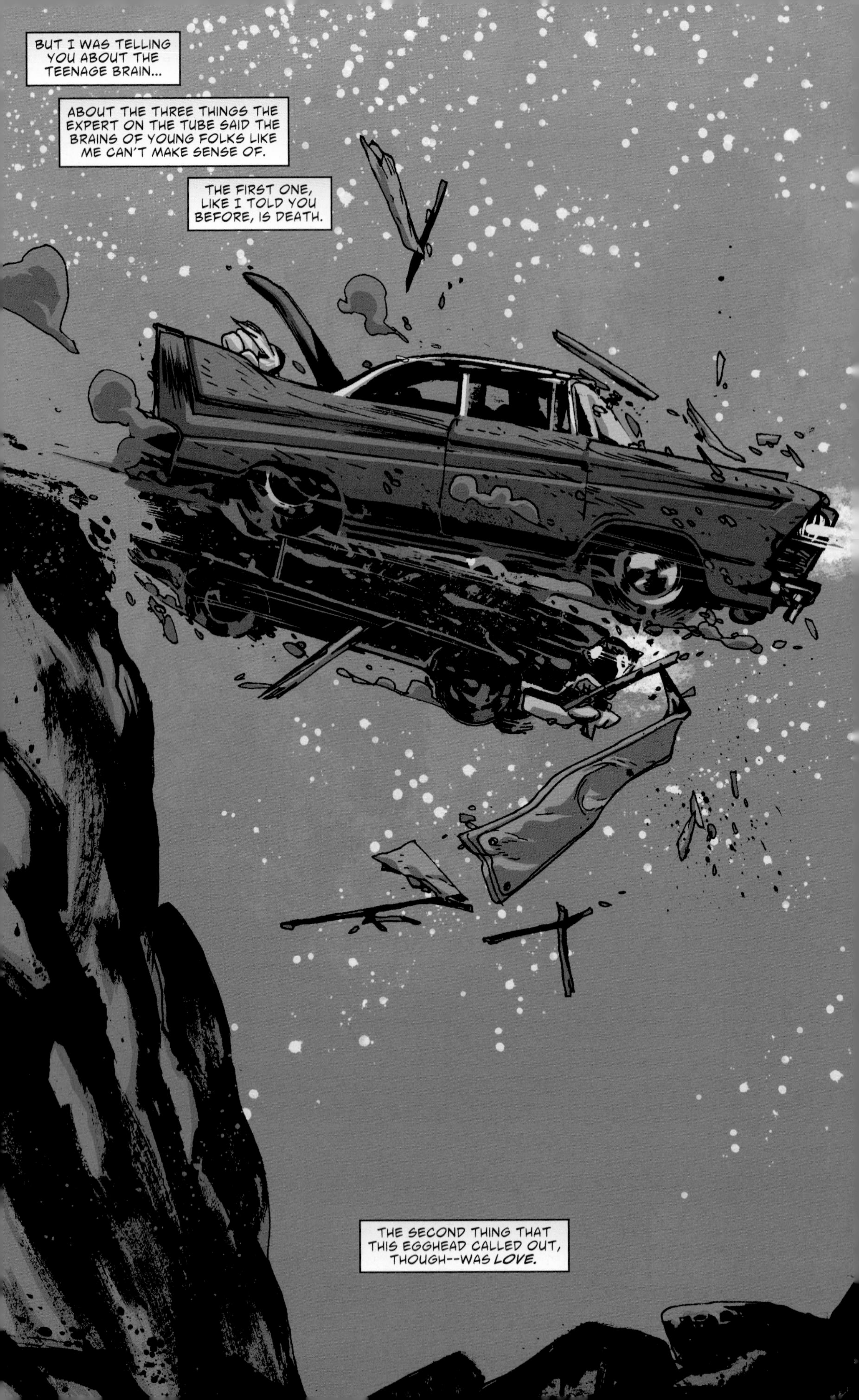
BUT I WAS TELLING YOU ABOUT THE TEENAGE BRAIN...
ABOUT THE THREE THINGS THE EXPERT ON THE TUBE SAID THE BRAINS OF YOUNG FOLKS LIKE ME CAN'T MAKE SENSE OF.
THE FIRST ONE, LIKE I TOLD YOU BEFORE, IS DEATH.
THE SECOND THING THAT THIS EGGHEAD CALLED OUT, THOUGH--WAS *LOVE.*

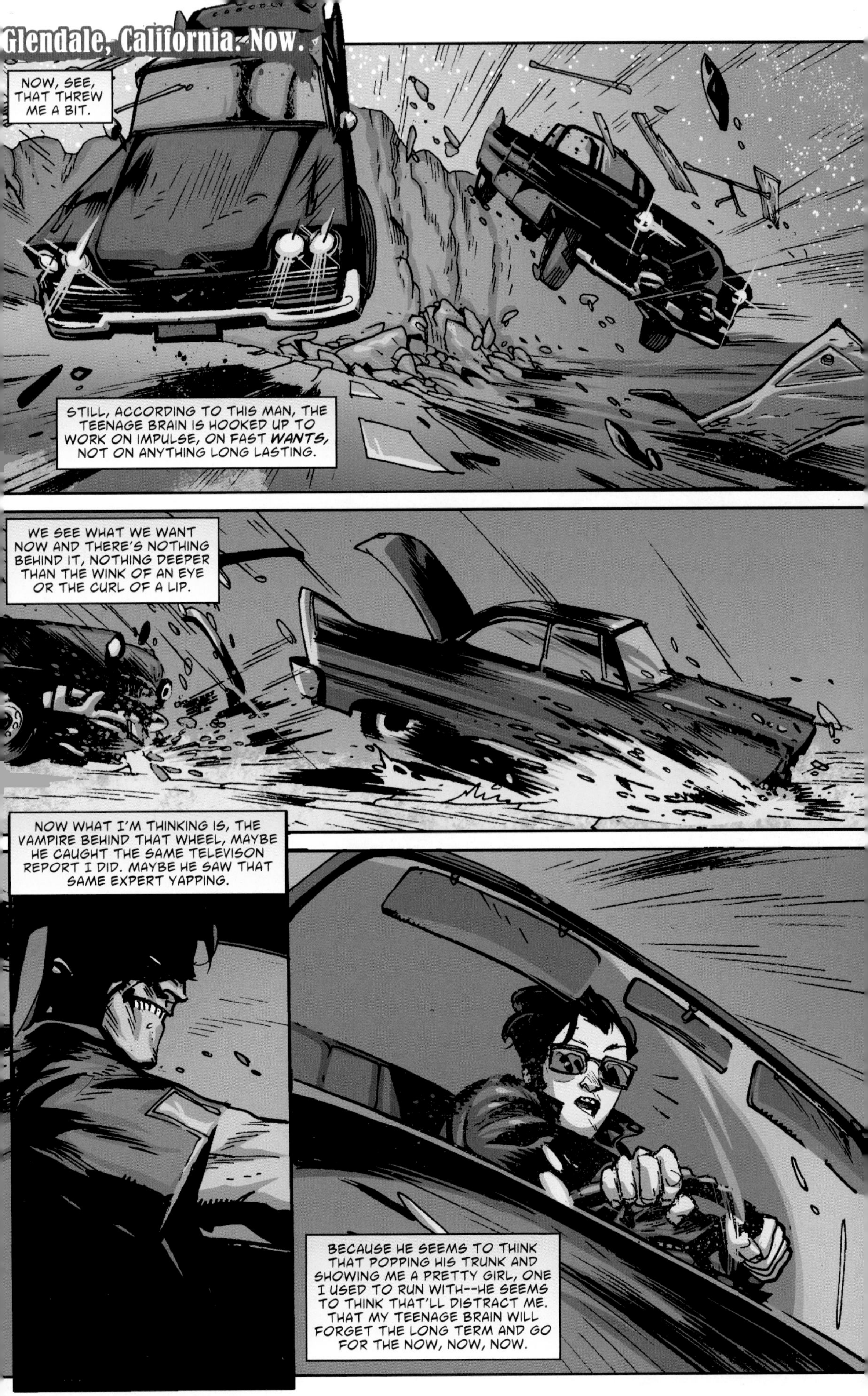
Glendale, California. Now.
NOW, SEE, THAT THREW ME A BIT.
STILL, ACCORDING TO THIS MAN, THE TEENAGE BRAIN IS HOOKED UP TO WORK ON IMPULSE, ON FAST WANTS, NOT ON ANYTHING LONG LASTING.
WE SEE WHAT WE WANT NOW AND THERE'S NOTHING BEHIND IT, NOTHING DEEPER THAN THE WINK OF AN EYE OR THE CURL OF A LIP.
NOW WHAT I'M THINKING IS, THE VAMPIRE BEHIND THAT WHEEL, MAYBE HE CAUGHT THE SAME TELEVISON REPORT I DID. MAYBE HE SAW THAT SAME EXPERT YAPPING.
BECAUSE HE SEEMS TO THINK THAT POPPING HIS TRUNK AND SHOWING ME A PRETTY GIRL, ONE I USED TO RUN WITH--HE SEEMS TO THINK THAT'LL DISTRACT ME. THAT MY TEENAGE BRAIN WILL FORGET THE LONG TERM AND GO FOR THE NOW, NOW, NOW.

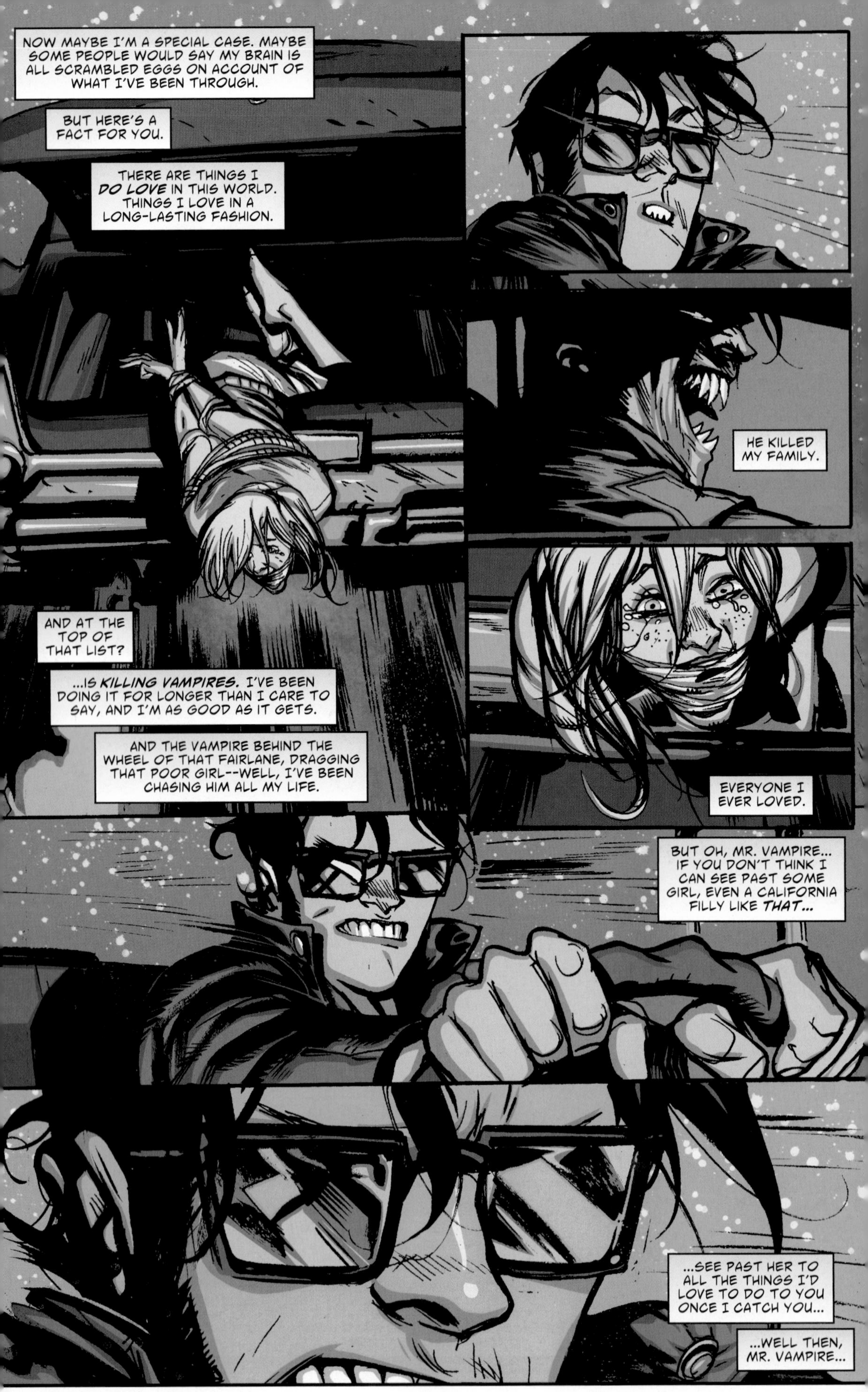
NOW MAYBE I'M A SPECIAL CASE. MAYBE SOME PEOPLE WOULD SAY MY BRAIN IS ALL SCRAMBLED EGGS ON ACCOUNT OF WHAT I'VE BEEN THROUGH.
BUT HERE'S A FACT FOR YOU.
THERE ARE THINGS I *DO LOVE* IN THIS WORLD. THINGS I LOVE IN A LONG-LASTING FASHION.
HE KILLED MY FAMILY.
AND AT THE TOP OF THAT LIST?
...IS *KILLING VAMPIRES.* I'VE BEEN DOING IT FOR LONGER THAN I CARE TO SAY, AND I'M AS GOOD AS IT GETS.
AND THE VAMPIRE BEHIND THE WHEEL OF THAT FAIRLANE, DRAGGING THAT POOR GIRL--WELL, I'VE BEEN CHASING HIM ALL MY LIFE.
EVERYONE I EVER LOVED.
BUT OH, MR. VAMPIRE... IF YOU DON'T THINK I CAN SEE PAST SOME GIRL, EVEN A CALIFORNIA FILLY LIKE *THAT*...
...SEE PAST HER TO ALL THE THINGS I'D LOVE TO DO TO YOU ONCE I CATCH YOU...
...WELL THEN, MR. VAMPIRE...

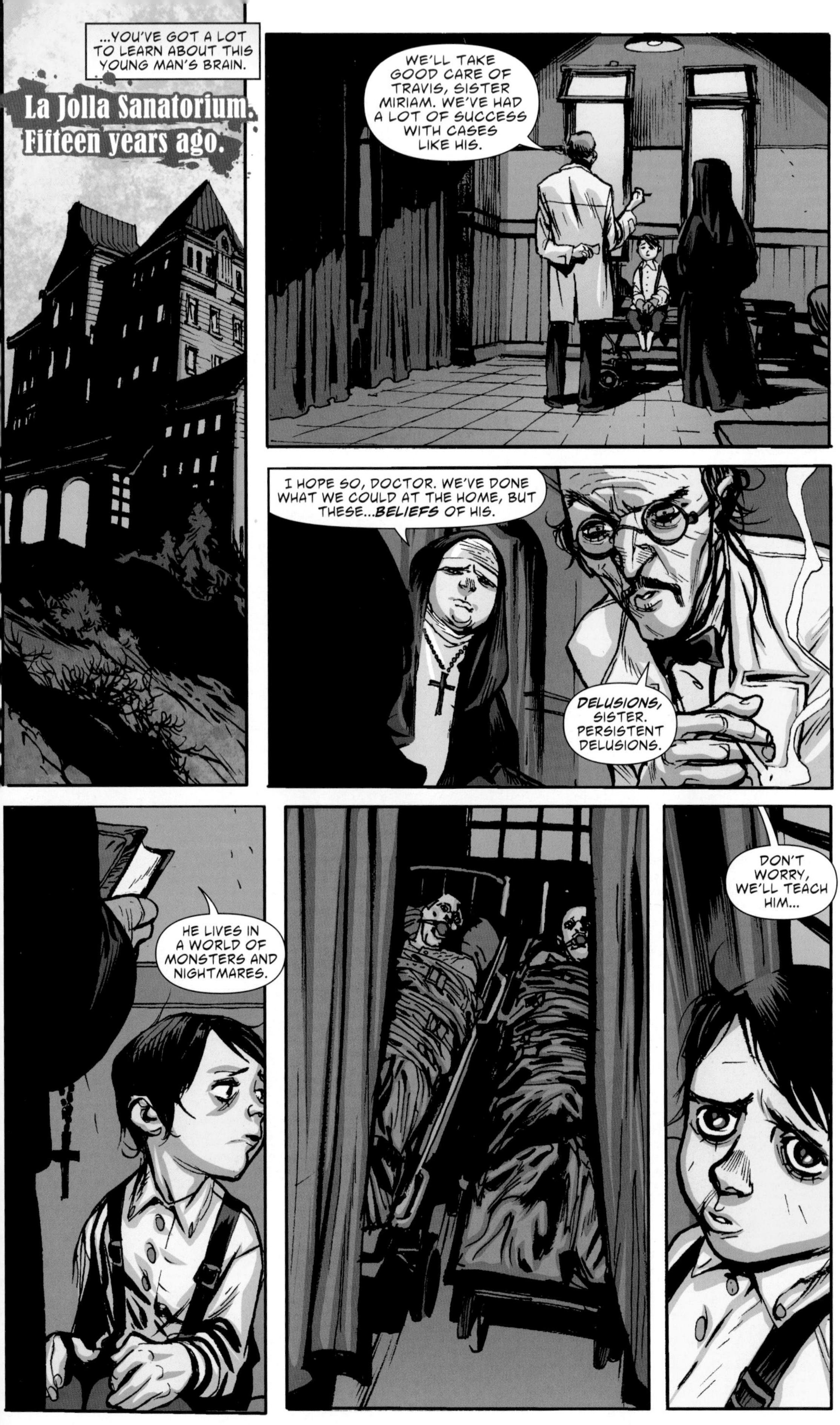
...YOU'VE GOT A LOT TO LEARN ABOUT THIS YOUNG MAN'S BRAIN.
La Jolla Sanatorium. Fifteen years ago.
WE'LL TAKE GOOD CARE OF TRAVIS, SISTER MIRIAM. WE'VE HAD A LOT OF SUCCESS WITH CASES LIKE HIS.
I HOPE SO, DOCTOR. WE'VE DONE WHAT WE COULD AT THE HOME, BUT THESE...BELIEFS OF HIS.
DELUSIONS, SISTER. PERSISTENT DELUSIONS.
HE LIVES IN A WORLD OF MONSTERS AND NIGHTMARES.
DON'T WORRY, WE'LL TEACH HIM...

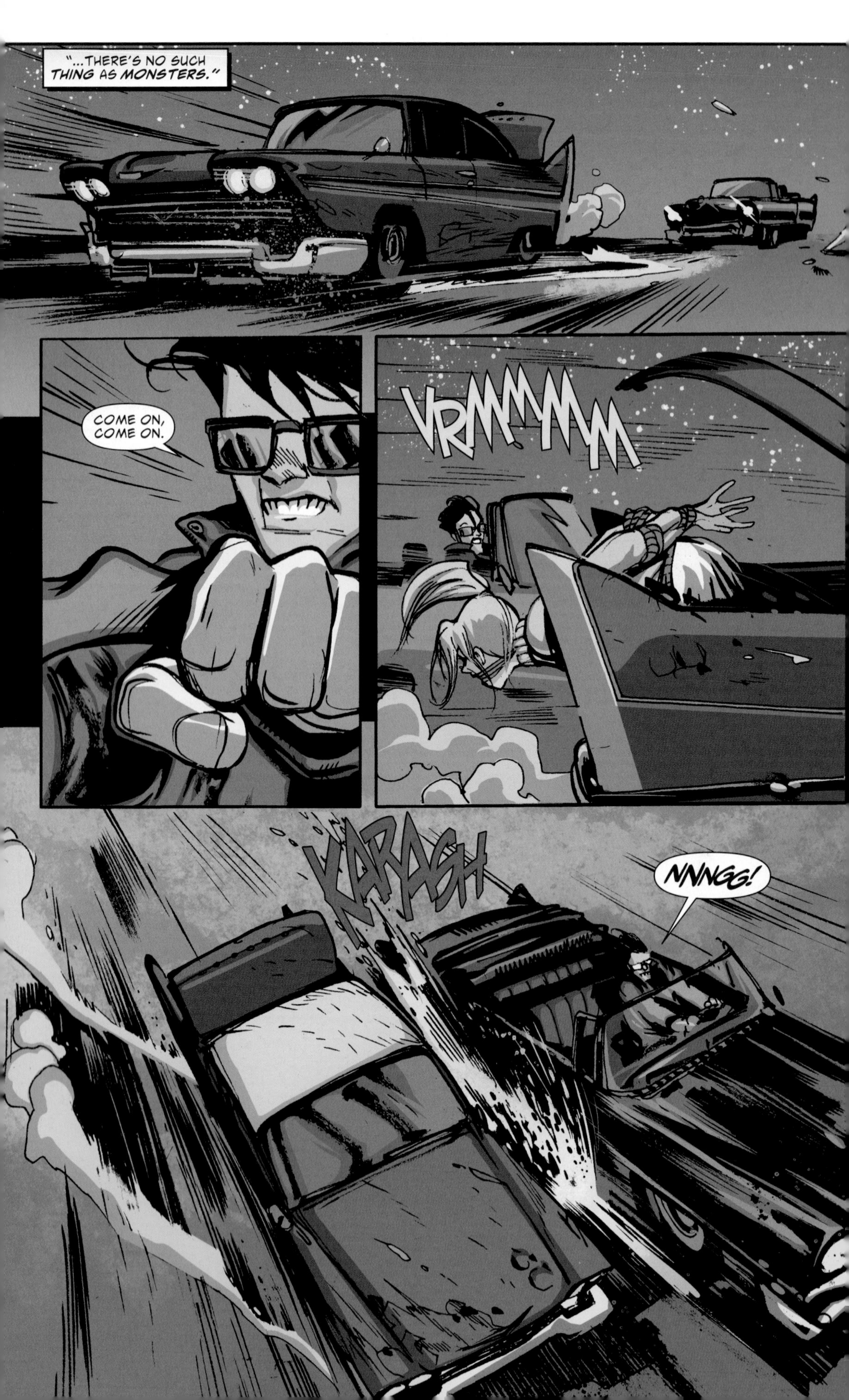
"...THERE'S NO SUCH THING AS MONSTERS."
COME ON, COME ON.
VRMMMM
KARASH
NNNGG!

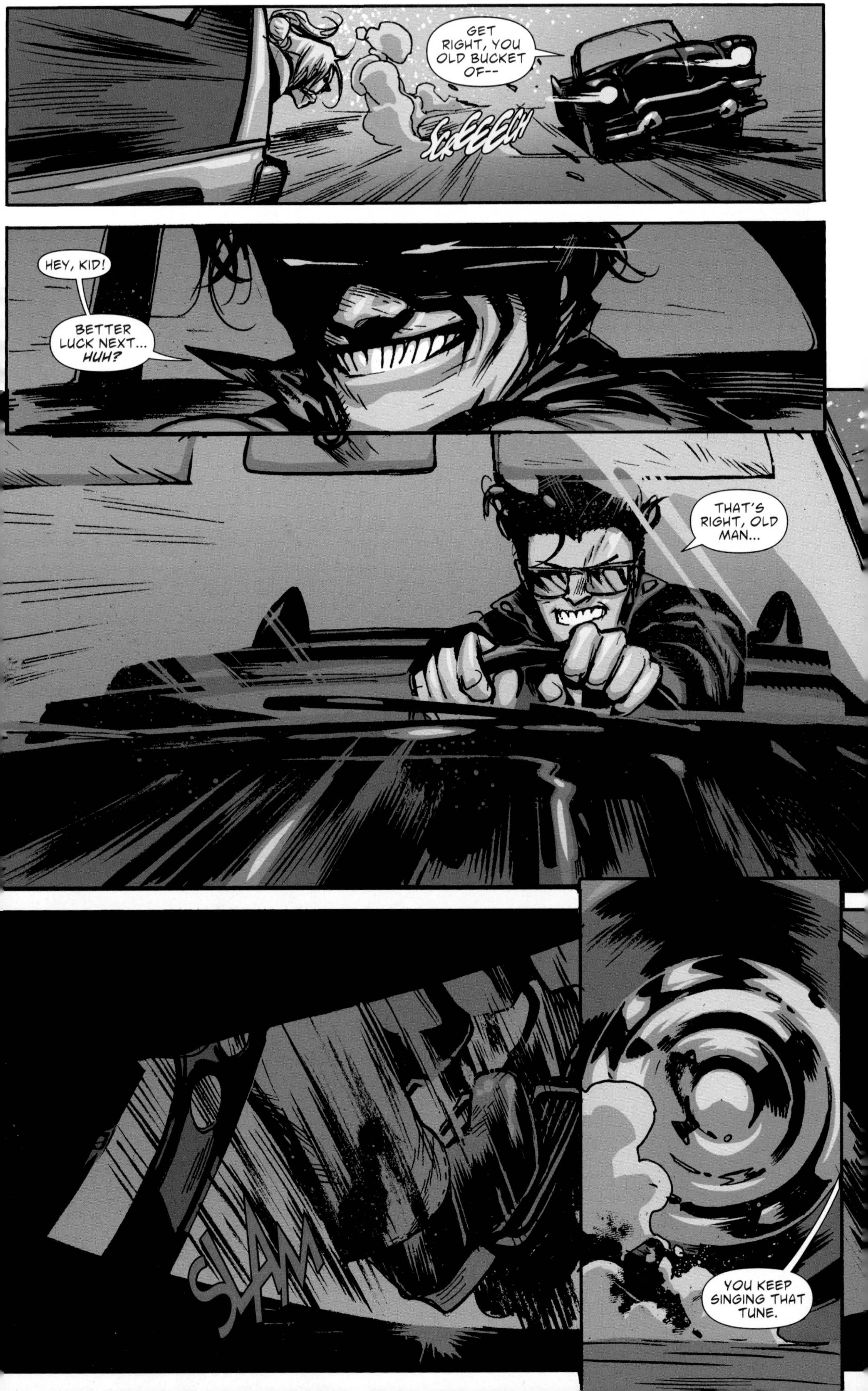
GET RIGHT, YOU OLD BUCKET OF--
SCREEEECH
HEY, KID!
BETTER LUCK NEXT... HUH?
THAT'S RIGHT, OLD MAN...
SLAM
YOU KEEP SINGING THAT TUNE.

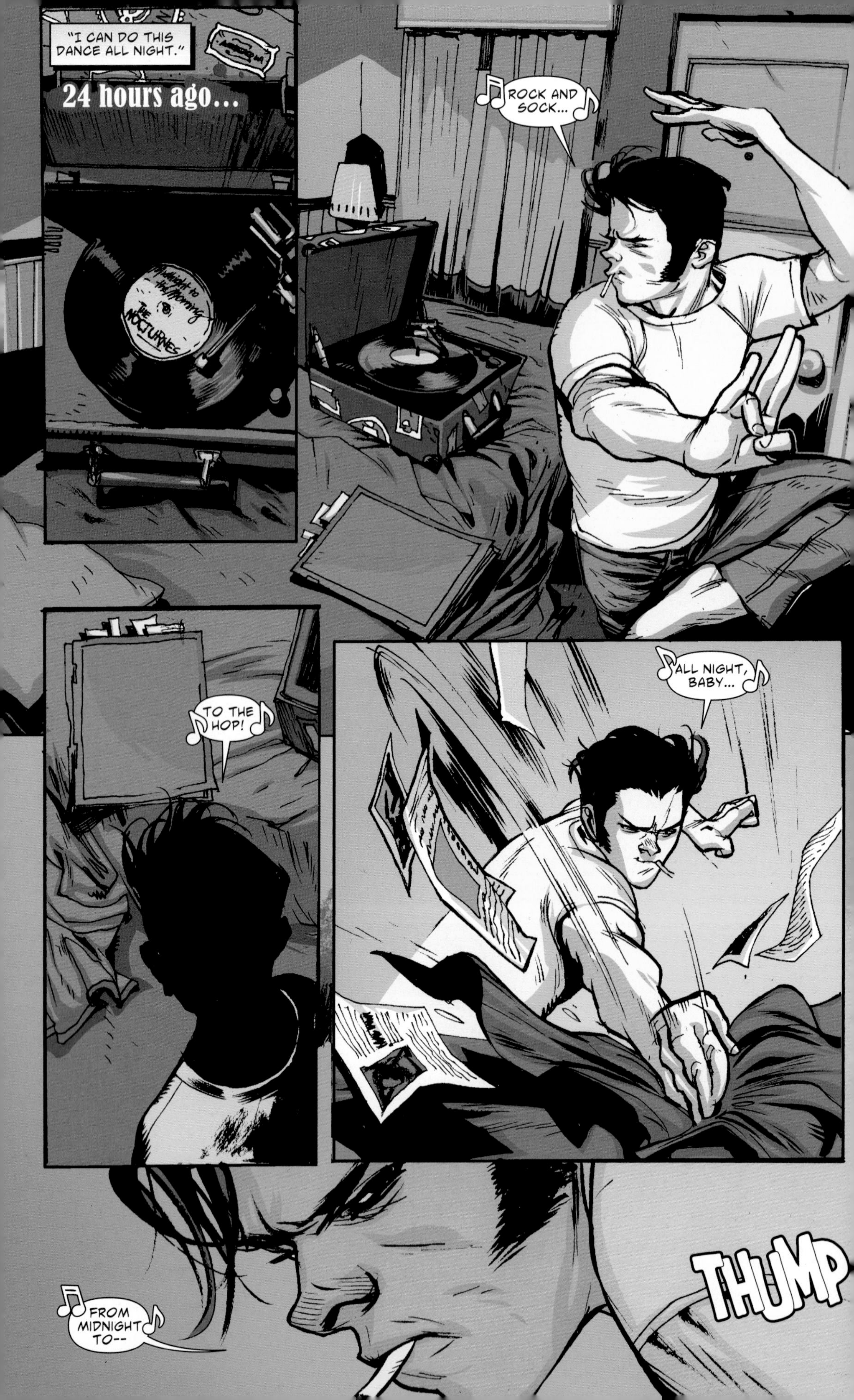
"I CAN DO THIS DANCE ALL NIGHT."
24 hours ago...
ROCK AND SOCK...
TO THE HOP!
ALL NIGHT, BABY...
FROM MIDNIGHT TO--
THUMP

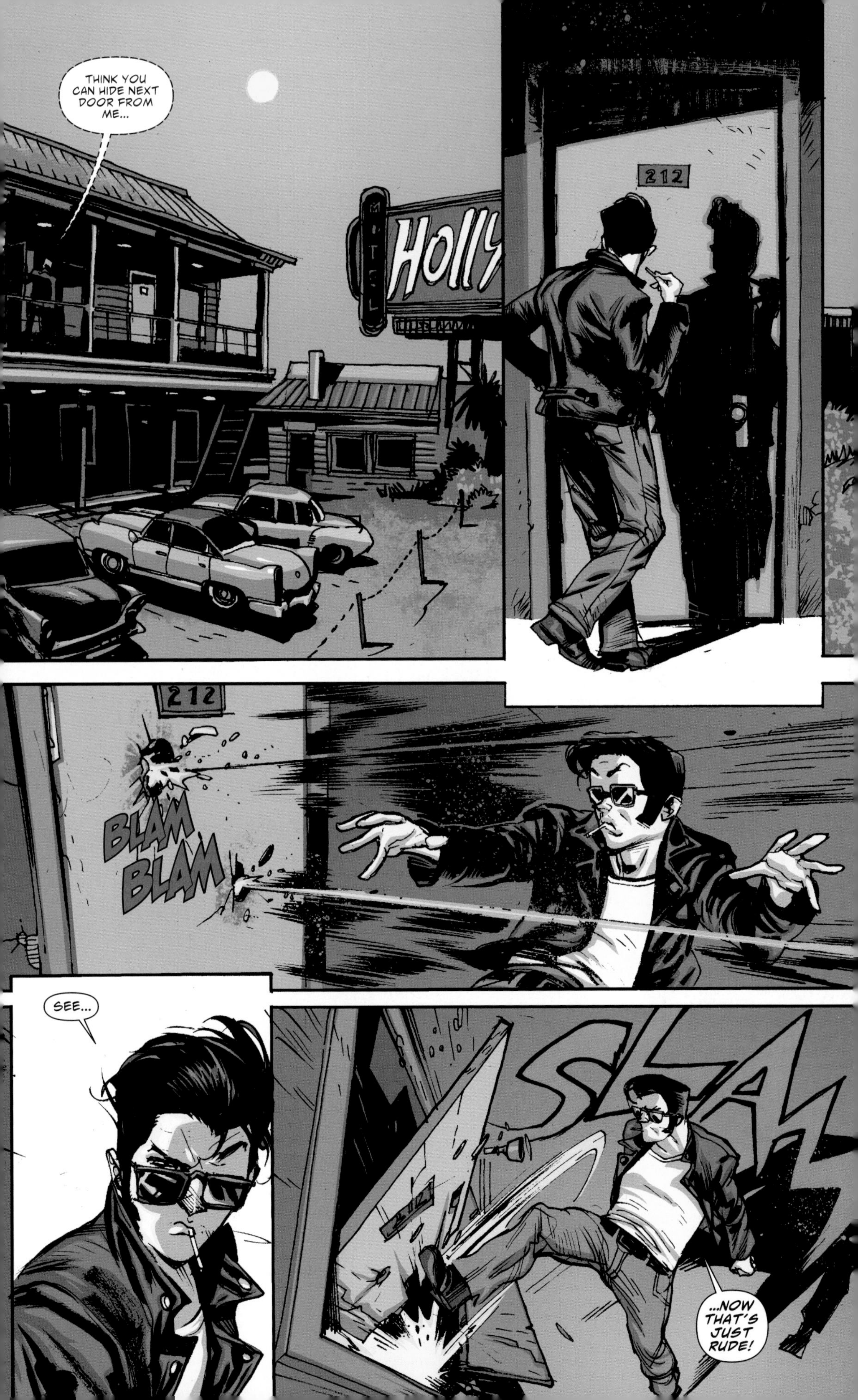
THINK YOU CAN HIDE NEXT DOOR FROM ME...
Holly
212
BLAM
BLAM
SEE...
...NOW THAT'S JUST RUDE!

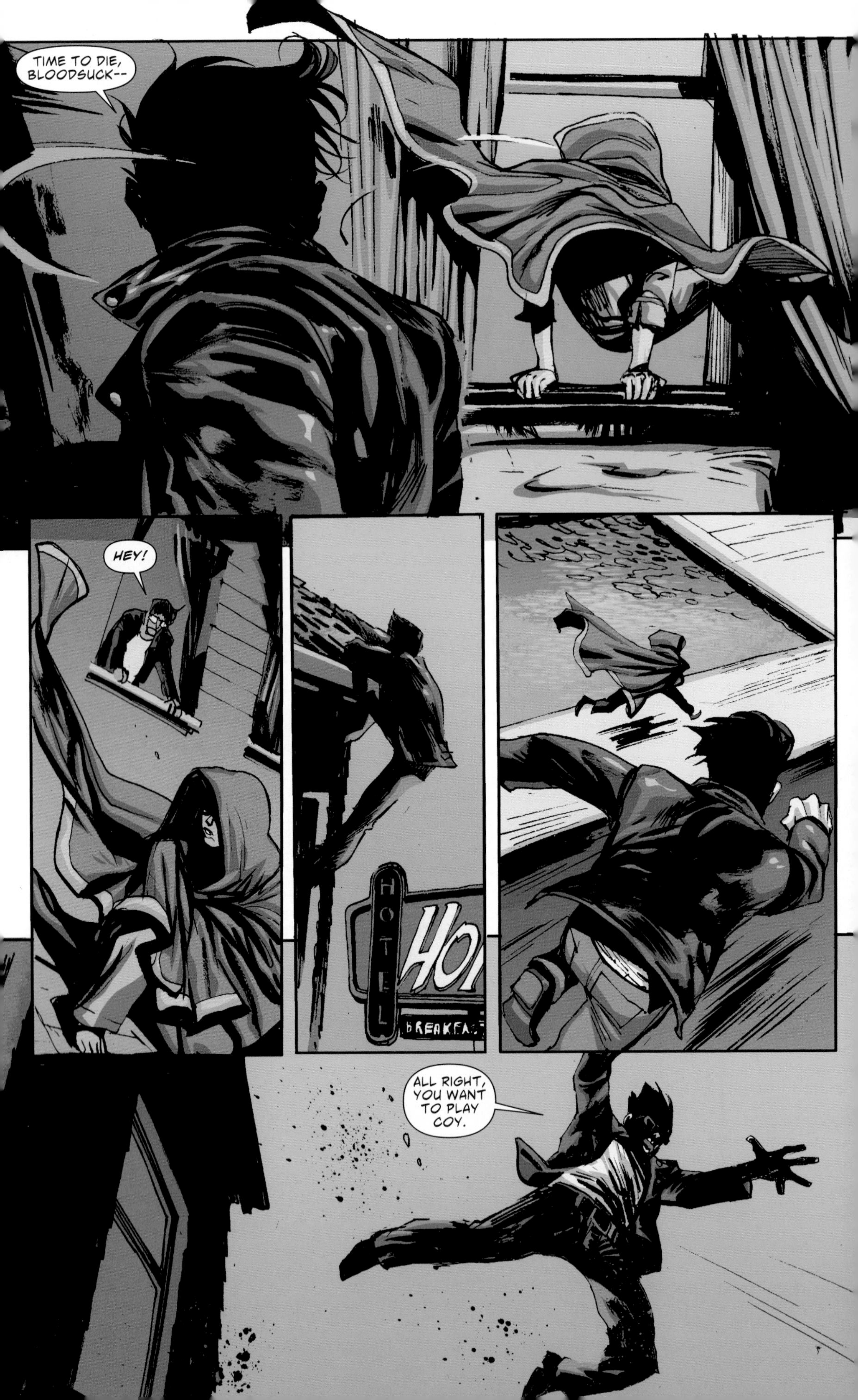
TIME TO DIE, BLOODSUCK--
HEY!
HOTEL
HOT
BREAKFA
ALL RIGHT, YOU WANT TO PLAY COY.

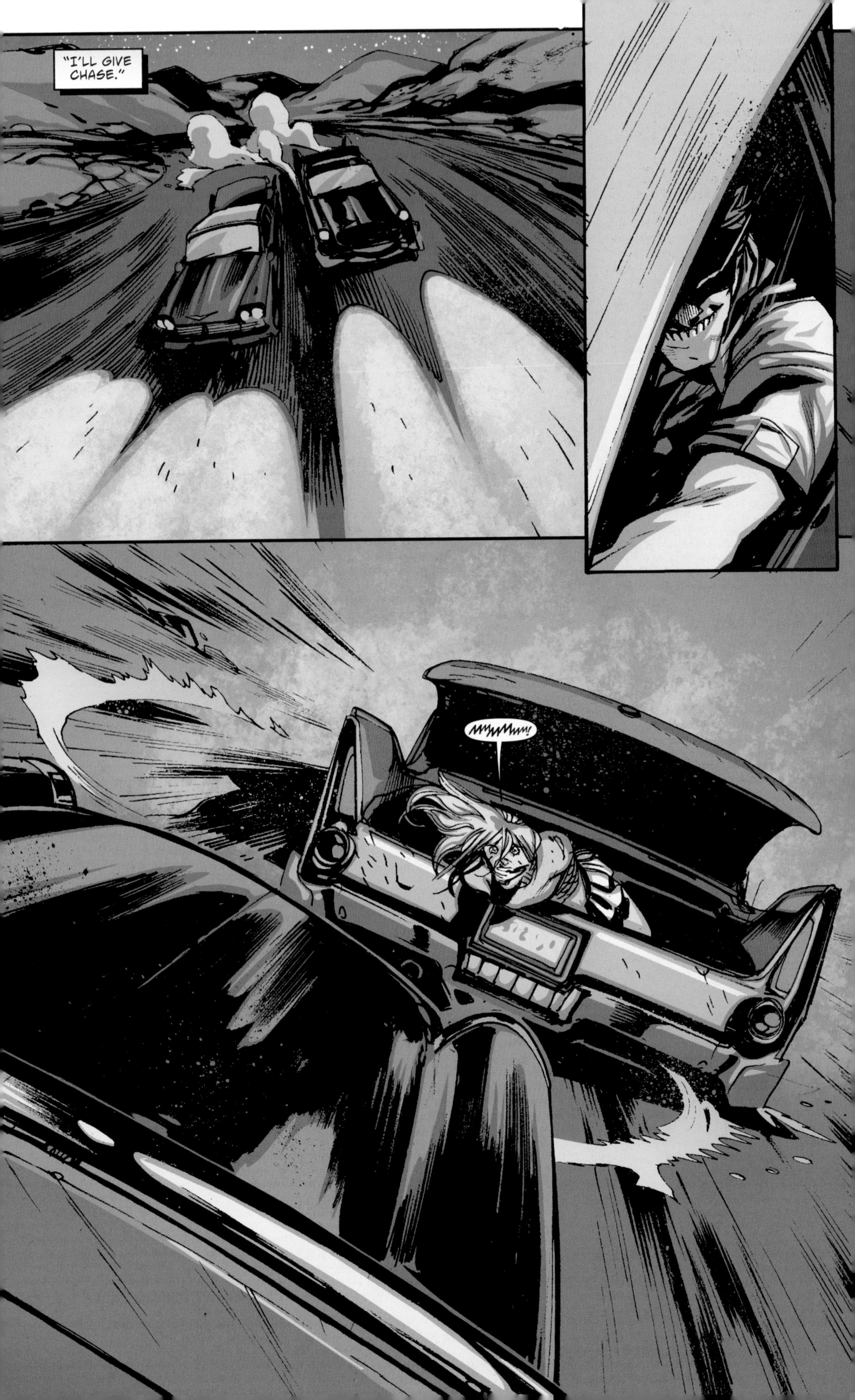
"I'LL GIVE CHASE."
MMMMMM!

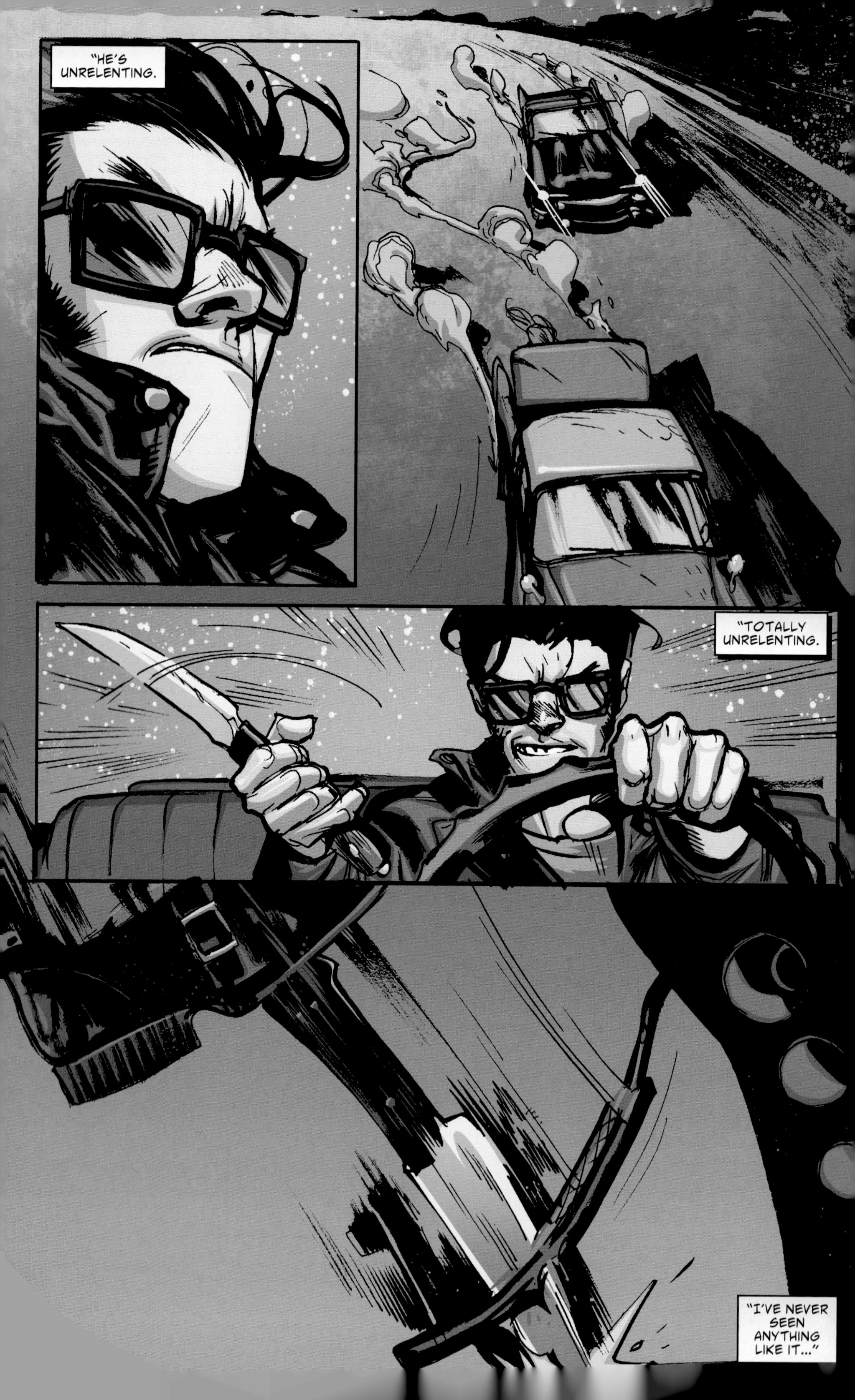
"HE'S
UNRELENTING.
"TOTALLY
UNRELENTING.
"I'VE NEVER
SEEN
ANYTHING
LIKE IT..."

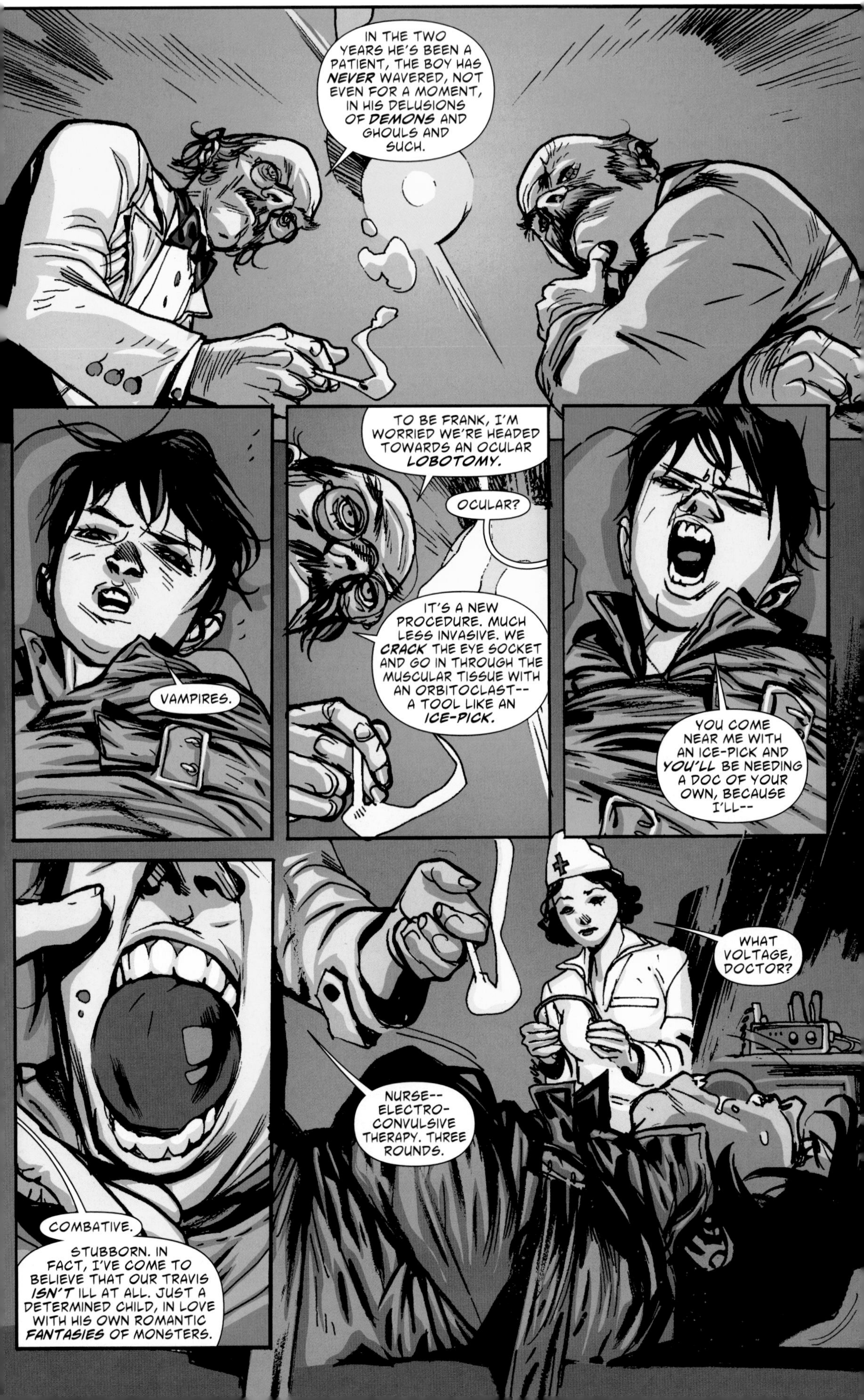
IN THE TWO YEARS HE'S BEEN A PATIENT, THE BOY HAS NEVER WAVERED, NOT EVEN FOR A MOMENT, IN HIS DELUSIONS OF DEMONS AND GHOULS AND SUCH.
VAMPIRES.
TO BE FRANK, I'M WORRIED WE'RE HEADED TOWARDS AN OCULAR LOBOTOMY.
OCULAR?
IT'S A NEW PROCEDURE. MUCH LESS INVASIVE. WE CRACK THE EYE SOCKET AND GO IN THROUGH THE MUSCULAR TISSUE WITH AN ORBITOCLAST-- A TOOL LIKE AN ICE-PICK.
YOU COME NEAR ME WITH AN ICE-PICK AND YOU'LL BE NEEDING A DOC OF YOUR OWN, BECAUSE I'LL--
COMBATIVE.
STUBBORN. IN FACT, I'VE COME TO BELIEVE THAT OUR TRAVIS ISN'T ILL AT ALL. JUST A DETERMINED CHILD, IN LOVE WITH HIS OWN ROMANTIC FANTASIES OF MONSTERS.
NURSE-- ELECTRO-CONVULSIVE THERAPY. THREE ROUNDS.
WHAT VOLTAGE, DOCTOR?

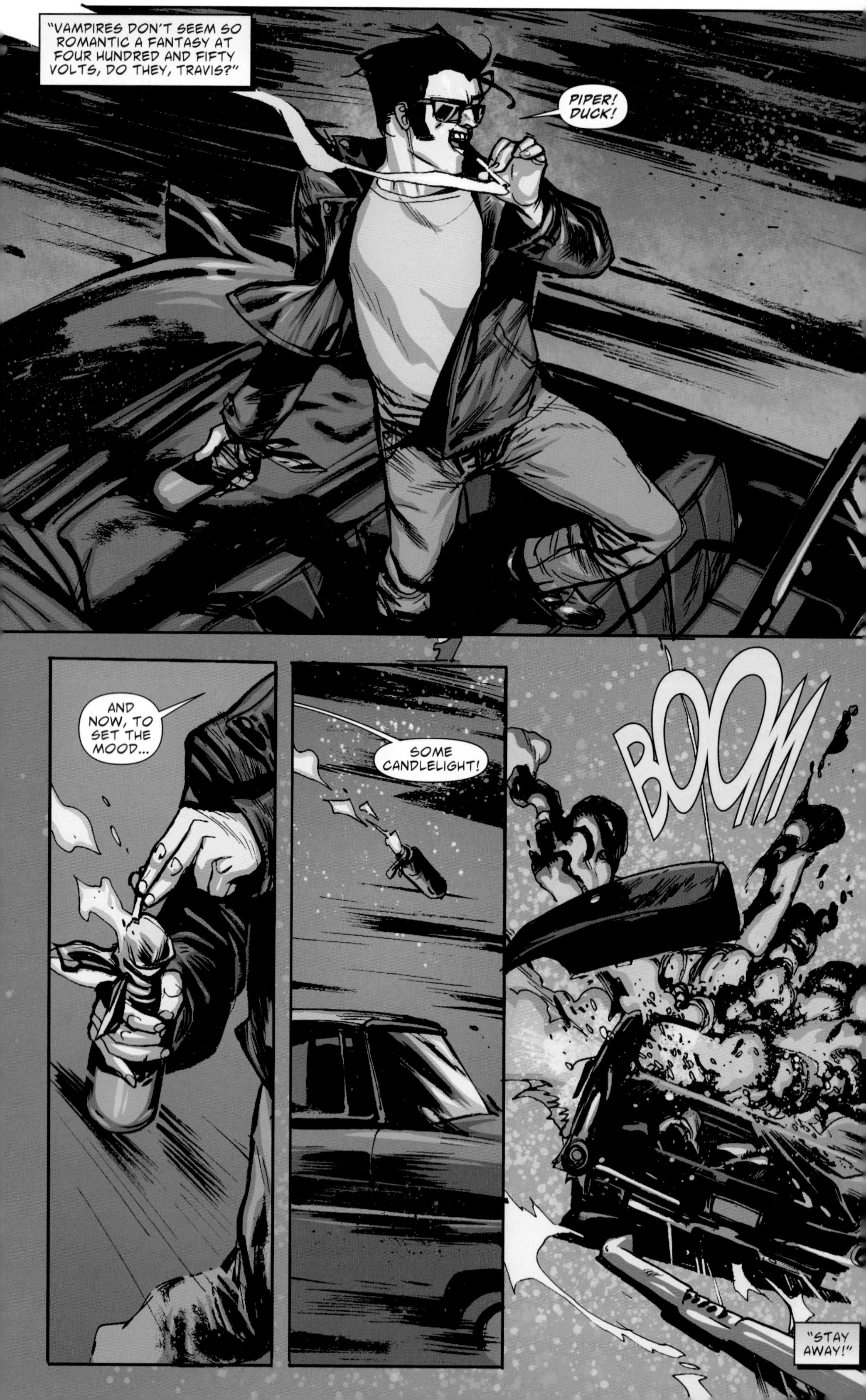
"VAMPIRES DON'T SEEM SO ROMANTIC A FANTASY AT FOUR HUNDRED AND FIFTY VOLTS, DO THEY, TRAVIS?"
PIPER! DUCK!
AND NOW, TO SET THE MOOD...
SOME CANDLELIGHT!
BOOM
"STAY AWAY!"

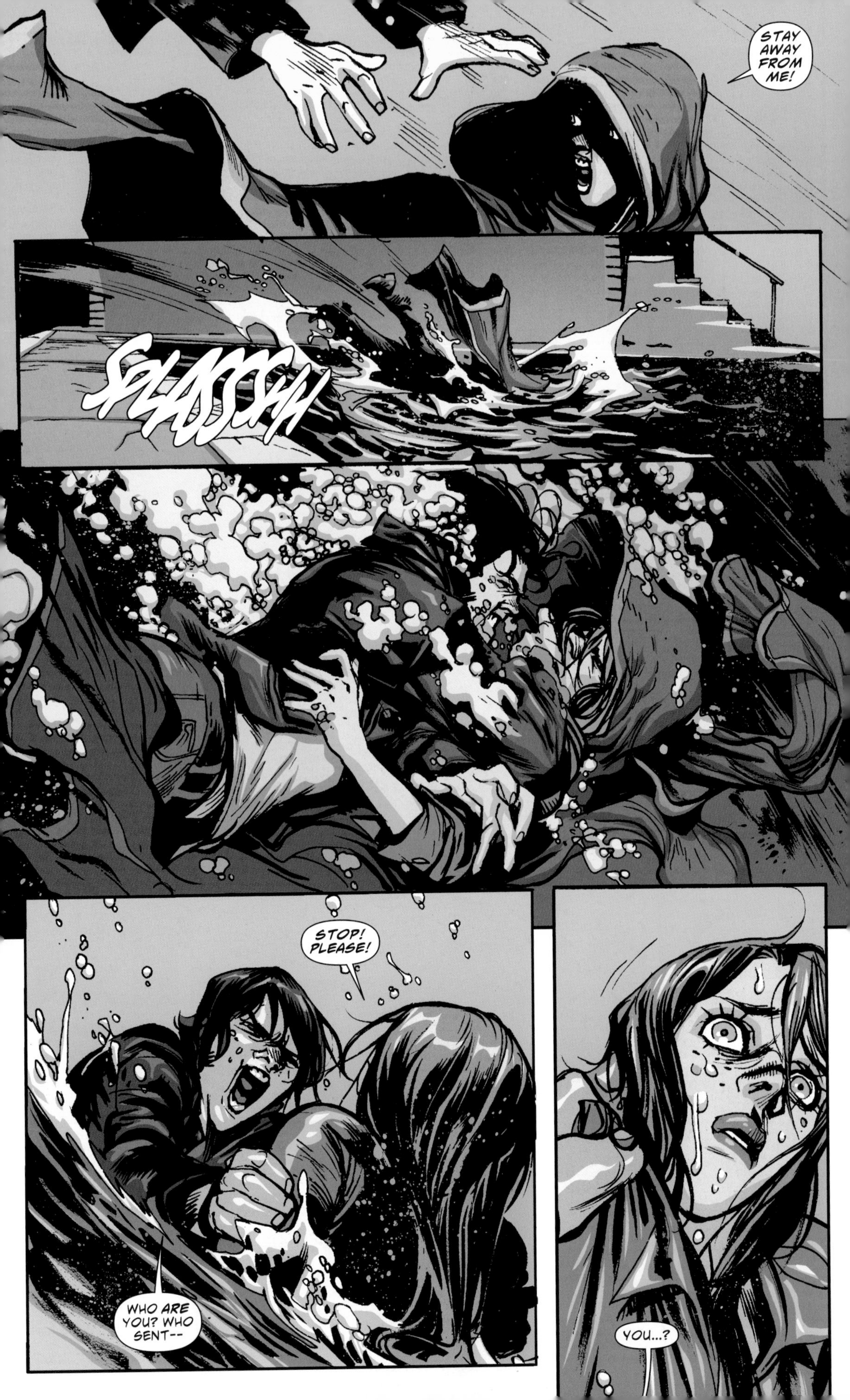
STAY AWAY FROM ME!
SPLOOSH
STOP! PLEASE!
WHO ARE YOU? WHO SENT--
YOU...?

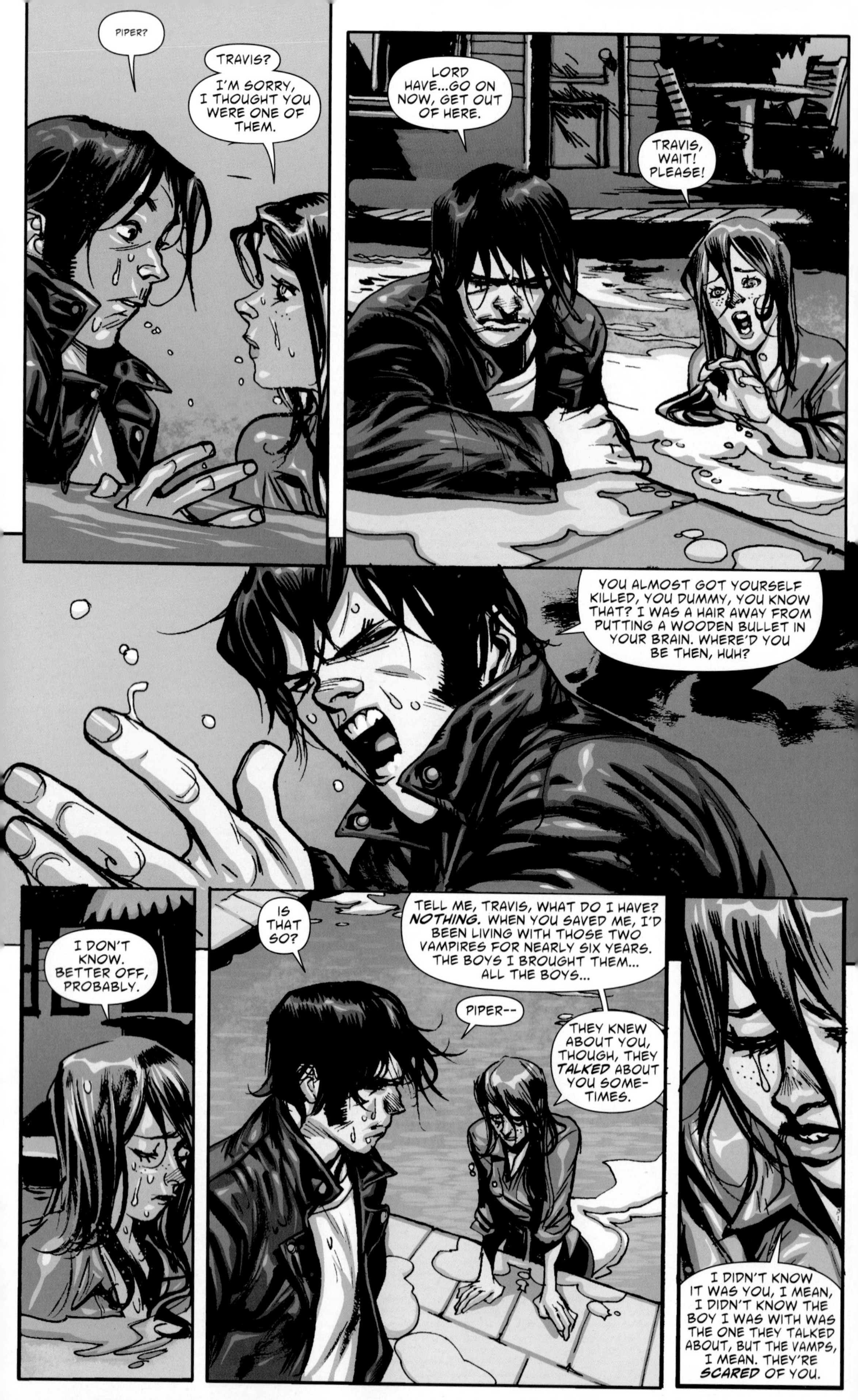
PIPER?
TRAVIS? I'M SORRY, I THOUGHT YOU WERE ONE OF THEM.
LORD HAVE...GO ON NOW, GET OUT OF HERE.
TRAVIS, WAIT! PLEASE!
YOU ALMOST GOT YOURSELF KILLED, YOU DUMMY, YOU KNOW THAT? I WAS A HAIR AWAY FROM PUTTING A WOODEN BULLET IN YOUR BRAIN. WHERE'D YOU BE THEN, HUH?
I DON'T KNOW. BETTER OFF, PROBABLY.
IS THAT SO?
TELL ME, TRAVIS, WHAT DO I HAVE? NOTHING. WHEN YOU SAVED ME, I'D BEEN LIVING WITH THOSE TWO VAMPIRES FOR NEARLY SIX YEARS. THE BOYS I BROUGHT THEM... ALL THE BOYS...
PIPER--
THEY KNEW ABOUT YOU, THOUGH, THEY TALKED ABOUT YOU SOME-TIMES.
I DIDN'T KNOW IT WAS YOU, I MEAN, I DIDN'T KNOW THE BOY I WAS WITH WAS THE ONE THEY TALKED ABOUT, BUT THE VAMPS, I MEAN. THEY'RE SCARED OF YOU.

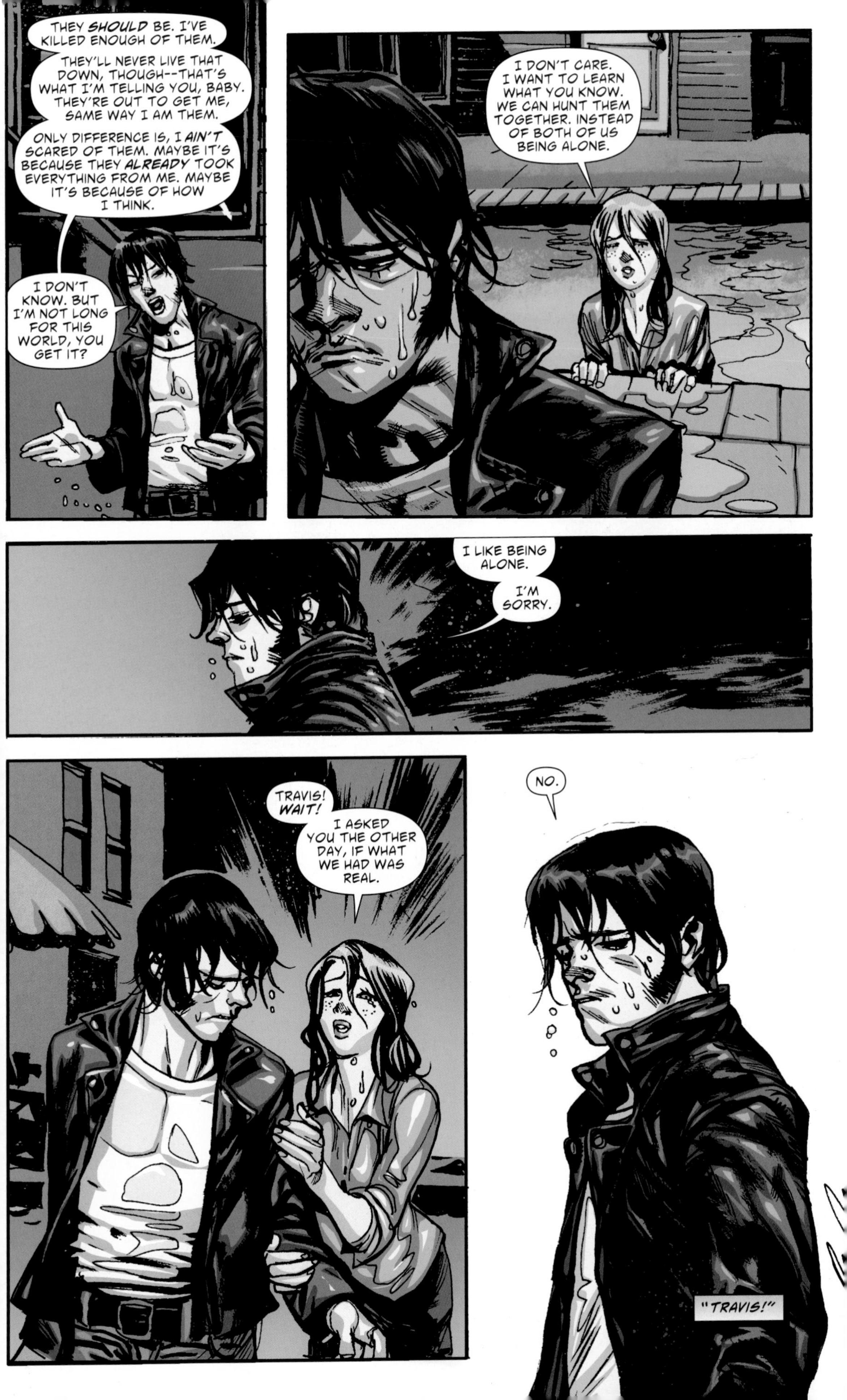
THEY **SHOULD** BE. I'VE KILLED ENOUGH OF THEM.
THEY'LL NEVER LIVE THAT DOWN, THOUGH--THAT'S WHAT I'M TELLING YOU, BABY. THEY'RE OUT TO GET ME, SAME WAY I AM THEM.
ONLY DIFFERENCE IS, I **AIN'T** SCARED OF THEM. MAYBE IT'S BECAUSE THEY **ALREADY** TOOK EVERYTHING FROM ME. MAYBE IT'S BECAUSE OF HOW I THINK.
I DON'T KNOW. BUT I'M NOT LONG FOR THIS WORLD, YOU GET IT?
I DON'T CARE. I WANT TO LEARN WHAT YOU KNOW. WE CAN HUNT THEM TOGETHER. INSTEAD OF BOTH OF US BEING ALONE.
I LIKE BEING ALONE.
I'M SORRY.
TRAVIS! **WAIT!**
I ASKED YOU THE OTHER DAY, IF WHAT WE HAD WAS REAL.
NO.
"TRAVIS!"

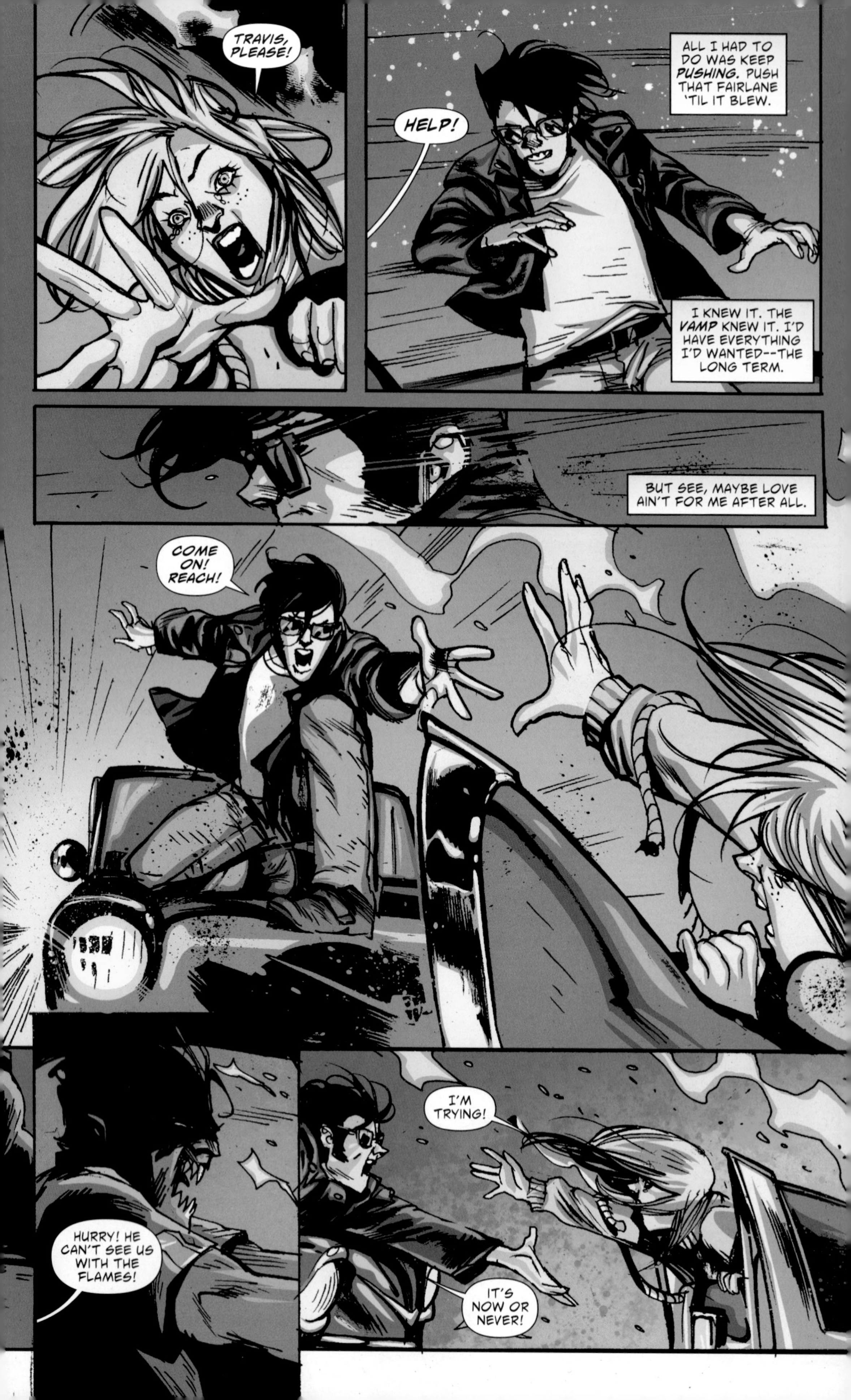
TRAVIS, PLEASE!
ALL I HAD TO DO WAS KEEP PUSHING. PUSH THAT FAIRLANE 'TIL IT BLEW.
HELP!
I KNEW IT. THE VAMP KNEW IT. I'D HAVE EVERYTHING I'D WANTED--THE LONG TERM.
BUT SEE, MAYBE LOVE AIN'T FOR ME AFTER ALL.
COME ON! REACH!
I'M TRYING!
HURRY! HE CAN'T SEE US WITH THE FLAMES!
IT'S NOW OR NEVER!

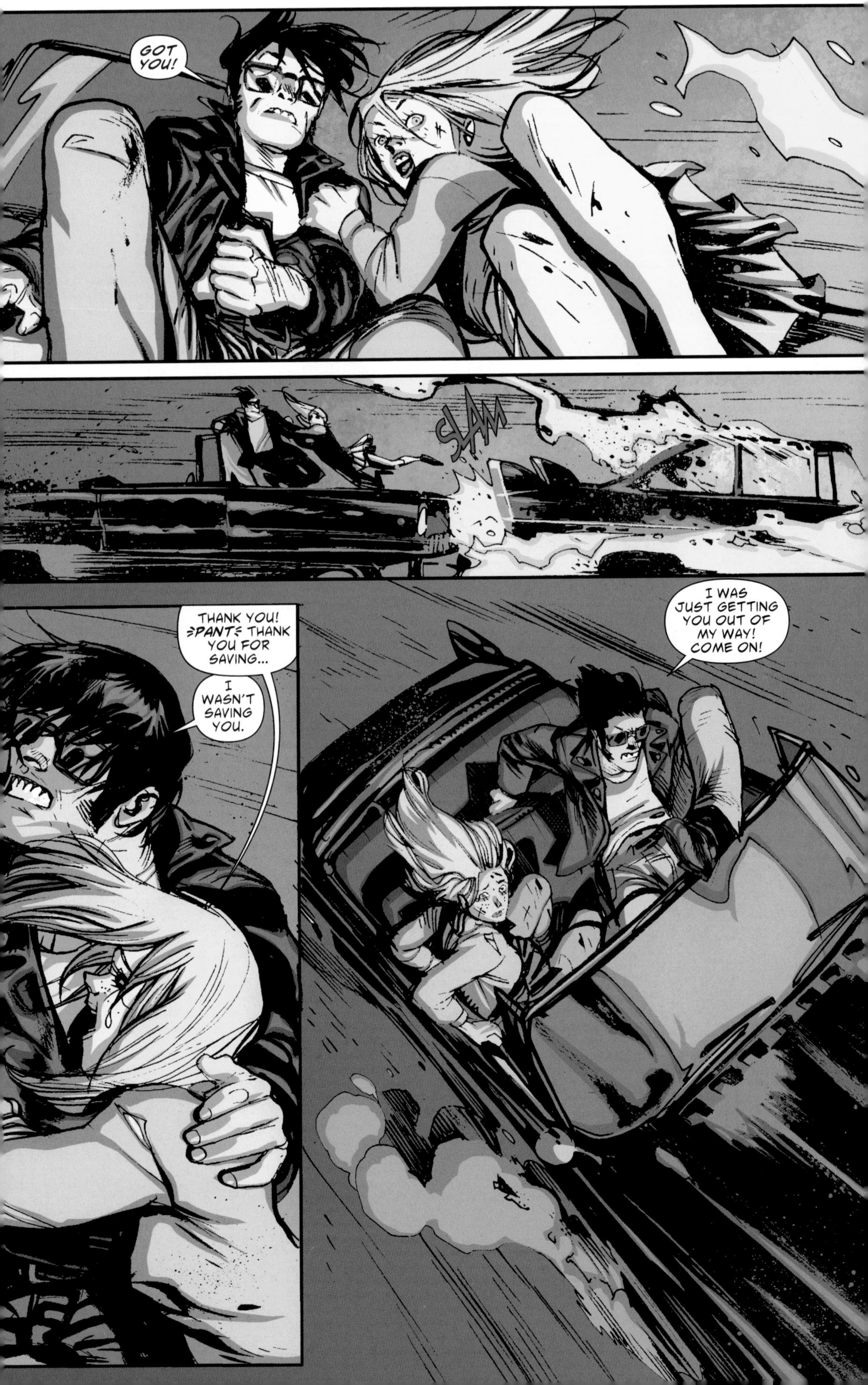
GOT YOU!
SLAM
THANK YOU! =PANT= THANK YOU FOR SAVING...
I WASN'T SAVING YOU.
I WAS JUST GETTING YOU OUT OF MY WAY! COME ON!

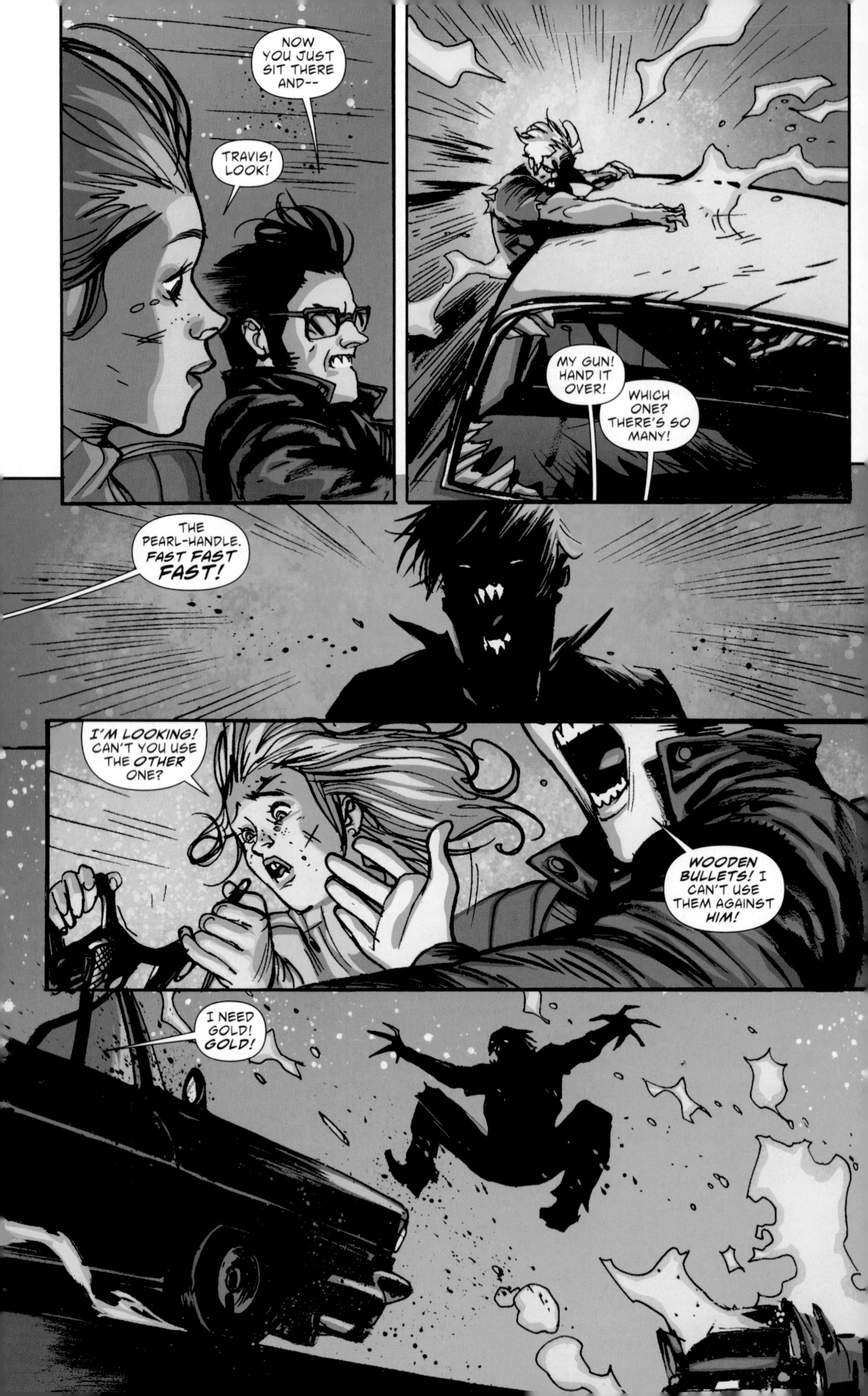
NOW YOU JUST SIT THERE AND--
TRAVIS! LOOK!
MY GUN! HAND IT OVER!
WHICH ONE? THERE'S SO MANY!
THE PEARL-HANDLE. *FAST FAST FAST!*
I'M LOOKING! CAN'T YOU USE THE *OTHER* ONE?
WOODEN BULLETS! I CAN'T USE THEM AGAINST *HIM!*
I NEED GOLD! *GOLD!*

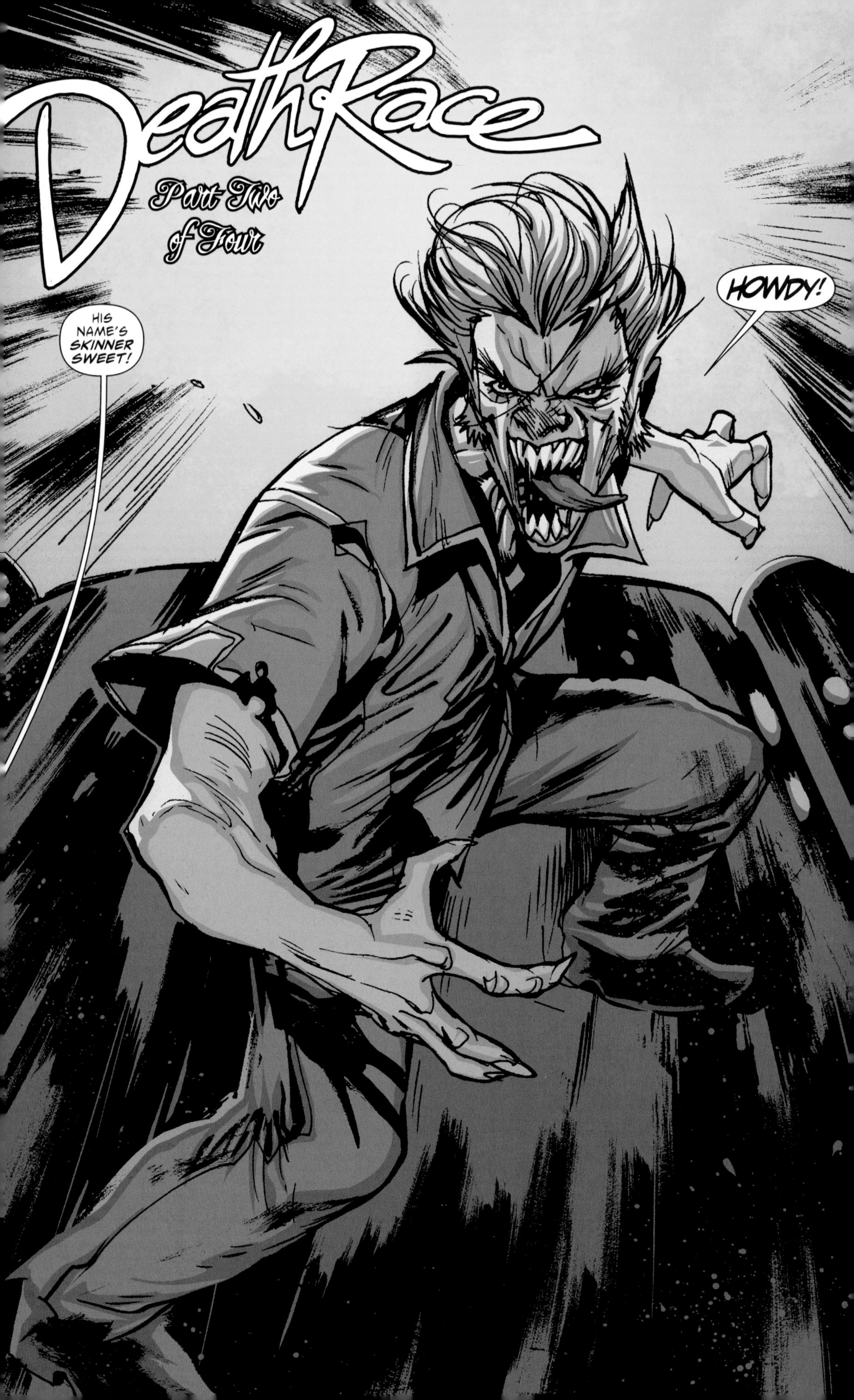

Death Race
Part Two of Four
HIS NAME'S SKINNER SWEET!
HOWDY!

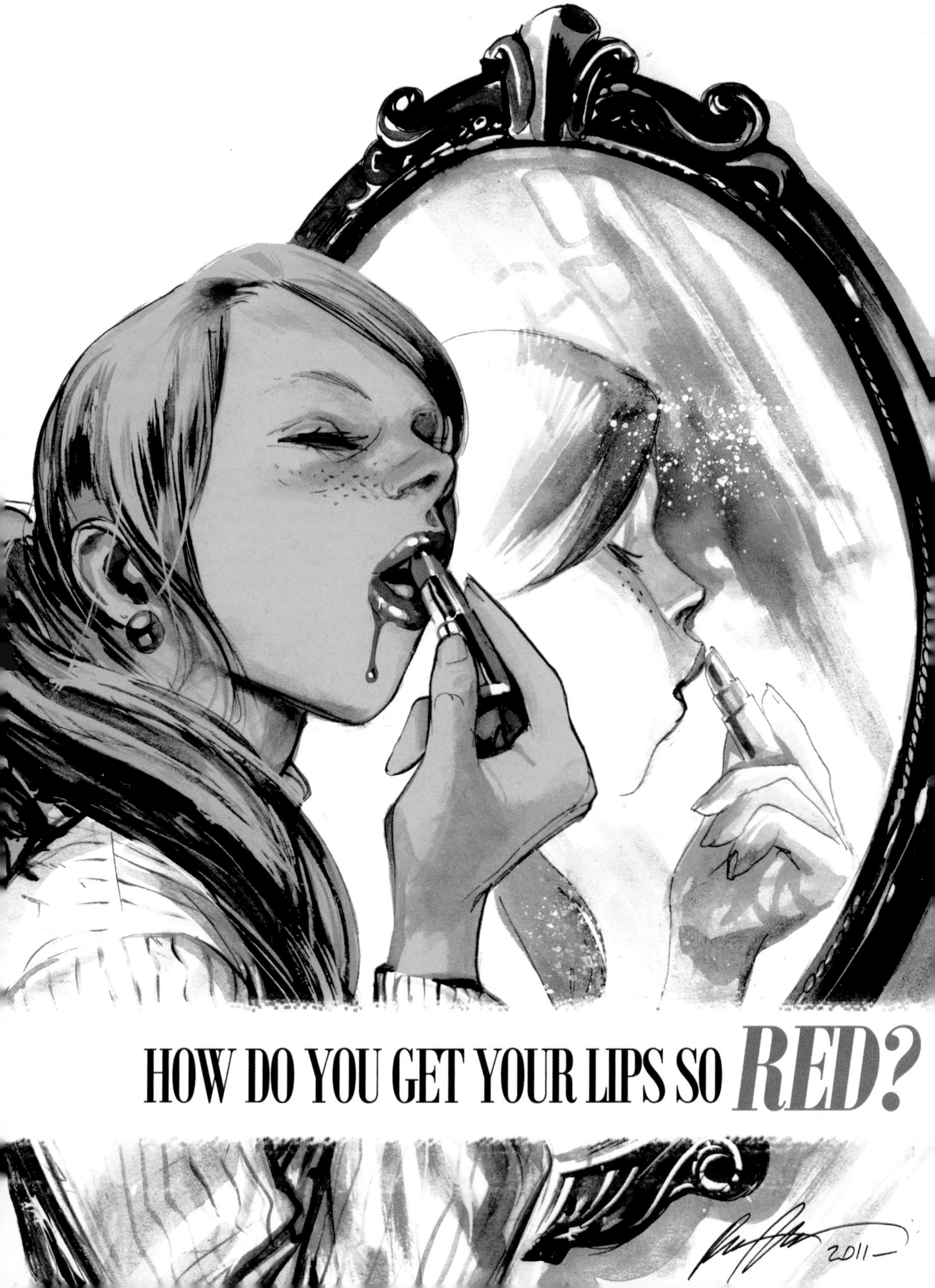
HOW DO YOU GET YOUR LIPS SO RED?
2011

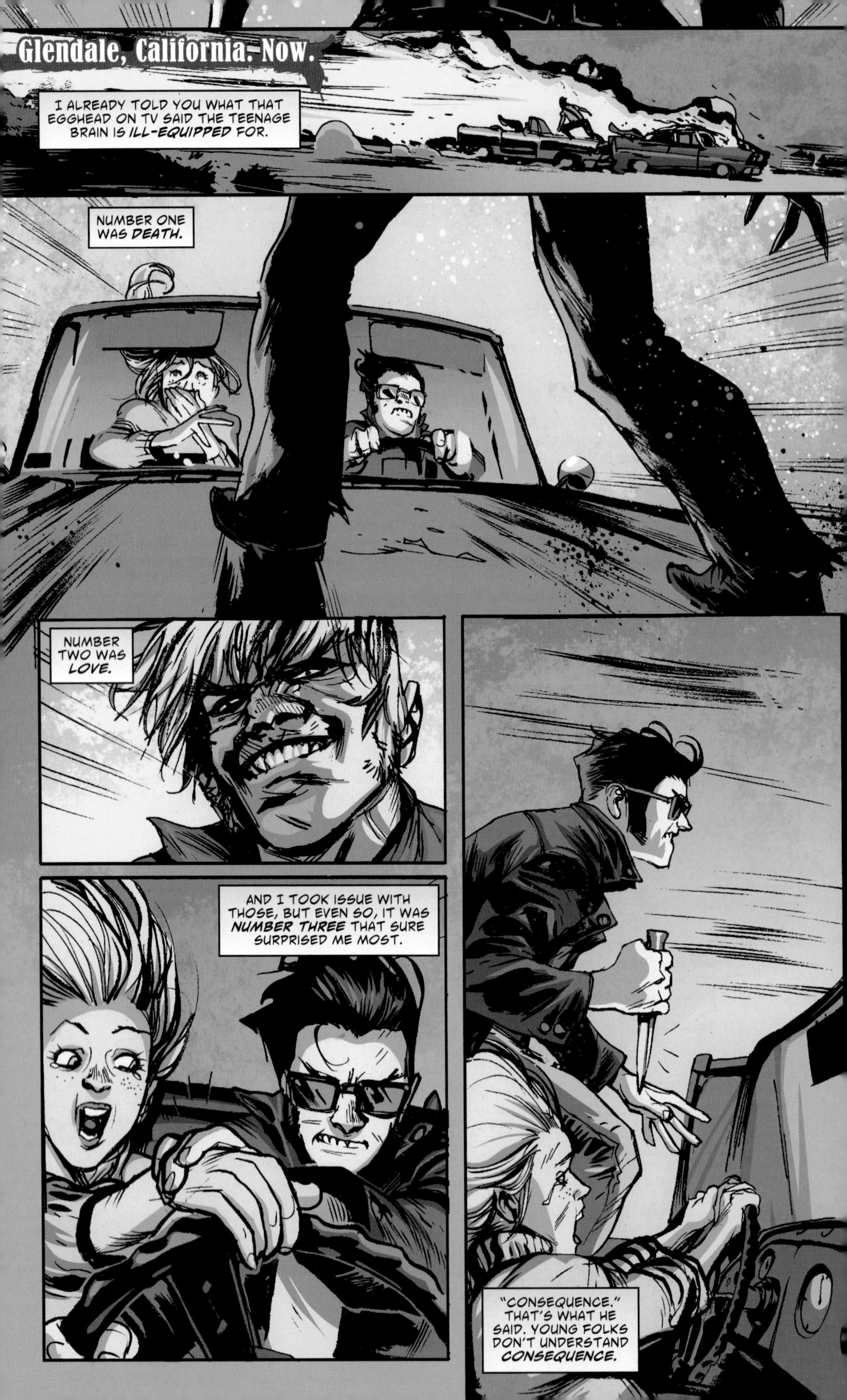
Glendale, California. Now.
I ALREADY TOLD YOU WHAT THAT EGGHEAD ON TV SAID THE TEENAGE BRAIN IS ILL-EQUIPPED FOR.
NUMBER ONE WAS DEATH.
NUMBER TWO WAS LOVE.
AND I TOOK ISSUE WITH THOSE, BUT EVEN SO, IT WAS NUMBER THREE THAT SURE SURPRISED ME MOST.
"CONSEQUENCE." THAT'S WHAT HE SAID. YOUNG FOLKS DON'T UNDERSTAND CONSEQUENCE.

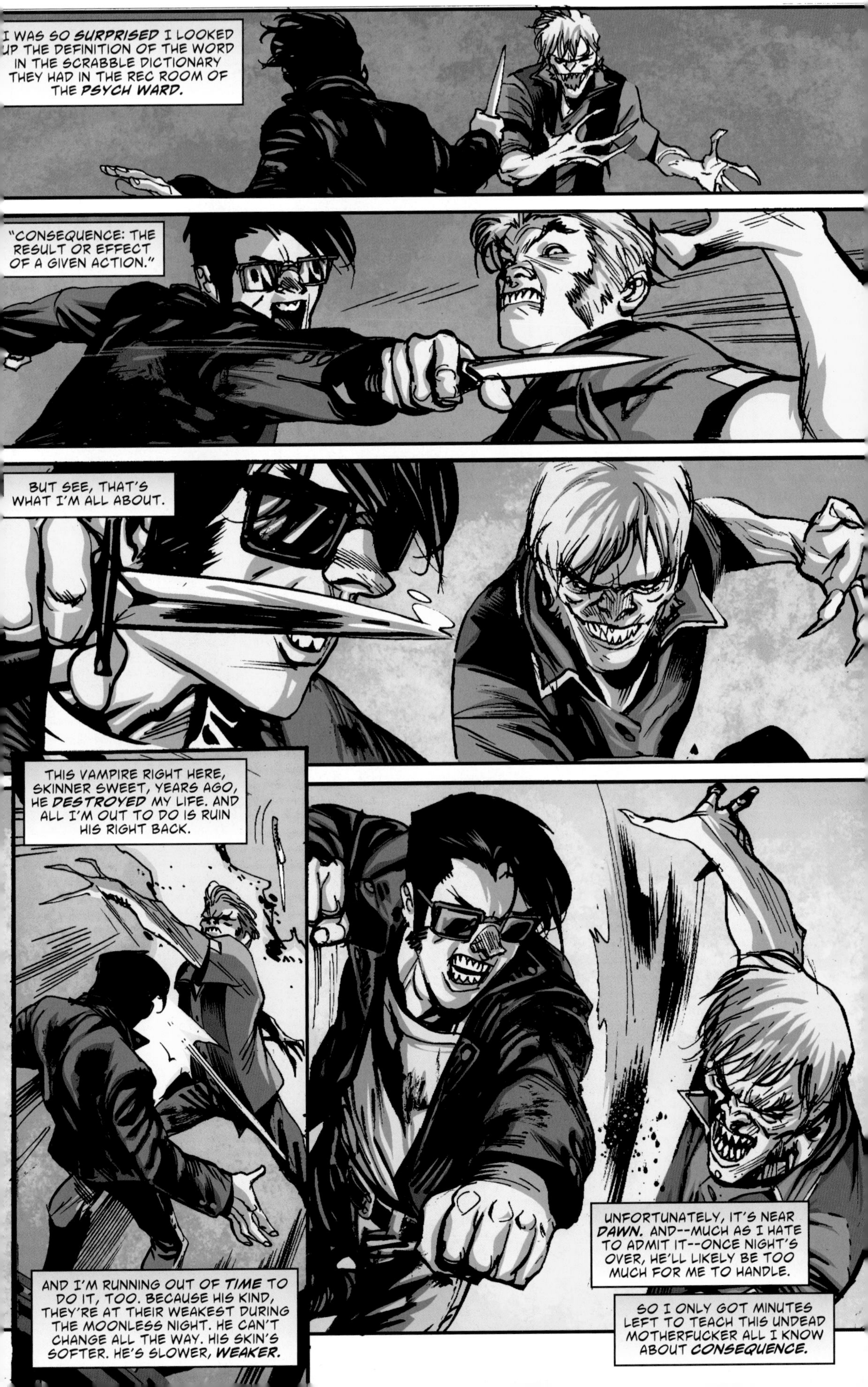
I WAS SO SURPRISED I LOOKED UP THE DEFINITION OF THE WORD IN THE SCRABBLE DICTIONARY THEY HAD IN THE REC ROOM OF THE PSYCH WARD.
"CONSEQUENCE: THE RESULT OR EFFECT OF A GIVEN ACTION."
BUT SEE, THAT'S WHAT I'M ALL ABOUT.
THIS VAMPIRE RIGHT HERE, SKINNER SWEET, YEARS AGO, HE DESTROYED MY LIFE. AND ALL I'M OUT TO DO IS RUIN HIS RIGHT BACK.
AND I'M RUNNING OUT OF TIME TO DO IT, TOO. BECAUSE HIS KIND, THEY'RE AT THEIR WEAKEST DURING THE MOONLESS NIGHT. HE CAN'T CHANGE ALL THE WAY. HIS SKIN'S SOFTER. HE'S SLOWER, WEAKER.
UNFORTUNATELY, IT'S NEAR DAWN. AND--MUCH AS I HATE TO ADMIT IT--ONCE NIGHT'S OVER, HE'LL LIKELY BE TOO MUCH FOR ME TO HANDLE.
SO I ONLY GOT MINUTES LEFT TO TEACH THIS UNDEAD MOTHERFUCKER ALL I KNOW ABOUT CONSEQUENCE.

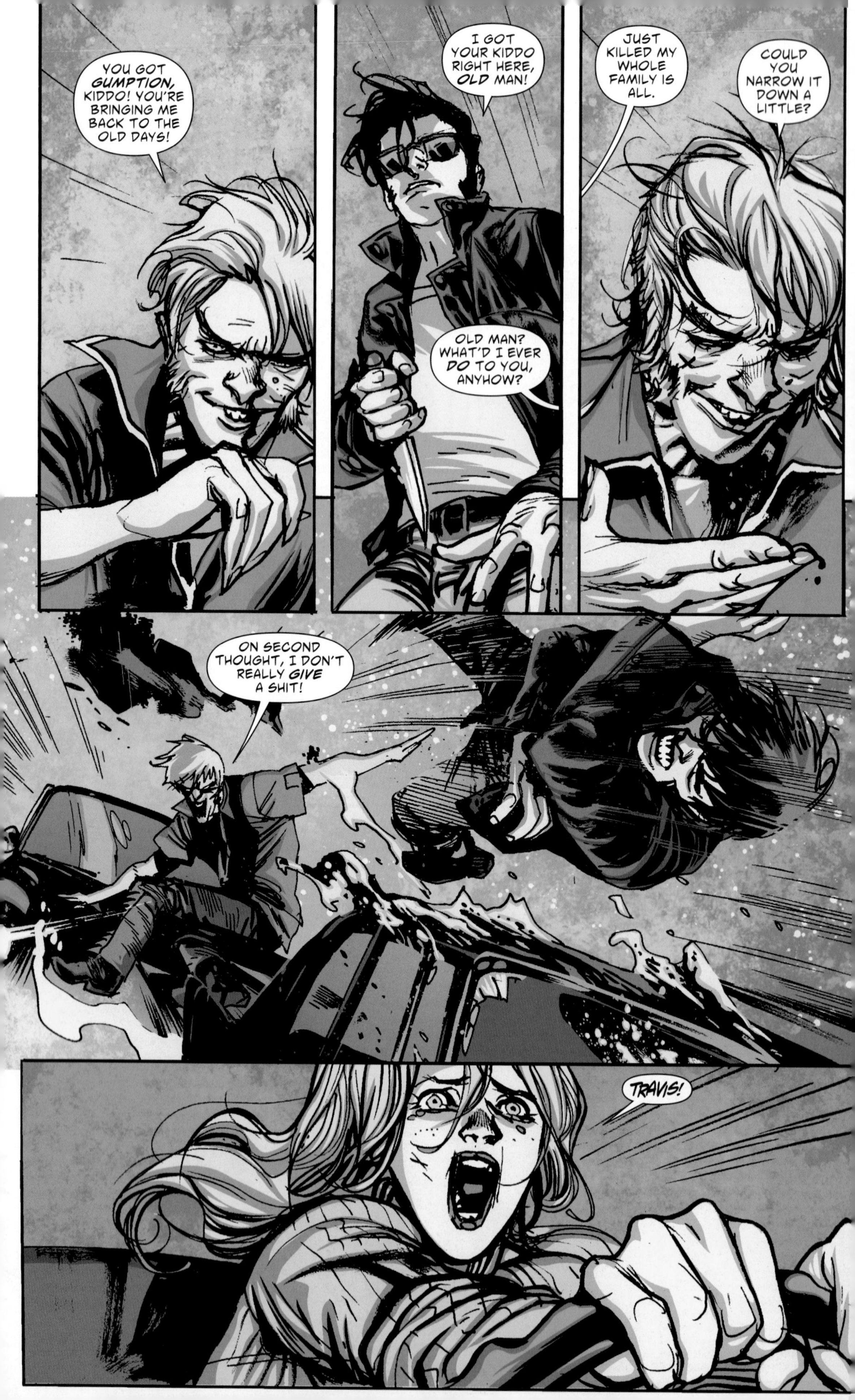
YOU GOT GUMPTION, KIDDO! YOU'RE BRINGING ME BACK TO THE OLD DAYS!
I GOT YOUR KIDDO RIGHT HERE, OLD MAN!
OLD MAN? WHAT'D I EVER DO TO YOU, ANYHOW?
JUST KILLED MY WHOLE FAMILY IS ALL.
COULD YOU NARROW IT DOWN A LITTLE?
ON SECOND THOUGHT, I DON'T REALLY GIVE A SHIT!
TRAVIS!

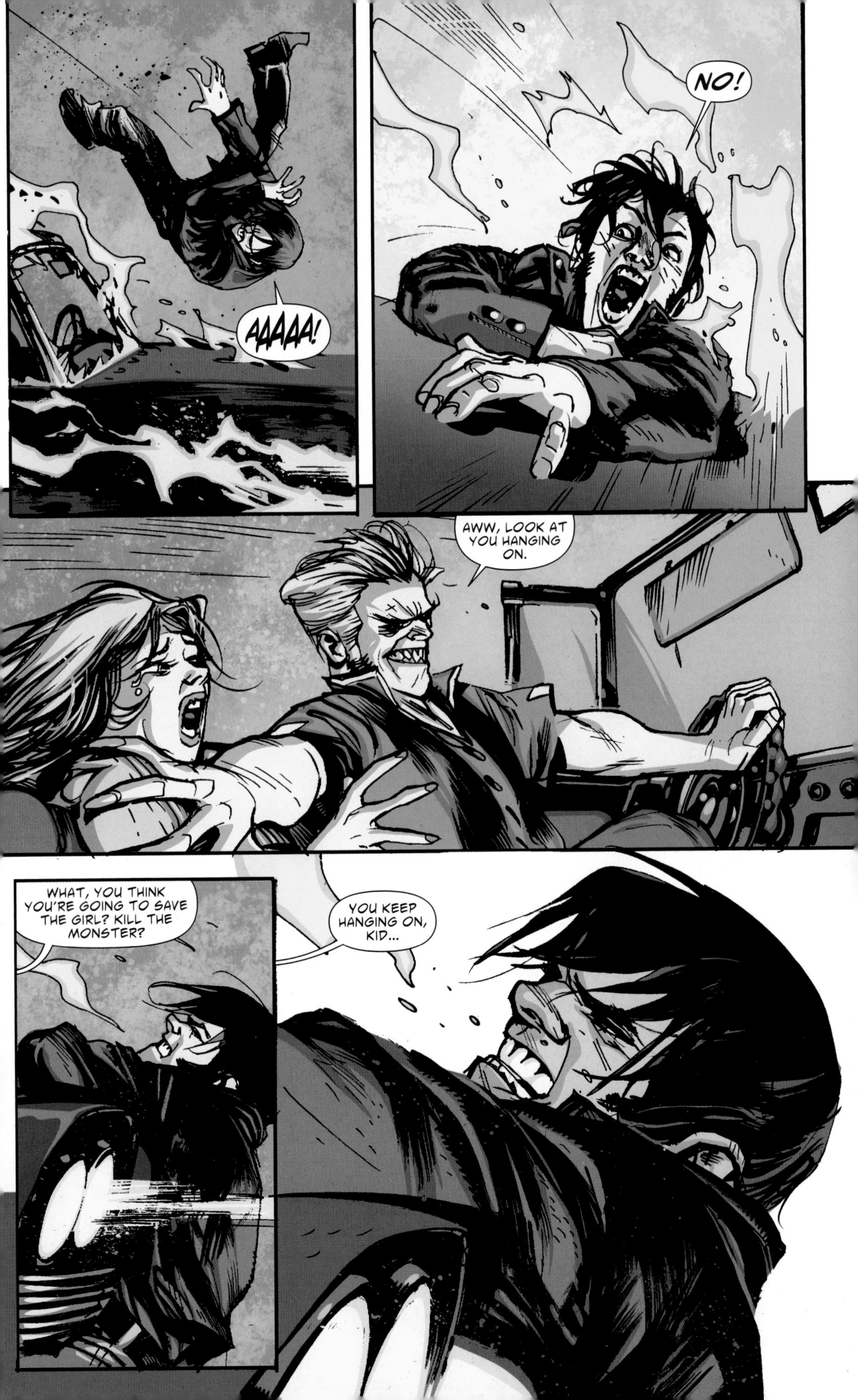
AAAAA!
NO!
AWW, LOOK AT YOU HANGING ON.
WHAT, YOU THINK YOU'RE GOING TO SAVE THE GIRL? KILL THE MONSTER?
YOU KEEP HANGING ON, KID...

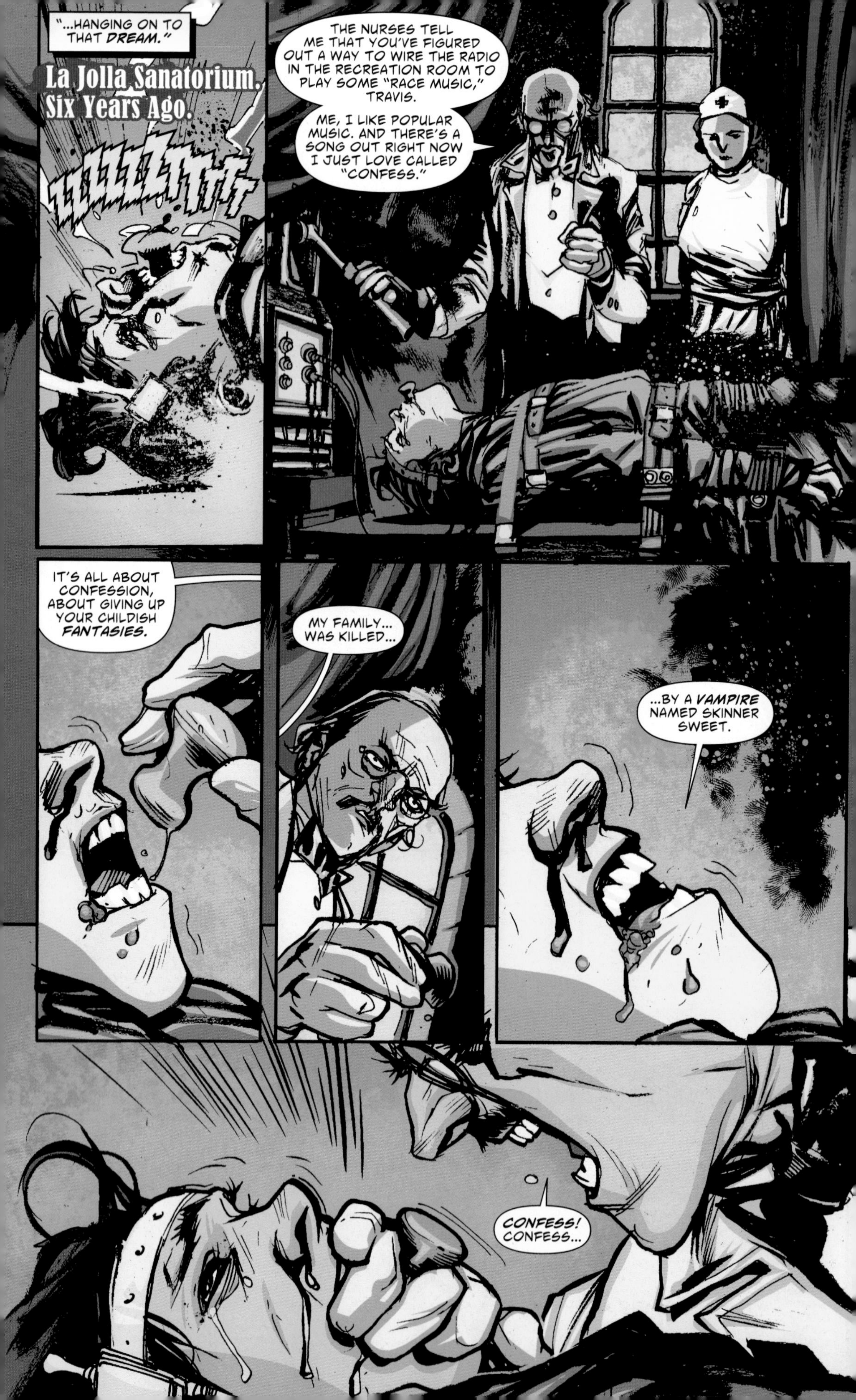
"...HANGING ON TO THAT DREAM."
La Jolla Sanatorium. Six Years Ago.
ZZZZZZTTTTT
THE NURSES TELL ME THAT YOU'VE FIGURED OUT A WAY TO WIRE THE RADIO IN THE RECREATION ROOM TO PLAY SOME "RACE MUSIC," TRAVIS.
ME, I LIKE POPULAR MUSIC. AND THERE'S A SONG OUT RIGHT NOW I JUST LOVE CALLED "CONFESS."
IT'S ALL ABOUT CONFESSION, ABOUT GIVING UP YOUR CHILDISH FANTASIES.
MY FAMILY... WAS KILLED...
...BY A VAMPIRE NAMED SKINNER SWEET.
CONFESS! CONFESS...

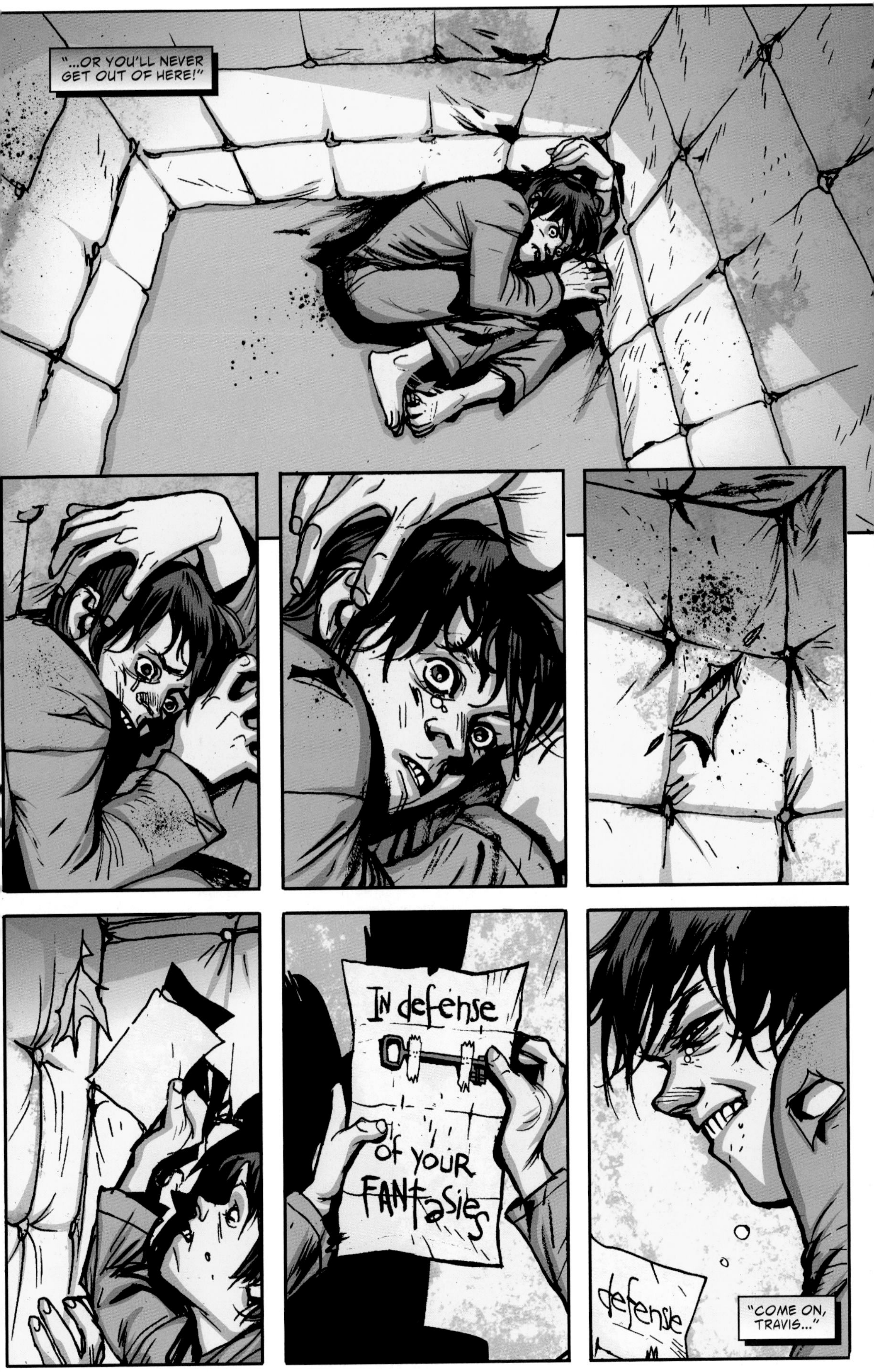
"...OR YOU'LL NEVER GET OUT OF HERE!"
IN defense
of YOUR FANTasies
defense
"COME ON, TRAVIS..."

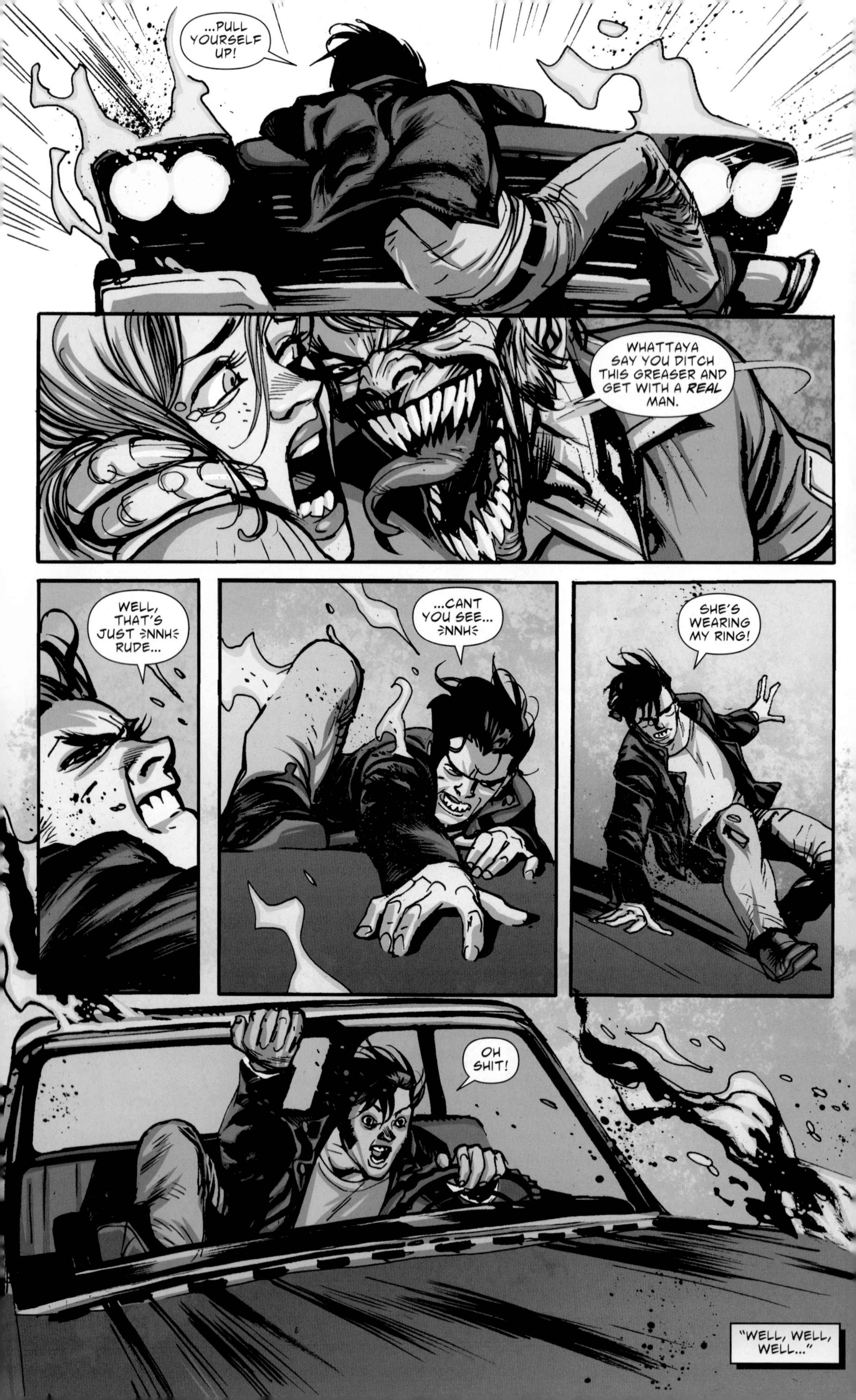
...PULL YOURSELF UP!
WHATTAYA SAY YOU DITCH THIS GREASER AND GET WITH A REAL MAN.
WELL, THAT'S JUST NNH RUDE...
...CANT YOU SEE... NNH
SHE'S WEARING MY RING!
OH SHIT!
"WELL, WELL, WELL..."

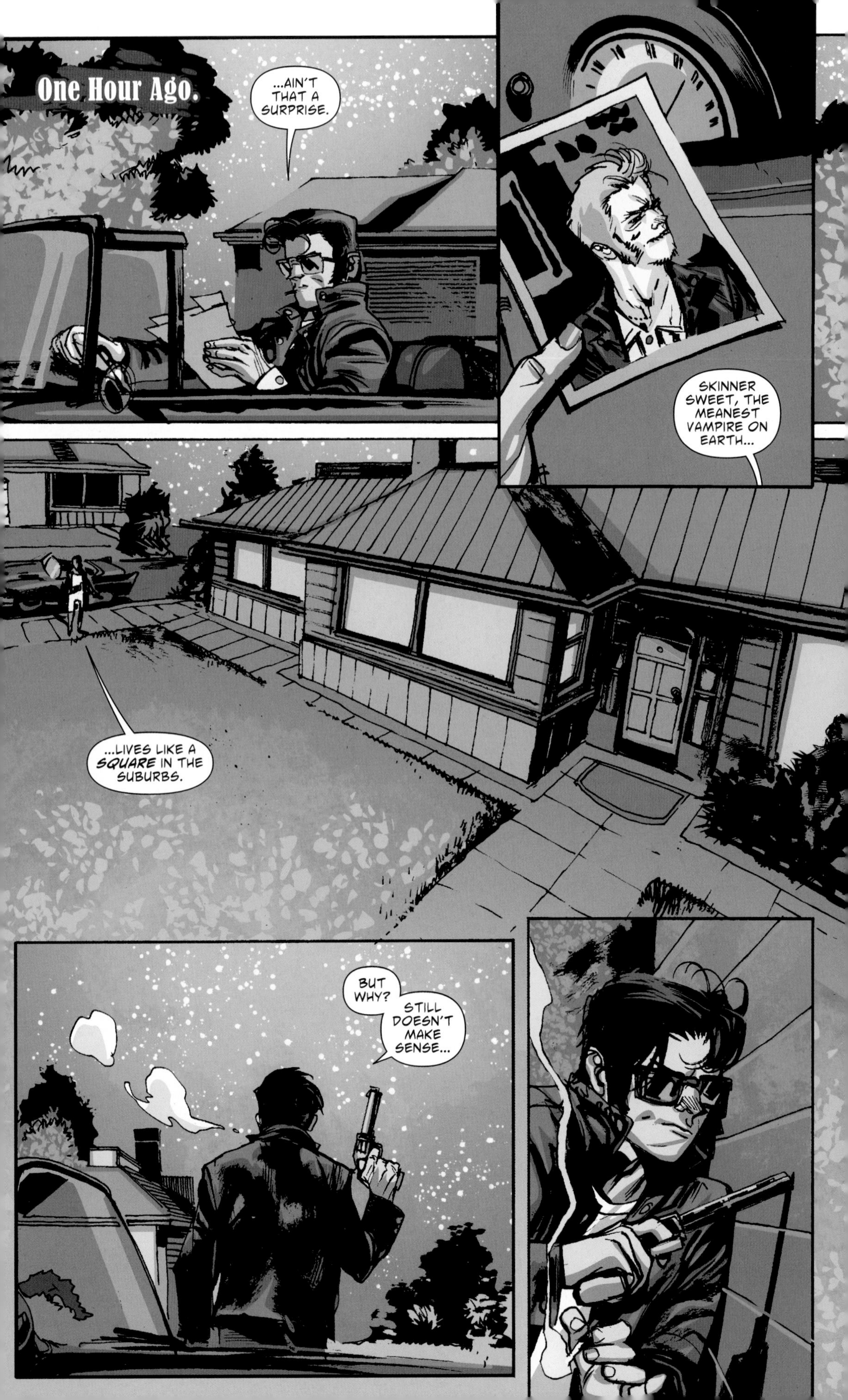
One Hour Ago.
...AIN'T THAT A SURPRISE.
SKINNER SWEET, THE MEANEST VAMPIRE ON EARTH...
...LIVES LIKE A *SQUARE* IN THE SUBURBS.
BUT WHY?
STILL DOESN'T MAKE SENSE...

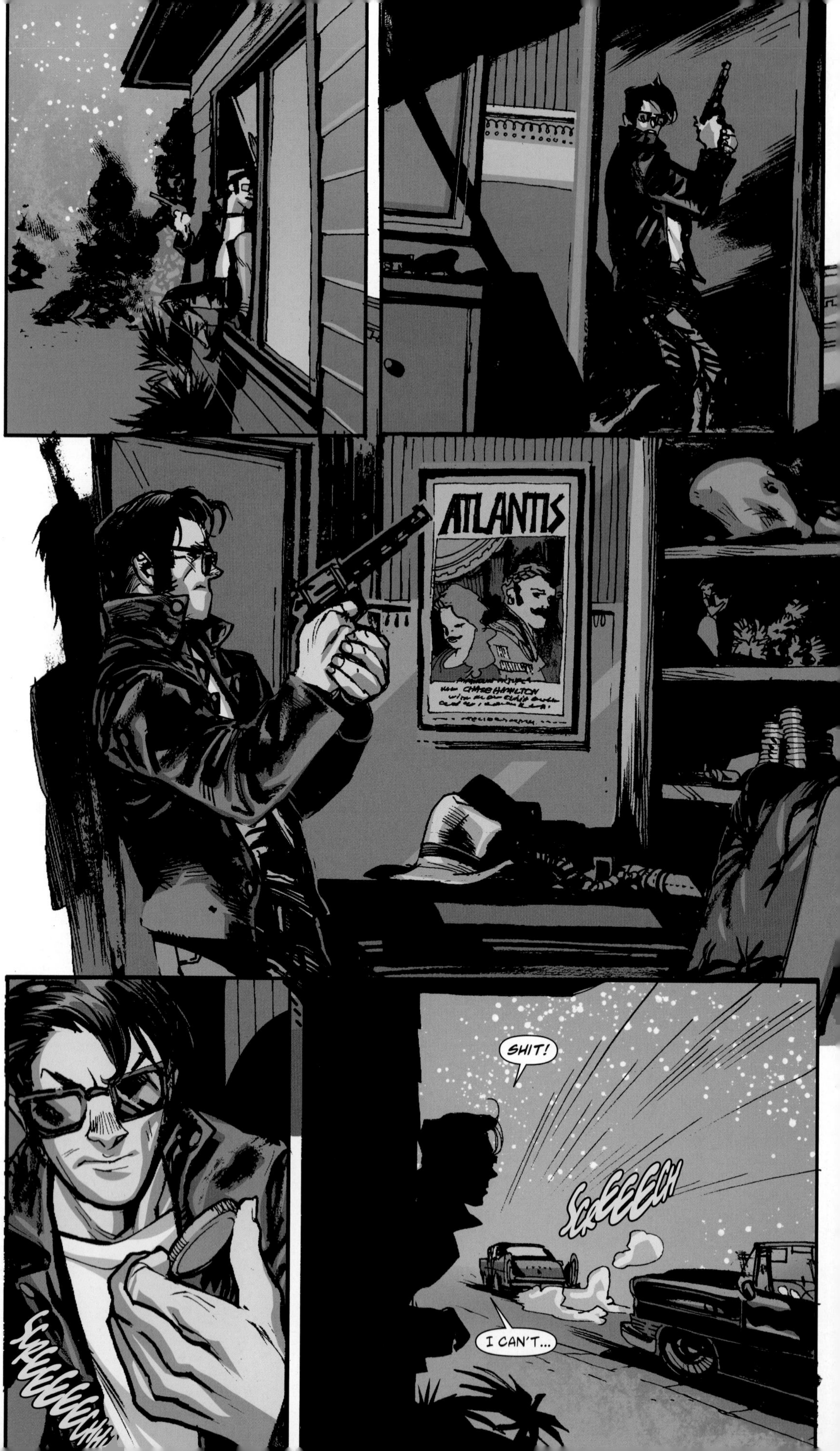

ATLANTIS
CHASE HAMILTON
SHIT!
SCREEECH
I CAN'T...

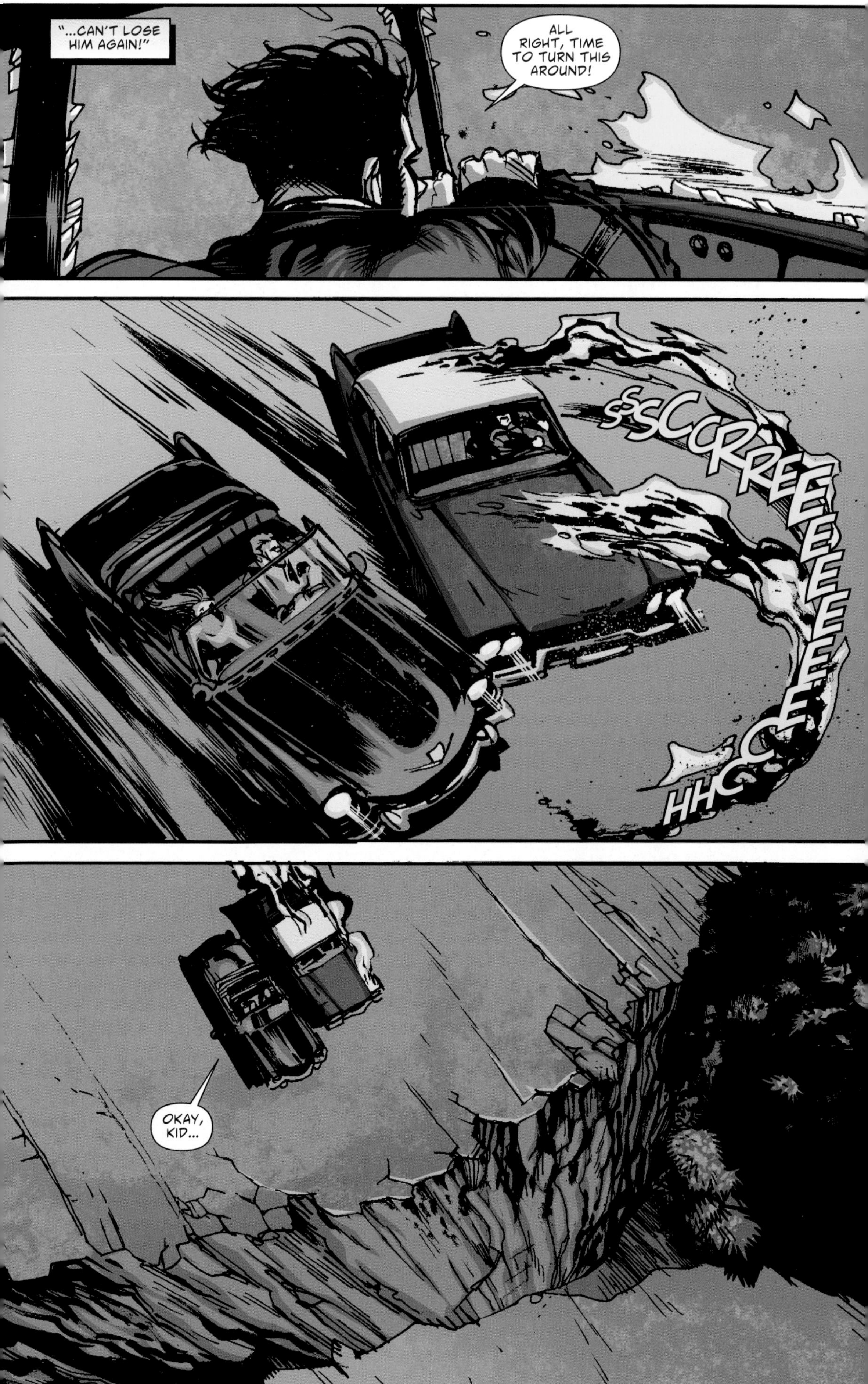
"...CAN'T LOSE HIM AGAIN!"
ALL RIGHT, TIME TO TURN THIS AROUND!
SSSCCRREEEEEEEEEECCHH
OKAY, KID...

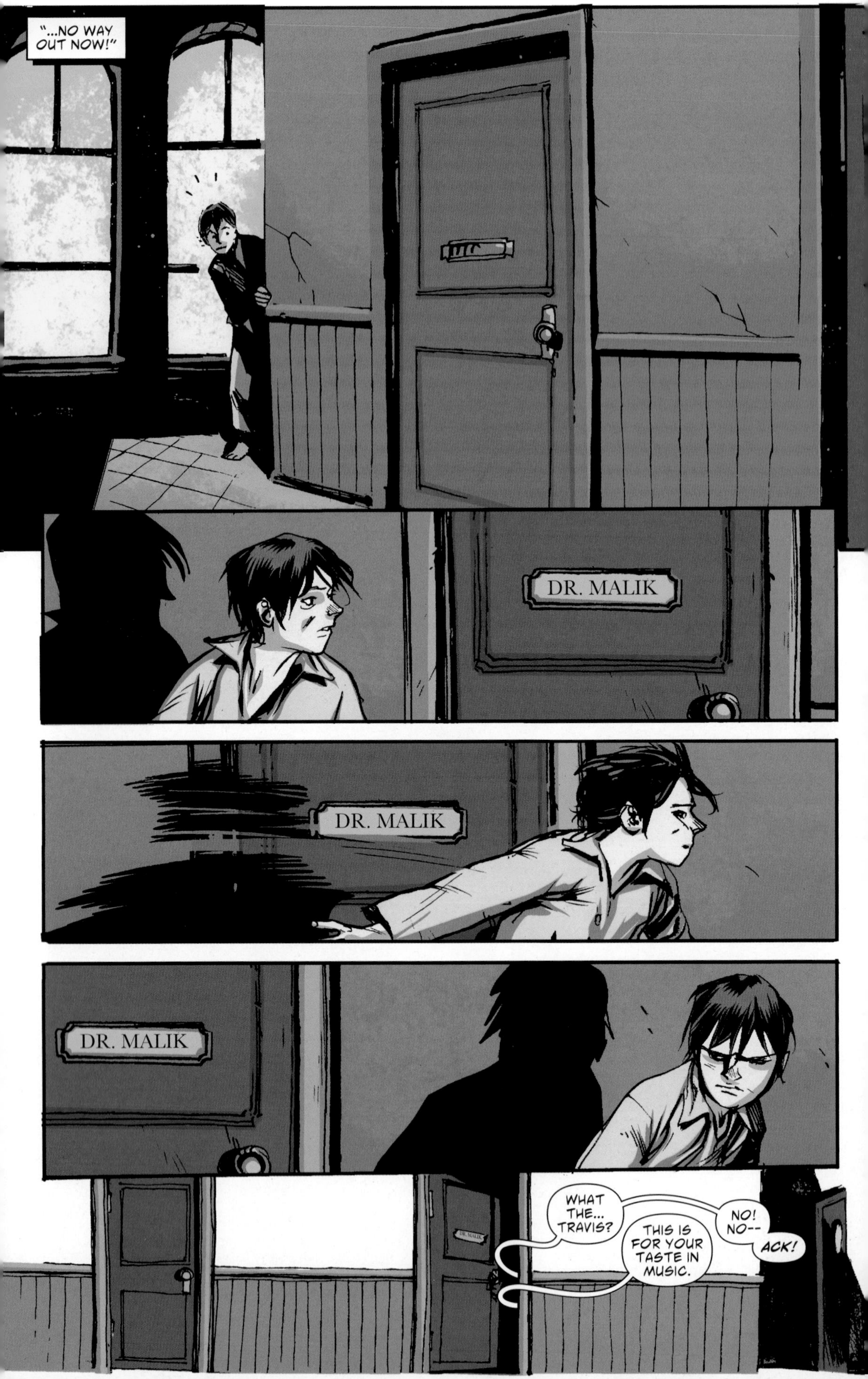
"...NO WAY OUT NOW!"
DR. MALIK
DR. MALIK
DR. MALIK
WHAT THE... TRAVIS?
THIS IS FOR YOUR TASTE IN MUSIC.
NO! NO--
ACK!

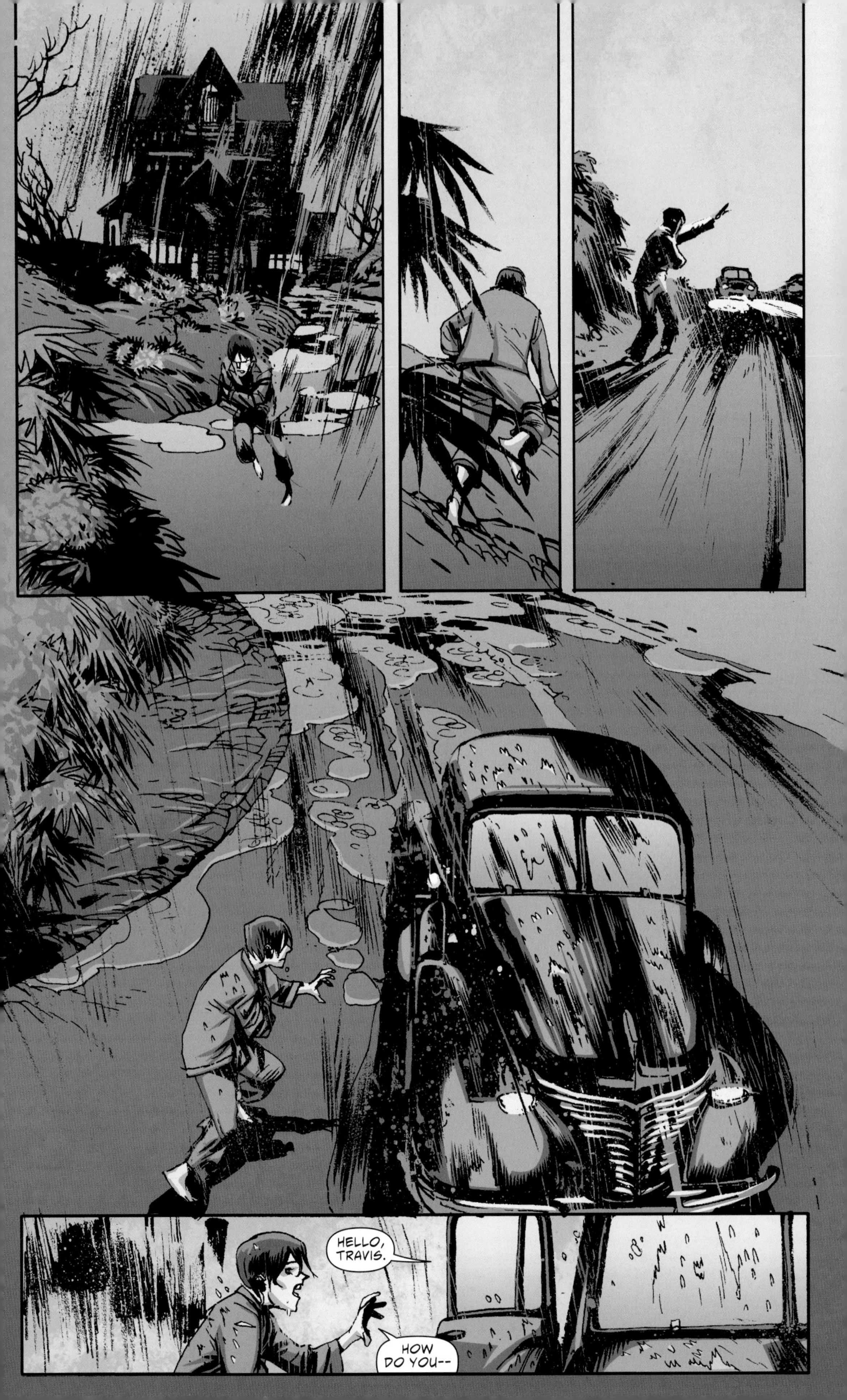
HELLO, TRAVIS.
HOW DO YOU--

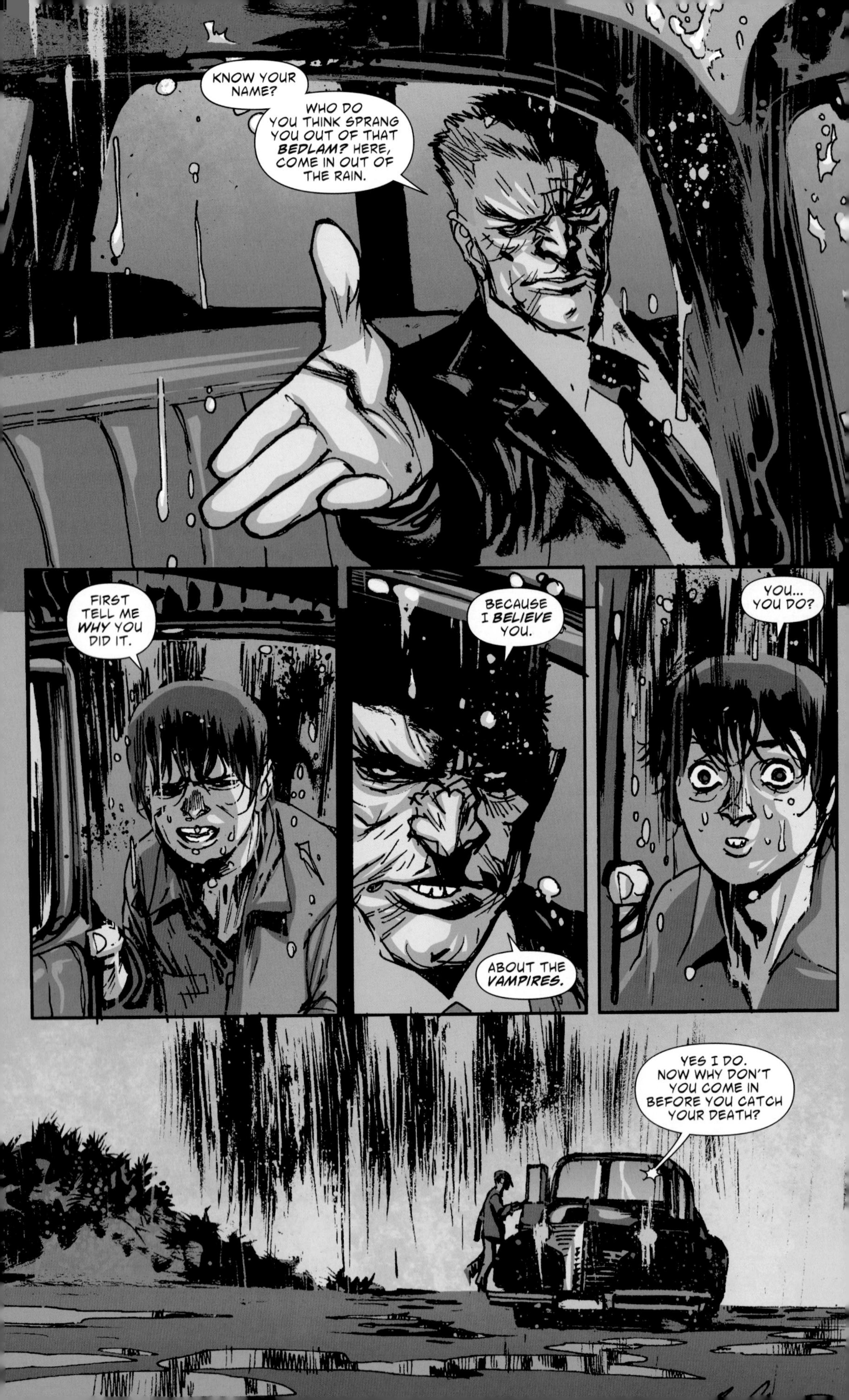
KNOW YOUR NAME?
WHO DO YOU THINK SPRANG YOU OUT OF THAT BEDLAM? HERE, COME IN OUT OF THE RAIN.
FIRST TELL ME WHY YOU DID IT.
BECAUSE I BELIEVE YOU.
ABOUT THE VAMPIRES.
YOU... YOU DO?
YES I DO. NOW WHY DON'T YOU COME IN BEFORE YOU CATCH YOUR DEATH?

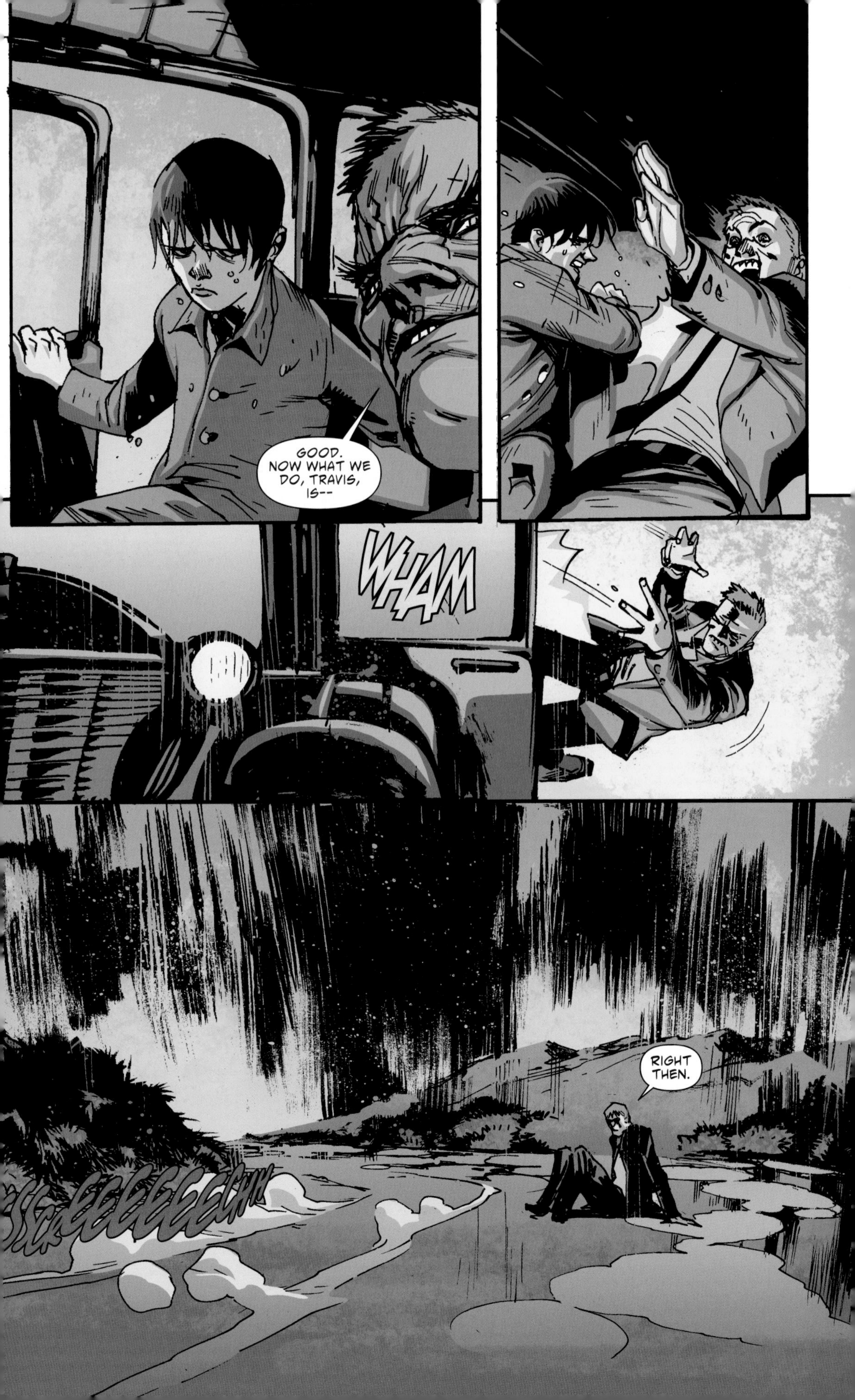
GOOD. NOW WHAT WE DO, TRAVIS, IS--
WHAM
RIGHT THEN.

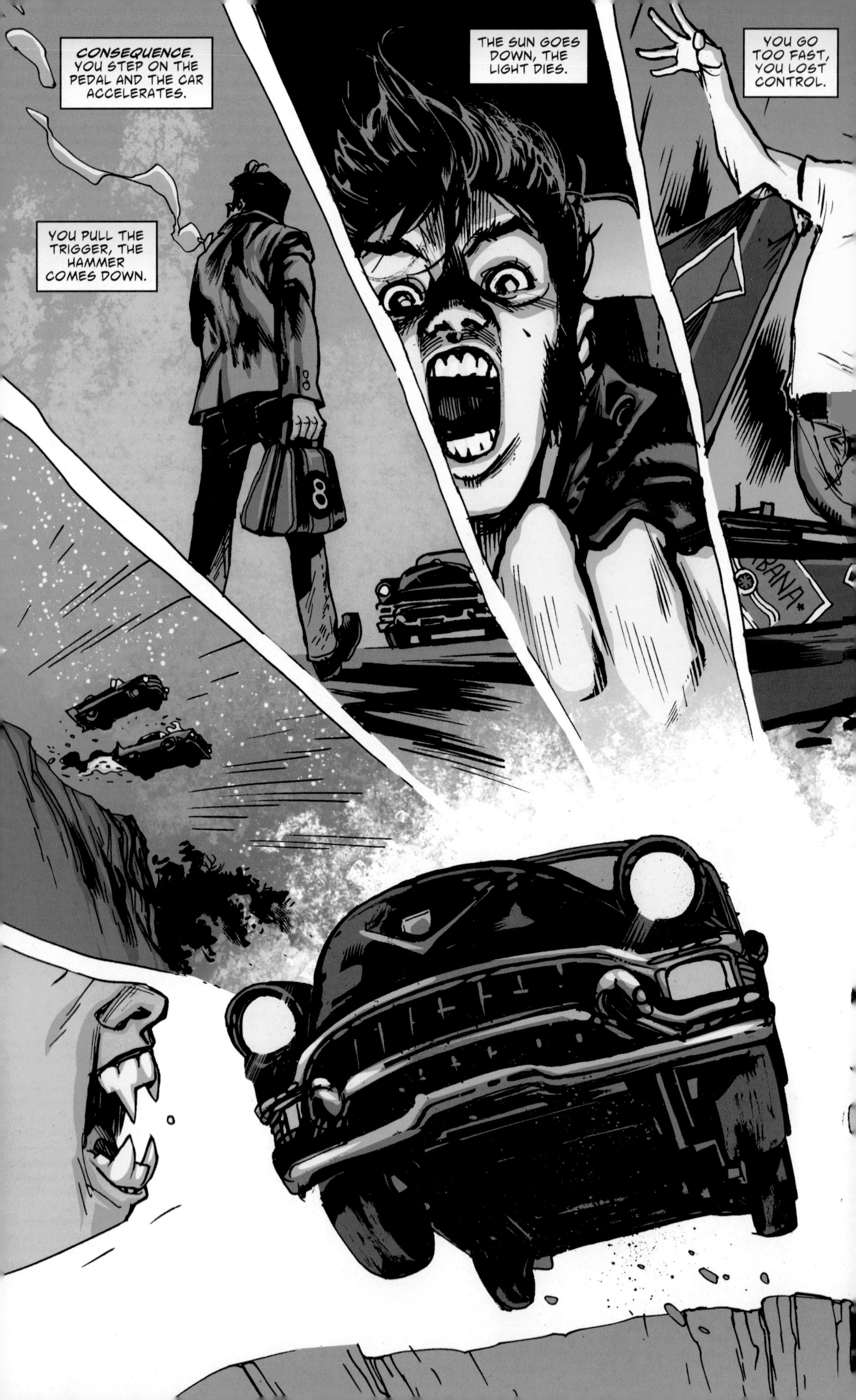
CONSEQUENCE. YOU STEP ON THE PEDAL AND THE CAR ACCELERATES.
YOU PULL THE TRIGGER, THE HAMMER COMES DOWN.
THE SUN GOES DOWN, THE LIGHT DIES.
YOU GO TOO FAST, YOU LOST CONTROL.

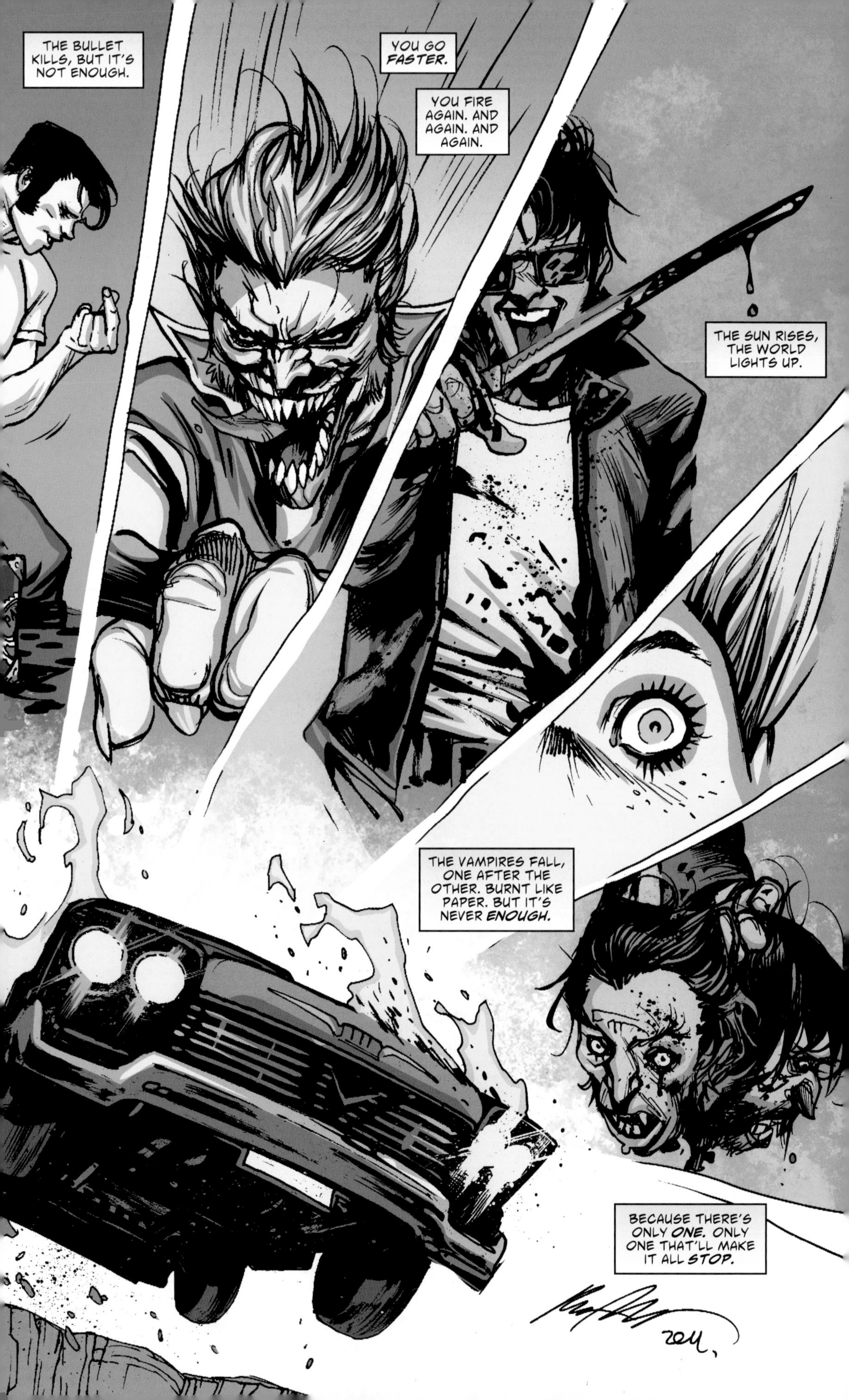
THE BULLET KILLS, BUT IT'S NOT ENOUGH.
YOU GO *FASTER.*
YOU FIRE AGAIN. AND AGAIN. AND AGAIN.
THE SUN RISES, THE WORLD LIGHTS UP.
THE VAMPIRES FALL, ONE AFTER THE OTHER. BURNT LIKE PAPER. BUT IT'S NEVER *ENOUGH.*
BECAUSE THERE'S ONLY *ONE.* ONLY ONE THAT'LL MAKE IT ALL *STOP.*
2011.

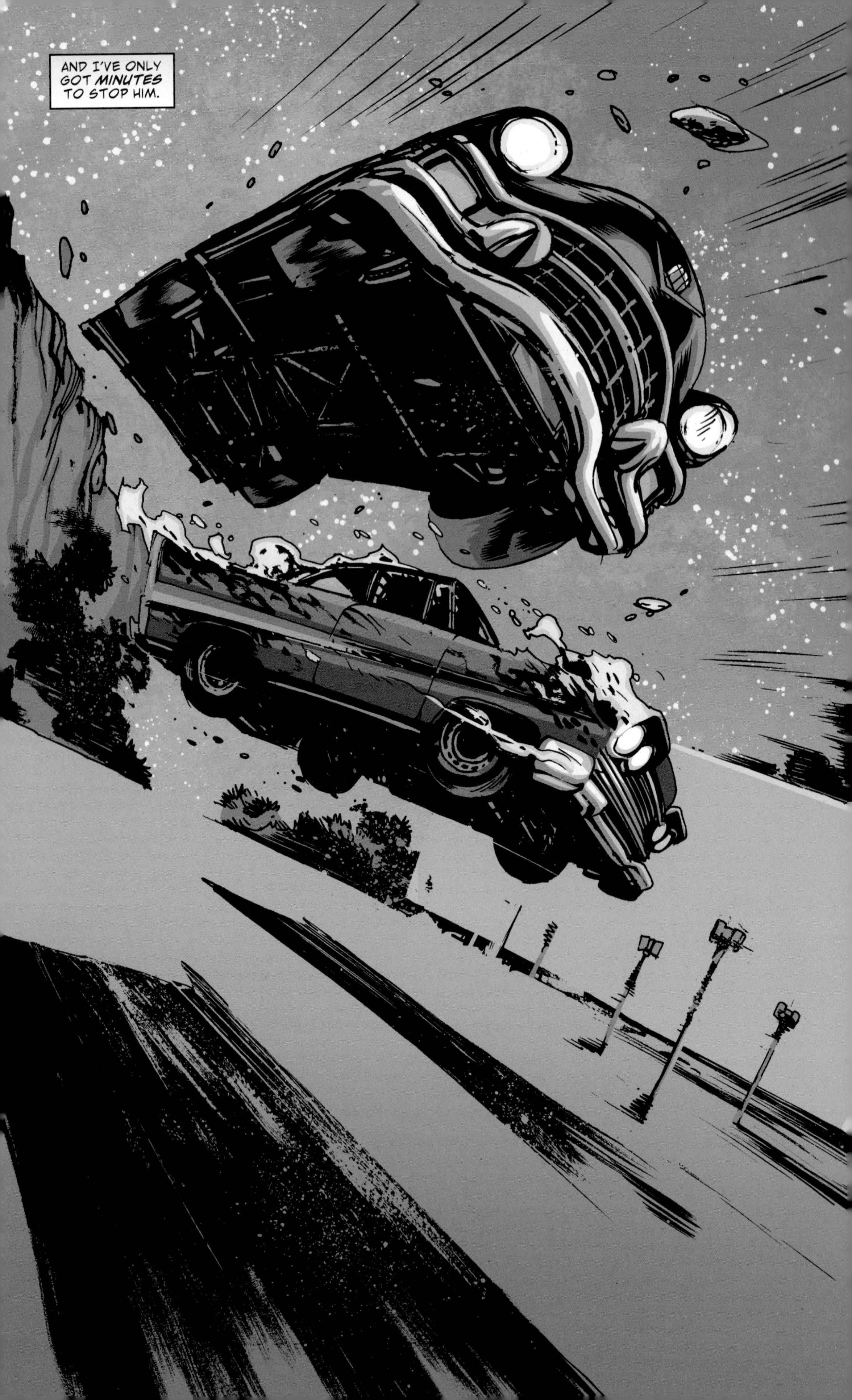
AND I'VE ONLY GOT MINUTES TO STOP HIM.

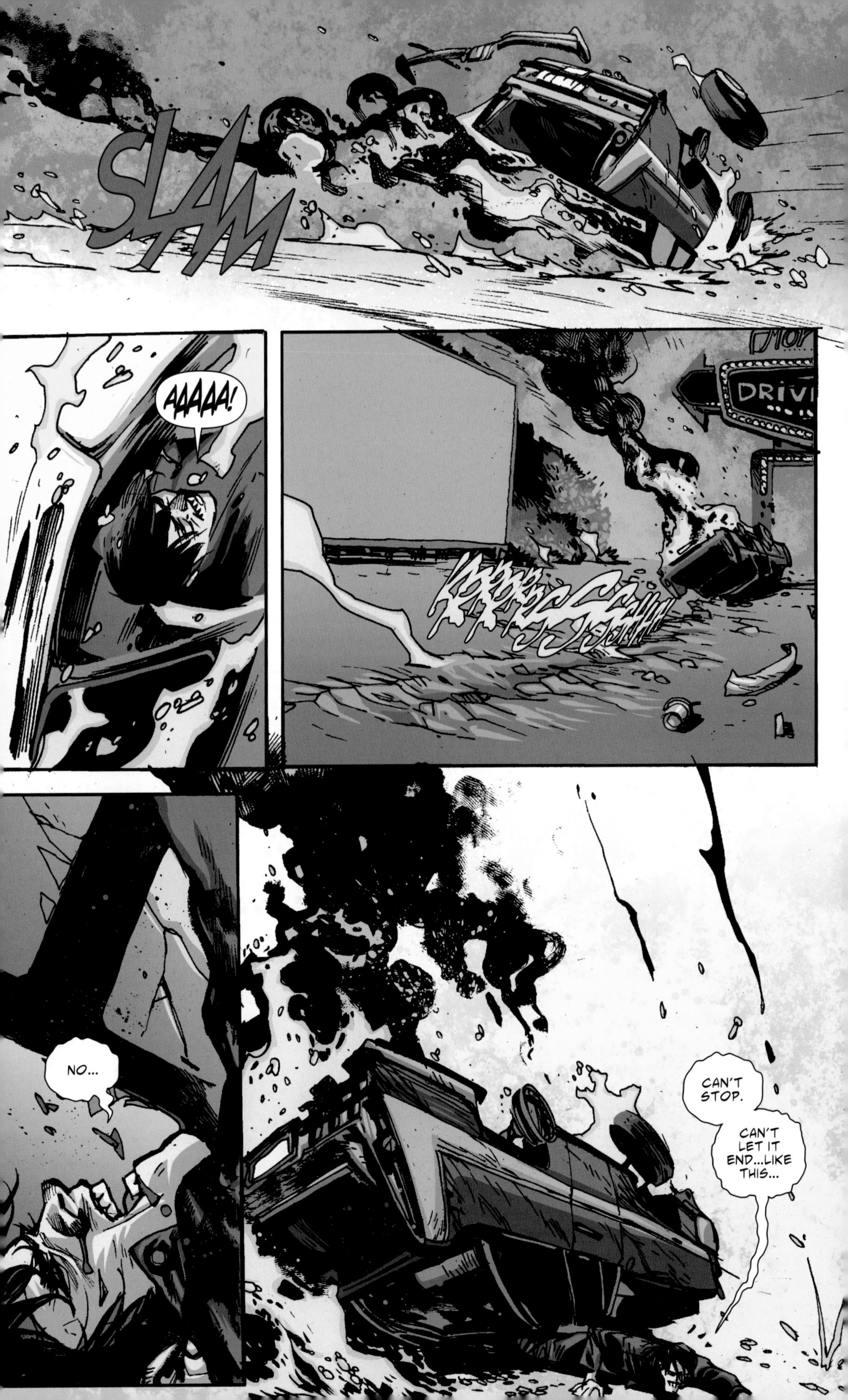
SLAM
AAAAA!
DRIV
KRRRRSSSHH!!
NO...
CAN'T STOP.
CAN'T LET IT END...LIKE THIS...

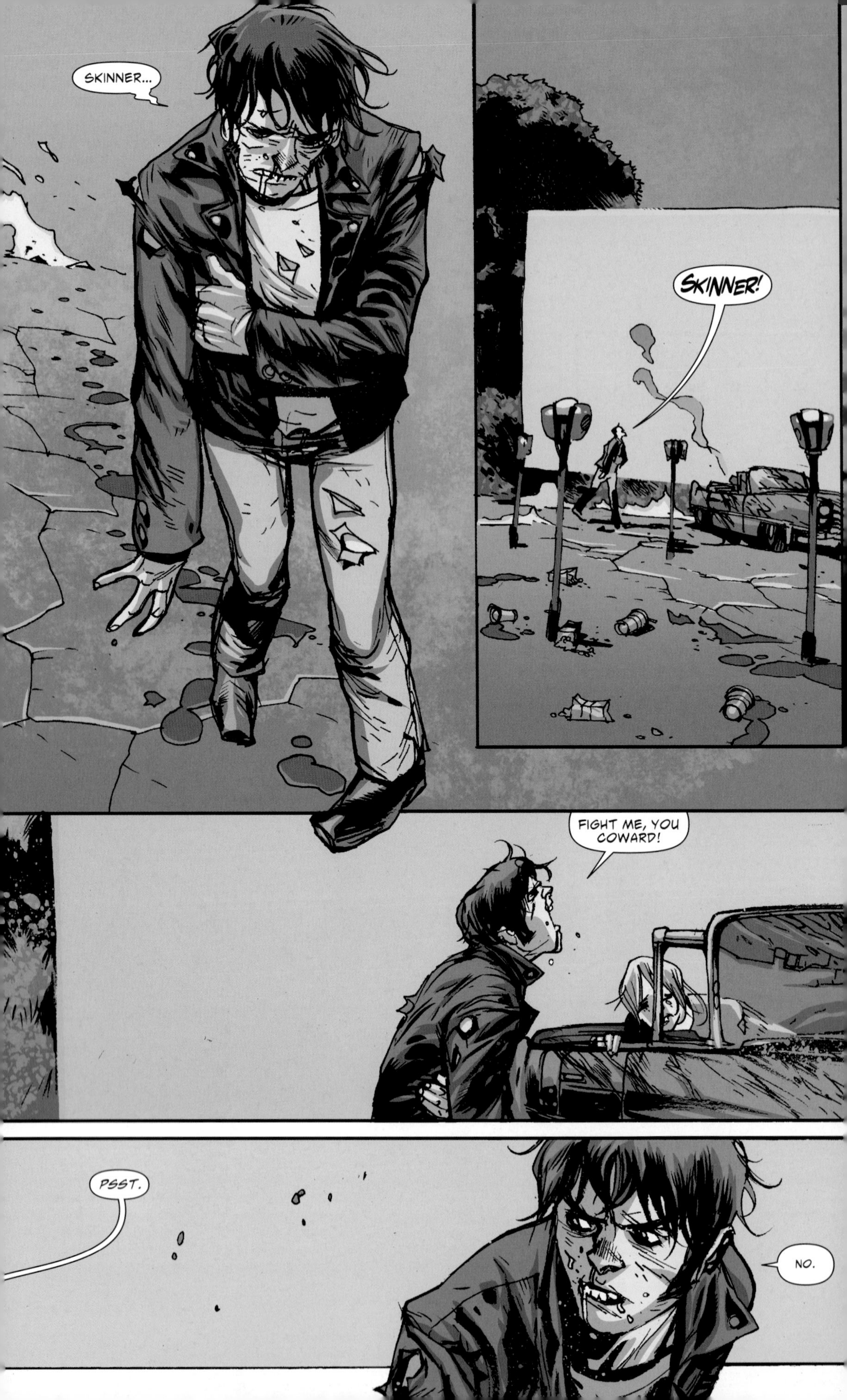
SKINNER...
SKINNER!
FIGHT ME, YOU COWARD!
PSST.
NO.

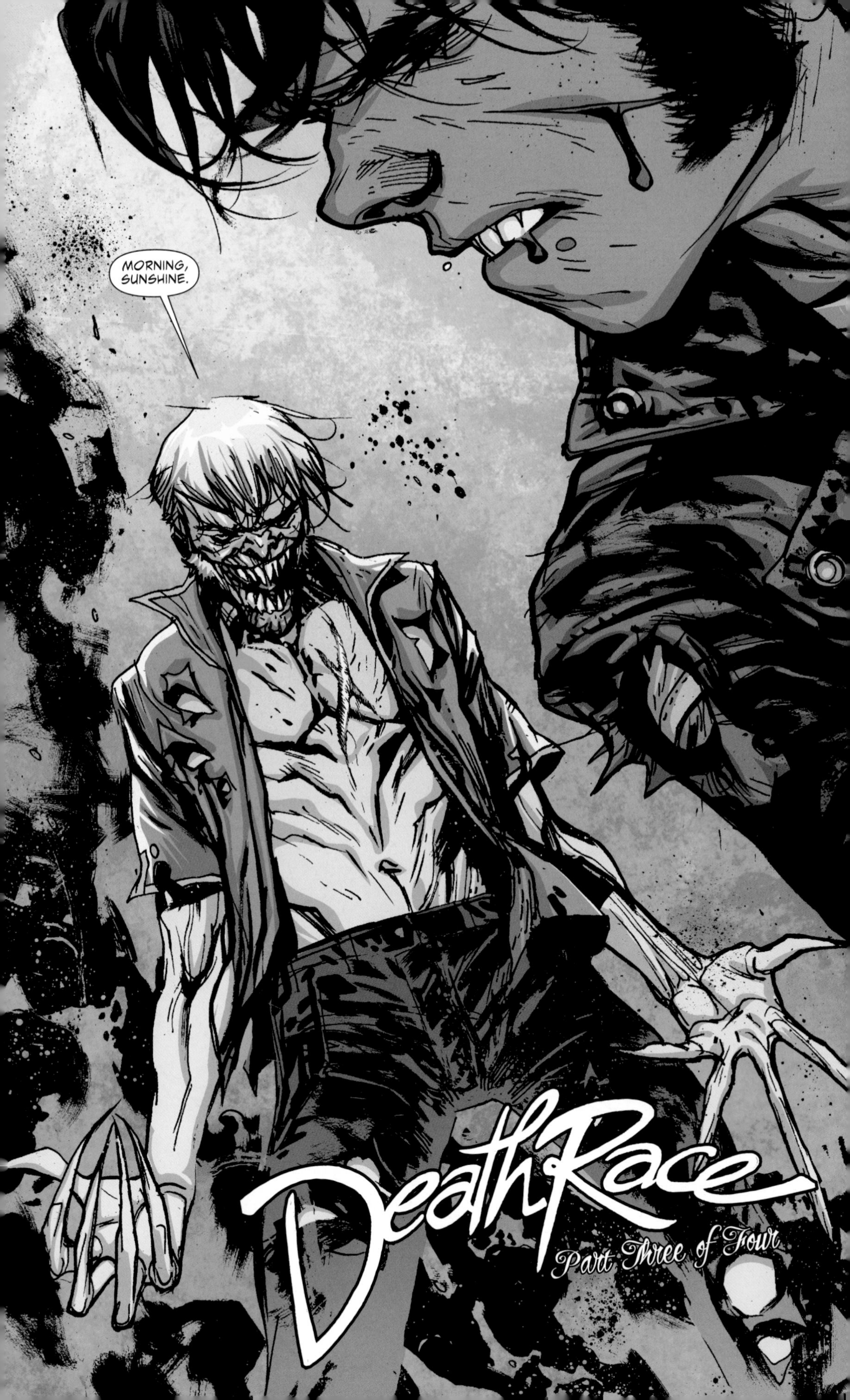
MORNING, SUNSHINE.
Death Race
Part Three of Four

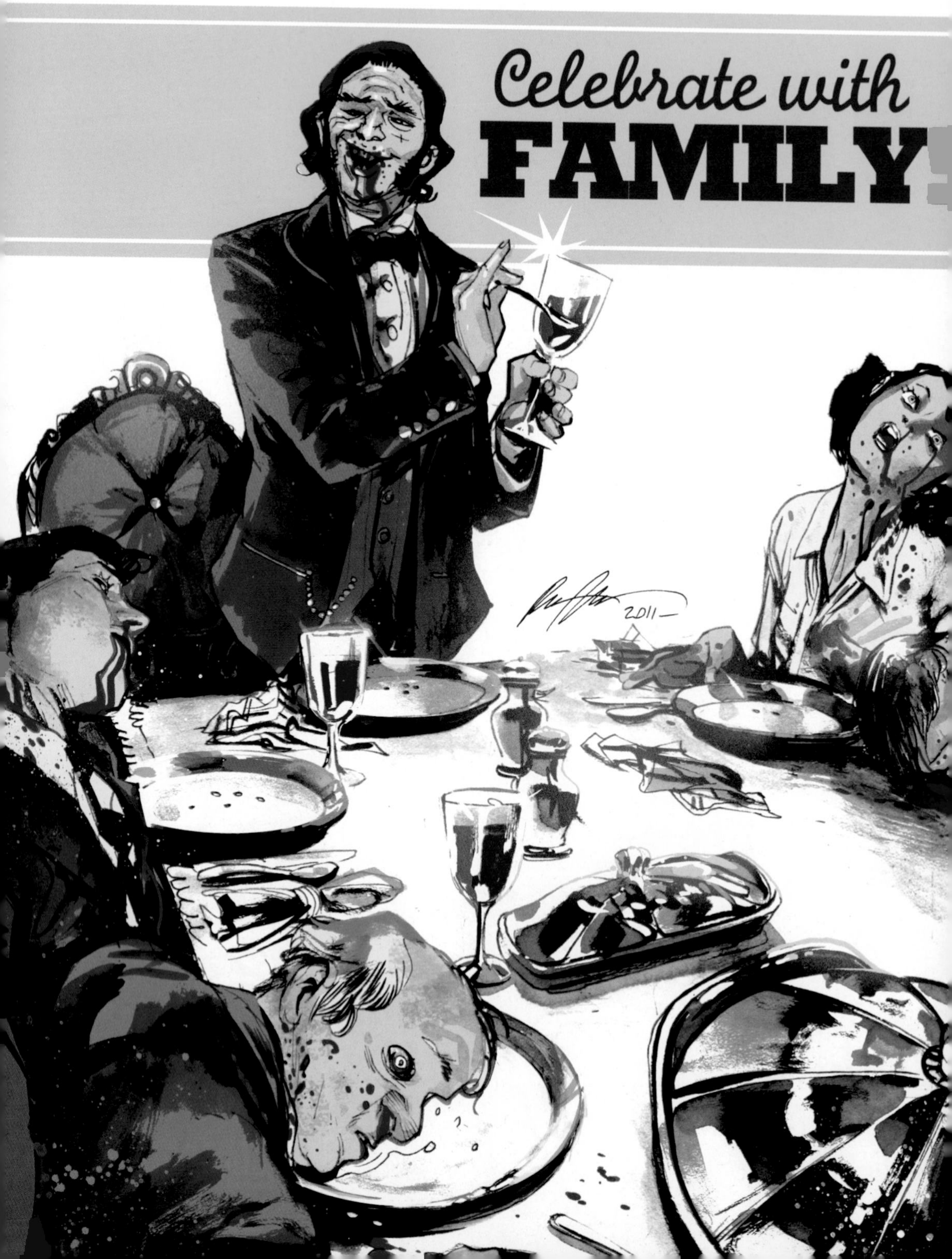

Celebrate with
FAMILY
2011

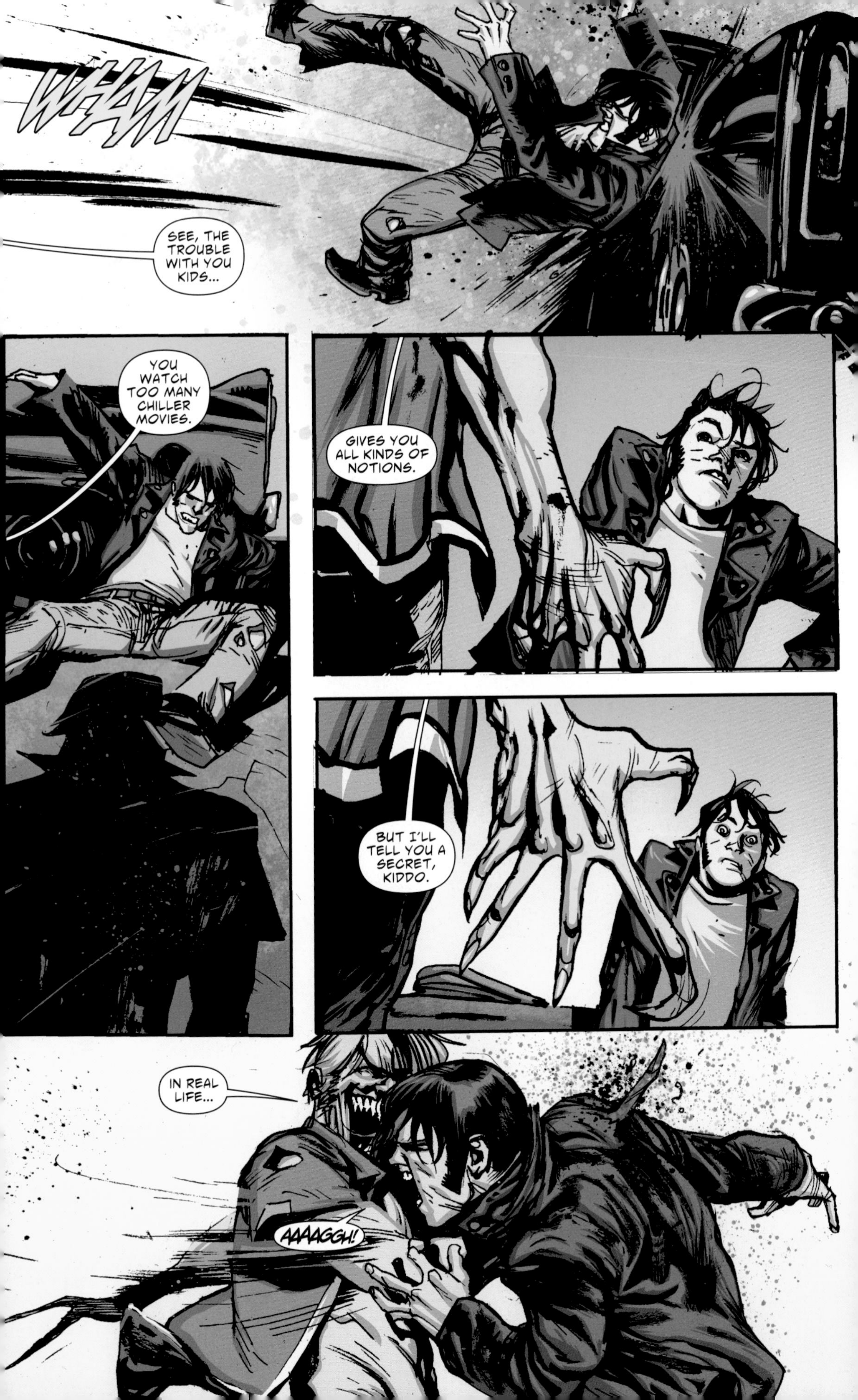
WHAM
SEE, THE TROUBLE WITH YOU KIDS...
YOU WATCH TOO MANY CHILLER MOVIES.
GIVES YOU ALL KINDS OF NOTIONS.
BUT I'LL TELL YOU A SECRET, KIDDO.
IN REAL LIFE...
AAAAGGH!

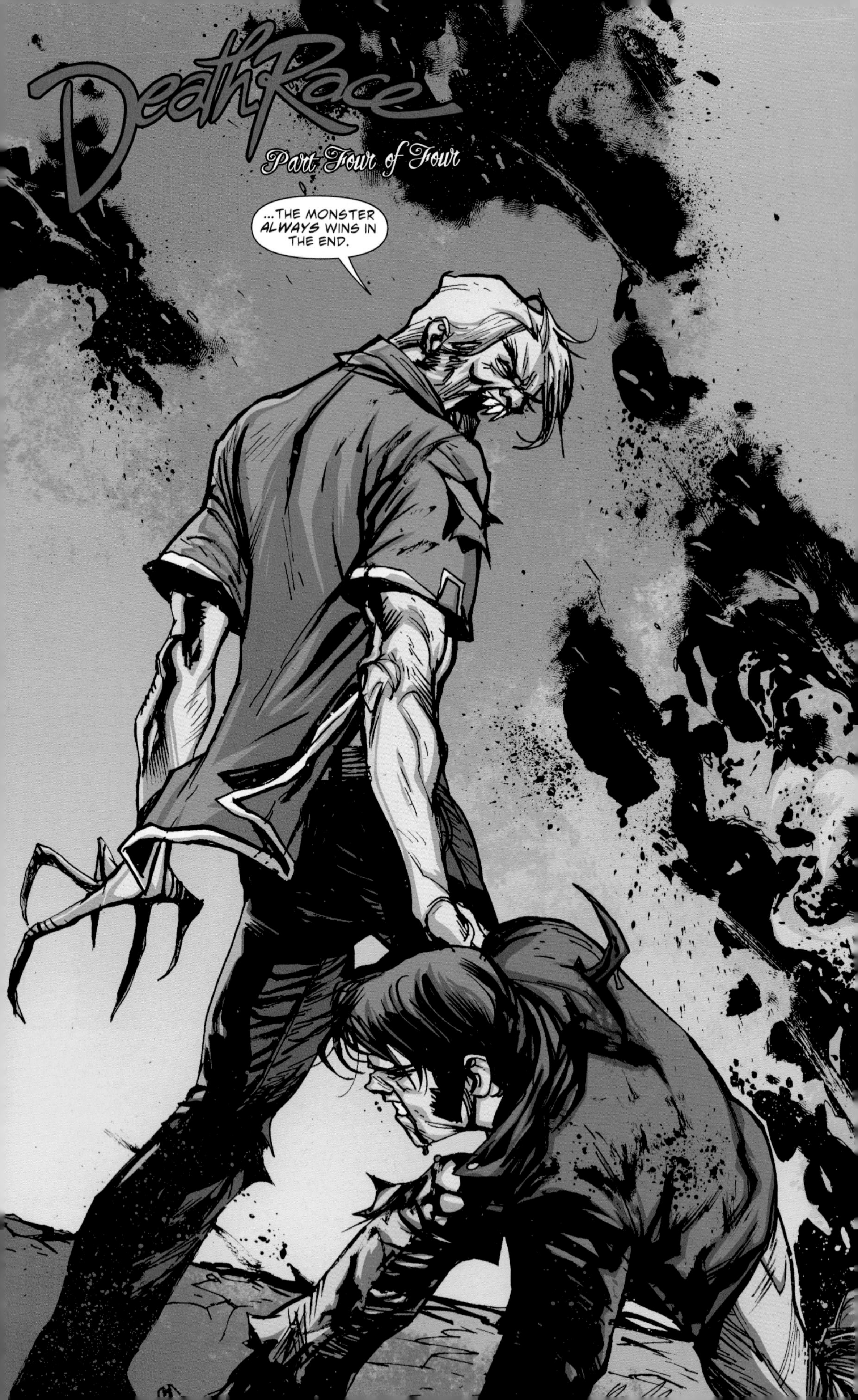
Death Race
Part Four of Four
...THE MONSTER ALWAYS WINS IN THE END.

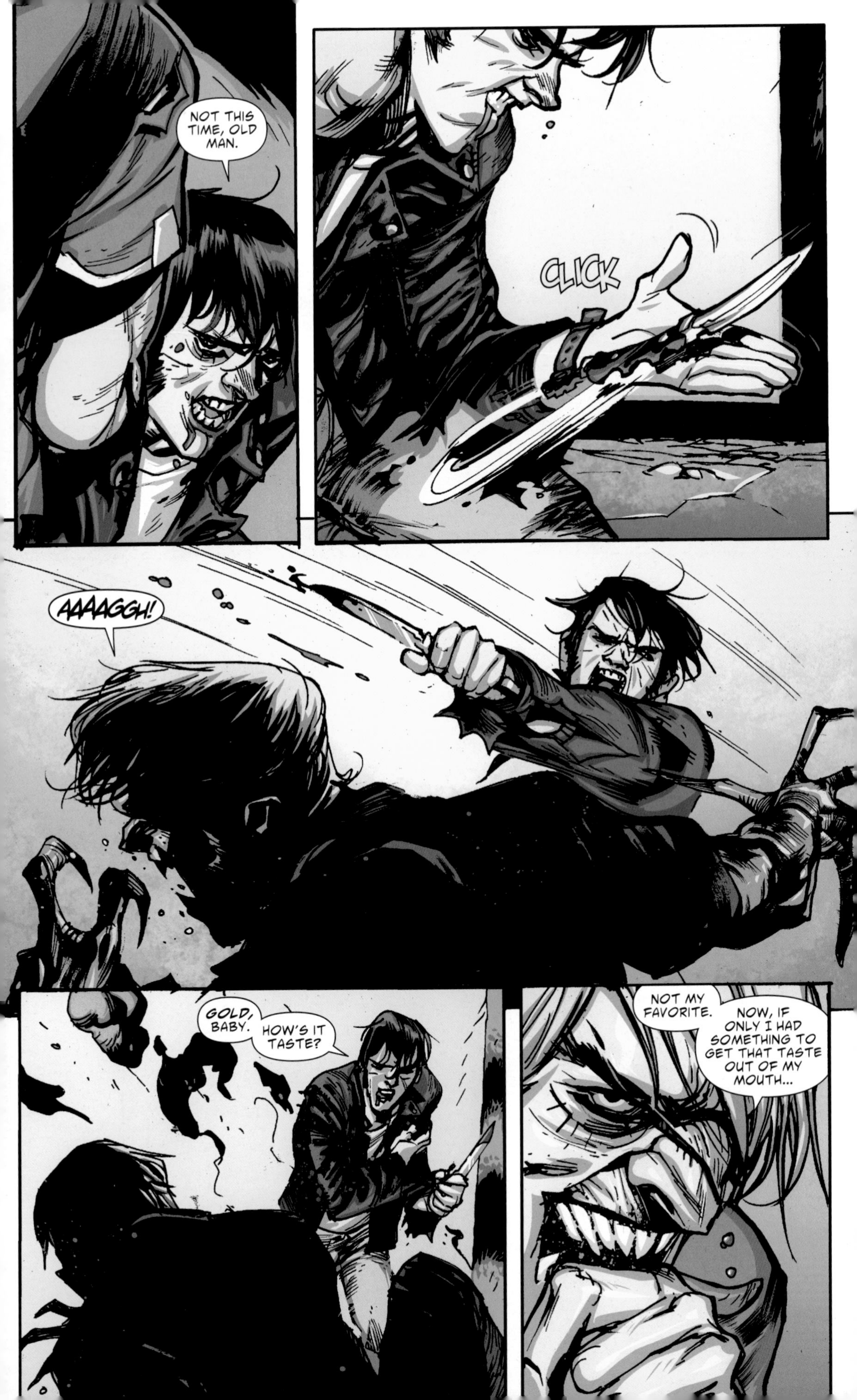
NOT THIS TIME, OLD MAN.
CLICK
AAAAGGH!
GOLD, BABY.
HOW'S IT TASTE?
NOT MY FAVORITE.
NOW, IF ONLY I HAD SOMETHING TO GET THAT TASTE OUT OF MY MOUTH...

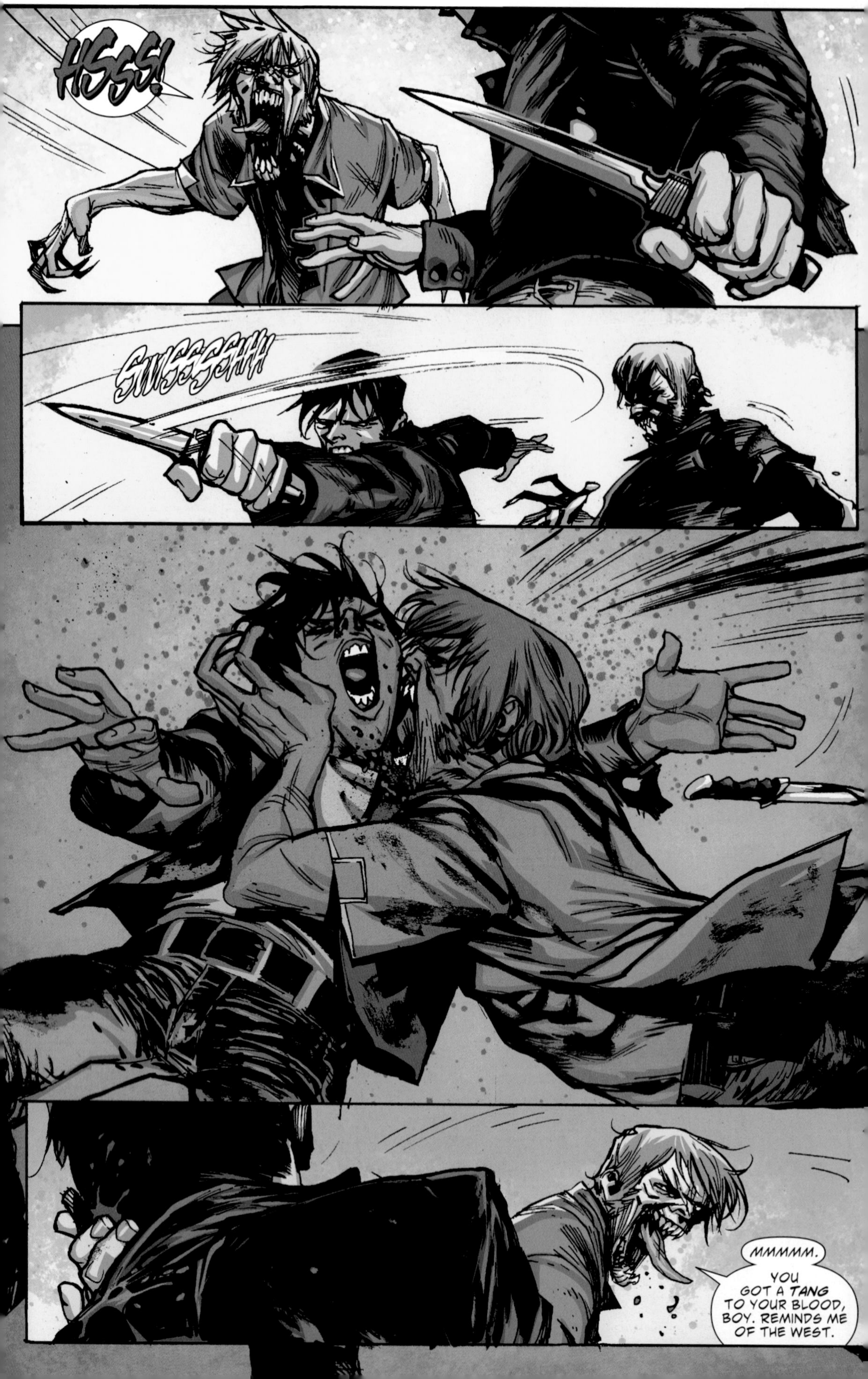
HSSS!
SWISSSHH
MMMMM.
YOU GOT A TANG TO YOUR BLOOD, BOY. REMINDS ME OF THE WEST.

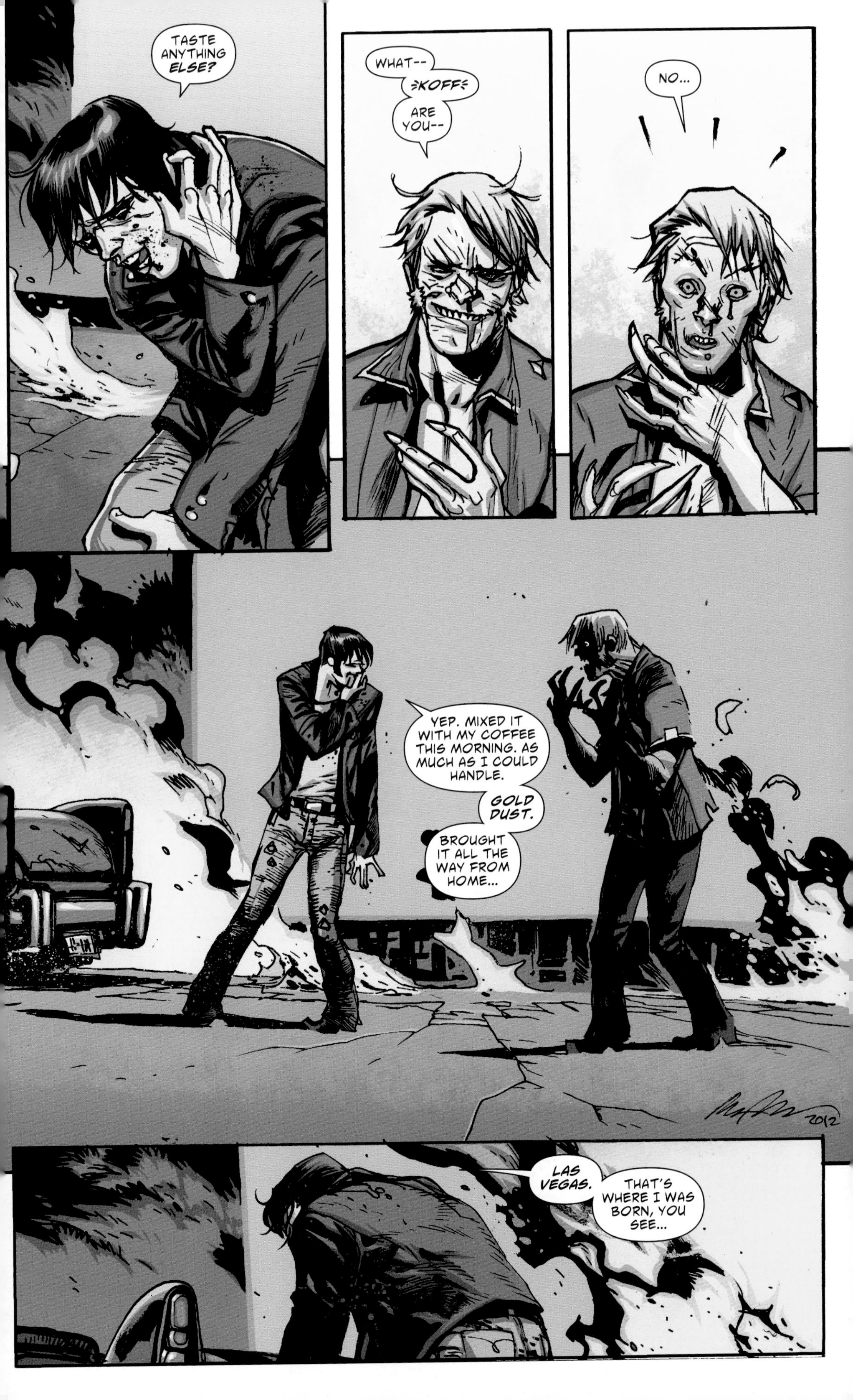
TASTE ANYTHING ELSE?
WHAT--
KOFF
ARE YOU--
NO...
YEP. MIXED IT WITH MY COFFEE THIS MORNING. AS MUCH AS I COULD HANDLE.
GOLD DUST.
BROUGHT IT ALL THE WAY FROM HOME...
LAS VEGAS.
THAT'S WHERE I WAS BORN, YOU SEE...

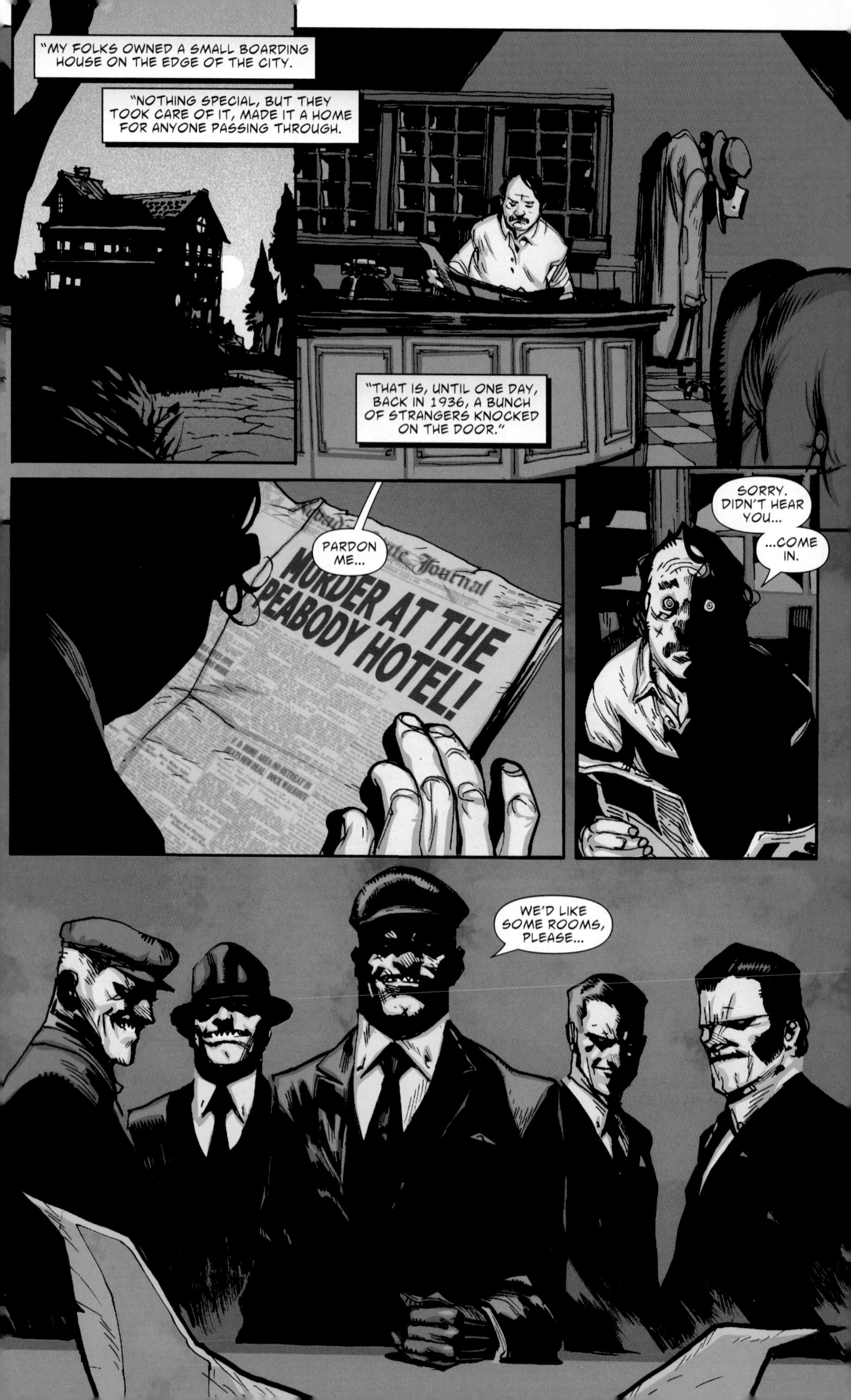
"MY FOLKS OWNED A SMALL BOARDING HOUSE ON THE EDGE OF THE CITY.
"NOTHING SPECIAL, BUT THEY TOOK CARE OF IT, MADE IT A HOME FOR ANYONE PASSING THROUGH.
"THAT IS, UNTIL ONE DAY, BACK IN 1936, A BUNCH OF STRANGERS KNOCKED ON THE DOOR."
PARDON ME...
MURDER AT THE PEABODY HOTEL!
SORRY. DIDN'T HEAR YOU...
...COME IN.
WE'D LIKE SOME ROOMS, PLEASE...

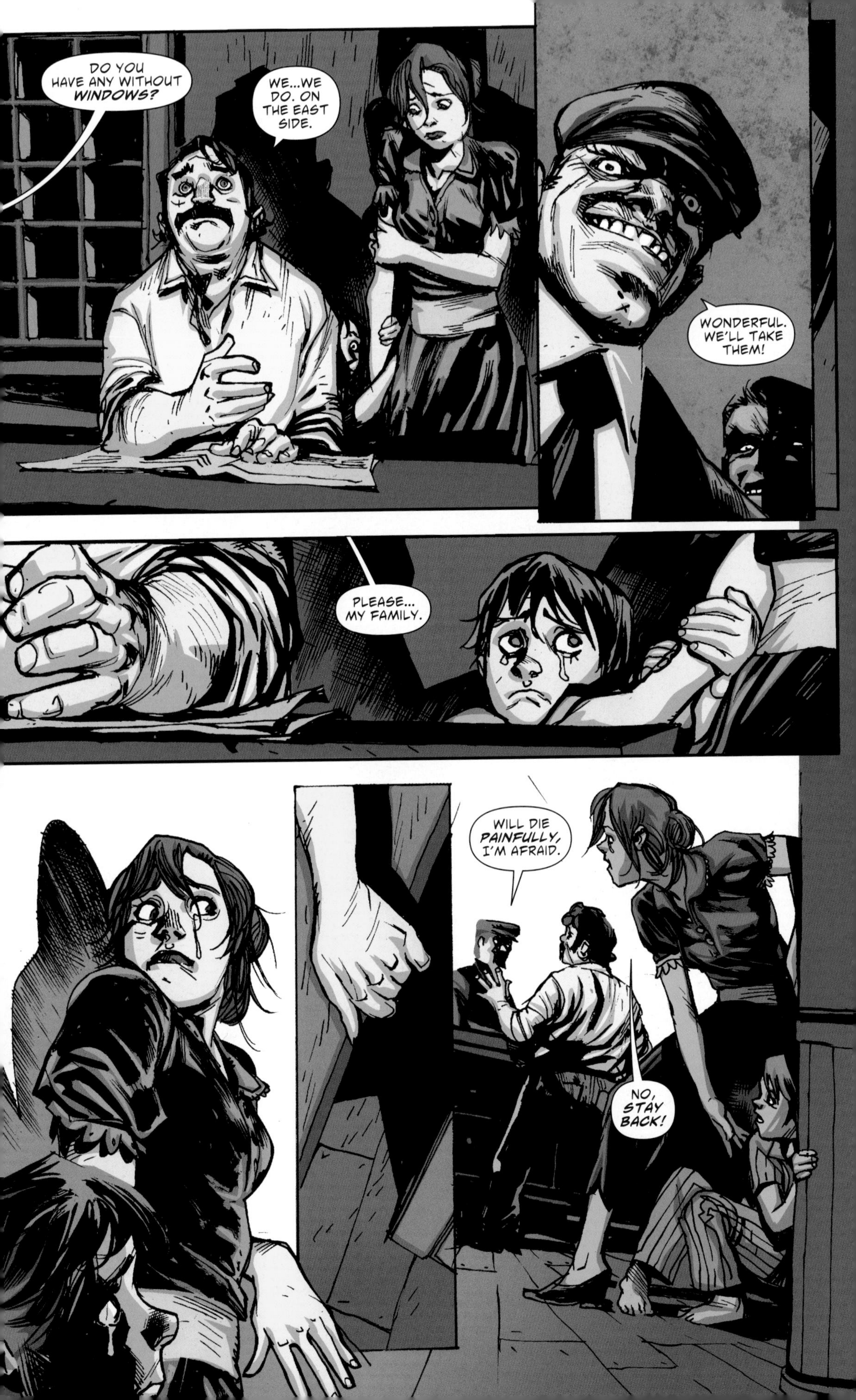
DO YOU HAVE ANY WITHOUT WINDOWS?
WE...WE DO. ON THE EAST SIDE.
WONDERFUL. WE'LL TAKE THEM!
PLEASE... MY FAMILY.
WILL DIE PAINFULLY, I'M AFRAID.
NO, STAY BACK!

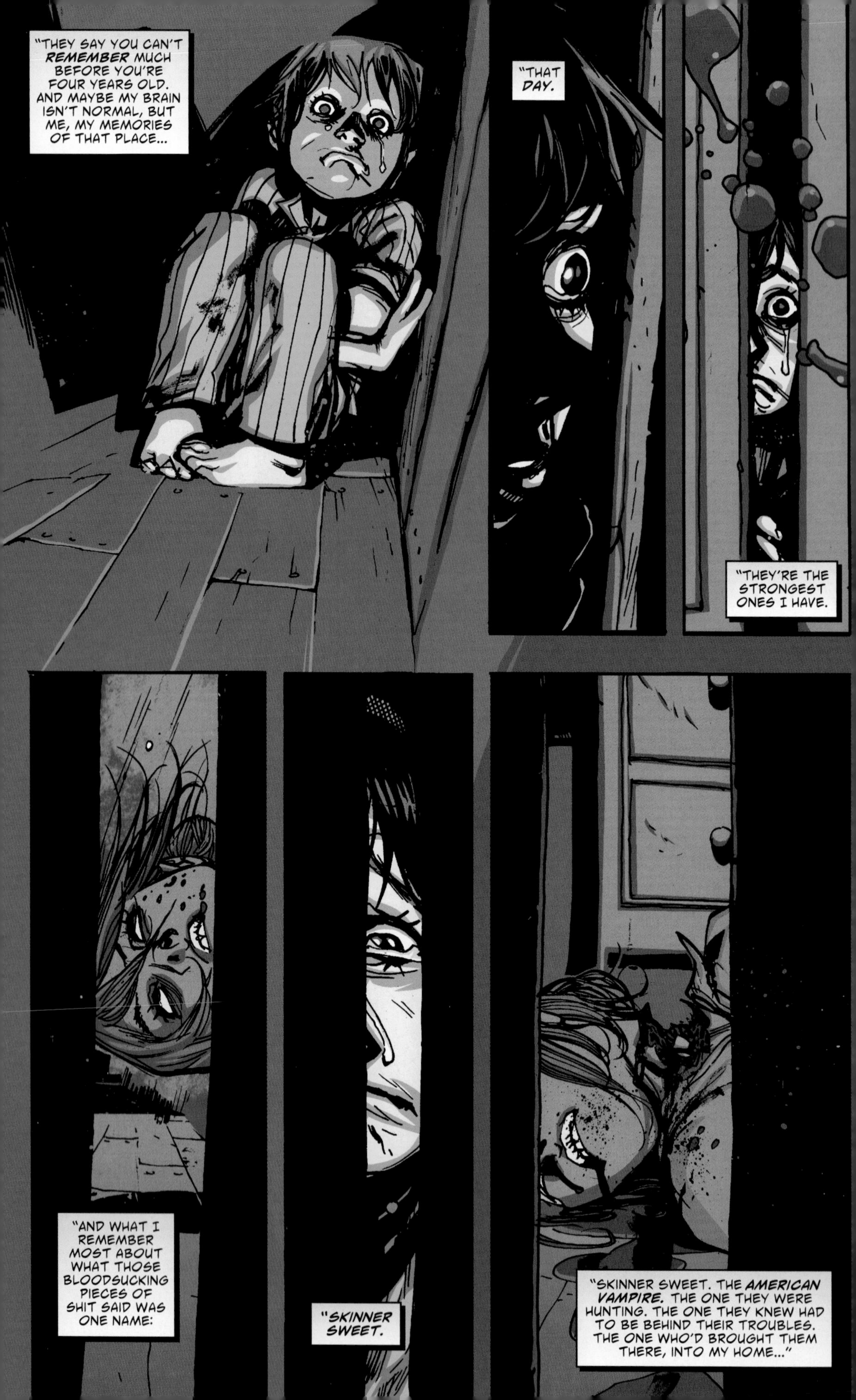
"THEY SAY YOU CAN'T **REMEMBER** MUCH BEFORE YOU'RE FOUR YEARS OLD. AND MAYBE MY BRAIN ISN'T NORMAL, BUT ME, MY MEMORIES OF THAT PLACE...
"THAT **DAY.**
"THEY'RE THE STRONGEST ONES I HAVE.
"AND WHAT I REMEMBER MOST ABOUT WHAT THOSE BLOODSUCKING PIECES OF SHIT SAID WAS ONE NAME:
"**SKINNER SWEET.**
"SKINNER SWEET. THE **AMERICAN VAMPIRE.** THE ONE THEY WERE HUNTING. THE ONE THEY KNEW HAD TO BE BEHIND THEIR TROUBLES. THE ONE WHO'D BROUGHT THEM THERE, INTO MY HOME..."

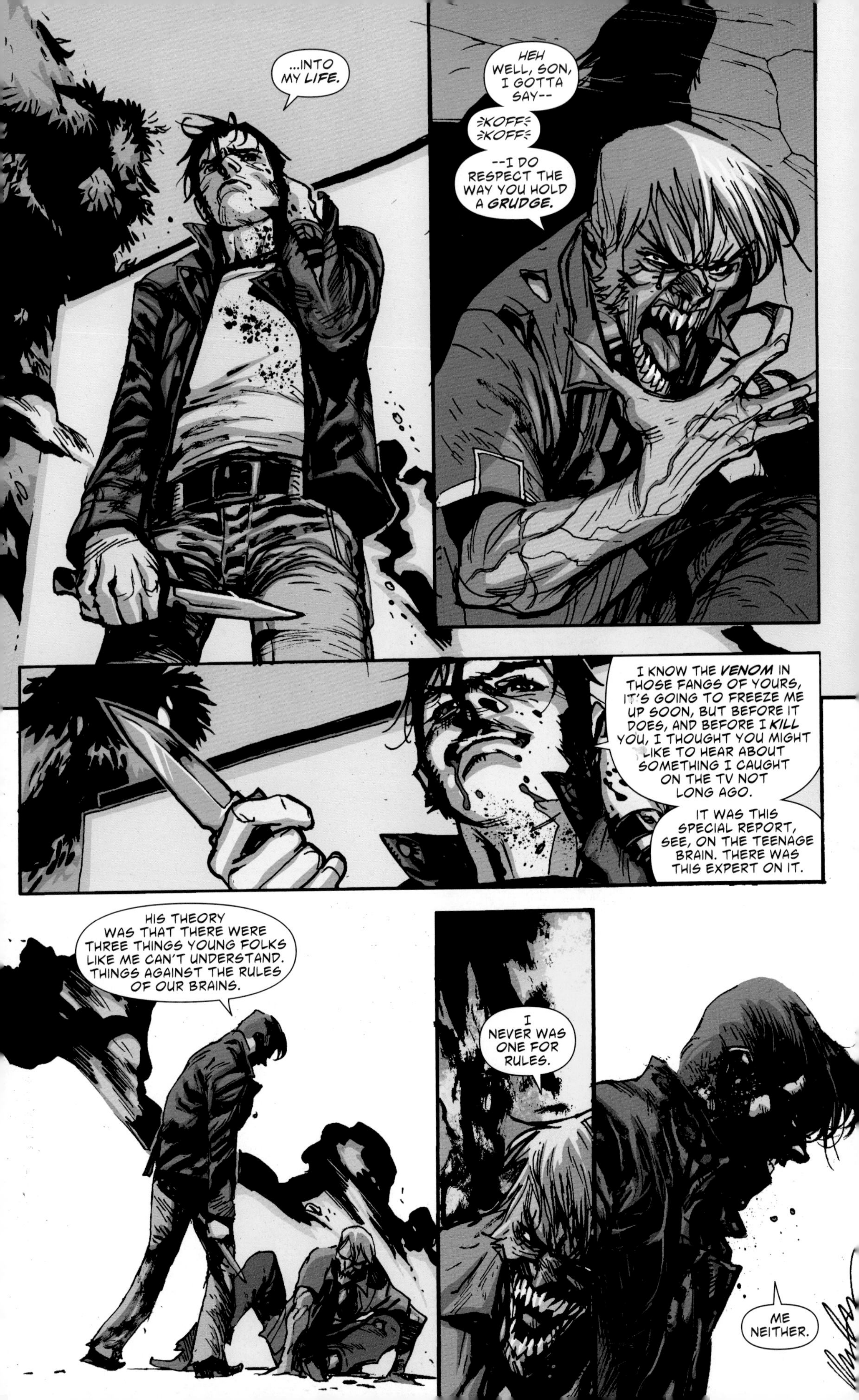

...INTO MY LIFE.
HEH WELL, SON, I GOTTA SAY--
KOFF KOFF
--I DO RESPECT THE WAY YOU HOLD A GRUDGE.
I KNOW THE VENOM IN THOSE FANGS OF YOURS, IT'S GOING TO FREEZE ME UP SOON, BUT BEFORE IT DOES, AND BEFORE I KILL YOU, I THOUGHT YOU MIGHT LIKE TO HEAR ABOUT SOMETHING I CAUGHT ON THE TV NOT LONG AGO.
IT WAS THIS SPECIAL REPORT, SEE, ON THE TEENAGE BRAIN. THERE WAS THIS EXPERT ON IT.
HIS THEORY WAS THAT THERE WERE THREE THINGS YOUNG FOLKS LIKE ME CAN'T UNDERSTAND. THINGS AGAINST THE RULES OF OUR BRAINS.
I NEVER WAS ONE FOR RULES.
ME NEITHER.

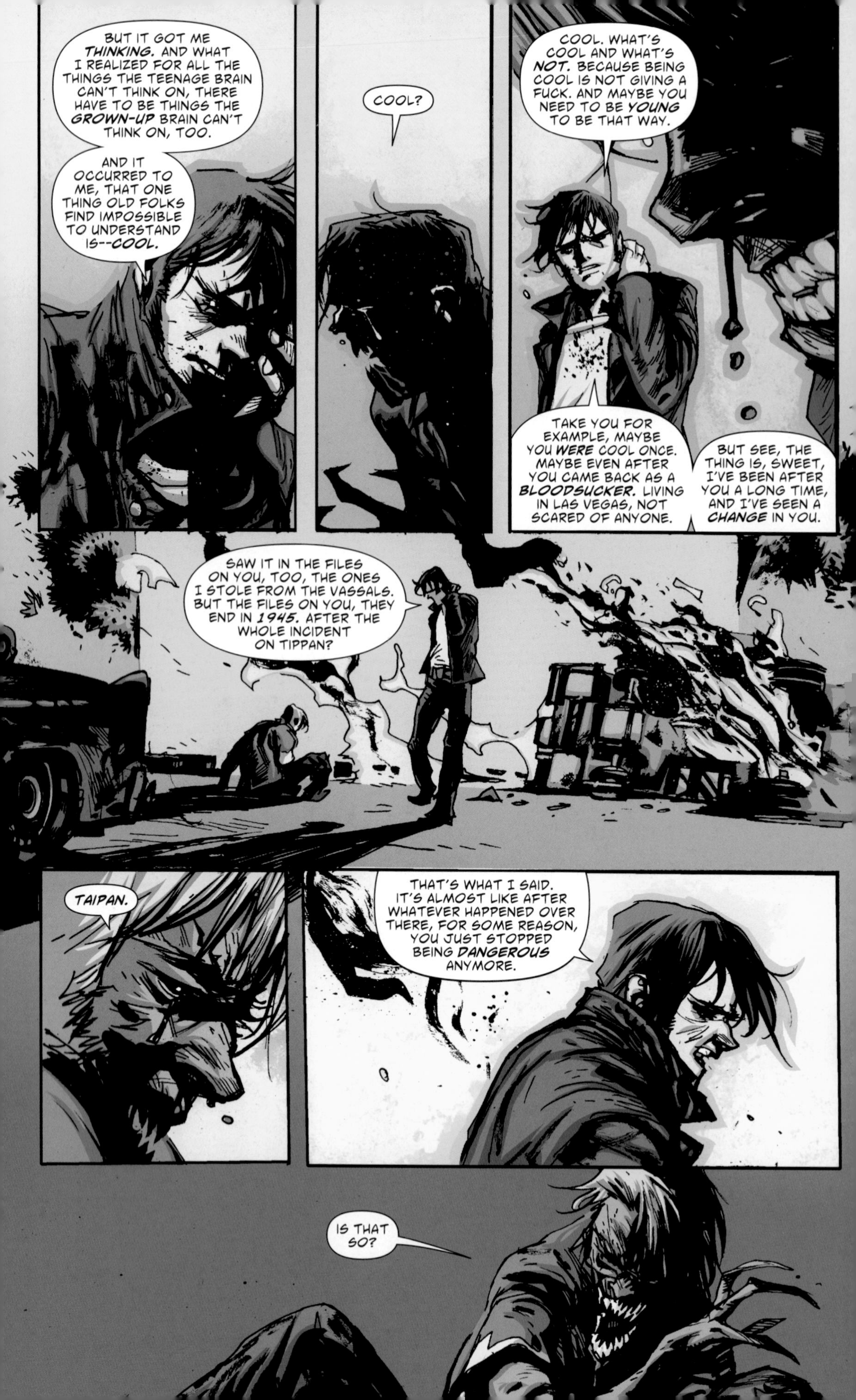
BUT IT GOT ME THINKING. AND WHAT I REALIZED FOR ALL THE THINGS THE TEENAGE BRAIN CAN'T THINK ON, THERE HAVE TO BE THINGS THE GROWN-UP BRAIN CAN'T THINK ON, TOO.
AND IT OCCURRED TO ME, THAT ONE THING OLD FOLKS FIND IMPOSSIBLE TO UNDERSTAND IS--COOL.
COOL?
COOL. WHAT'S COOL AND WHAT'S NOT. BECAUSE BEING COOL IS NOT GIVING A FUCK. AND MAYBE YOU NEED TO BE YOUNG TO BE THAT WAY.
TAKE YOU FOR EXAMPLE, MAYBE YOU WERE COOL ONCE. MAYBE EVEN AFTER YOU CAME BACK AS A BLOODSUCKER. LIVING IN LAS VEGAS, NOT SCARED OF ANYONE.
BUT SEE, THE THING IS, SWEET, I'VE BEEN AFTER YOU A LONG TIME, AND I'VE SEEN A CHANGE IN YOU.
SAW IT IN THE FILES ON YOU, TOO, THE ONES I STOLE FROM THE VASSALS. BUT THE FILES ON YOU, THEY END IN 1945. AFTER THE WHOLE INCIDENT ON TIPPAN?
TAIPAN.
THAT'S WHAT I SAID. IT'S ALMOST LIKE AFTER WHATEVER HAPPENED OVER THERE, FOR SOME REASON, YOU JUST STOPPED BEING DANGEROUS ANYMORE.
IS THAT SO?

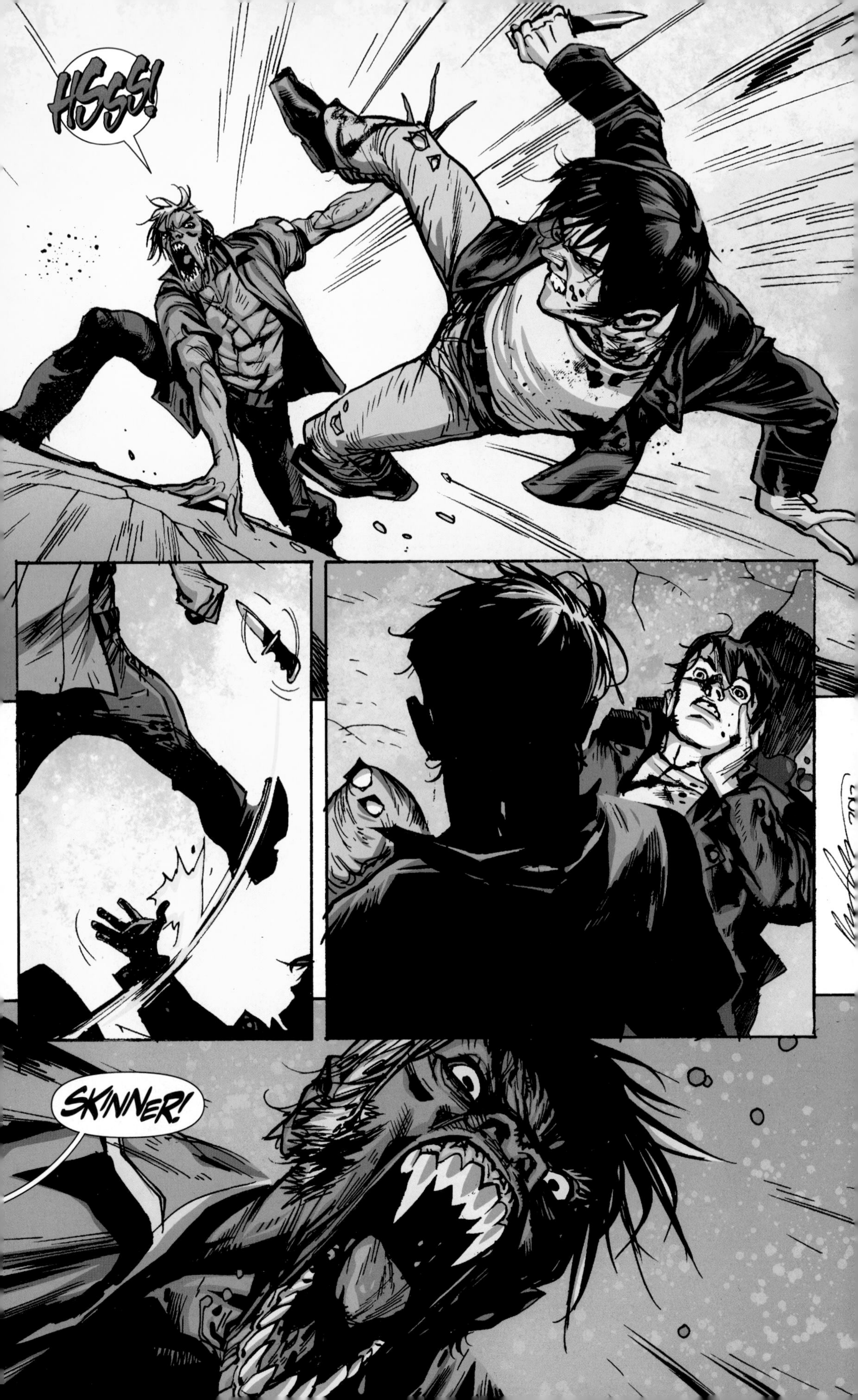
HSSS!
SKINNER!

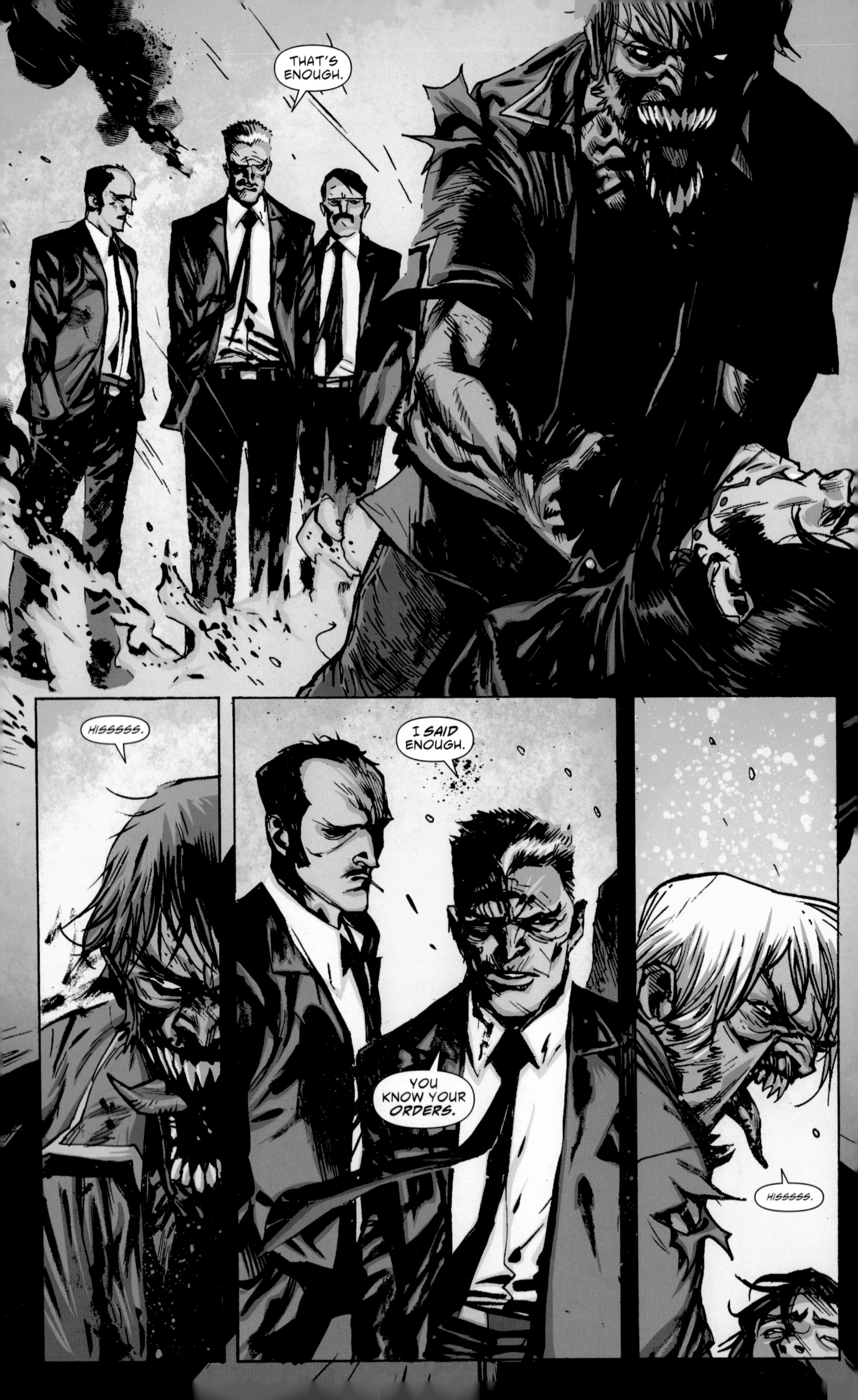
THAT'S ENOUGH.
HISSSSS.
I SAID ENOUGH.
YOU KNOW YOUR ORDERS.
HISSSSS.

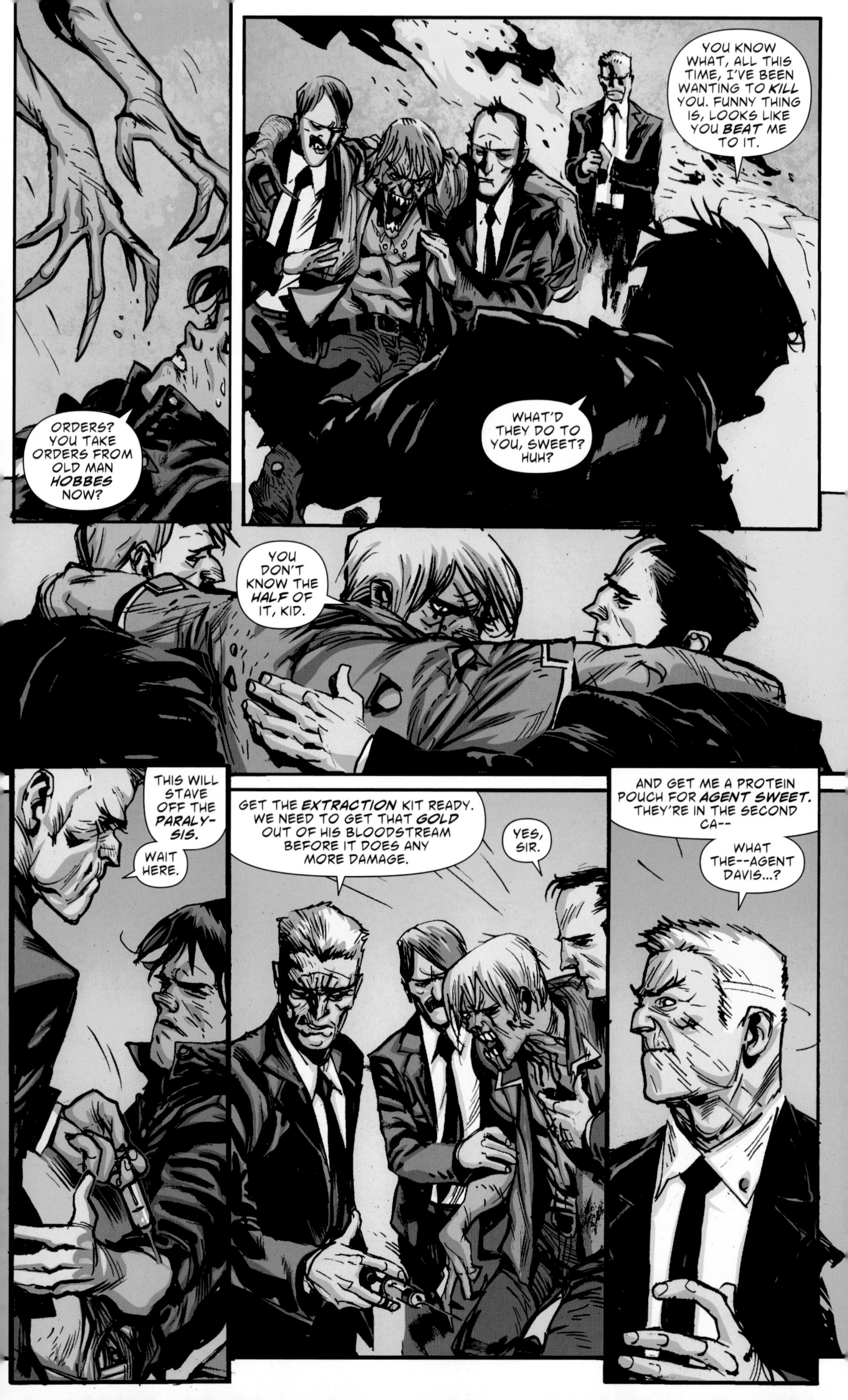
ORDERS? YOU TAKE ORDERS FROM OLD MAN HOBBES NOW?
YOU KNOW WHAT, ALL THIS TIME, I'VE BEEN WANTING TO KILL YOU. FUNNY THING IS, LOOKS LIKE YOU BEAT ME TO IT.
WHAT'D THEY DO TO YOU, SWEET? HUH?
YOU DON'T KNOW THE HALF OF IT, KID.
THIS WILL STAVE OFF THE PARALY-SIS.
WAIT HERE.
GET THE EXTRACTION KIT READY. WE NEED TO GET THAT GOLD OUT OF HIS BLOODSTREAM BEFORE IT DOES ANY MORE DAMAGE.
YES, SIR.
AND GET ME A PROTEIN POUCH FOR AGENT SWEET. THEY'RE IN THE SECOND CA--
WHAT THE--AGENT DAVIS...?

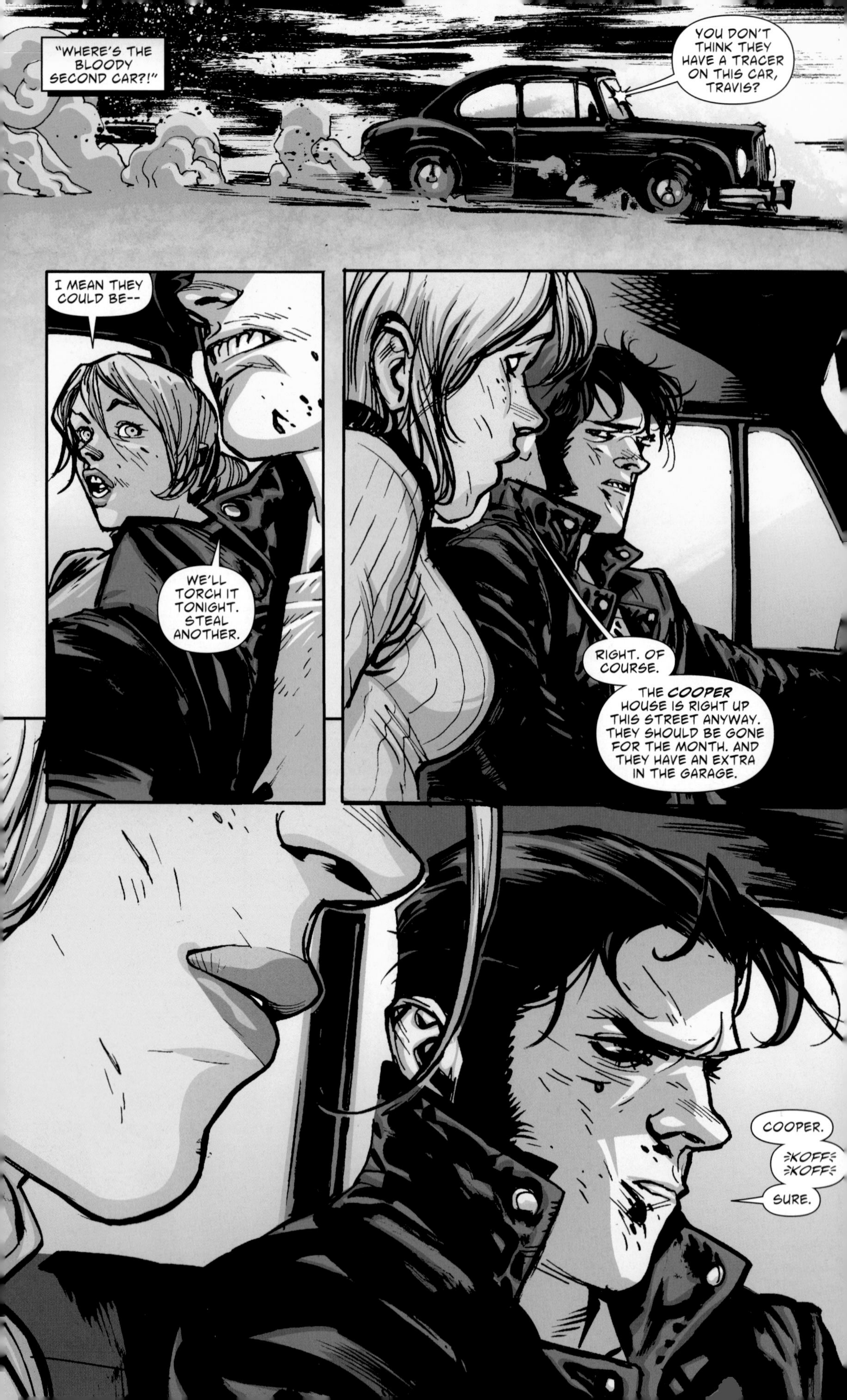
"WHERE'S THE BLOODY SECOND CAR?!"
YOU DON'T THINK THEY HAVE A TRACER ON THIS CAR, TRAVIS?
I MEAN THEY COULD BE--
WE'LL TORCH IT TONIGHT. STEAL ANOTHER.
RIGHT. OF COURSE.
THE *COOPER* HOUSE IS RIGHT UP THIS STREET ANYWAY. THEY SHOULD BE GONE FOR THE MONTH. AND THEY HAVE AN EXTRA IN THE GARAGE.
COOPER.
KOFF KOFF
SURE.

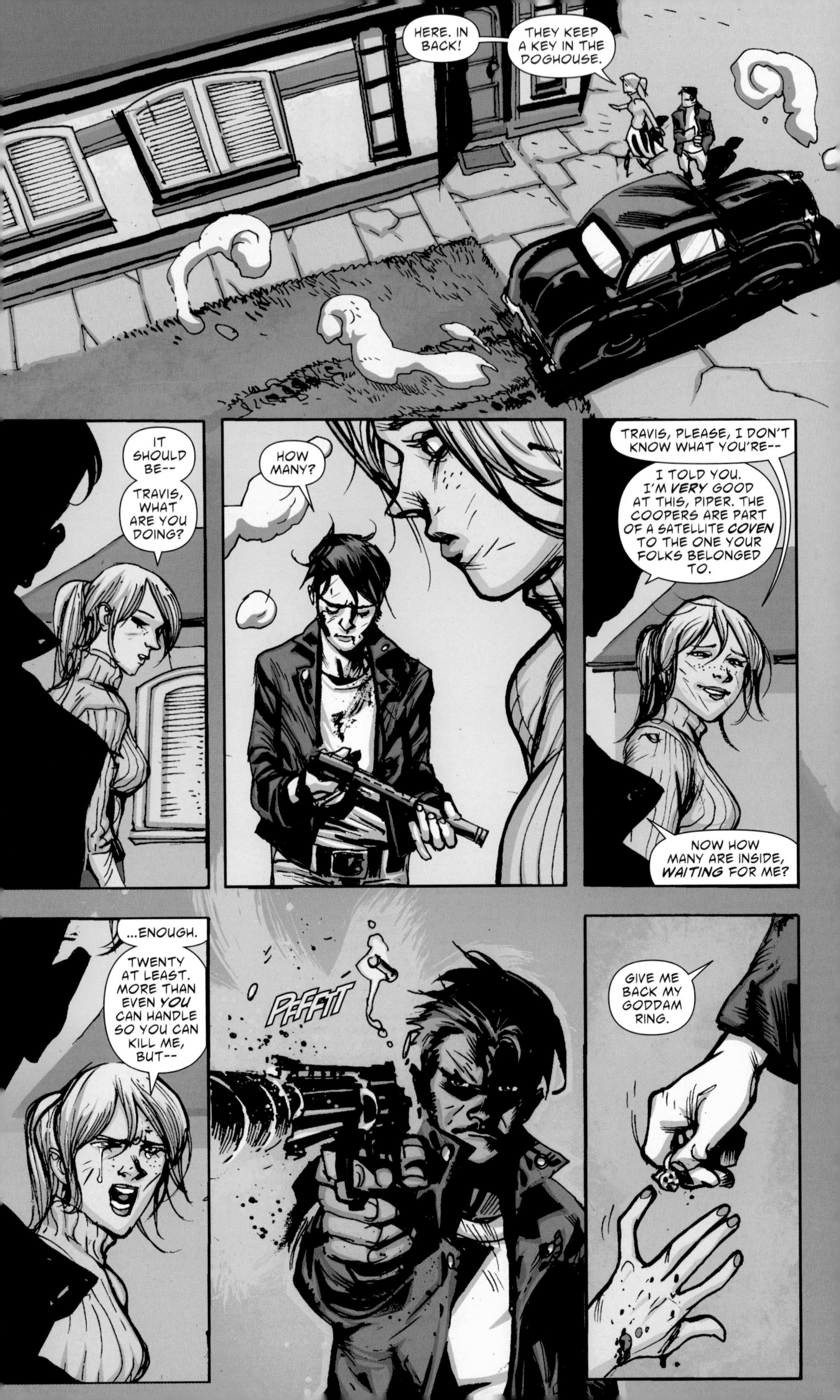
HERE. IN BACK!
THEY KEEP A KEY IN THE DOGHOUSE.
IT SHOULD BE--
TRAVIS, WHAT ARE YOU DOING?
HOW MANY?
TRAVIS, PLEASE, I DON'T KNOW WHAT YOU'RE--
I TOLD YOU. I'M *VERY* GOOD AT THIS, PIPER. THE COOPERS ARE PART OF A SATELLITE *COVEN* TO THE ONE YOUR FOLKS BELONGED TO.
NOW HOW MANY ARE INSIDE, *WAITING* FOR ME?
...ENOUGH.
TWENTY AT LEAST. MORE THAN EVEN *YOU* CAN HANDLE SO YOU CAN KILL ME, BUT--
PFFFTT
GIVE ME BACK MY GODDAM RING.

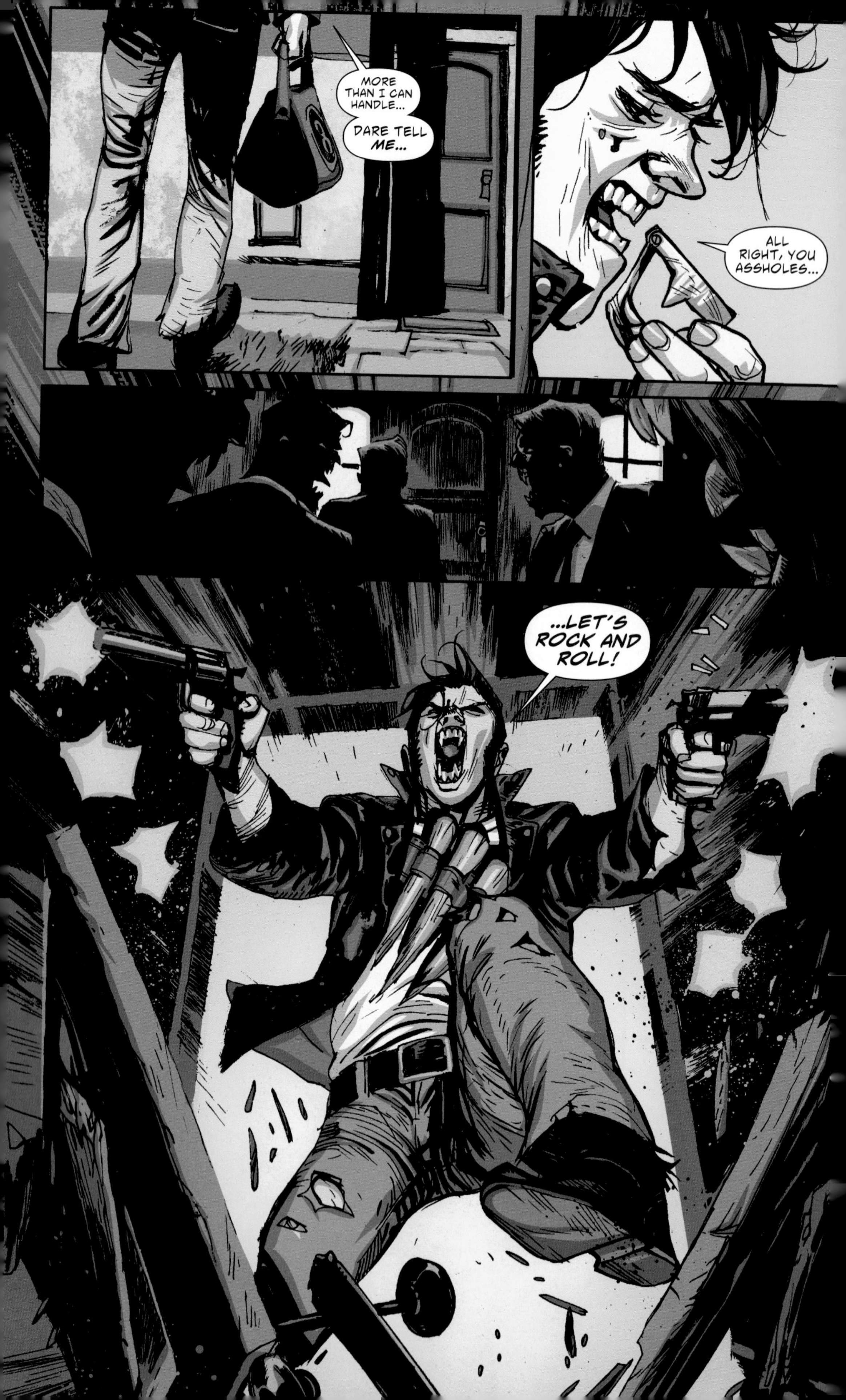
MORE THAN I CAN HANDLE...
DARE TELL ME...
ALL RIGHT, YOU ASSHOLES...
...LET'S ROCK AND ROLL!

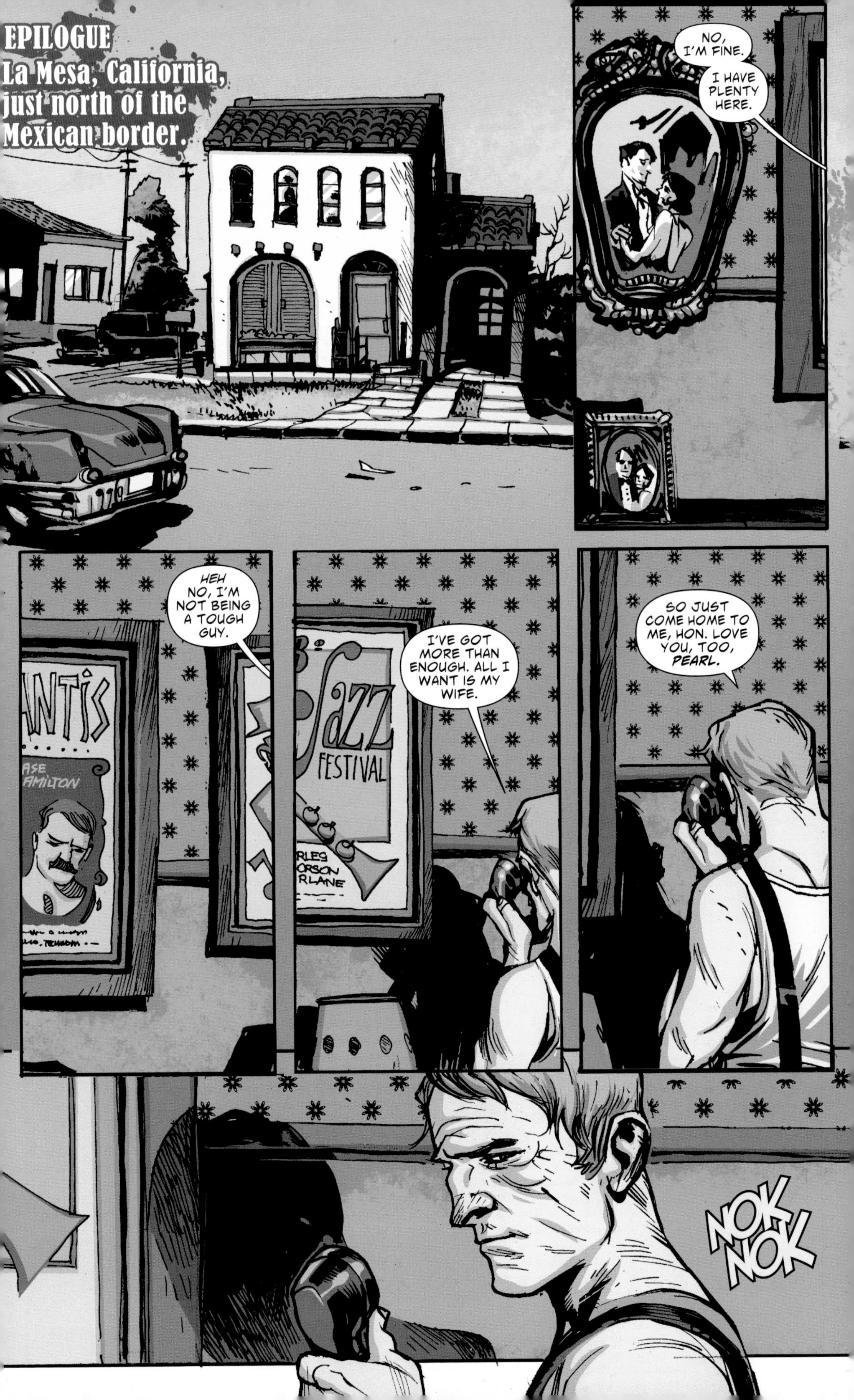
EPILOGUE
La Mesa, California, just north of the Mexican border.
NO, I'M FINE.
I HAVE PLENTY HERE.
HEH NO, I'M NOT BEING A TOUGH GUY.
I'VE GOT MORE THAN ENOUGH. ALL I WANT IS MY WIFE.
SO JUST COME HOME TO ME, HON. LOVE YOU, TOO, PEARL.
NOK NOK

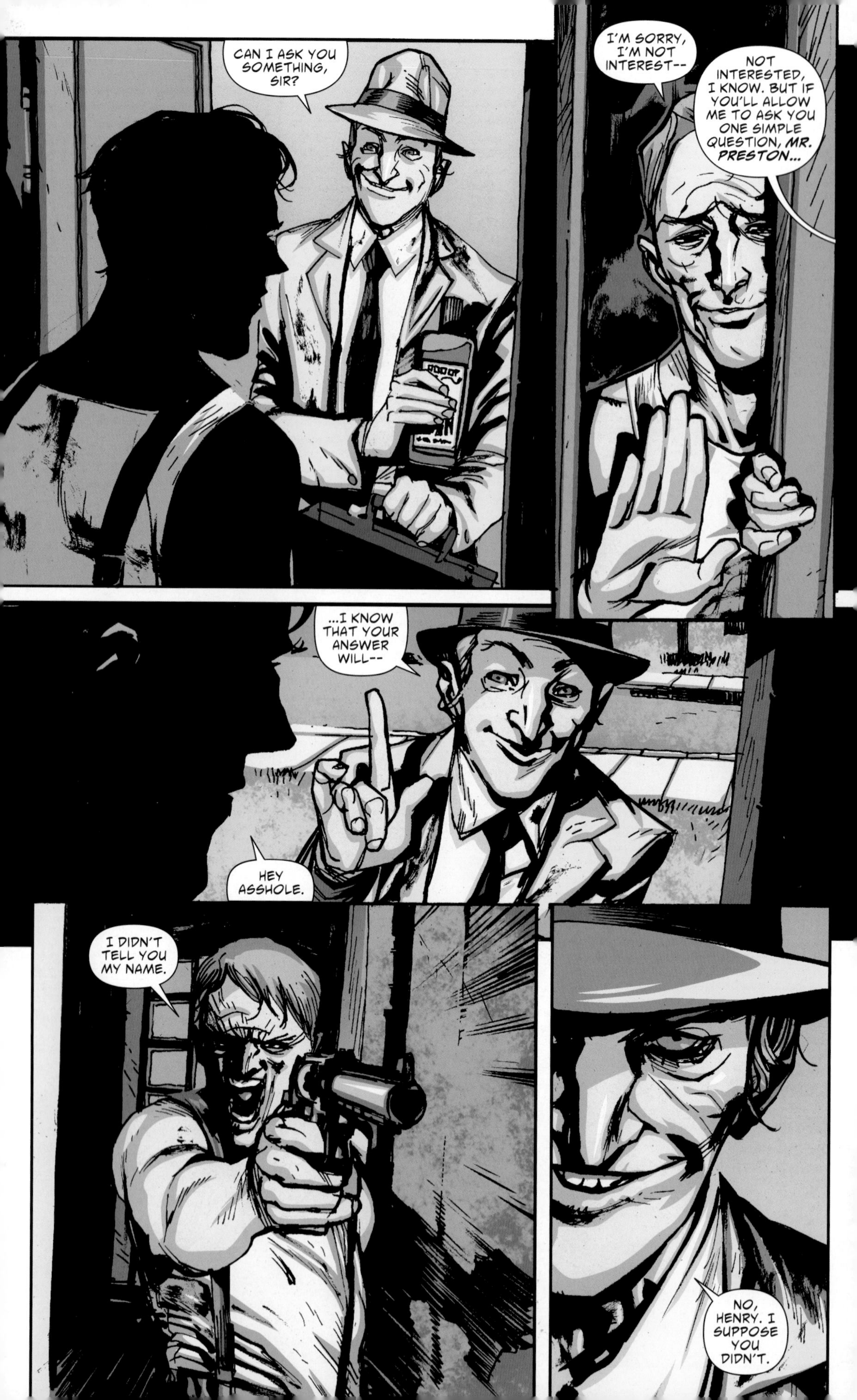
CAN I ASK YOU SOMETHING, SIR?
I'M SORRY, I'M NOT INTEREST--
NOT INTERESTED, I KNOW. BUT IF YOU'LL ALLOW ME TO ASK YOU ONE SIMPLE QUESTION, MR. PRESTON...
...I KNOW THAT YOUR ANSWER WILL--
HEY ASSHOLE.
I DIDN'T TELL YOU MY NAME.
NO, HENRY. I SUPPOSE YOU DIDN'T.

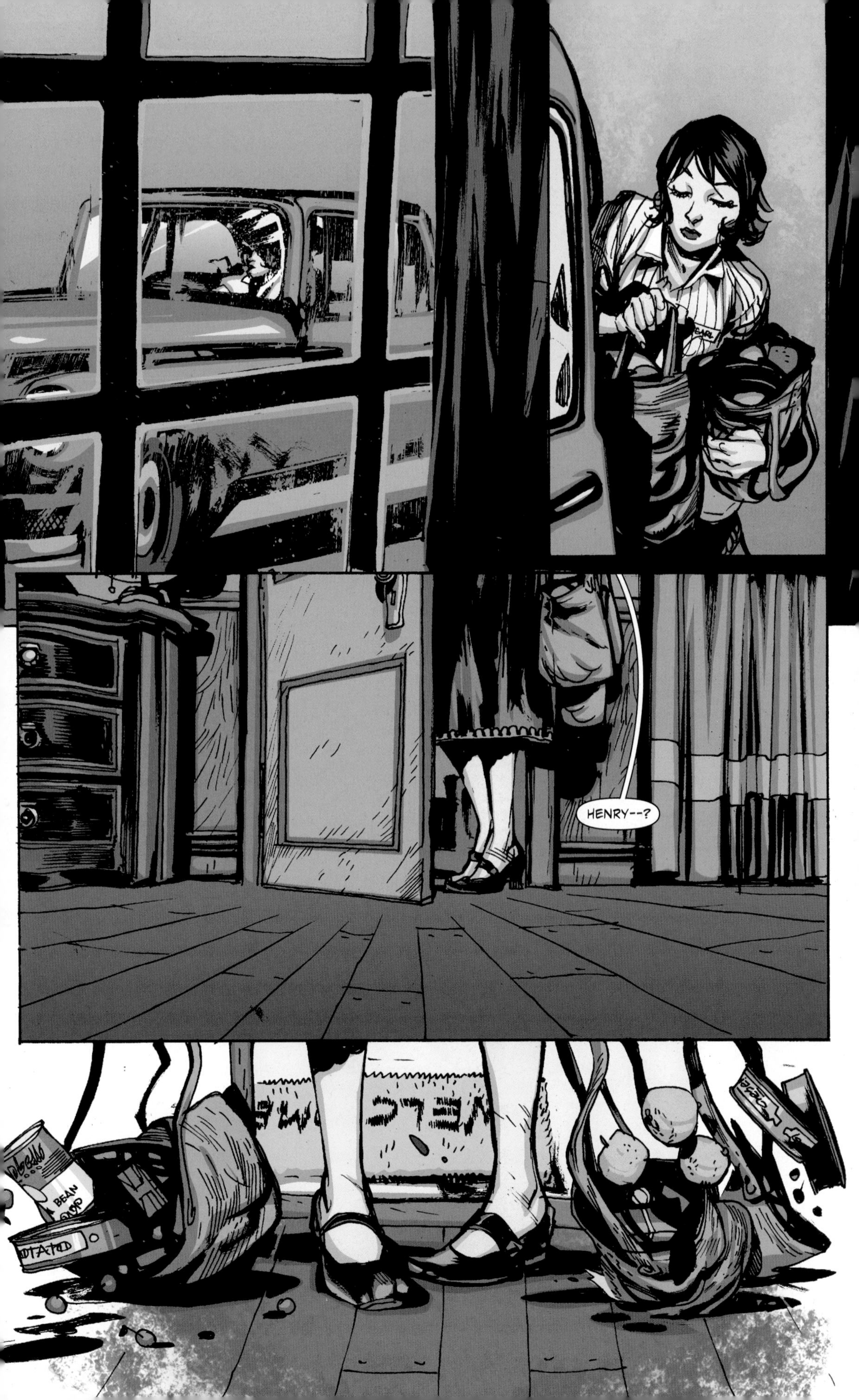
HENRY--?

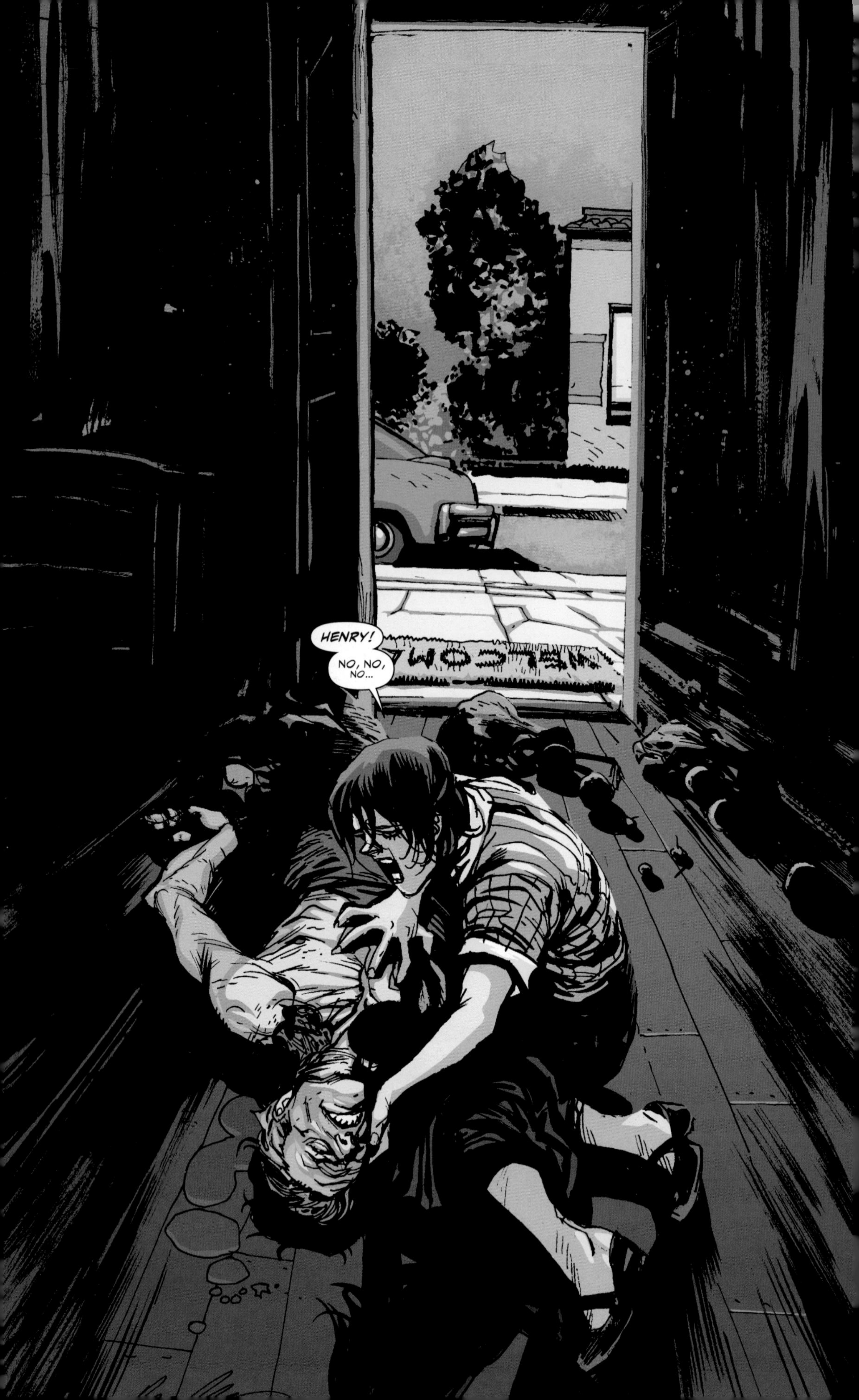
HENRY!
NO, NO, NO...

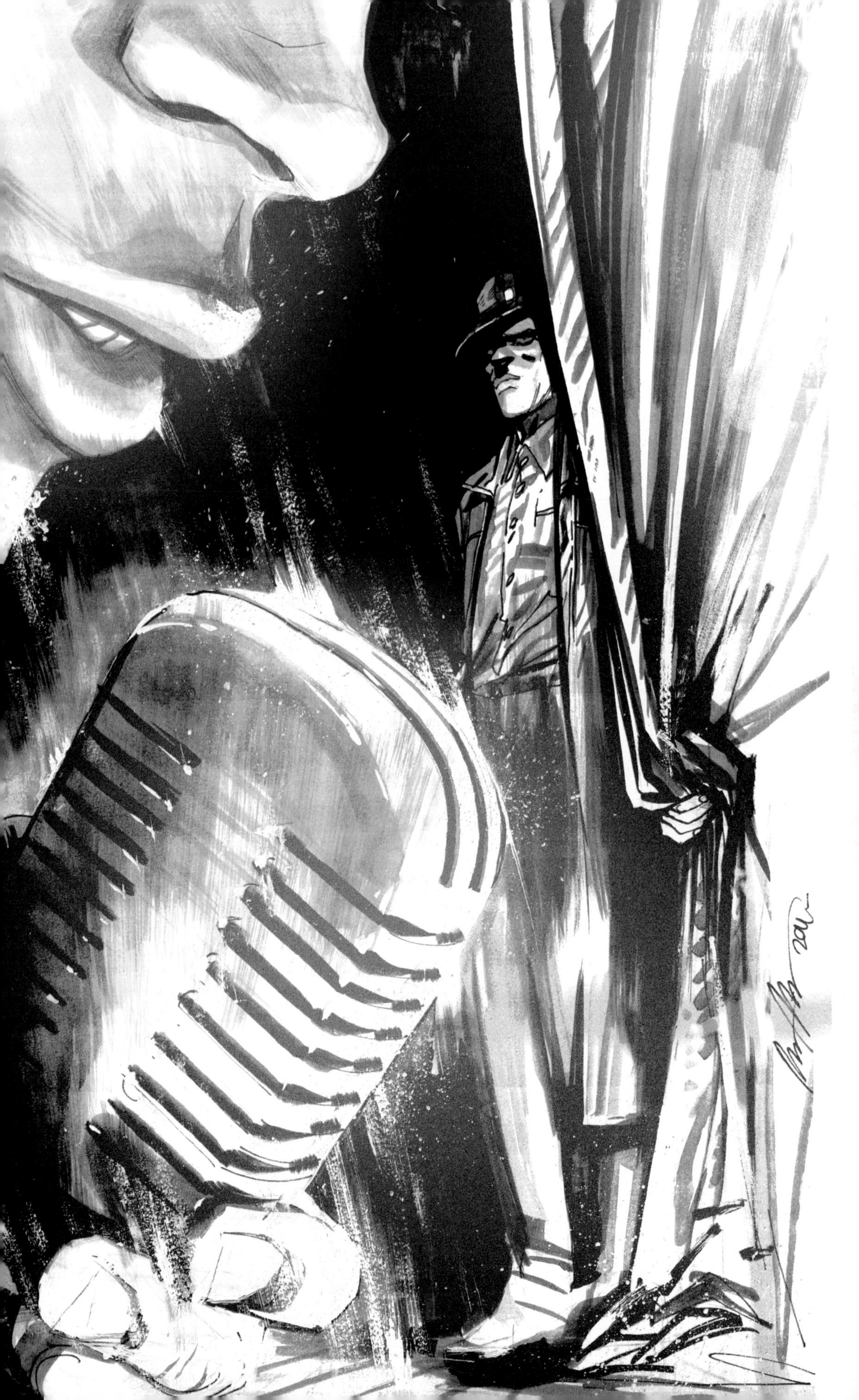

The Nocturnes

Part One
Roger Cruz
Artist

Part Two
Riccardo Burchielli
Artist

Rafael Albuquerque
Covers

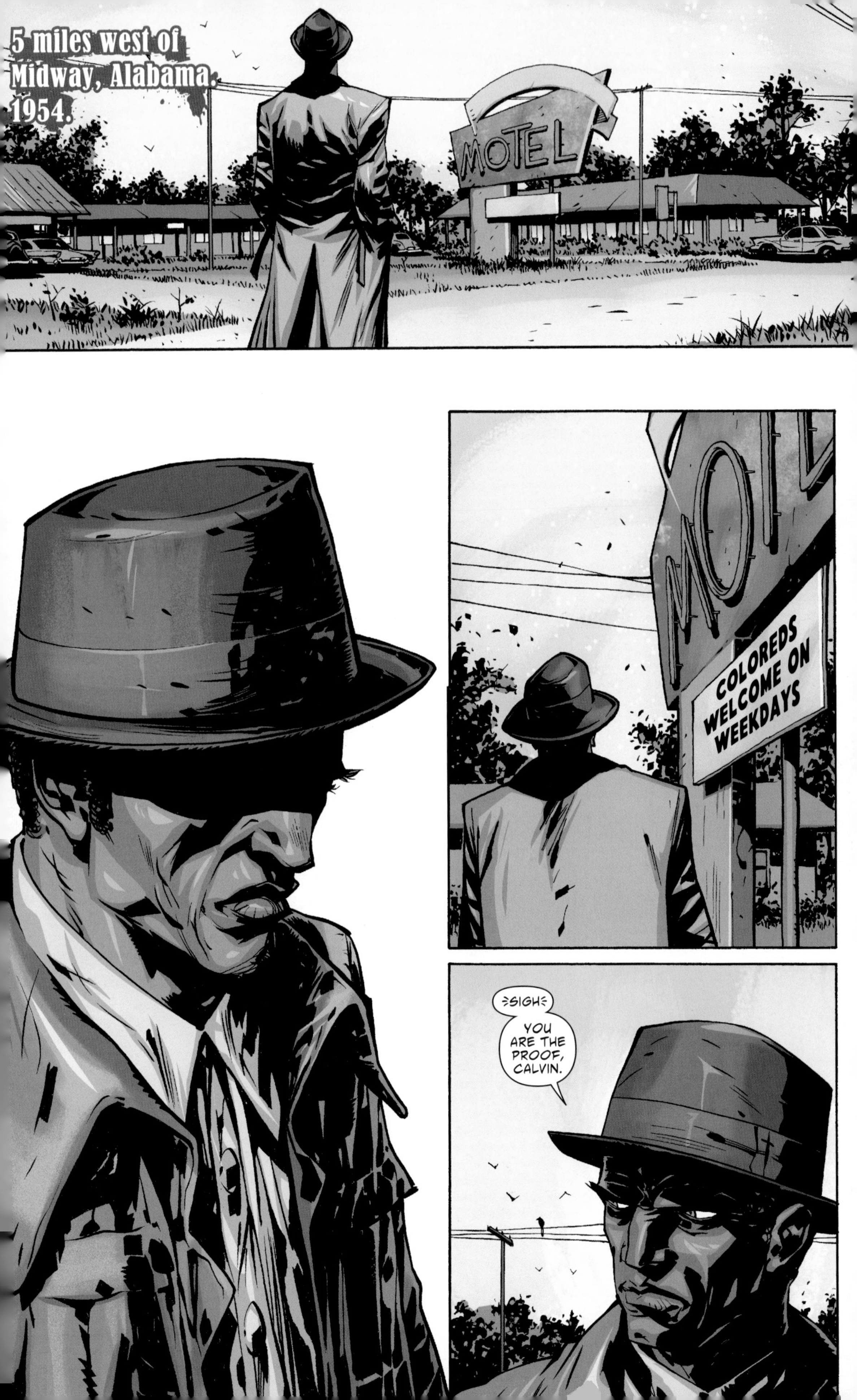
5 miles west of Midway, Alabama. 1954.
MOTEL
COLOREDS WELCOME ON WEEKDAYS
SIGH
YOU ARE THE PROOF, CALVIN.

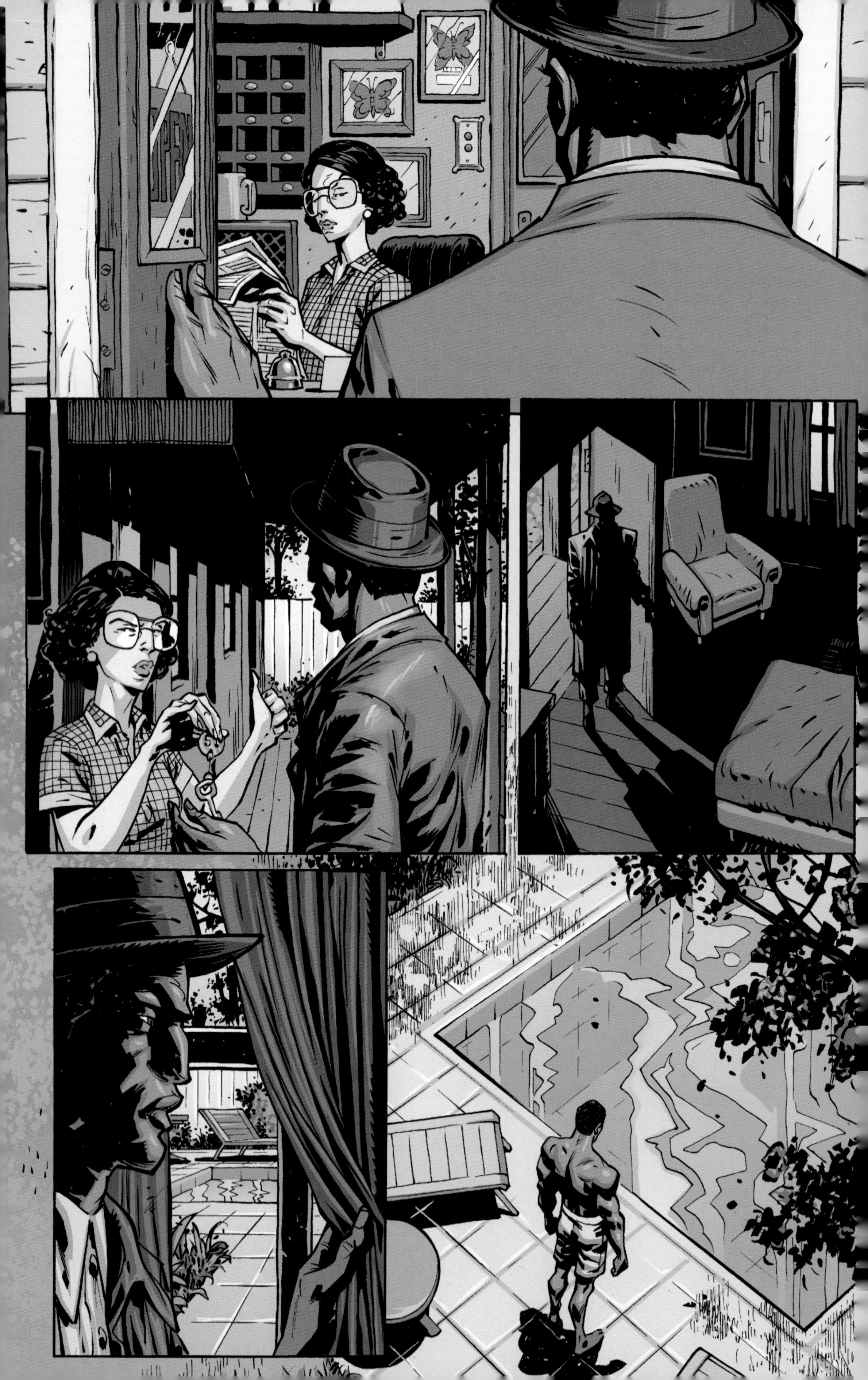

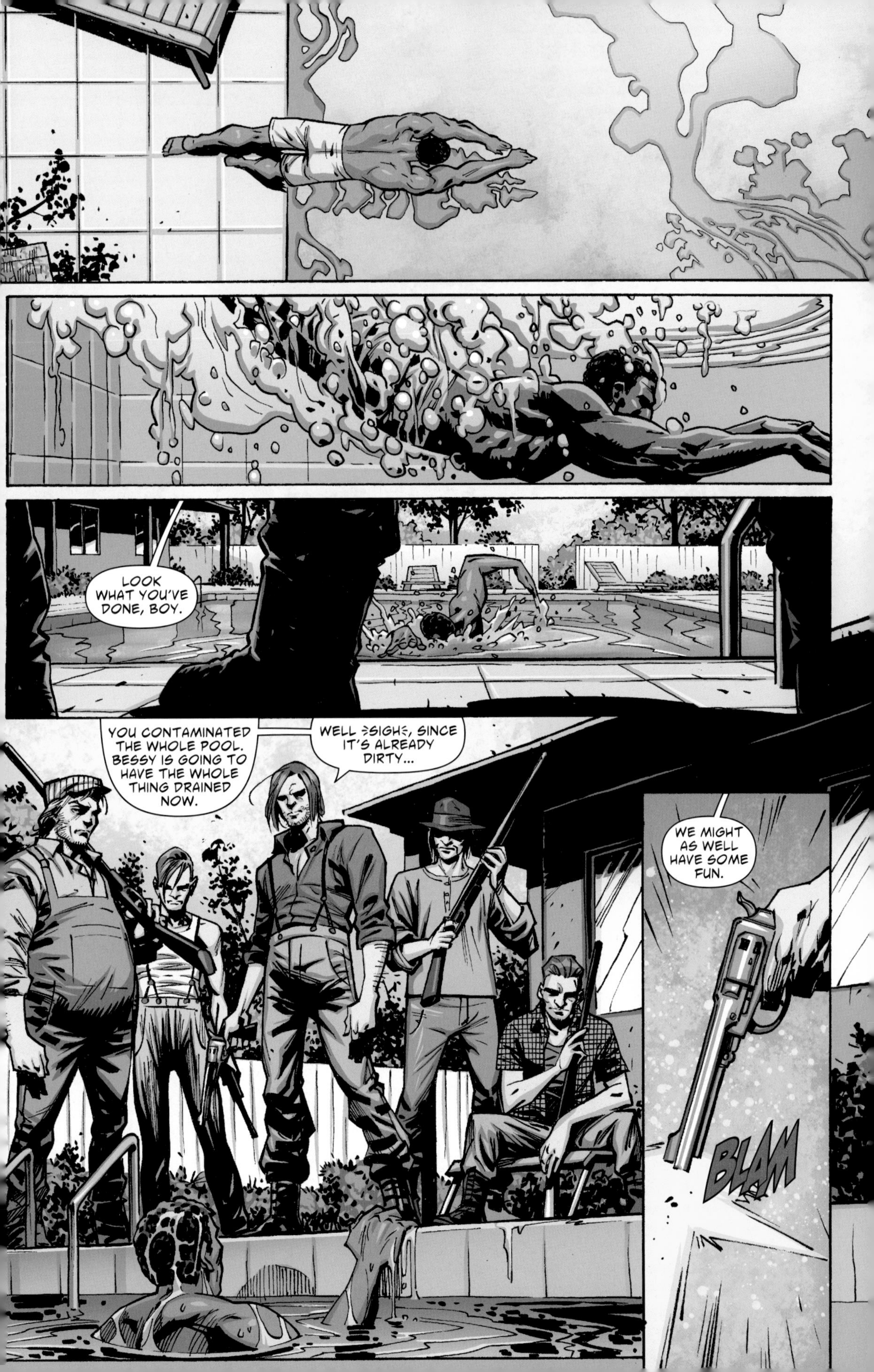
LOOK WHAT YOU'VE DONE, BOY.
YOU CONTAMINATED THE WHOLE POOL. BESSY IS GOING TO HAVE THE WHOLE THING DRAINED NOW.
WELL *SIGH*, SINCE IT'S ALREADY DIRTY...
WE MIGHT AS WELL HAVE SOME FUN.
BLAM

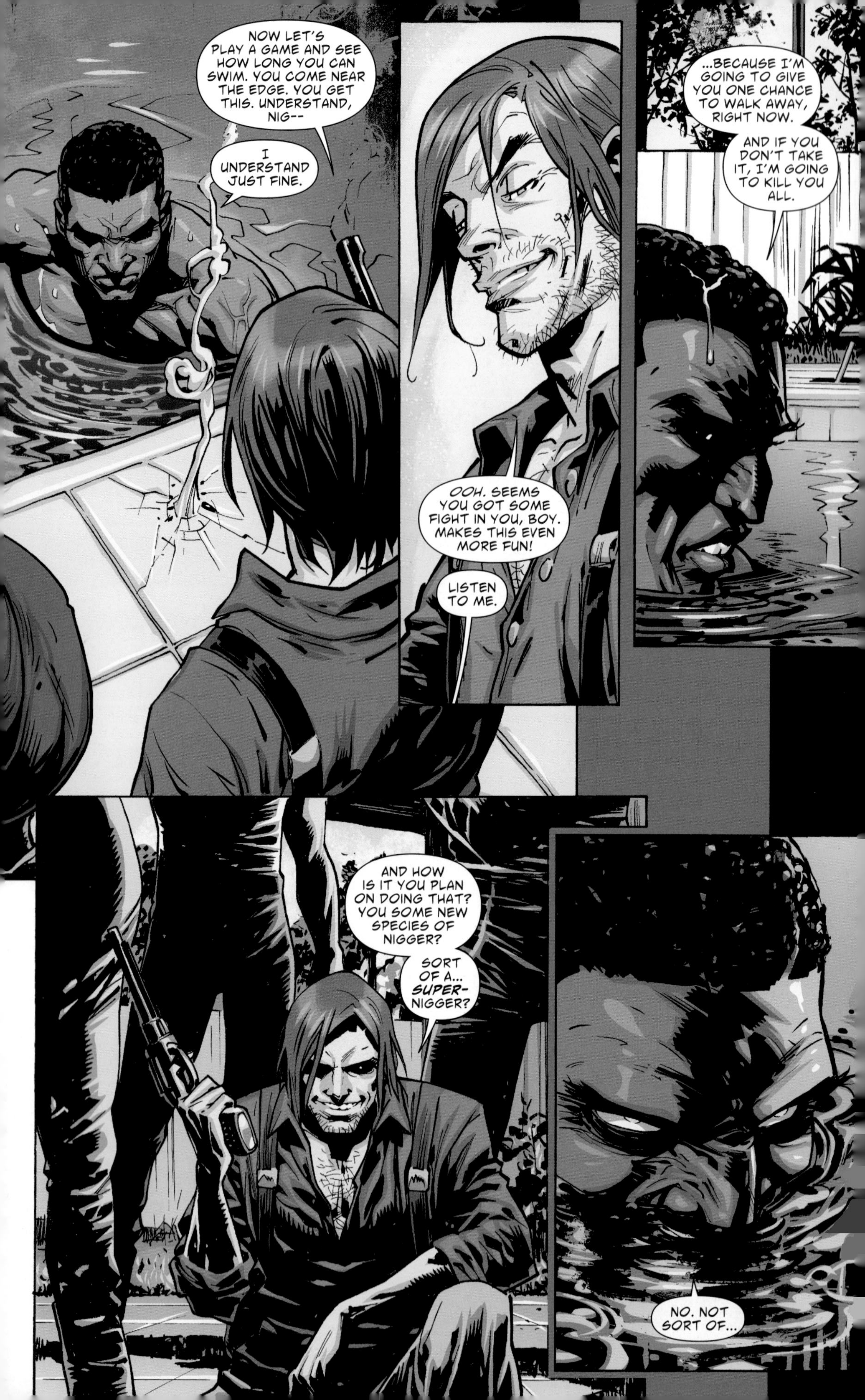
NOW LET'S PLAY A GAME AND SEE HOW LONG YOU CAN SWIM. YOU COME NEAR THE EDGE. YOU GET THIS. UNDERSTAND, NIG--
I UNDERSTAND JUST FINE.
OOH. SEEMS YOU GOT SOME FIGHT IN YOU, BOY. MAKES THIS EVEN MORE FUN!
LISTEN TO ME.
...BECAUSE I'M GOING TO GIVE YOU ONE CHANCE TO WALK AWAY, RIGHT NOW.
AND IF YOU DON'T TAKE IT, I'M GOING TO KILL YOU ALL.
AND HOW IS IT YOU PLAN ON DOING THAT? YOU SOME NEW SPECIES OF NIGGER?
SORT OF A... *SUPER*-NIGGER?
NO. NOT SORT OF...

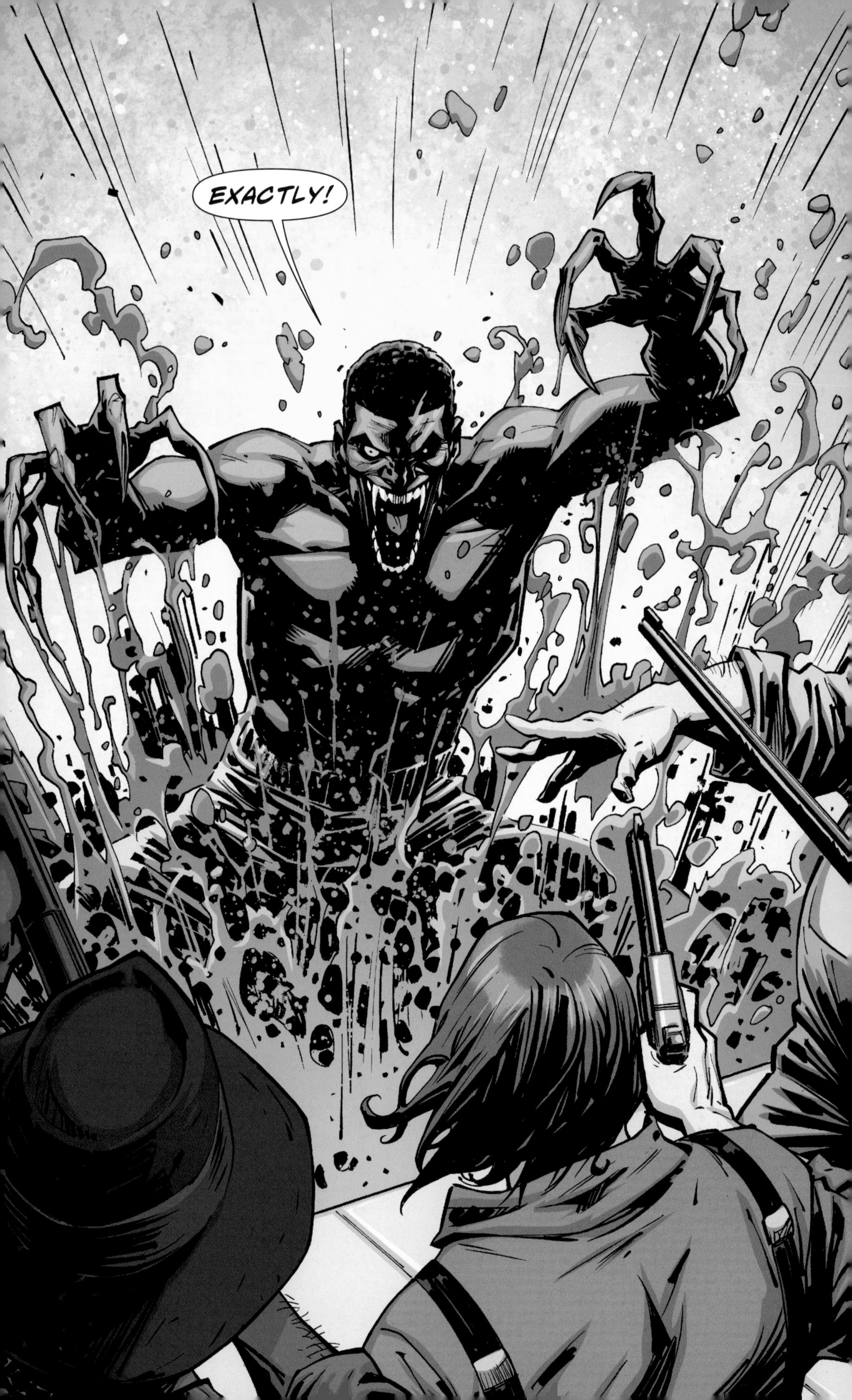
EXACTLY!

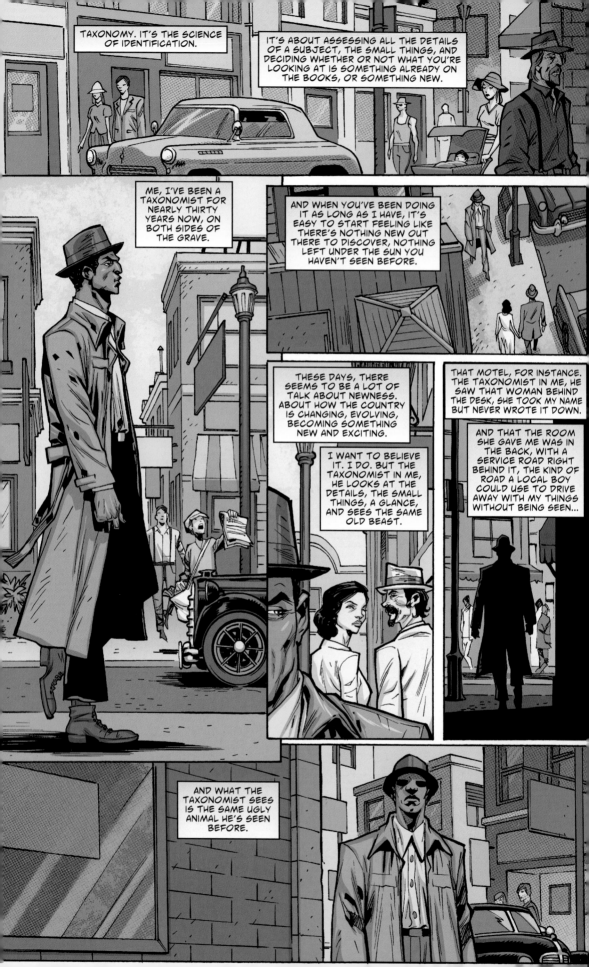

TAXONOMY. IT'S THE SCIENCE OF IDENTIFICATION.

IT'S ABOUT ASSESSING ALL THE DETAILS OF A SUBJECT, THE SMALL THINGS, AND DECIDING WHETHER OR NOT WHAT YOU'RE LOOKING AT IS SOMETHING ALREADY ON THE BOOKS, OR SOMETHING NEW.

ME, I'VE BEEN A TAXONOMIST FOR NEARLY THIRTY YEARS NOW, ON BOTH SIDES OF THE GRAVE.

AND WHEN YOU'VE BEEN DOING IT AS LONG AS I HAVE, IT'S EASY TO START FEELING LIKE THERE'S NOTHING NEW OUT THERE TO DISCOVER, NOTHING LEFT UNDER THE SUN YOU HAVEN'T SEEN BEFORE.

THESE DAYS, THERE SEEMS TO BE A LOT OF TALK ABOUT NEWNESS. ABOUT HOW THE COUNTRY IS CHANGING, EVOLVING, BECOMING SOMETHING NEW AND EXCITING.

I WANT TO BELIEVE IT. I DO. BUT THE TAXONOMIST IN ME, HE LOOKS AT THE DETAILS, THE SMALL THINGS, A GLANCE, AND SEES THE SAME OLD BEAST.

THAT MOTEL, FOR INSTANCE. THE TAXONOMIST IN ME, HE SAW THAT WOMAN BEHIND THE DESK, SHE TOOK MY NAME BUT NEVER WROTE IT DOWN.

AND THAT THE ROOM SHE GAVE ME WAS IN THE BACK, WITH A SERVICE ROAD RIGHT BEHIND IT, THE KIND OF ROAD A LOCAL BOY COULD USE TO DRIVE AWAY WITH MY THINGS WITHOUT BEING SEEN...

AND WHAT THE TAXONOMIST SEES IS THE SAME UGLY ANIMAL HE'S SEEN BEFORE.

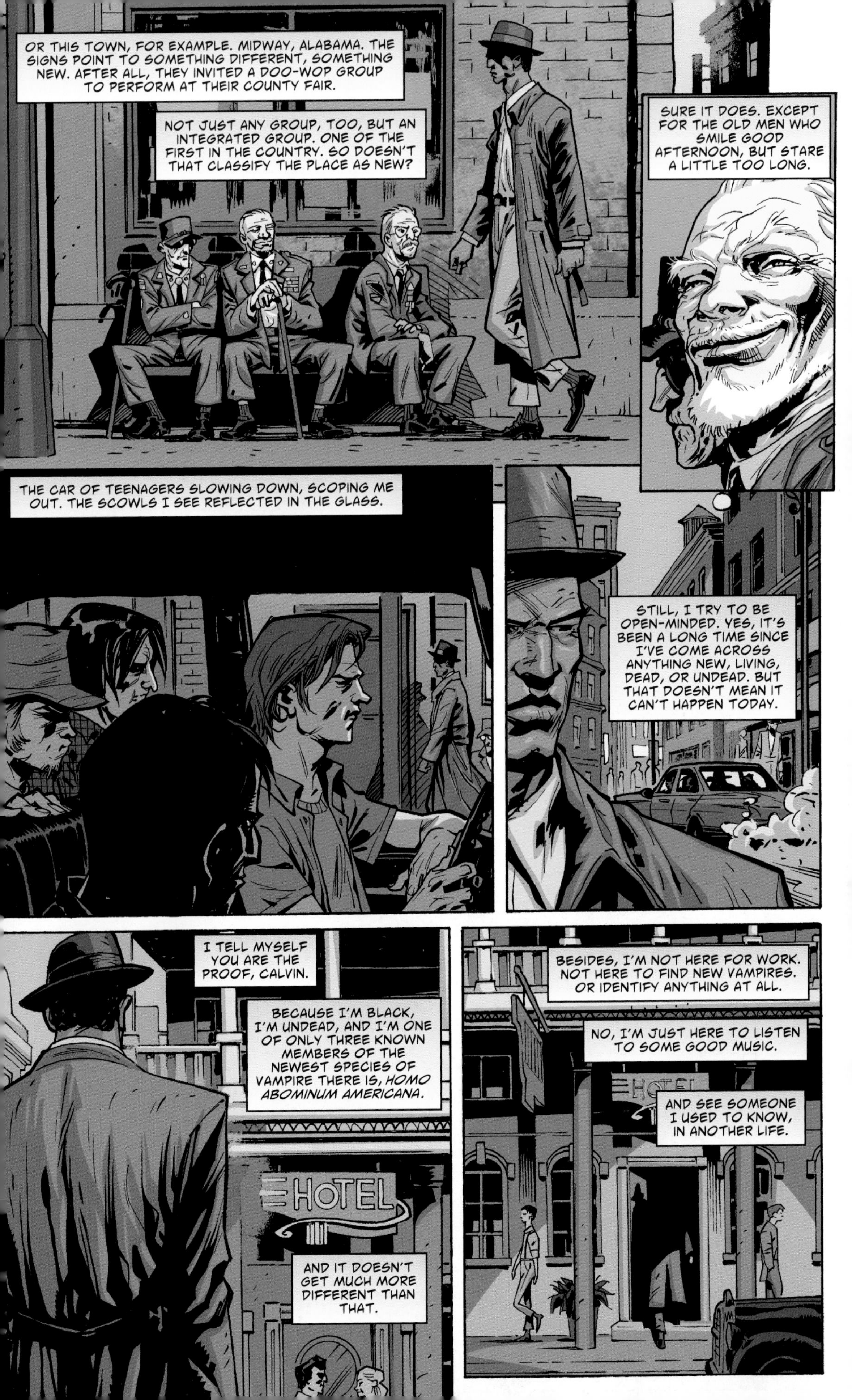
OR THIS TOWN, FOR EXAMPLE. MIDWAY, ALABAMA. THE SIGNS POINT TO SOMETHING DIFFERENT, SOMETHING NEW. AFTER ALL, THEY INVITED A DOO-WOP GROUP TO PERFORM AT THEIR COUNTY FAIR.
NOT JUST ANY GROUP, TOO, BUT AN INTEGRATED GROUP. ONE OF THE FIRST IN THE COUNTRY. SO DOESN'T THAT CLASSIFY THE PLACE AS NEW?
SURE IT DOES. EXCEPT FOR THE OLD MEN WHO SMILE GOOD AFTERNOON, BUT STARE A LITTLE TOO LONG.
THE CAR OF TEENAGERS SLOWING DOWN, SCOPING ME OUT. THE SCOWLS I SEE REFLECTED IN THE GLASS.
STILL, I TRY TO BE OPEN-MINDED. YES, IT'S BEEN A LONG TIME SINCE I'VE COME ACROSS ANYTHING NEW, LIVING, DEAD, OR UNDEAD. BUT THAT DOESN'T MEAN IT CAN'T HAPPEN TODAY.
I TELL MYSELF YOU ARE THE PROOF, CALVIN.
BECAUSE I'M BLACK, I'M UNDEAD, AND I'M ONE OF ONLY THREE KNOWN MEMBERS OF THE NEWEST SPECIES OF VAMPIRE THERE IS, *HOMO ABOMINUM AMERICANA*.
HOTEL
AND IT DOESN'T GET MUCH MORE DIFFERENT THAN THAT.
BESIDES, I'M NOT HERE FOR WORK. NOT HERE TO FIND NEW VAMPIRES. OR IDENTIFY ANYTHING AT ALL.
NO, I'M JUST HERE TO LISTEN TO SOME GOOD MUSIC.
AND SEE SOMEONE I USED TO KNOW, IN ANOTHER LIFE.

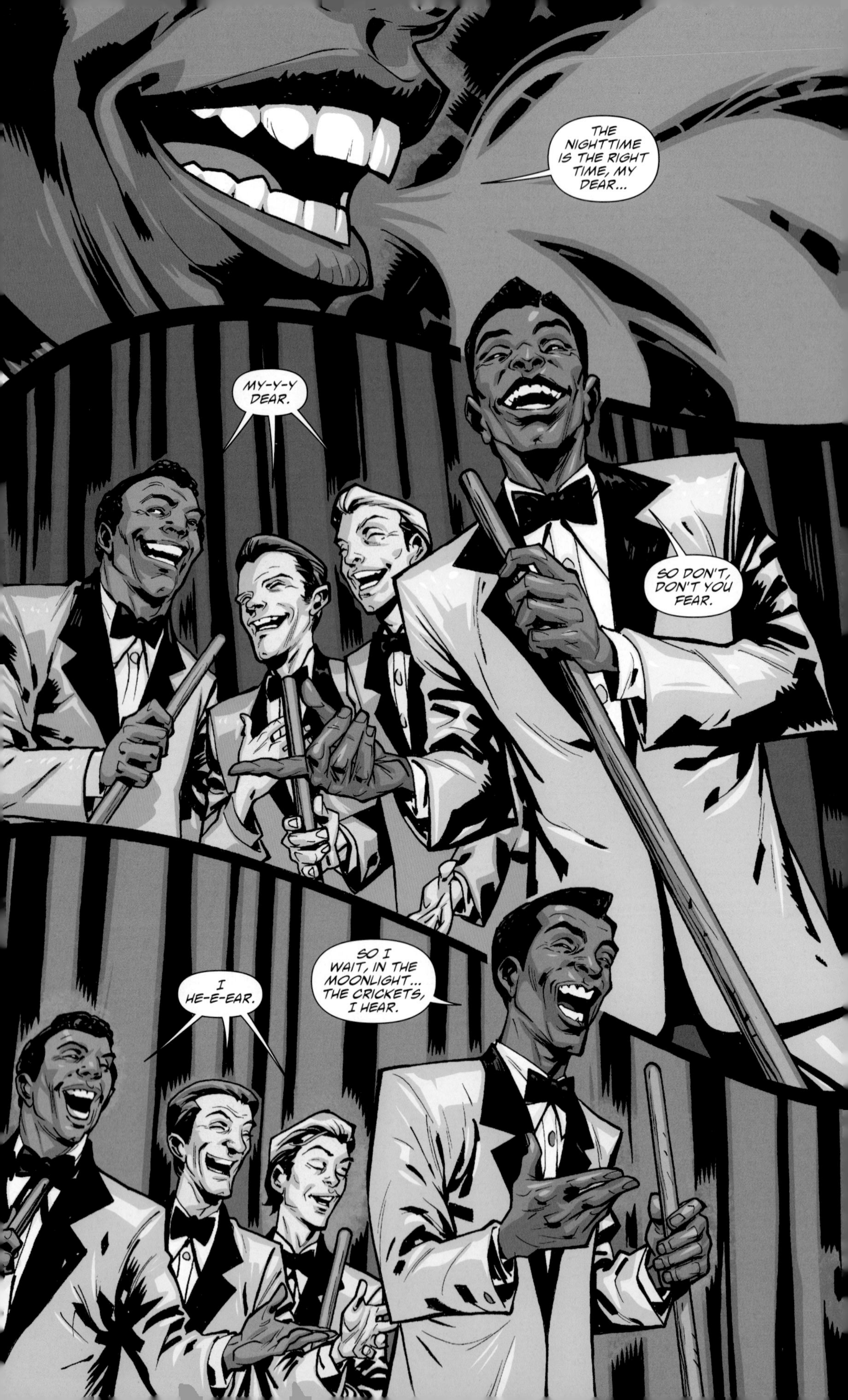
THE NIGHTTIME IS THE RIGHT TIME, MY DEAR...
MY-Y-Y DEAR.
SO DON'T, DON'T YOU FEAR.
SO I WAIT, IN THE MOONLIGHT... THE CRICKETS, I HEAR.
I HE-E-EAR.

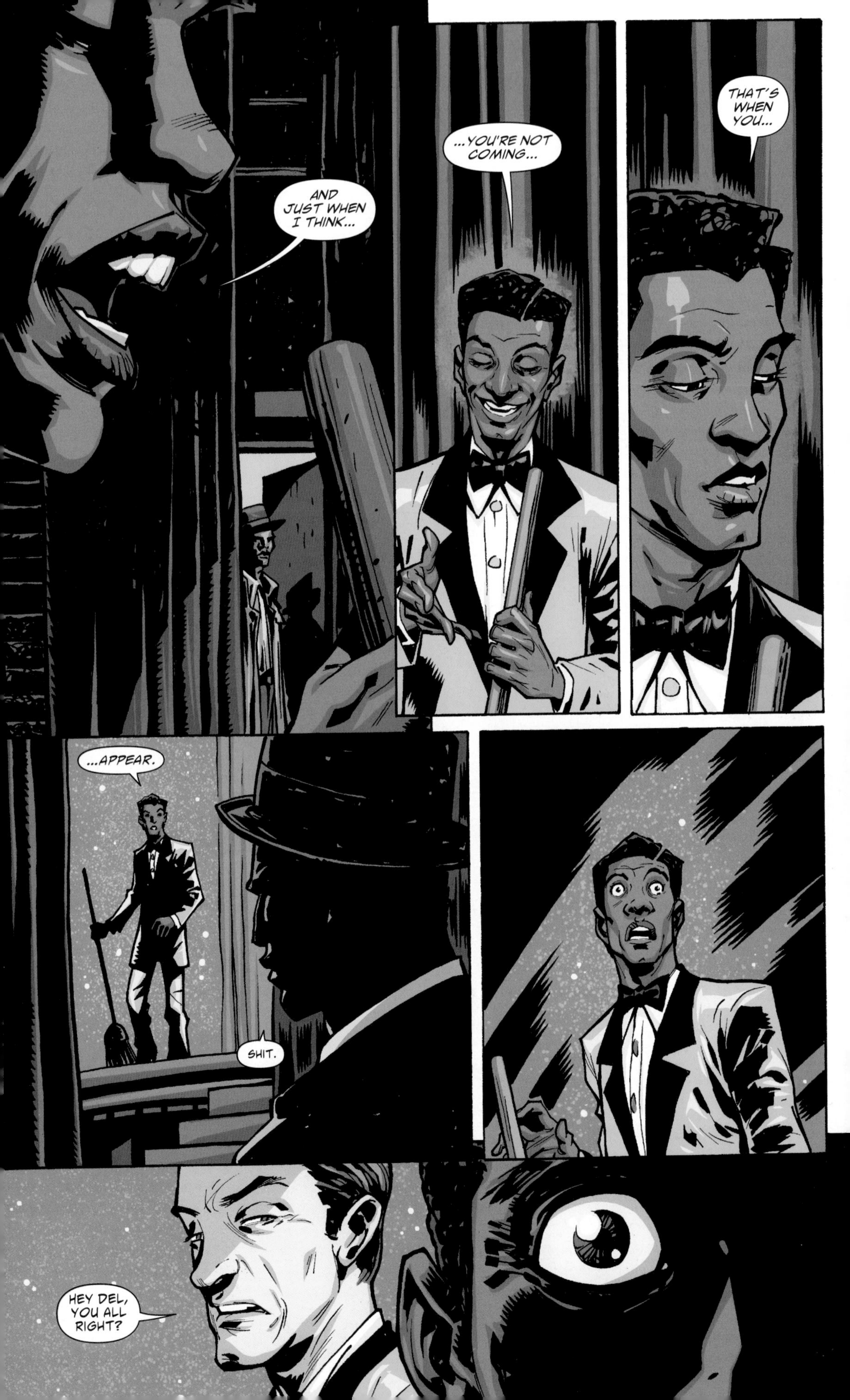
AND JUST WHEN I THINK...
...YOU'RE NOT COMING...
THAT'S WHEN YOU...
...APPEAR.
SHIT.
HEY DEL, YOU ALL RIGHT?

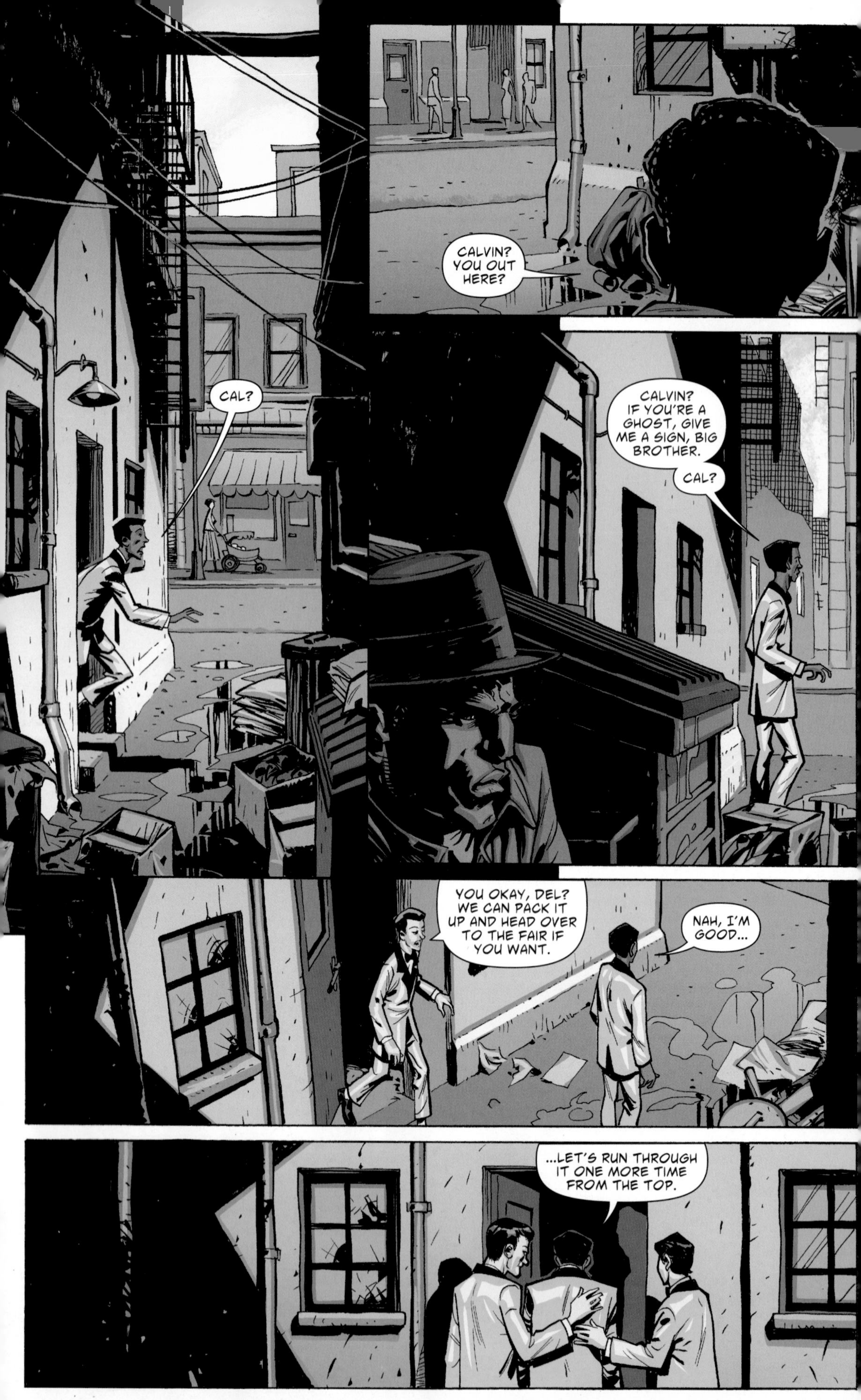
CAL?
CALVIN? YOU OUT HERE?
CALVIN? IF YOU'RE A GHOST, GIVE ME A SIGN, BIG BROTHER.
CAL?
YOU OKAY, DEL? WE CAN PACK IT UP AND HEAD OVER TO THE FAIR IF YOU WANT.
NAH, I'M GOOD...
...LET'S RUN THROUGH IT ONE MORE TIME FROM THE TOP.

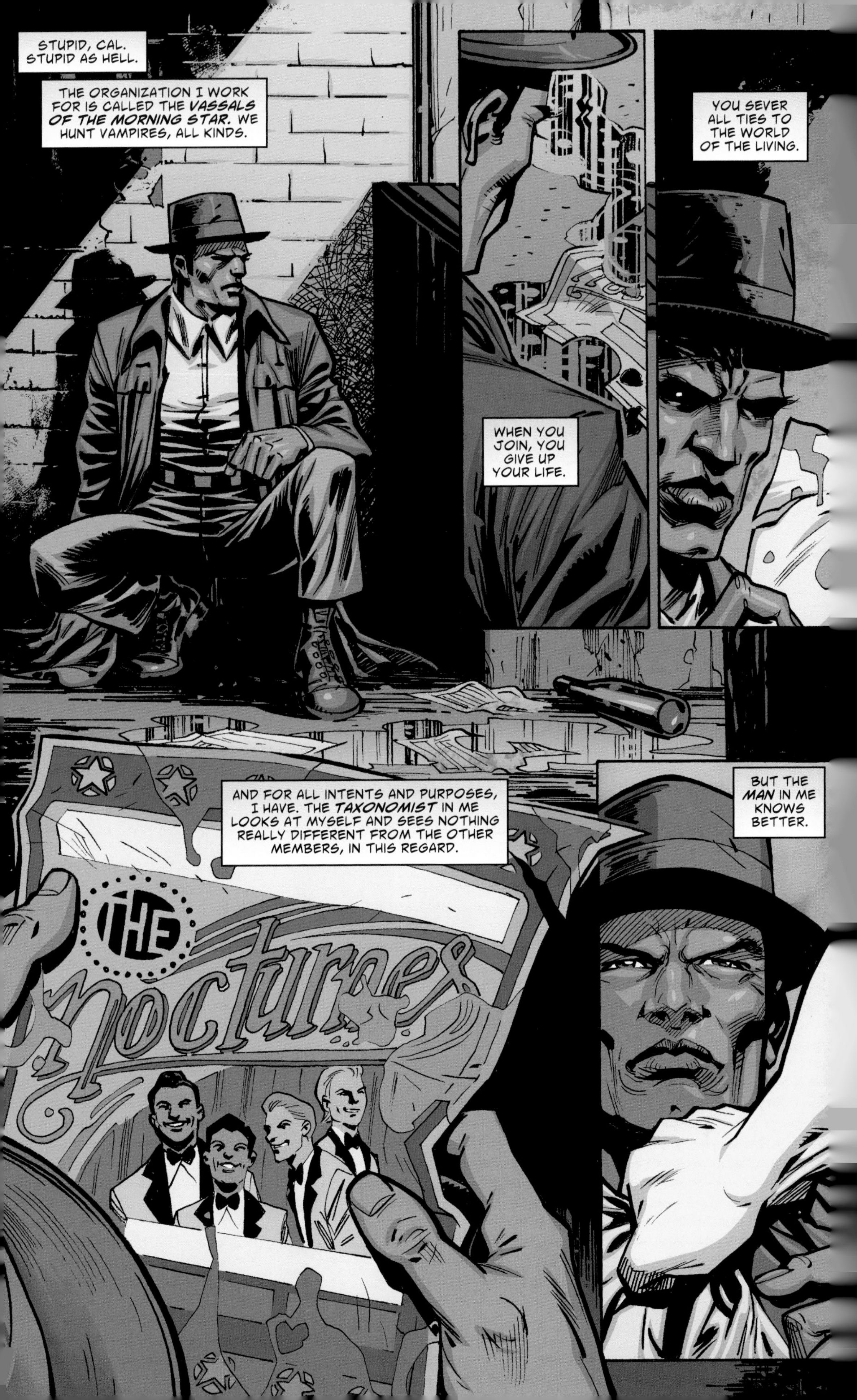

STUPID, CAL. STUPID AS HELL.
THE ORGANIZATION I WORK FOR IS CALLED THE *VASSALS OF THE MORNING STAR.* WE HUNT VAMPIRES, ALL KINDS.
WHEN YOU JOIN, YOU GIVE UP YOUR LIFE.
YOU SEVER ALL TIES TO THE WORLD OF THE LIVING.
AND FOR ALL INTENTS AND PURPOSES, I HAVE. THE *TAXONOMIST* IN ME LOOKS AT MYSELF AND SEES NOTHING REALLY DIFFERENT FROM THE OTHER MEMBERS, IN THIS REGARD.
THE Nocturnes
BUT THE *MAN* IN ME KNOWS BETTER.

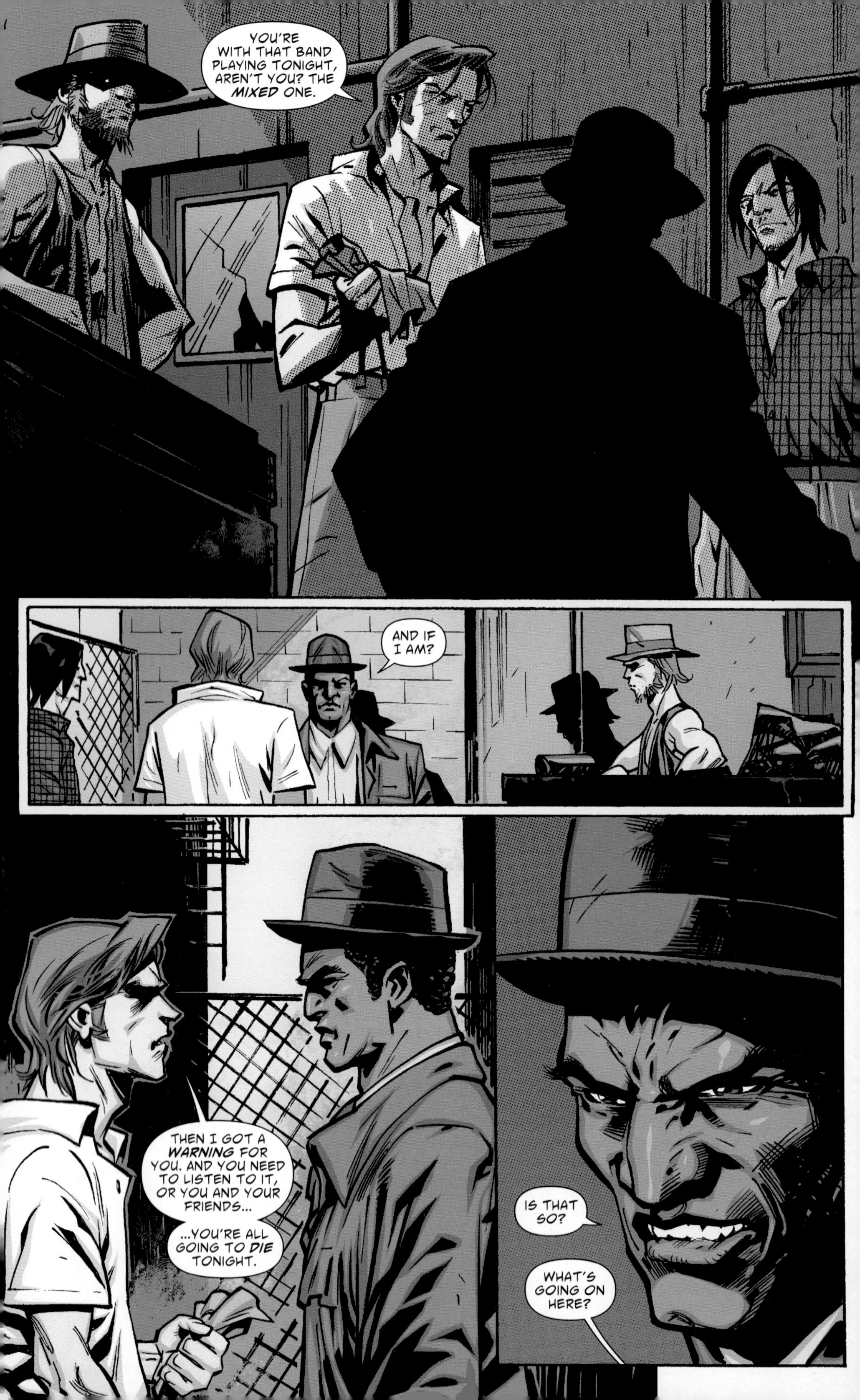
YOU'RE WITH THAT BAND PLAYING TONIGHT, AREN'T YOU? THE *MIXED* ONE.
AND IF I AM?
THEN I GOT A *WARNING* FOR YOU. AND YOU NEED TO LISTEN TO IT, OR YOU AND YOUR FRIENDS...
...YOU'RE ALL GOING TO *DIE* TONIGHT.
IS THAT SO?
WHAT'S GOING ON HERE?

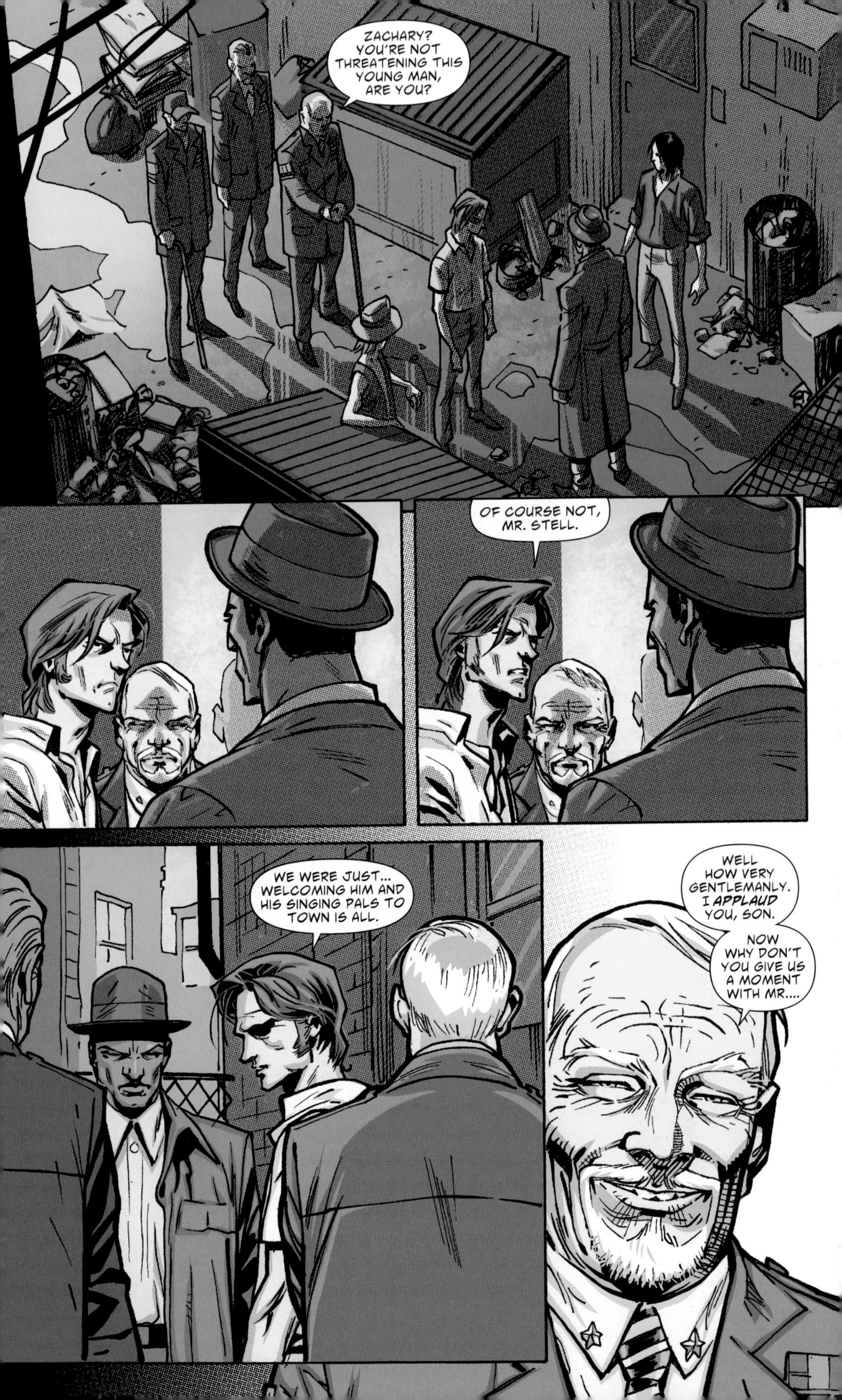
ZACHARY? YOU'RE NOT THREATENING THIS YOUNG MAN, ARE YOU?
OF COURSE NOT, MR. STELL.
WE WERE JUST... WELCOMING HIM AND HIS SINGING PALS TO TOWN IS ALL.
WELL HOW VERY GENTLEMANLY. I *APPLAUD* YOU, SON.
NOW WHY DON'T YOU GIVE US A MOMENT WITH MR....

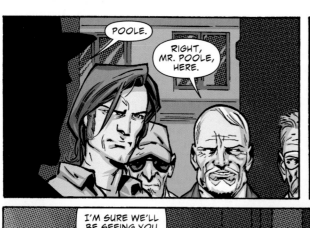

POOLE.

RIGHT, MR. POOLE, HERE.

I'M WARNING YOU TO--

ZACHARY?

I'M SURE WE'LL BE SEEING YOU ALL AT THE FAIR TONIGHT, ANYHOW.

YOU DIDN'T NEED TO DO THAT.

OF COURSE NOT. BUT WE LOOK OUT FOR OUR *OWN.*

YOUR "OWN"?

STARTS WITH A "V"...?

A VAM--

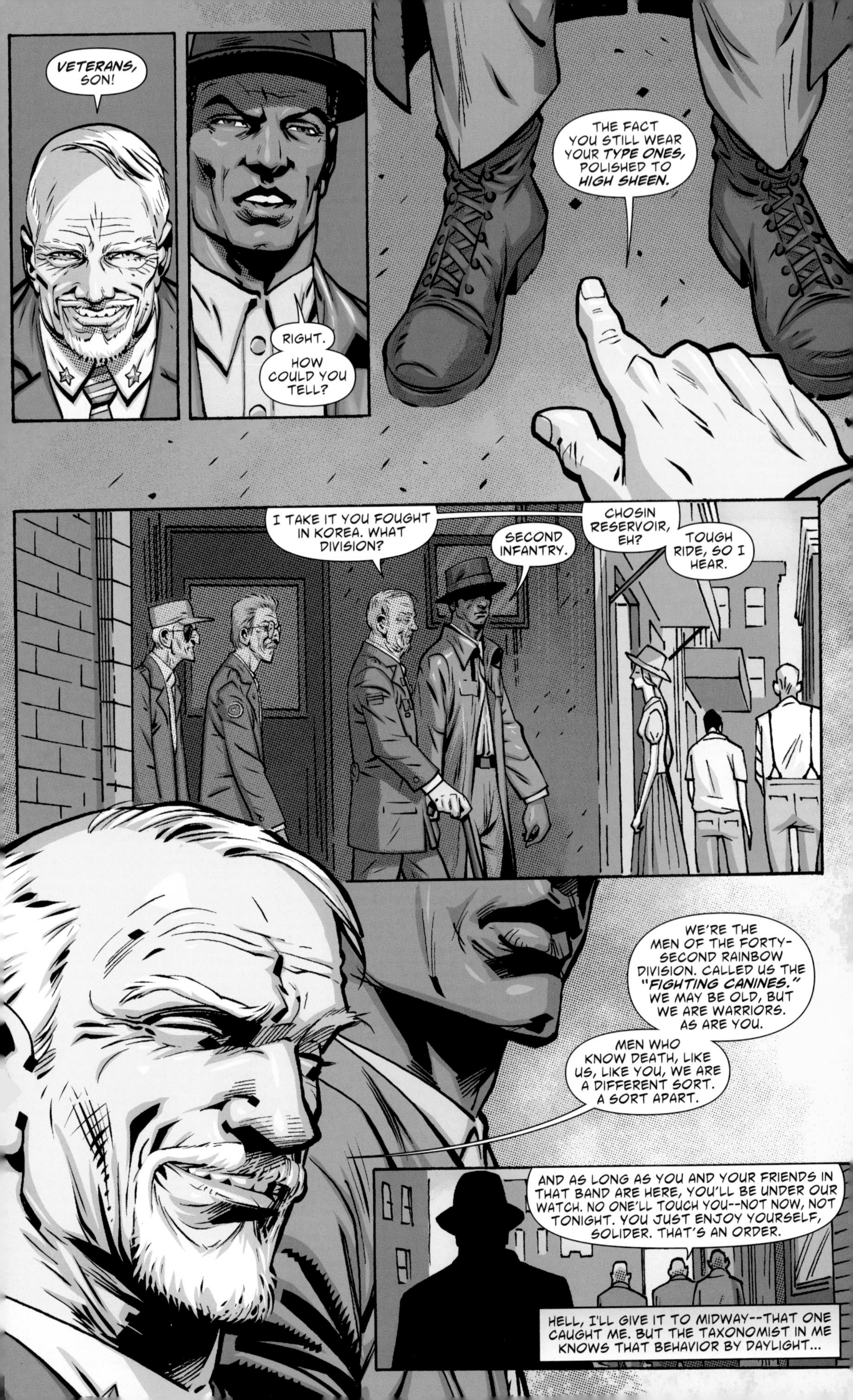
VETERANS, SON!
RIGHT.
HOW COULD YOU TELL?
THE FACT YOU STILL WEAR YOUR TYPE ONES, POLISHED TO HIGH SHEEN.
I TAKE IT YOU FOUGHT IN KOREA. WHAT DIVISION?
SECOND INFANTRY.
CHOSIN RESERVOIR, EH?
TOUGH RIDE, SO I HEAR.
WE'RE THE MEN OF THE FORTY-SECOND RAINBOW DIVISION. CALLED US THE "FIGHTING CANINES." WE MAY BE OLD, BUT WE ARE WARRIORS. AS ARE YOU.
MEN WHO KNOW DEATH, LIKE US, LIKE YOU, WE ARE A DIFFERENT SORT. A SORT APART.
AND AS LONG AS YOU AND YOUR FRIENDS IN THAT BAND ARE HERE, YOU'LL BE UNDER OUR WATCH. NO ONE'LL TOUCH YOU--NOT NOW, NOT TONIGHT. YOU JUST ENJOY YOURSELF, SOLIDER. THAT'S AN ORDER.
HELL, I'LL GIVE IT TO MIDWAY--THAT ONE CAUGHT ME. BUT THE TAXONOMIST IN ME KNOWS THAT BEHAVIOR BY DAYLIGHT...

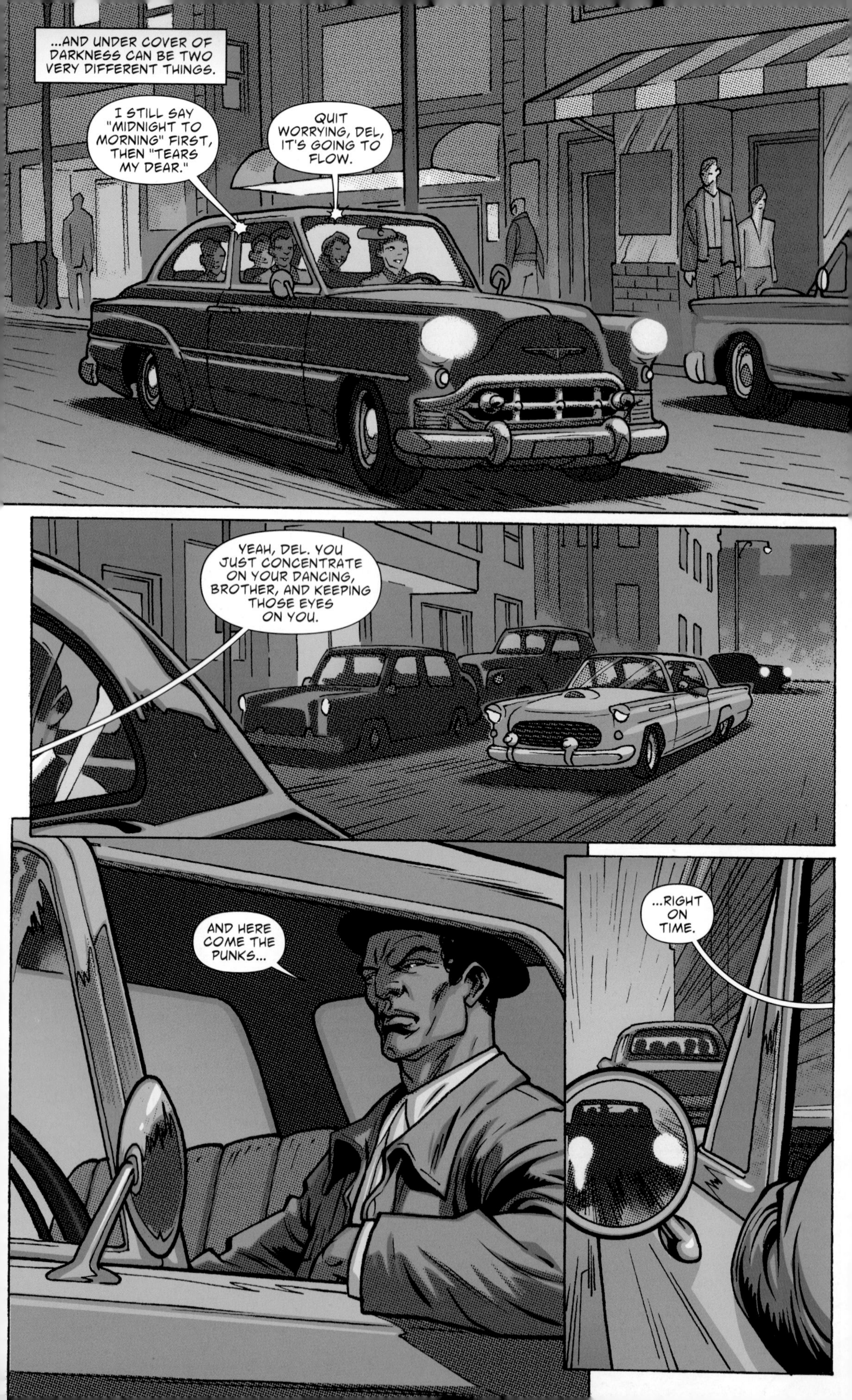
...AND UNDER COVER OF DARKNESS CAN BE TWO VERY DIFFERENT THINGS.
I STILL SAY "MIDNIGHT TO MORNING" FIRST, THEN "TEARS MY DEAR."
QUIT WORRYING, DEL, IT'S GOING TO FLOW.
YEAH, DEL. YOU JUST CONCENTRATE ON YOUR DANCING, BROTHER, AND KEEPING THOSE EYES ON YOU.
AND HERE COME THE PUNKS...
...RIGHT ON TIME.

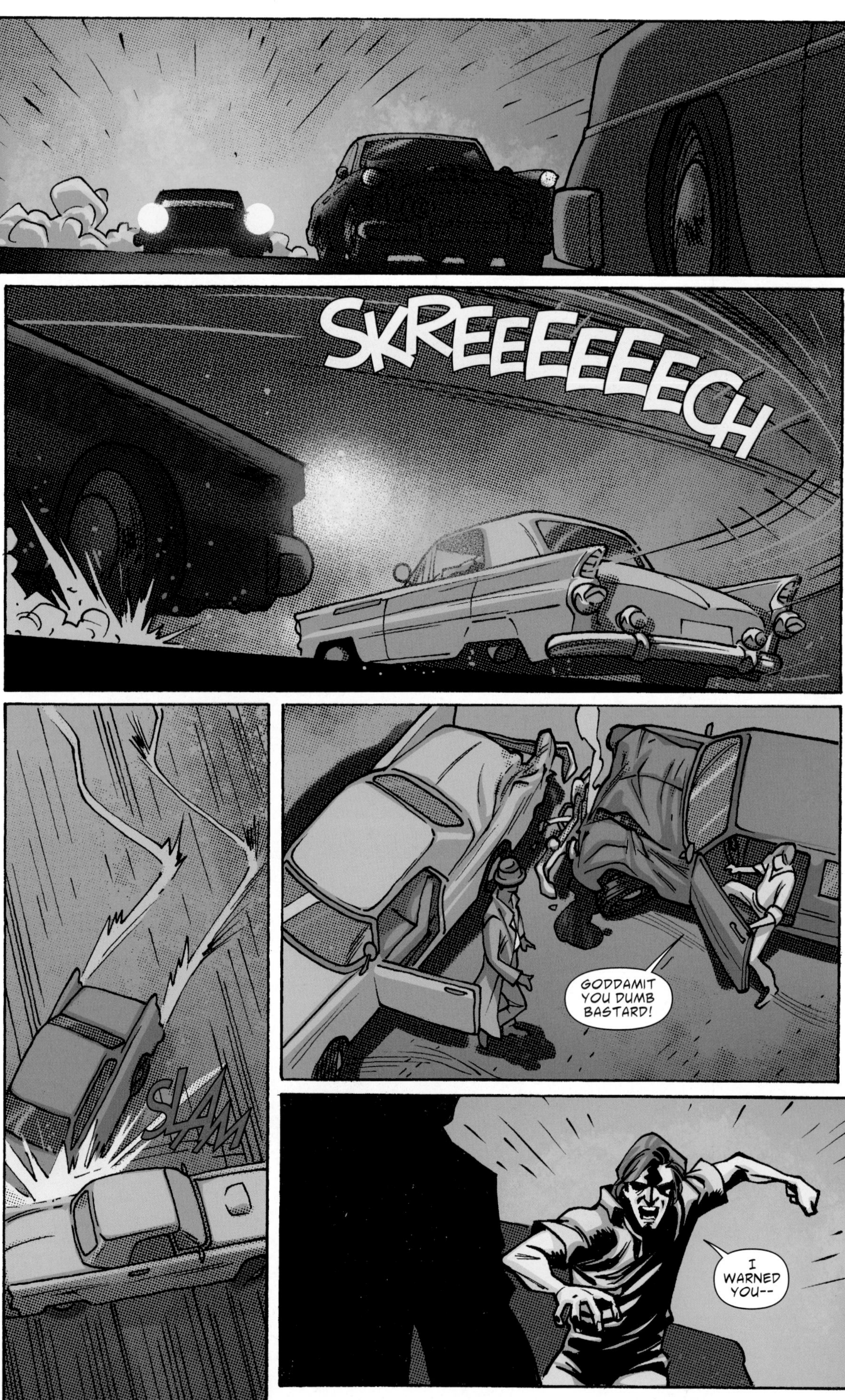
SKREEEEEEECH
SLAM
GODDAMIT YOU DUMB BASTARD!
I WARNED YOU--

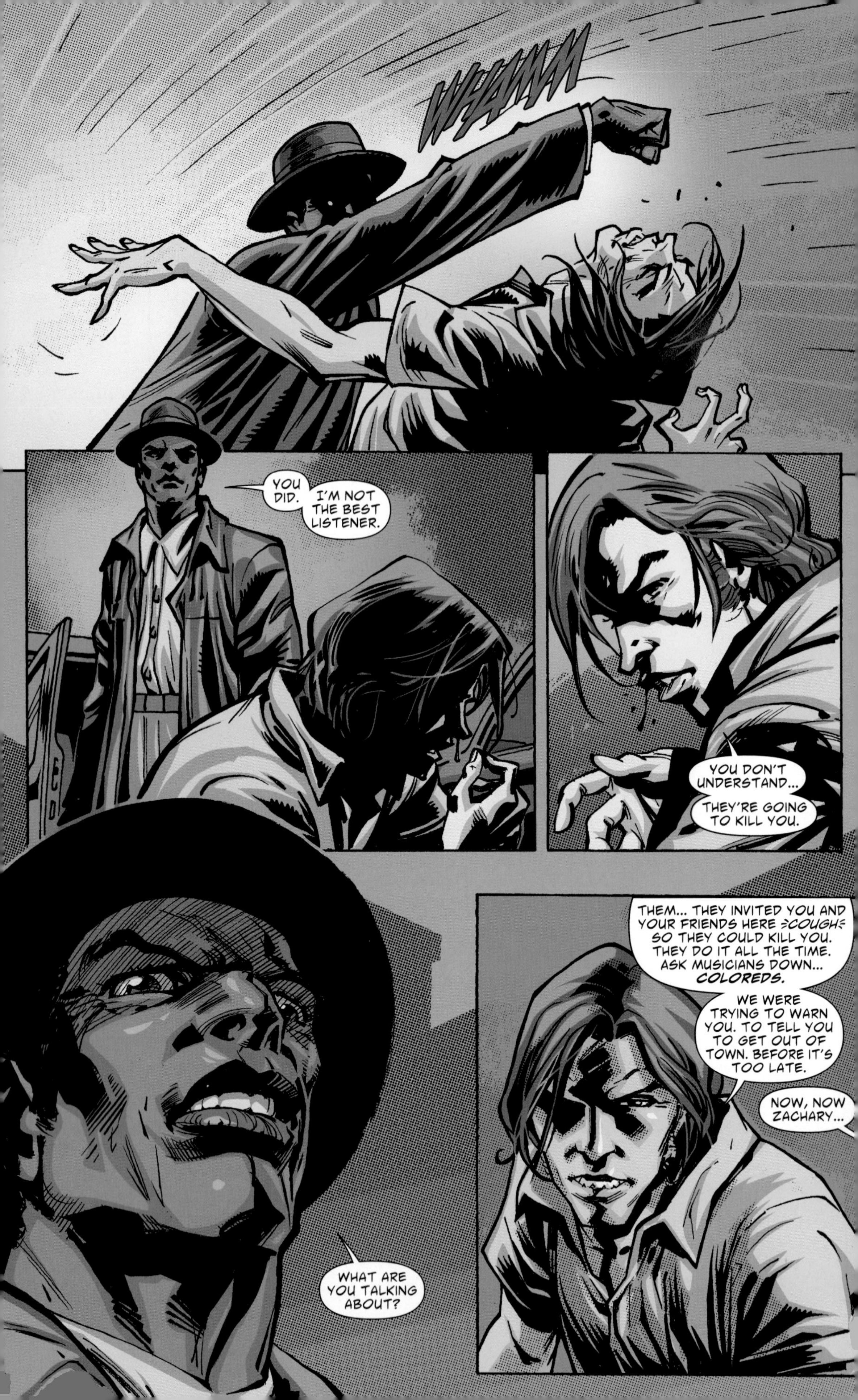
WHAMM
YOU DID.
I'M NOT THE BEST LISTENER.
YOU DON'T UNDERSTAND...
THEY'RE GOING TO KILL YOU.
WHAT ARE YOU TALKING ABOUT?
THEM... THEY INVITED YOU AND YOUR FRIENDS HERE *COUGH* SO THEY COULD KILL YOU. THEY DO IT ALL THE TIME. ASK MUSICIANS DOWN... **COLOREDS.**
WE WERE TRYING TO WARN YOU. TO TELL YOU TO GET OUT OF TOWN. BEFORE IT'S TOO LATE.
NOW, NOW ZACHARY...

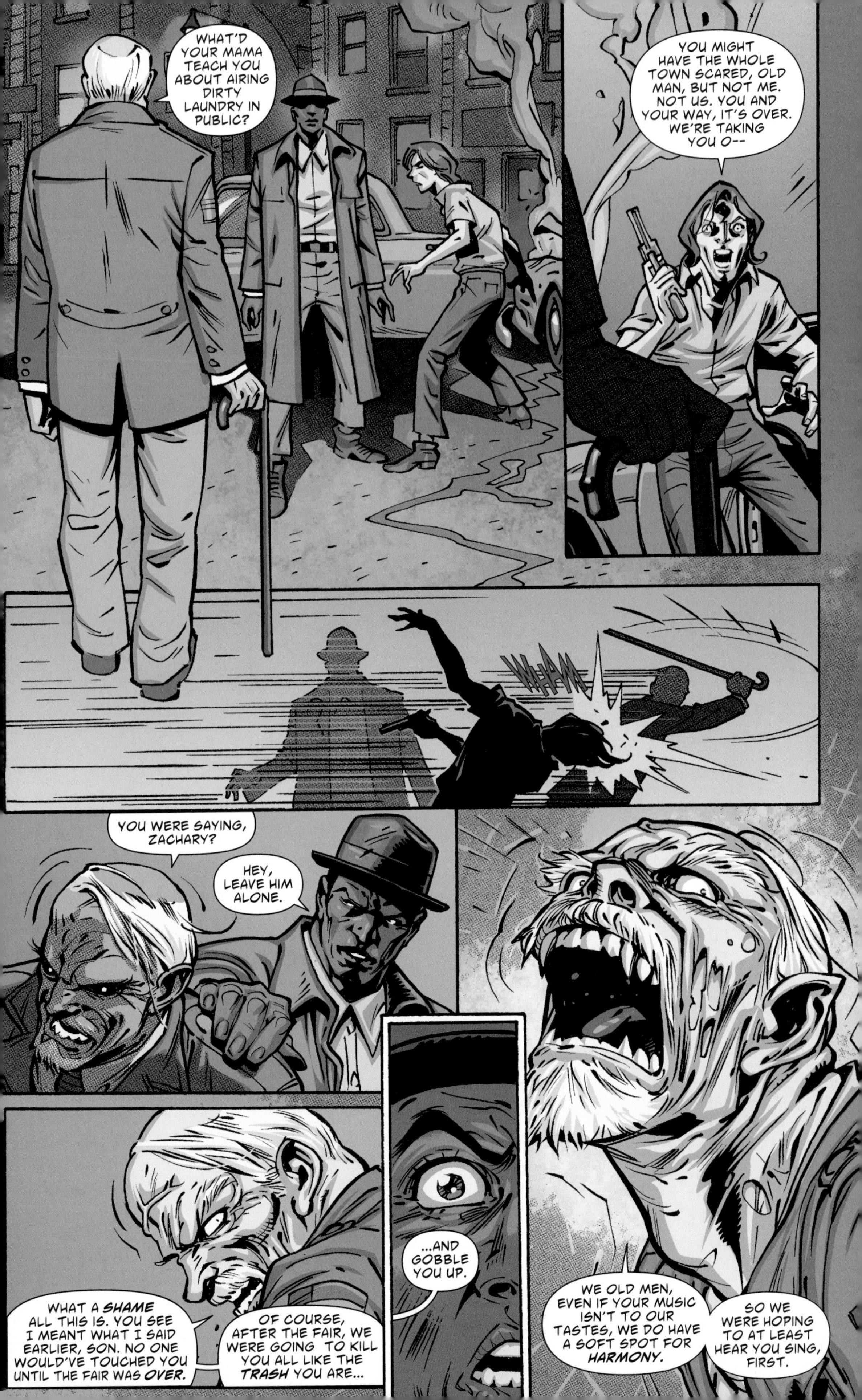
WHAT'D YOUR MAMA TEACH YOU ABOUT AIRING DIRTY LAUNDRY IN PUBLIC?
YOU MIGHT HAVE THE WHOLE TOWN SCARED, OLD MAN, BUT NOT ME. NOT US. YOU AND YOUR WAY, IT'S OVER. WE'RE TAKING YOU O--
WHAM
YOU WERE SAYING, ZACHARY?
HEY, LEAVE HIM ALONE.
WHAT A SHAME ALL THIS IS. YOU SEE I MEANT WHAT I SAID EARLIER, SON. NO ONE WOULD'VE TOUCHED YOU UNTIL THE FAIR WAS OVER.
OF COURSE, AFTER THE FAIR, WE WERE GOING TO KILL YOU ALL LIKE THE TRASH YOU ARE...
...AND GOBBLE YOU UP.
WE OLD MEN, EVEN IF YOUR MUSIC ISN'T TO OUR TASTES, WE DO HAVE A SOFT SPOT FOR HARMONY.
SO WE WERE HOPING TO AT LEAST HEAR YOU SING, FIRST.

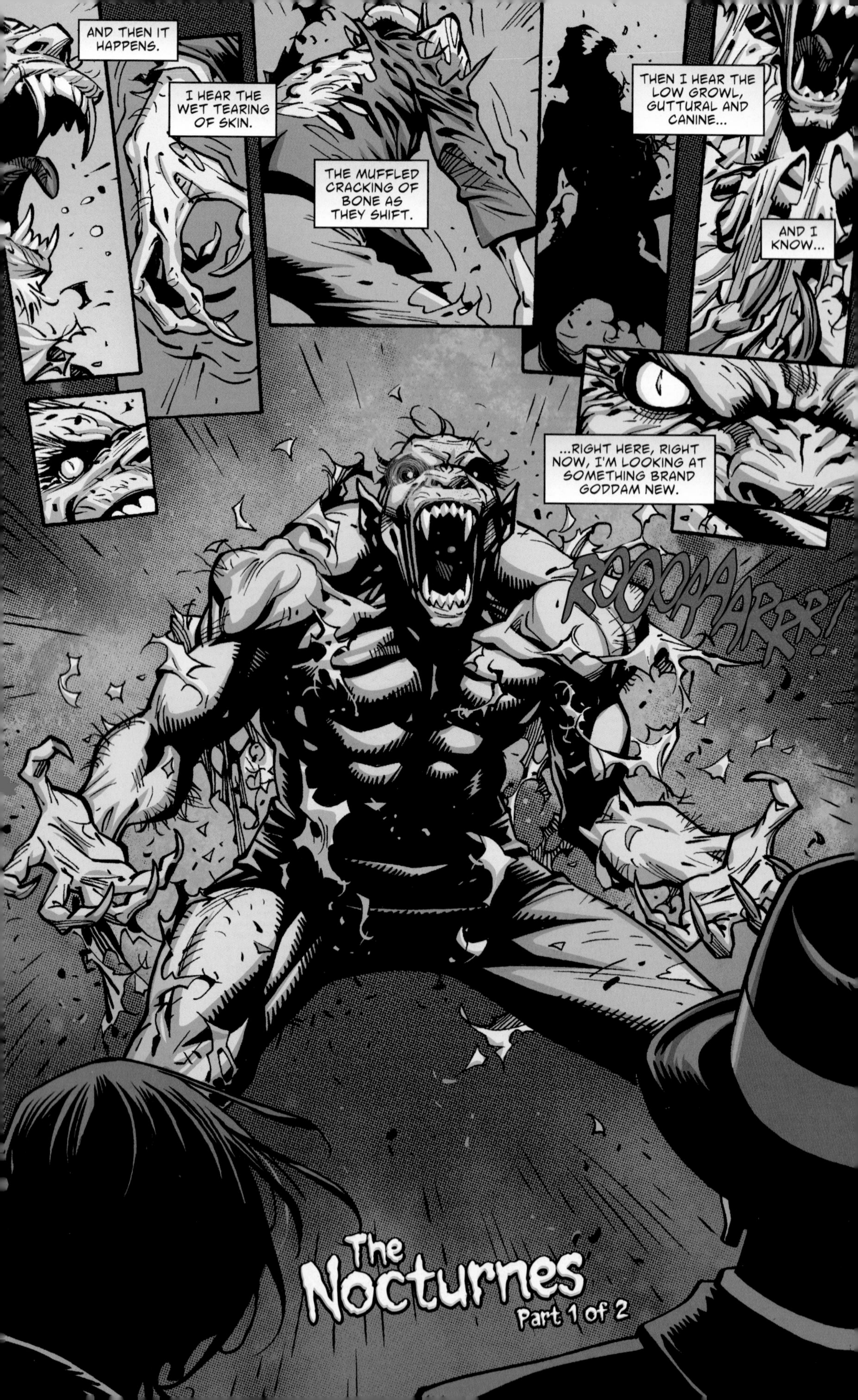
AND THEN IT HAPPENS.
I HEAR THE WET TEARING OF SKIN.
THE MUFFLED CRACKING OF BONE AS THEY SHIFT.
THEN I HEAR THE LOW GROWL, GUTTURAL AND CANINE...
AND I KNOW...
...RIGHT HERE, RIGHT NOW, I'M LOOKING AT SOMETHING BRAND GODDAM NEW.
ROOOAAARRR!
The Nocturnes
Part 1 of 2

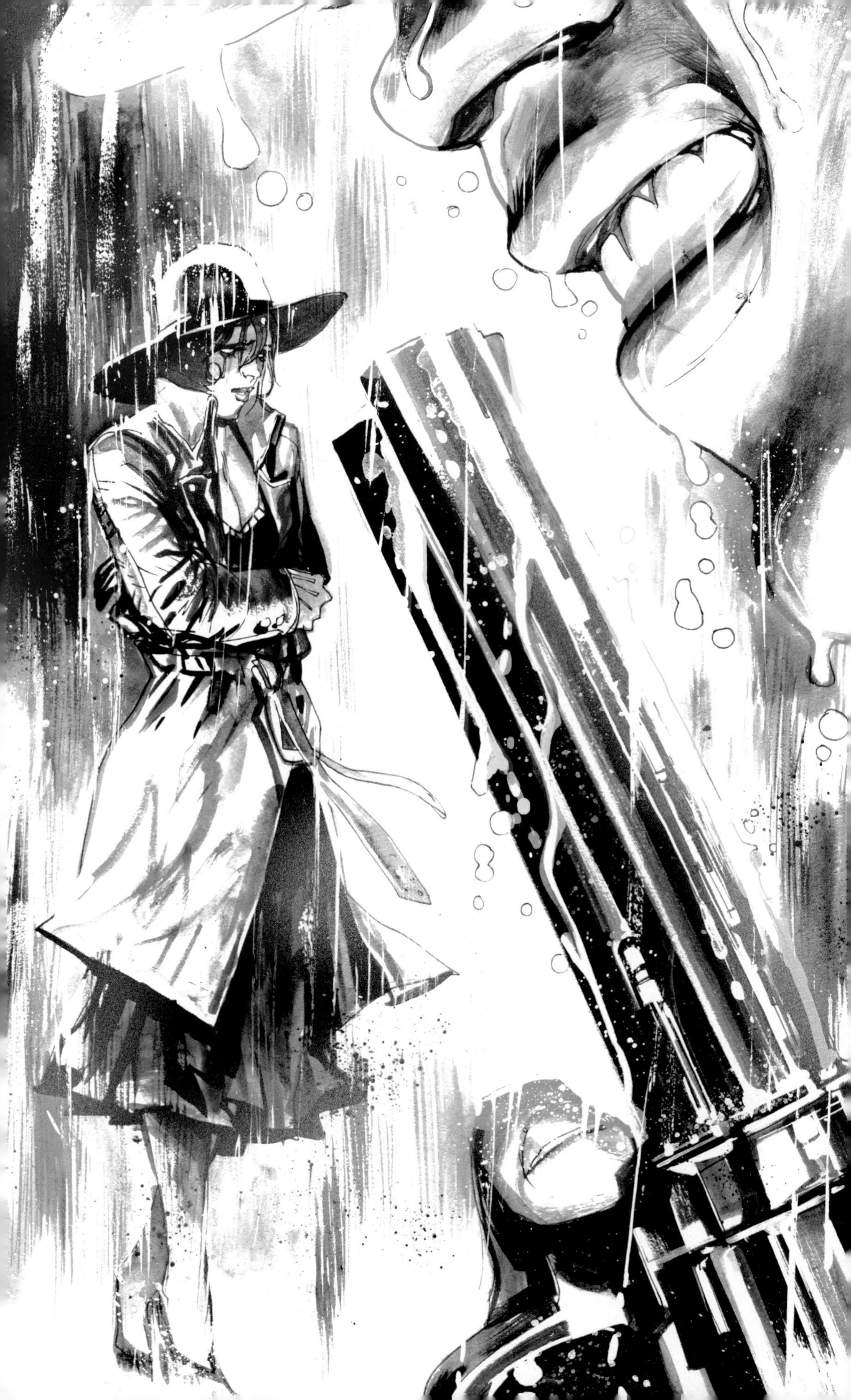

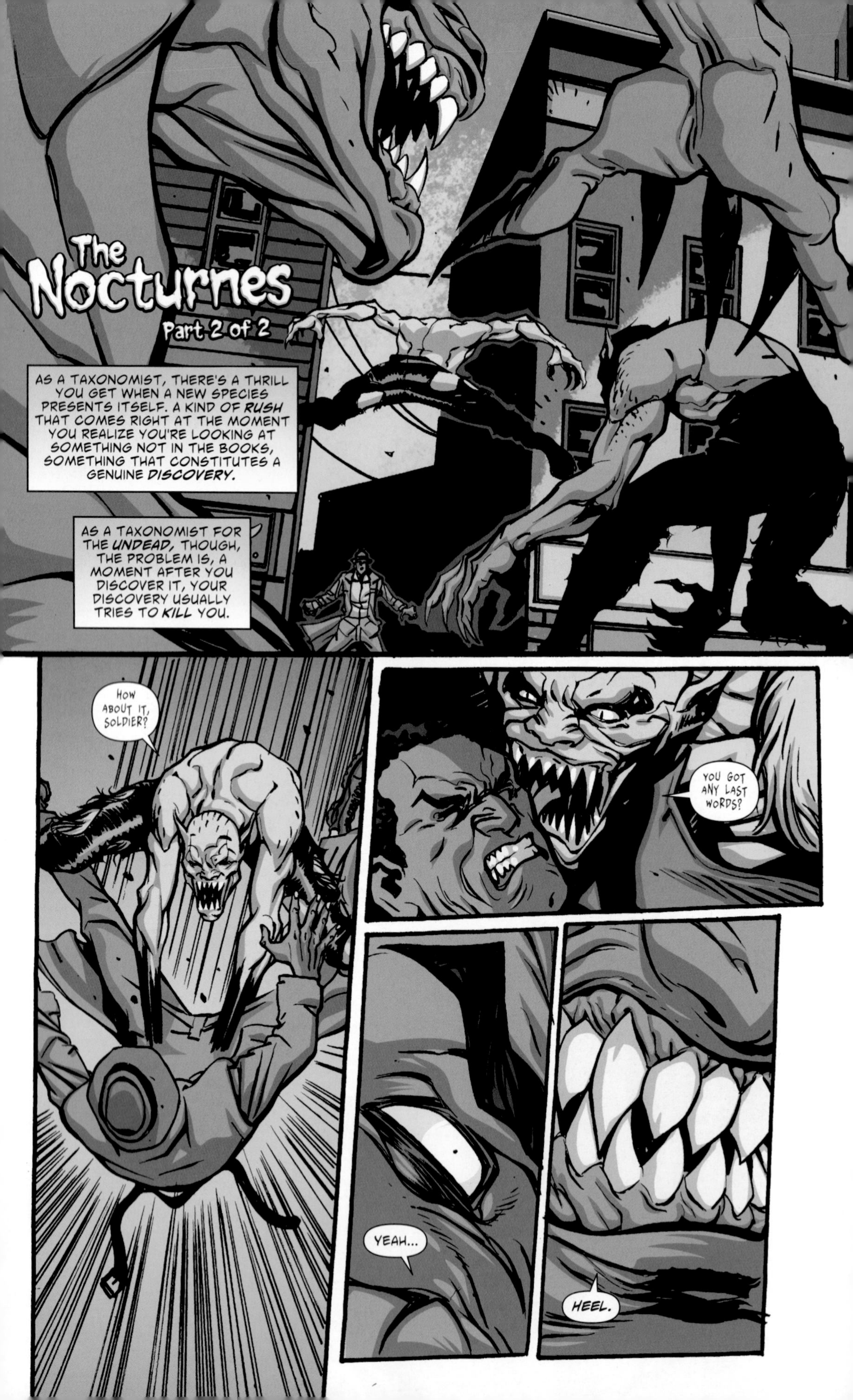
The Nocturnes
Part 2 of 2
AS A TAXONOMIST, THERE'S A THRILL YOU GET WHEN A NEW SPECIES PRESENTS ITSELF. A KIND OF RUSH THAT COMES RIGHT AT THE MOMENT YOU REALIZE YOU'RE LOOKING AT SOMETHING NOT IN THE BOOKS, SOMETHING THAT CONSTITUTES A GENUINE DISCOVERY.
AS A TAXONOMIST FOR THE UNDEAD, THOUGH, THE PROBLEM IS, A MOMENT AFTER YOU DISCOVER IT, YOUR DISCOVERY USUALLY TRIES TO KILL YOU.
HOW ABOUT IT, SOLDIER?
YOU GOT ANY LAST WORDS?
YEAH...
HEEL.

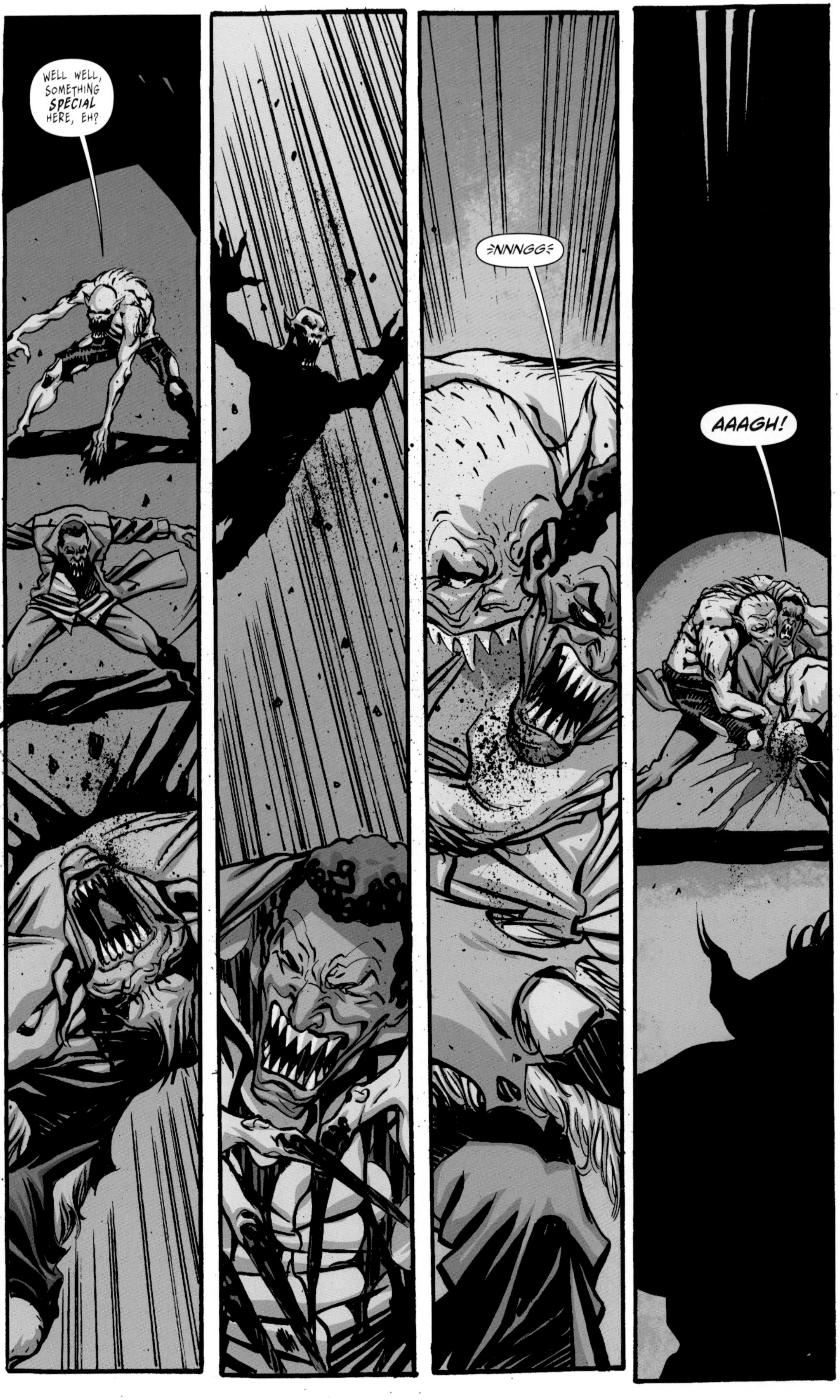
WELL WELL, SOMETHING SPECIAL HERE, EH?
NNNGG
AAAGH!

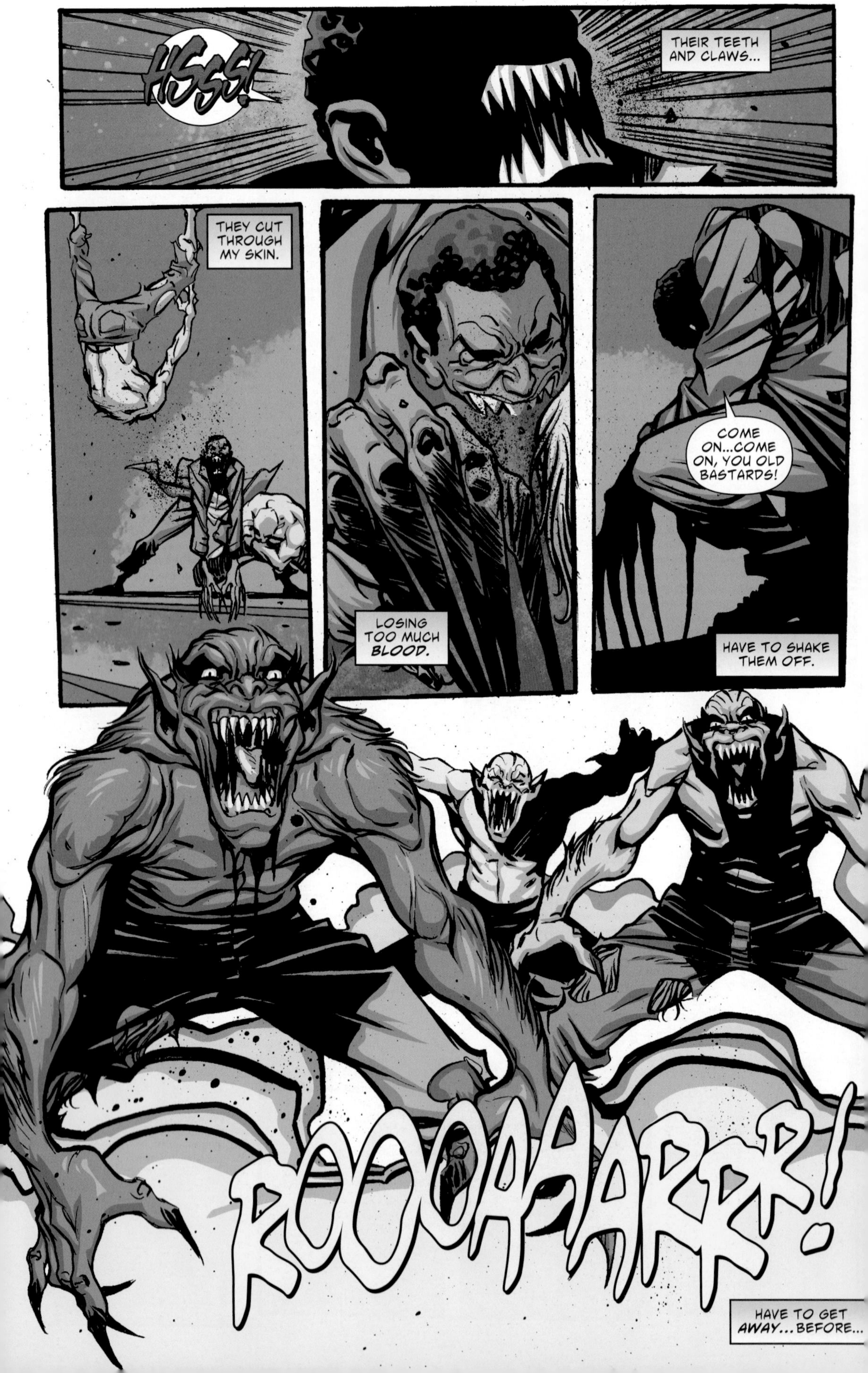
HSSS!
THEIR TEETH AND CLAWS...
THEY CUT THROUGH MY SKIN.
LOSING TOO MUCH *BLOOD.*
COME ON...COME ON, YOU OLD BASTARDS!
HAVE TO SHAKE THEM OFF.
ROOOAAARRR!
HAVE TO GET *AWAY*... BEFORE...

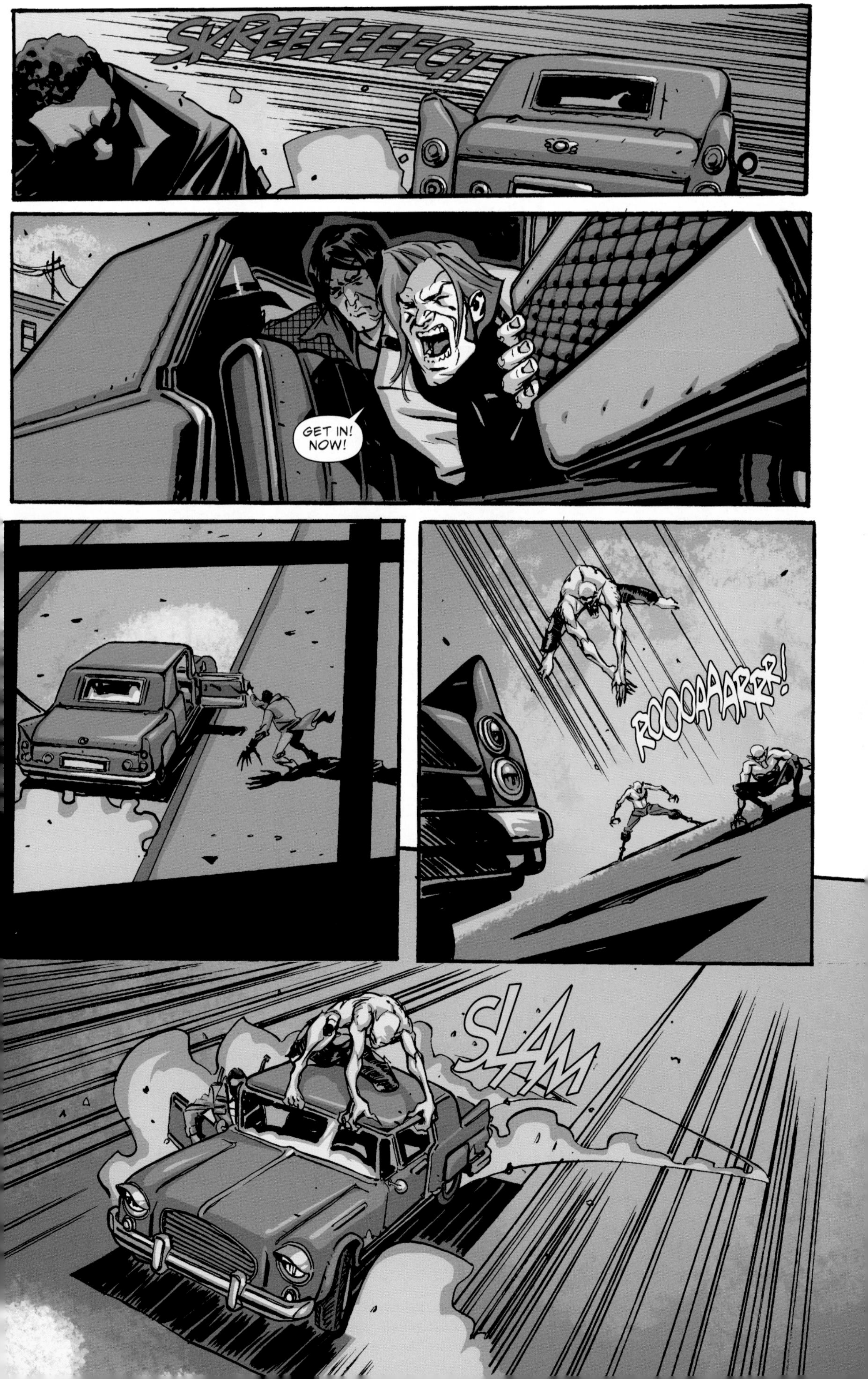
SKREEEEEEEECH
GET IN! NOW!
ROOOAAARRR!
SLAM

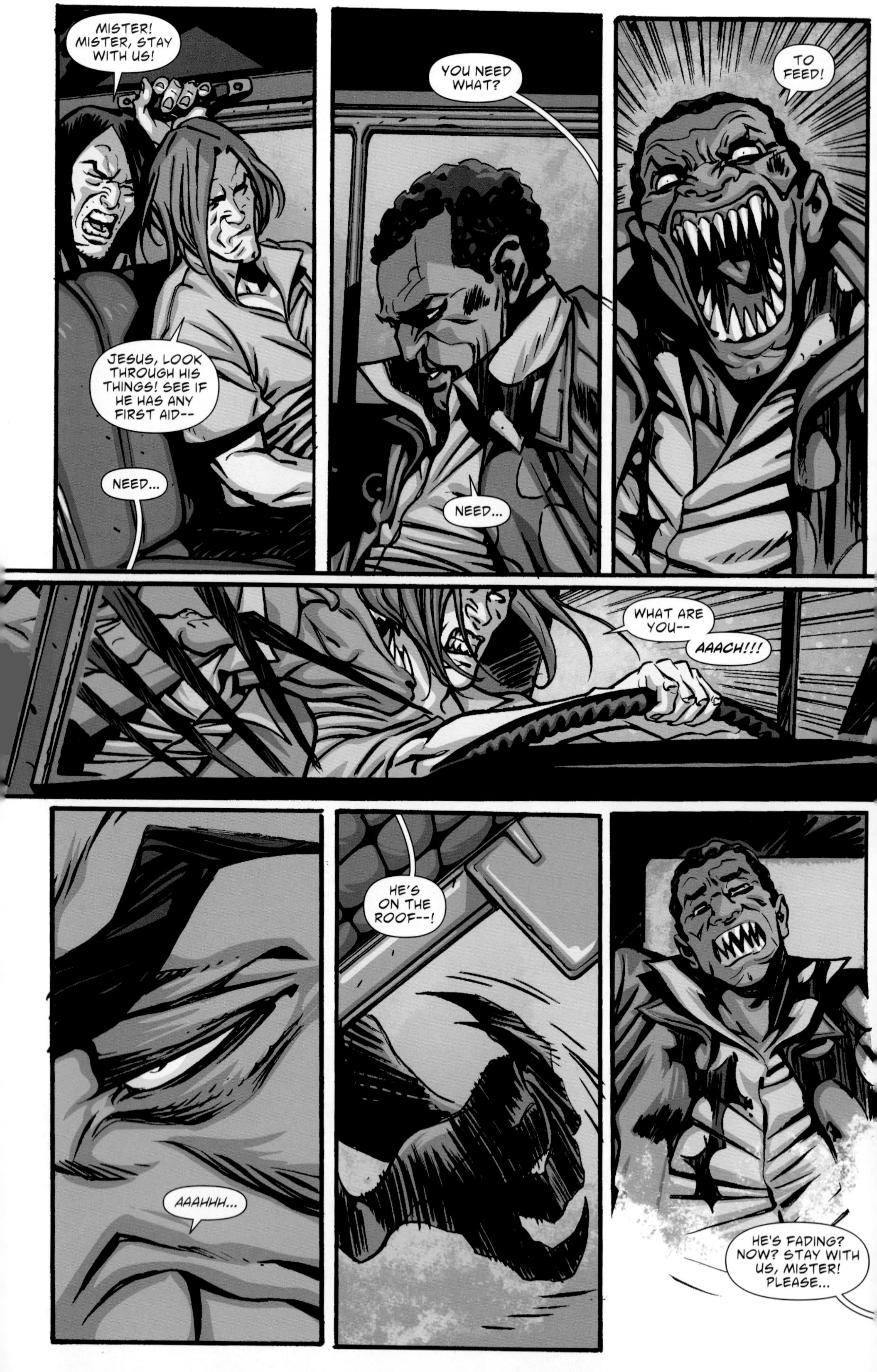

MISTER! MISTER, STAY WITH US!
JESUS, LOOK THROUGH HIS THINGS! SEE IF HE HAS ANY FIRST AID--
NEED...
YOU NEED WHAT?
NEED...
TO FEED!
WHAT ARE YOU--
AAACH!!!
AAAHHH...
HE'S ON THE ROOF--!
HE'S FADING? NOW? STAY WITH US, MISTER! PLEASE...

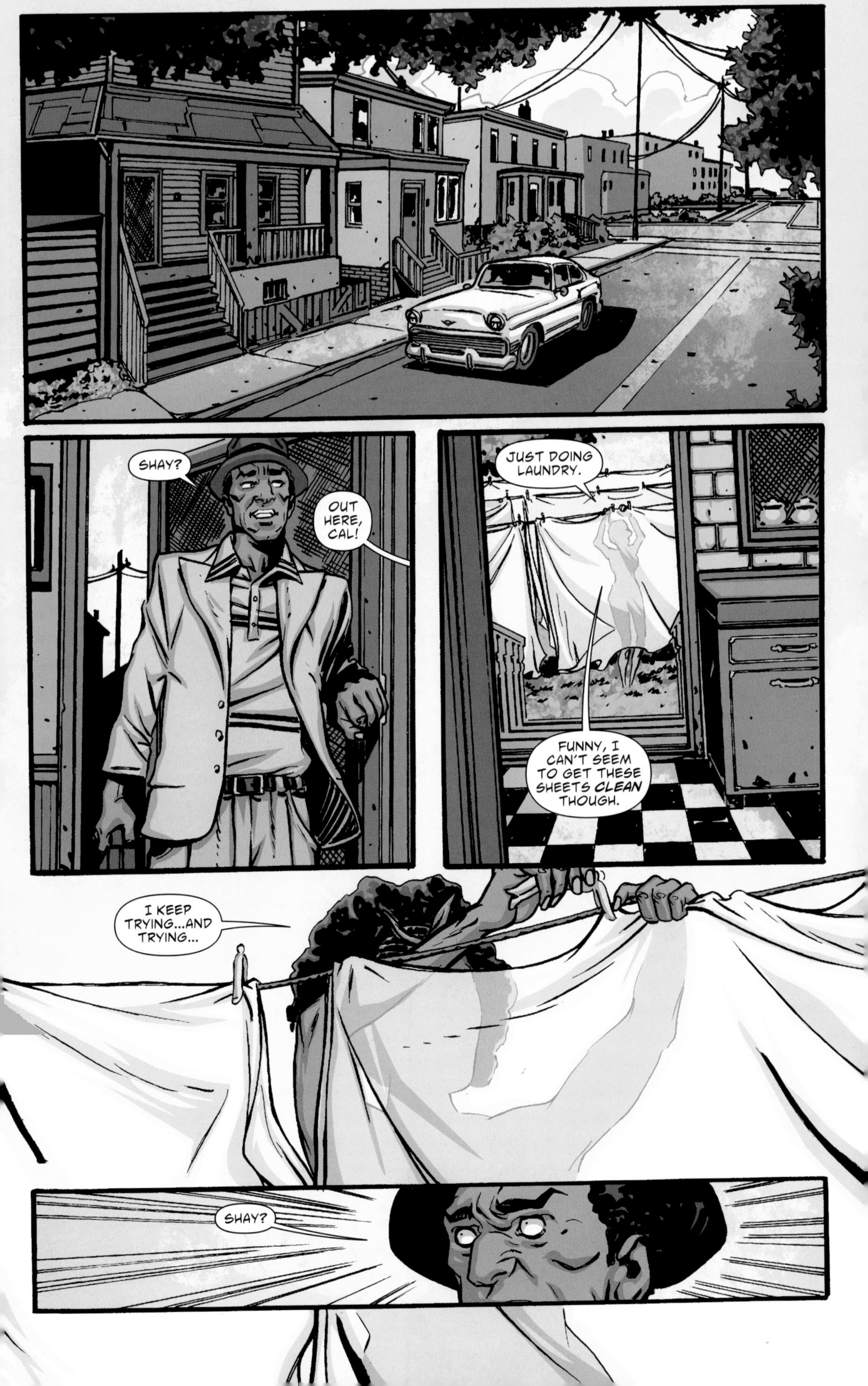
SHAY?
OUT HERE, CAL!
JUST DOING LAUNDRY.
FUNNY, I CAN'T SEEM TO GET THESE SHEETS *CLEAN* THOUGH.
I KEEP TRYING...AND TRYING...
SHAY?

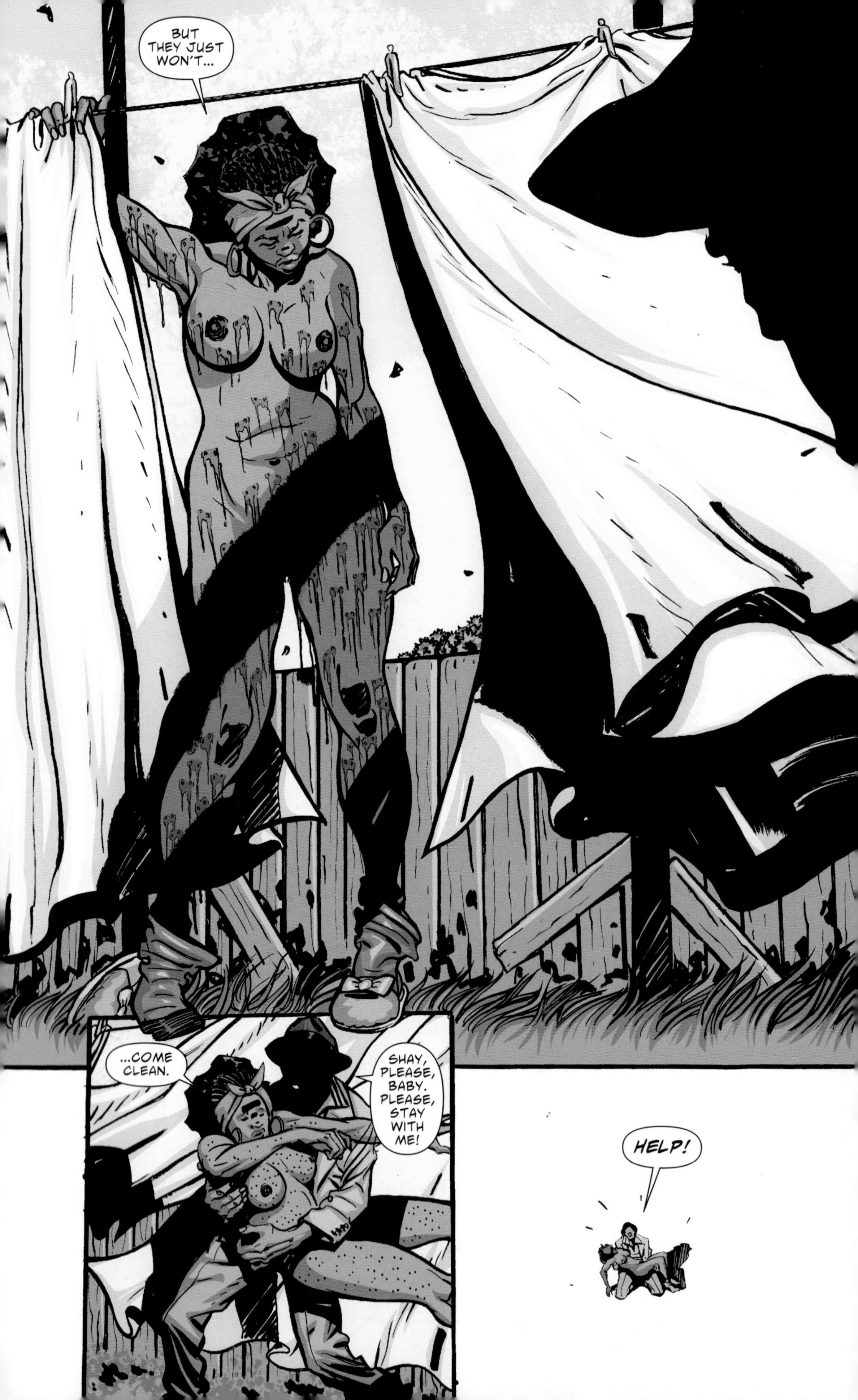
BUT THEY JUST WON'T...
...COME CLEAN.
SHAY, PLEASE, BABY. PLEASE, STAY WITH ME!
HELP!

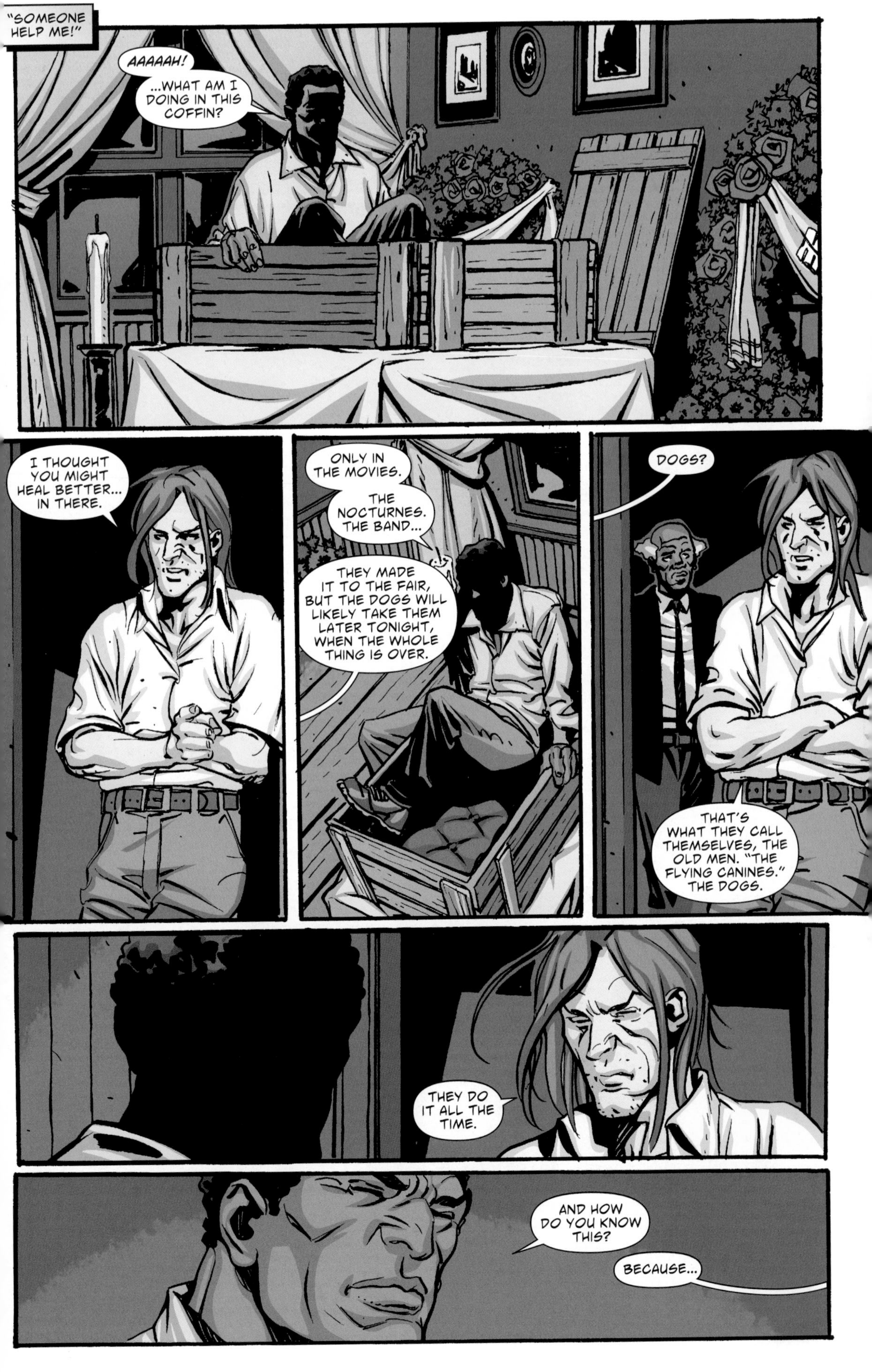
"SOMEONE HELP ME!"
AAAAAH!
...WHAT AM I DOING IN THIS COFFIN?
I THOUGHT YOU MIGHT HEAL BETTER... IN THERE.
ONLY IN THE MOVIES.
THE NOCTURNES. THE BAND...
THEY MADE IT TO THE FAIR, BUT THE DOGS WILL LIKELY TAKE THEM LATER TONIGHT, WHEN THE WHOLE THING IS OVER.
DOGS?
THAT'S WHAT THEY CALL THEMSELVES, THE OLD MEN. "THE FLYING CANINES." THE DOGS.
THEY DO IT ALL THE TIME.
AND HOW DO YOU KNOW THIS?
BECAUSE...

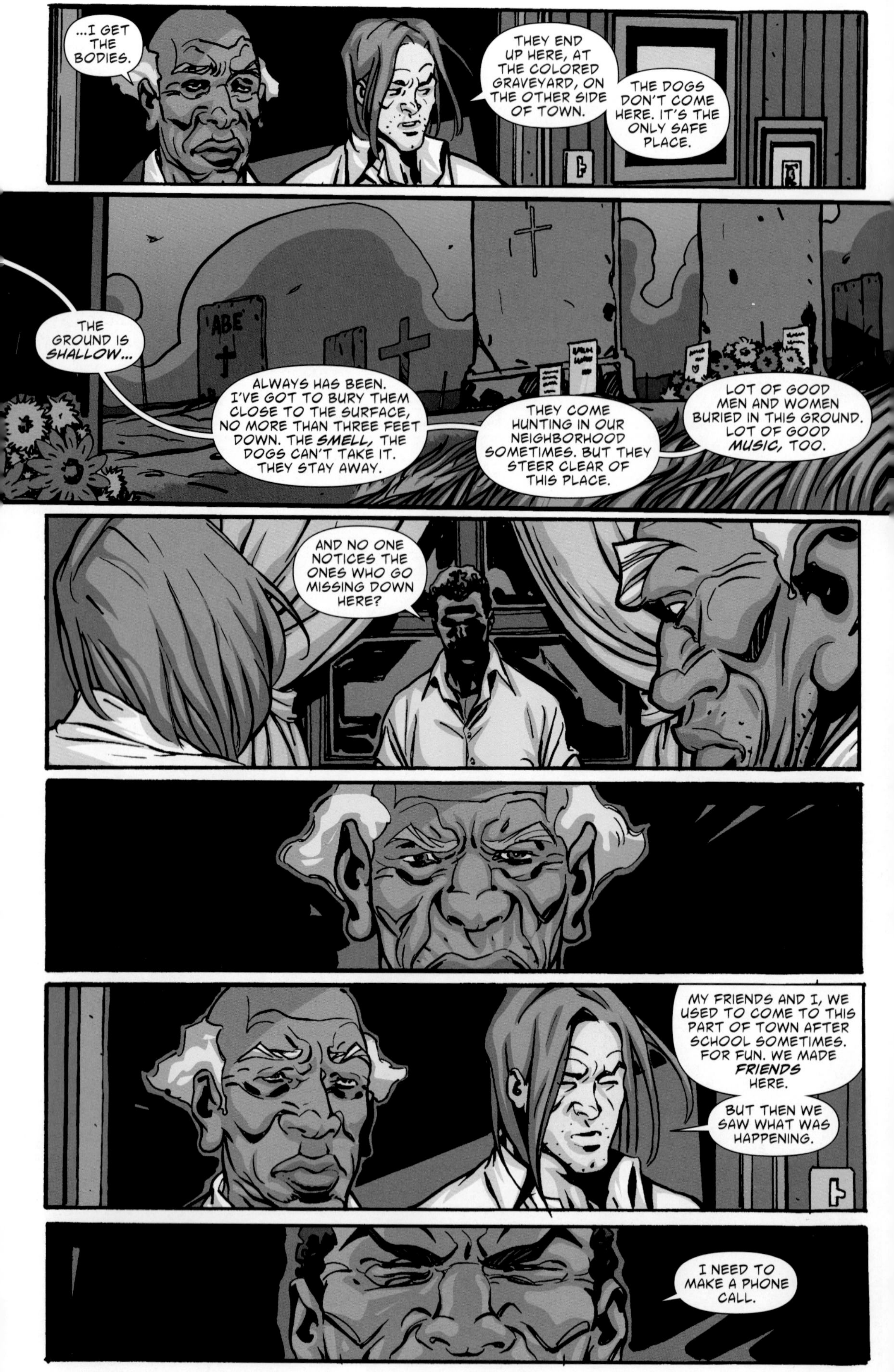
...I GET THE BODIES.
THEY END UP HERE, AT THE COLORED GRAVEYARD, ON THE OTHER SIDE OF TOWN.
THE DOGS DON'T COME HERE. IT'S THE ONLY SAFE PLACE.
ABE
THE GROUND IS *SHALLOW...*
ALWAYS HAS BEEN. I'VE GOT TO BURY THEM CLOSE TO THE SURFACE, NO MORE THAN THREE FEET DOWN. THE *SMELL,* THE DOGS CAN'T TAKE IT. THEY STAY AWAY.
THEY COME HUNTING IN OUR NEIGHBORHOOD SOMETIMES. BUT THEY STEER CLEAR OF THIS PLACE.
LOT OF GOOD MEN AND WOMEN BURIED IN THIS GROUND. LOT OF GOOD *MUSIC,* TOO.
AND NO ONE NOTICES THE ONES WHO GO MISSING DOWN HERE?
MY FRIENDS AND I, WE USED TO COME TO THIS PART OF TOWN AFTER SCHOOL SOMETIMES. FOR FUN. WE MADE *FRIENDS* HERE.
BUT THEN WE SAW WHAT WAS HAPPENING.
I NEED TO MAKE A PHONE CALL.

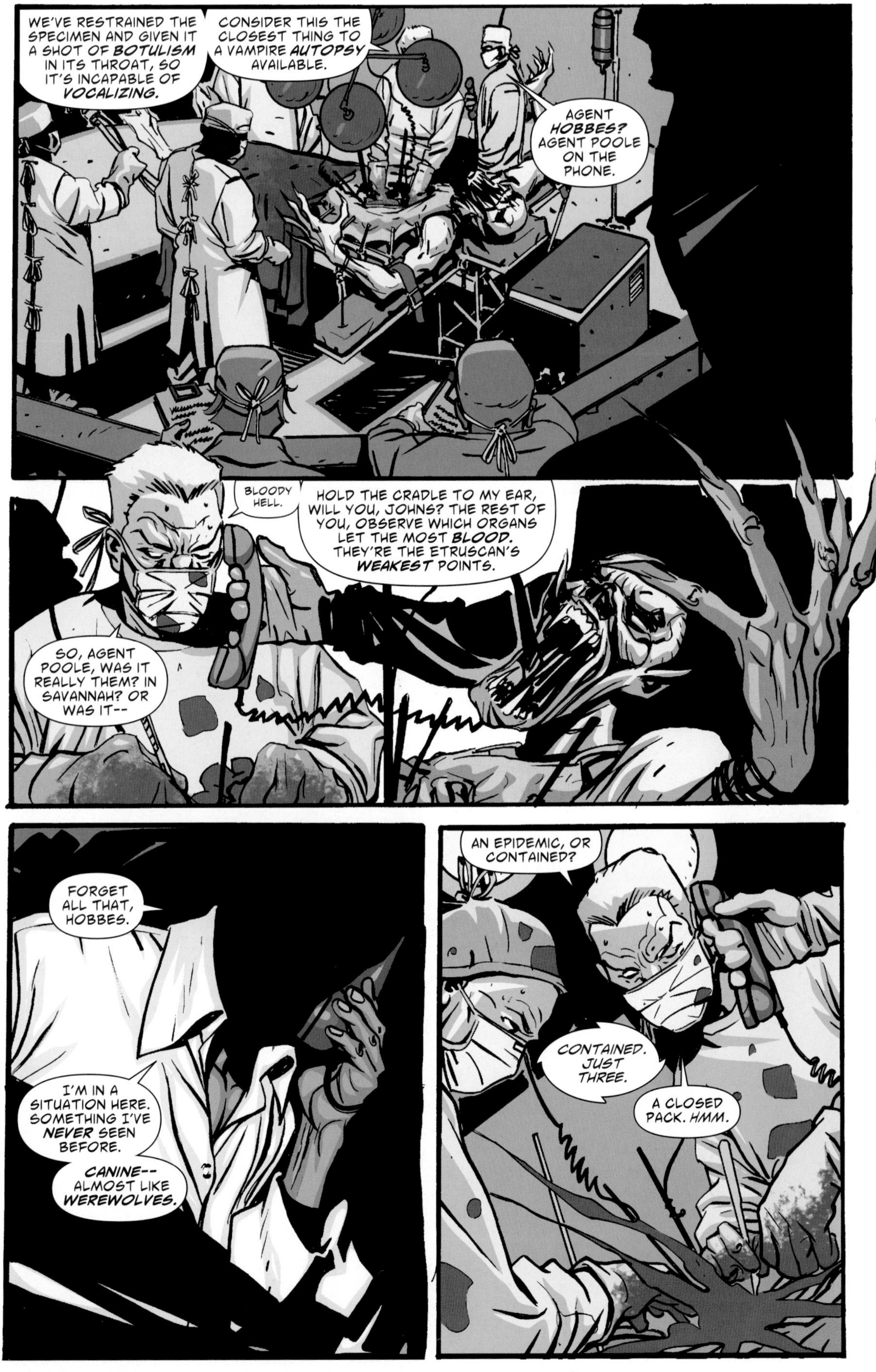
WE'VE RESTRAINED THE SPECIMEN AND GIVEN IT A SHOT OF BOTULISM IN ITS THROAT, SO IT'S INCAPABLE OF VOCALIZING.
CONSIDER THIS THE CLOSEST THING TO A VAMPIRE AUTOPSY AVAILABLE.
AGENT HOBBES? AGENT POOLE ON THE PHONE.
BLOODY HELL.
HOLD THE CRADLE TO MY EAR, WILL YOU, JOHNS? THE REST OF YOU, OBSERVE WHICH ORGANS LET THE MOST BLOOD. THEY'RE THE ETRUSCAN'S WEAKEST POINTS.
SO, AGENT POOLE, WAS IT REALLY THEM? IN SAVANNAH? OR WAS IT--
FORGET ALL THAT, HOBBES.
I'M IN A SITUATION HERE. SOMETHING I'VE NEVER SEEN BEFORE.
CANINE-- ALMOST LIKE WEREWOLVES.
AN EPIDEMIC, OR CONTAINED?
CONTAINED. JUST THREE.
A CLOSED PACK. HMM.

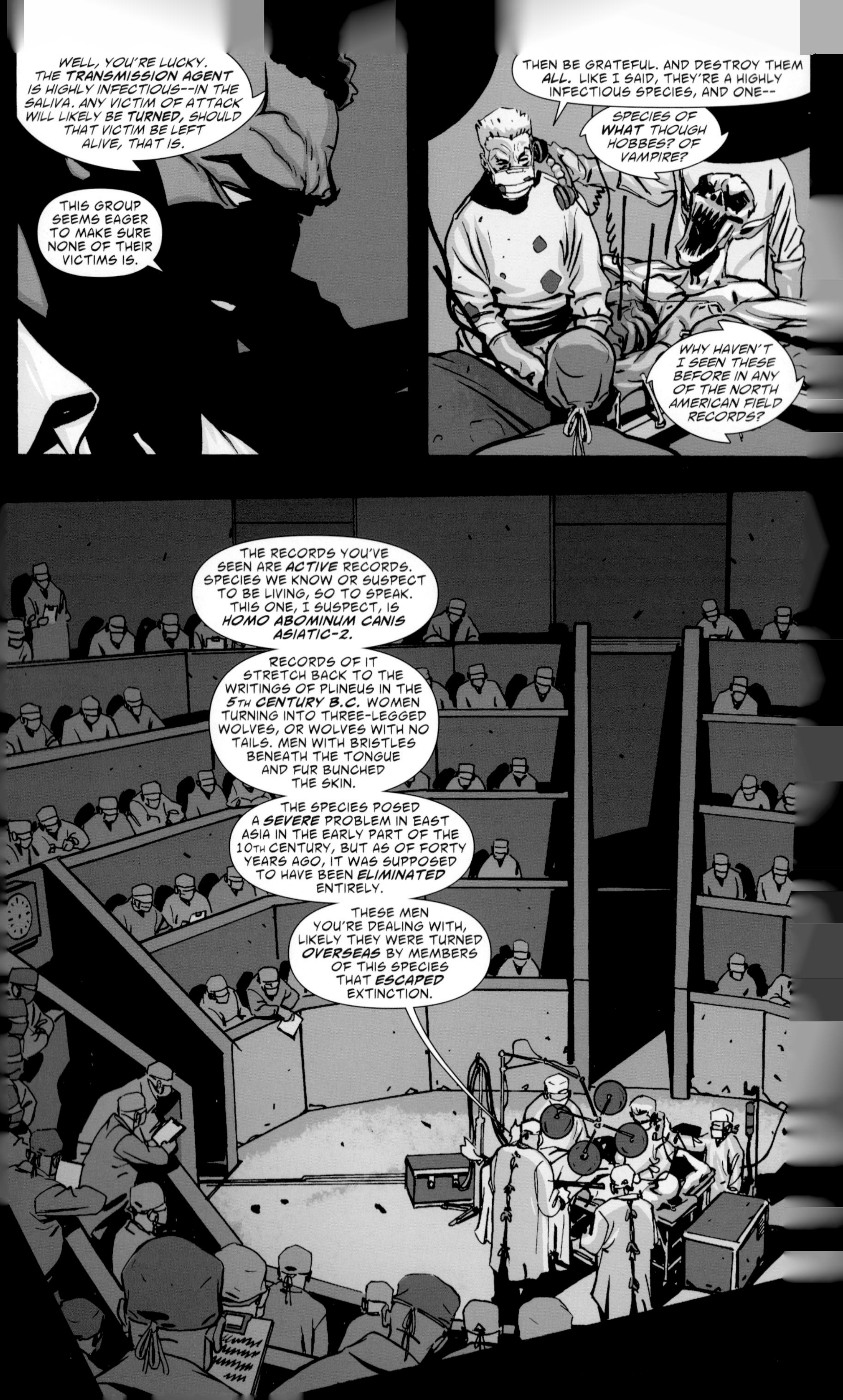
WELL, YOU'RE LUCKY. THE TRANSMISSION AGENT IS HIGHLY INFECTIOUS--IN THE SALIVA. ANY VICTIM OF ATTACK WILL LIKELY BE TURNED, SHOULD THAT VICTIM BE LEFT ALIVE, THAT IS.
THIS GROUP SEEMS EAGER TO MAKE SURE NONE OF THEIR VICTIMS IS.
THEN BE GRATEFUL. AND DESTROY THEM ALL. LIKE I SAID, THEY'RE A HIGHLY INFECTIOUS SPECIES, AND ONE--
SPECIES OF WHAT THOUGH HOBBES? OF VAMPIRE?
WHY HAVEN'T I SEEN THESE BEFORE IN ANY OF THE NORTH AMERICAN FIELD RECORDS?
THE RECORDS YOU'VE SEEN ARE ACTIVE RECORDS. SPECIES WE KNOW OR SUSPECT TO BE LIVING, SO TO SPEAK. THIS ONE, I SUSPECT, IS HOMO ABOMINUM CANIS ASIATIC-2.
RECORDS OF IT STRETCH BACK TO THE WRITINGS OF PLINEUS IN THE 5TH CENTURY B.C. WOMEN TURNING INTO THREE-LEGGED WOLVES, OR WOLVES WITH NO TAILS. MEN WITH BRISTLES BENEATH THE TONGUE AND FUR BUNCHED THE SKIN.
THE SPECIES POSED A SEVERE PROBLEM IN EAST ASIA IN THE EARLY PART OF THE 10TH CENTURY, BUT AS OF FORTY YEARS AGO, IT WAS SUPPOSED TO HAVE BEEN ELIMINATED ENTIRELY.
THESE MEN YOU'RE DEALING WITH, LIKELY THEY WERE TURNED OVERSEAS BY MEMBERS OF THIS SPECIES THAT ESCAPED EXTINCTION.

THEY SERVED OVERSEAS, YES. YOU'RE SAYING THEY'RE A FORM OF *ANCIENT* VAMPIRE?

THAT SPECIES YOU FERRETED OUT IN THE STATE OF GEORGIA. NEUROLOGICALLY IMPAIRED, WITHOUT FANGS... DID IT NOT RESEMBLE--

ZOMBIES. I SAID IT MYSELF, YES.

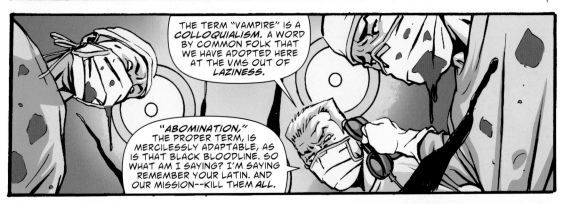

THE TERM "VAMPIRE" IS A *COLLOQUIALISM.* A WORD BY COMMON FOLK THAT WE HAVE ADOPTED HERE AT THE VMS OUT OF *LAZINESS.*

"ABOMINATION," THE PROPER TERM, IS MERCILESSLY ADAPTABLE, AS IS THAT BLACK BLOODLINE. SO WHAT AM I SAYING? I'M SAYING REMEMBER YOUR LATIN. AND OUR MISSION--KILL THEM *ALL.*

AND AGENT POOLE. I'M NOT GOING TO ASK YOU *WHY* YOU'RE IN ALABAMA CURRENTLY. I'M SIMPLY GOING TO REMIND YOU THAT THE LIVES YOU LEFT BEHIND, WHEN YOU MADE YOUR *CHOICE*--

I GET IT.

GOOD. THEY'RE SUSCEPTIBLE TO *SILVER.* GOOD LUCK, AGENT POOLE.

SILVER? WHERE AM I SUPPOSED TO FIND GODDAMN SILVER?

FOLLOW ME.

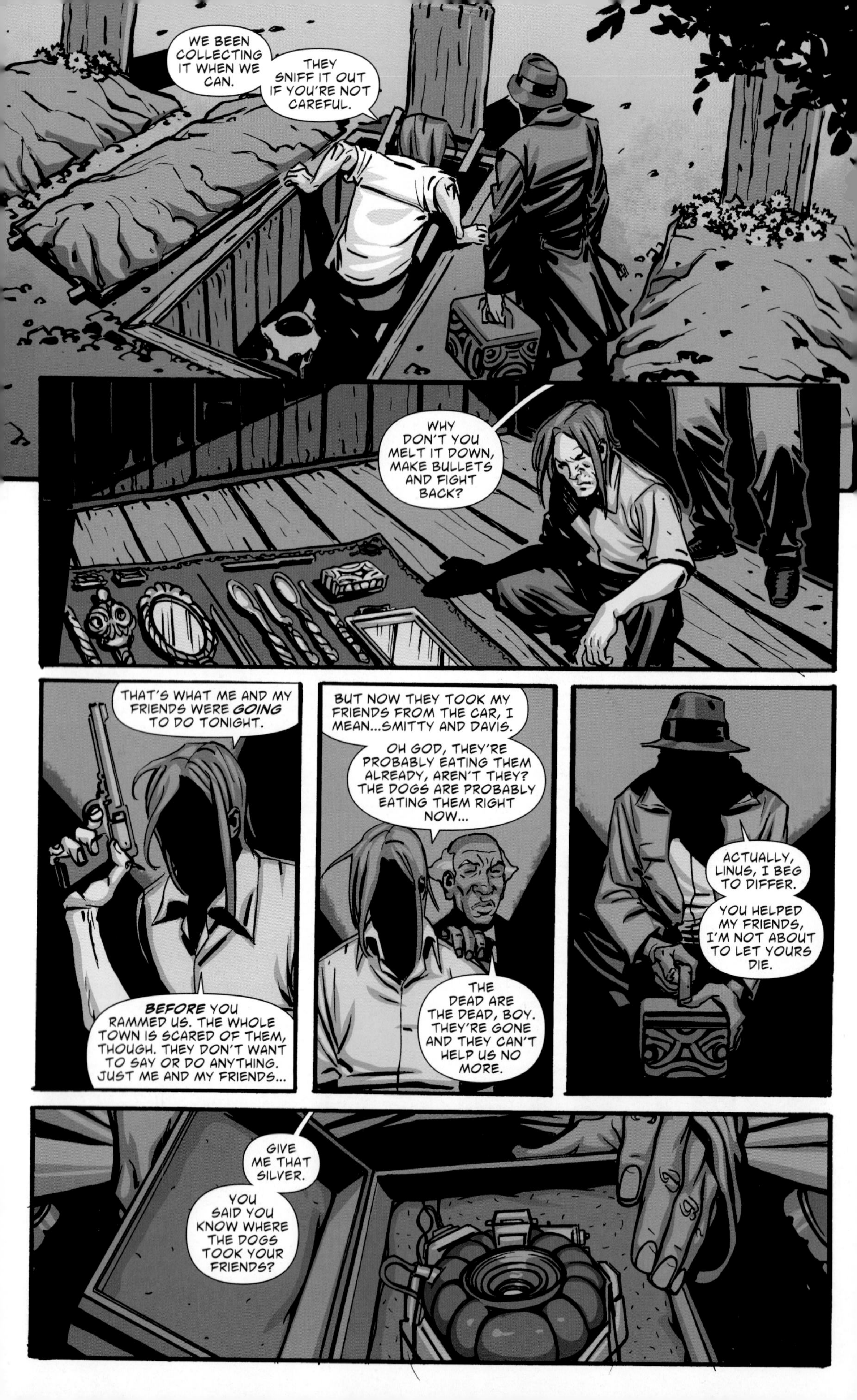
WE BEEN COLLECTING IT WHEN WE CAN.
THEY SNIFF IT OUT IF YOU'RE NOT CAREFUL.
WHY DON'T YOU MELT IT DOWN, MAKE BULLETS AND FIGHT BACK?
THAT'S WHAT ME AND MY FRIENDS WERE *GOING* TO DO TONIGHT.
BEFORE YOU RAMMED US. THE WHOLE TOWN IS SCARED OF THEM, THOUGH. THEY DON'T WANT TO SAY OR DO ANYTHING. JUST ME AND MY FRIENDS...
BUT NOW THEY TOOK MY FRIENDS FROM THE CAR, I MEAN...SMITTY AND DAVIS.
OH GOD, THEY'RE PROBABLY EATING THEM ALREADY, AREN'T THEY? THE DOGS ARE PROBABLY EATING THEM RIGHT NOW...
THE DEAD ARE THE DEAD, BOY. THEY'RE GONE AND THEY CAN'T HELP US NO MORE.
ACTUALLY, LINUS, I BEG TO DIFFER.
YOU HELPED MY FRIENDS, I'M NOT ABOUT TO LET YOURS DIE.
GIVE ME THAT SILVER.
YOU SAID YOU KNOW WHERE THE DOGS TOOK YOUR FRIENDS?

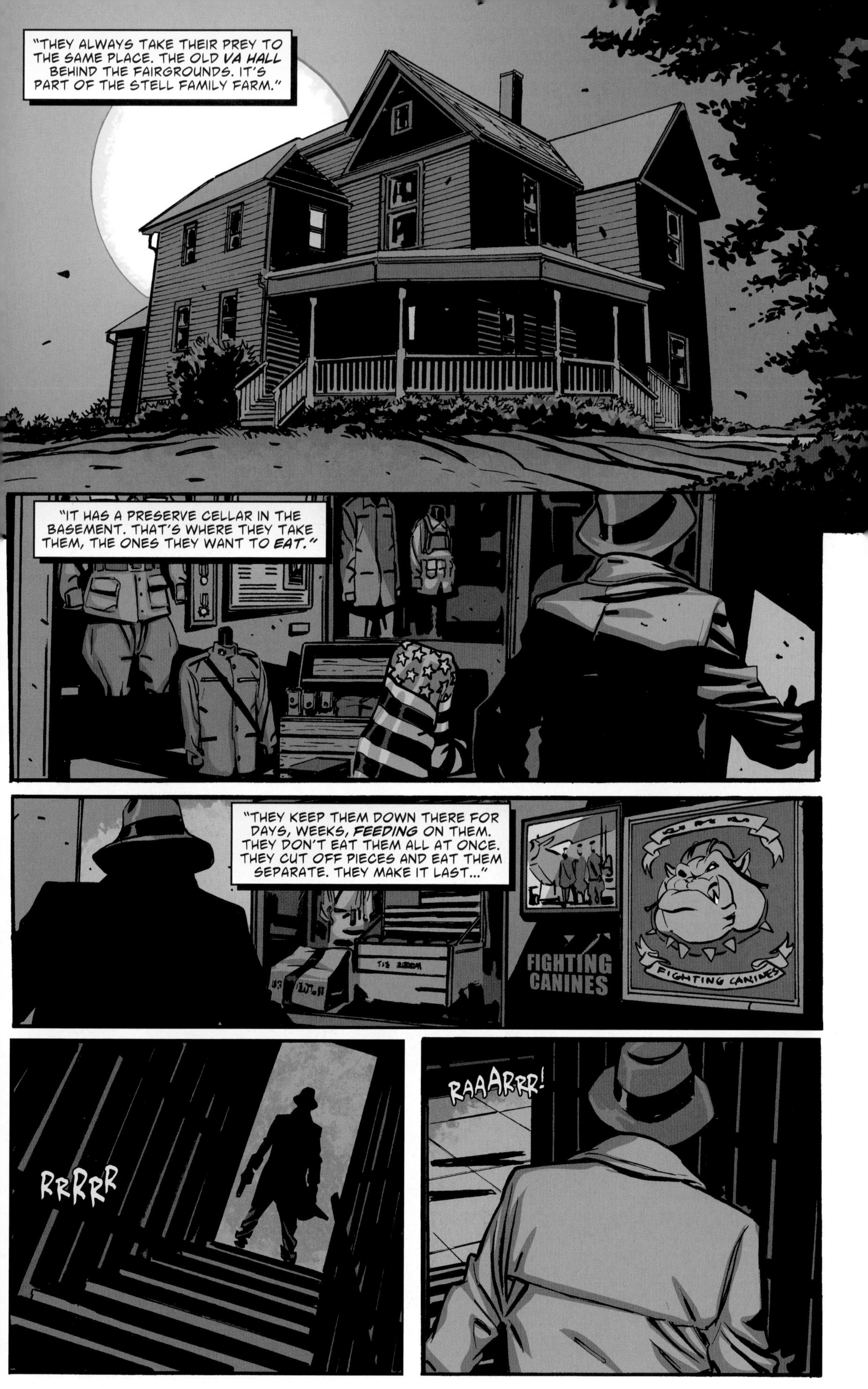
"THEY ALWAYS TAKE THEIR PREY TO THE SAME PLACE. THE OLD VA HALL BEHIND THE FAIRGROUNDS. IT'S PART OF THE STELL FAMILY FARM."
"IT HAS A PRESERVE CELLAR IN THE BASEMENT. THAT'S WHERE THEY TAKE THEM, THE ONES THEY WANT TO EAT."
"THEY KEEP THEM DOWN THERE FOR DAYS, WEEKS, FEEDING ON THEM. THEY DON'T EAT THEM ALL AT ONCE. THEY CUT OFF PIECES AND EAT THEM SEPARATE. THEY MAKE IT LAST..."
FIGHTING CANINES
FIGHTING CANINES
RRRRR
RAAARRR!

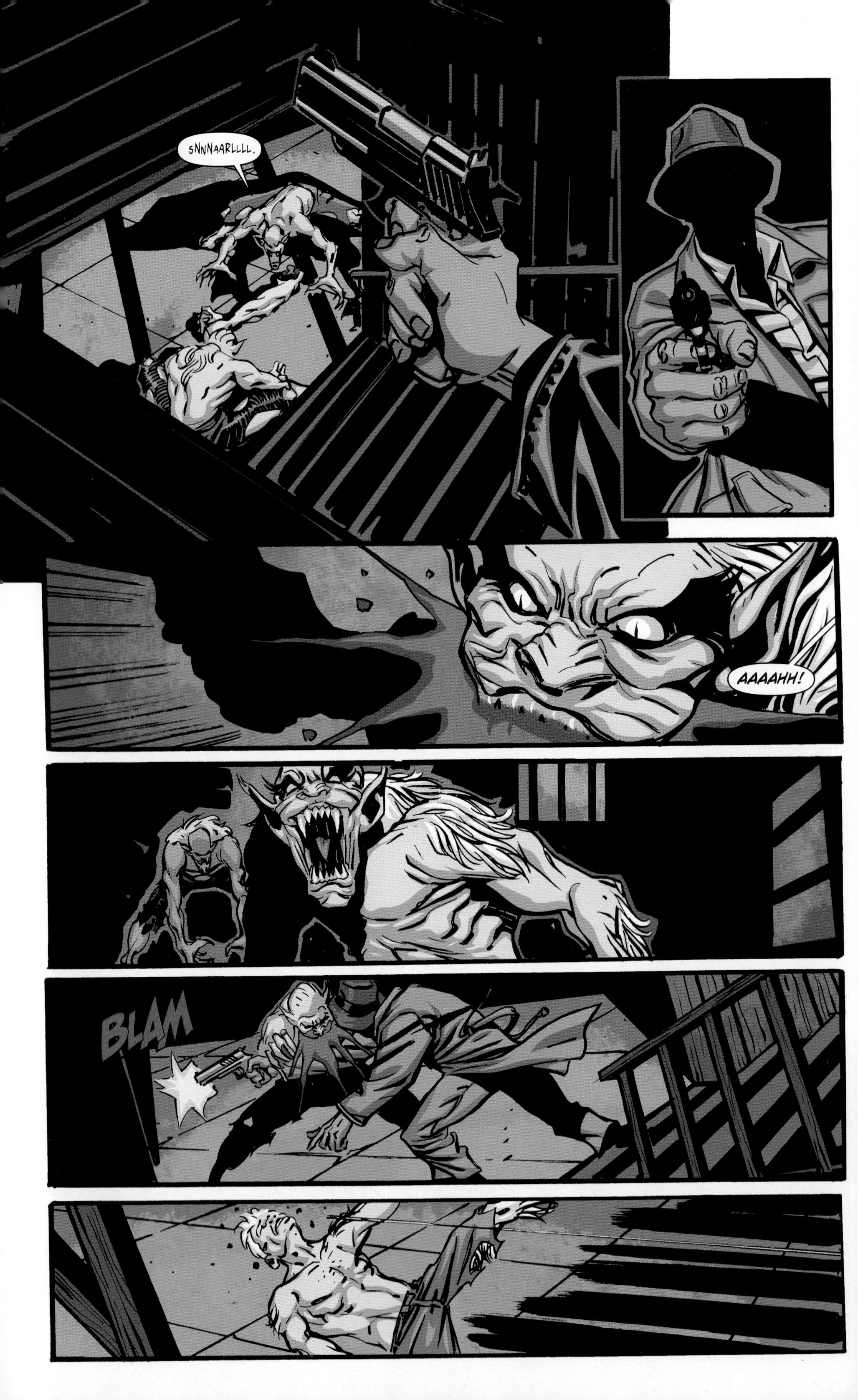
SNNNAARLLLL.
AAAAHH!
BLAM

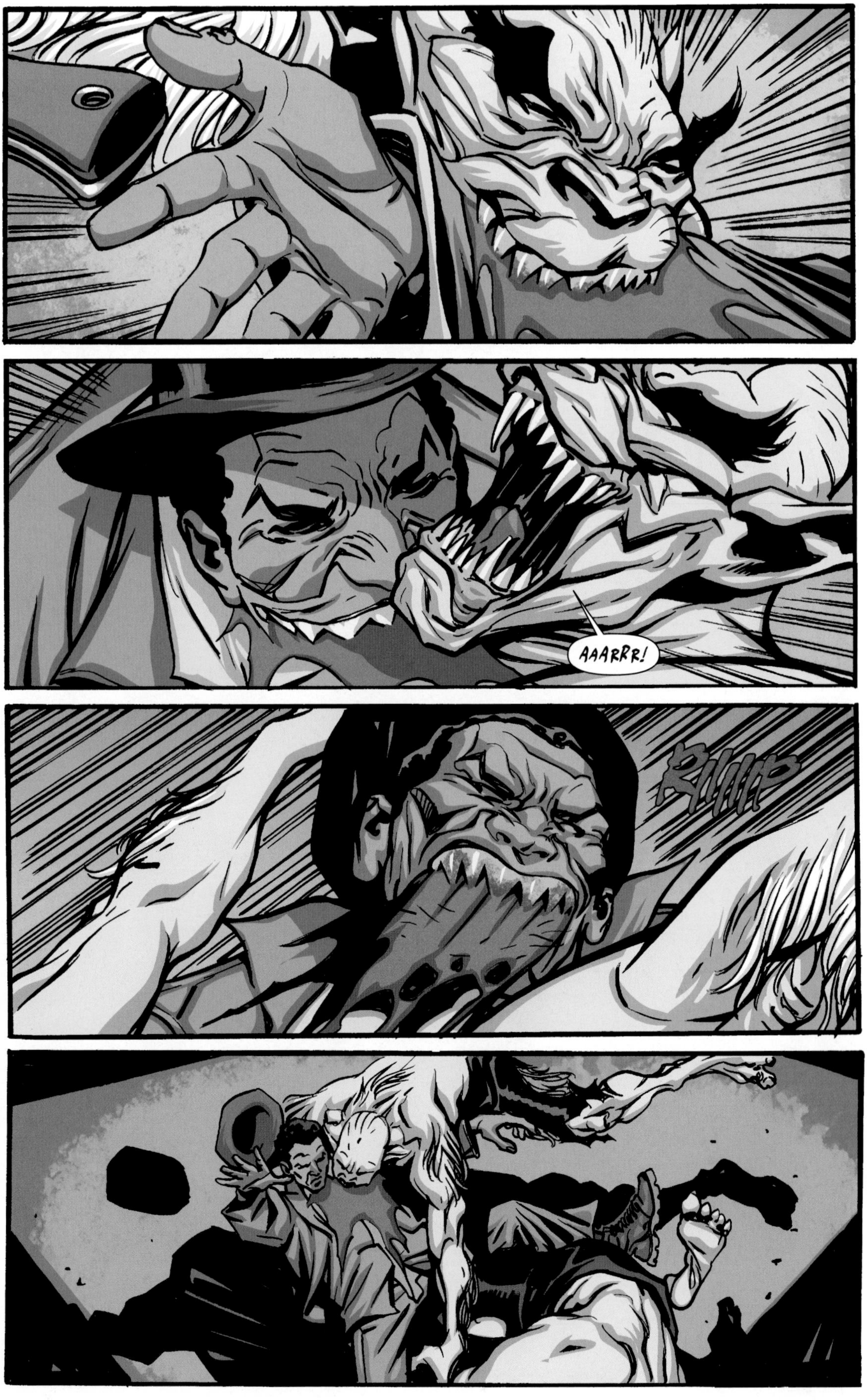
AAARRR!
RIIIIP

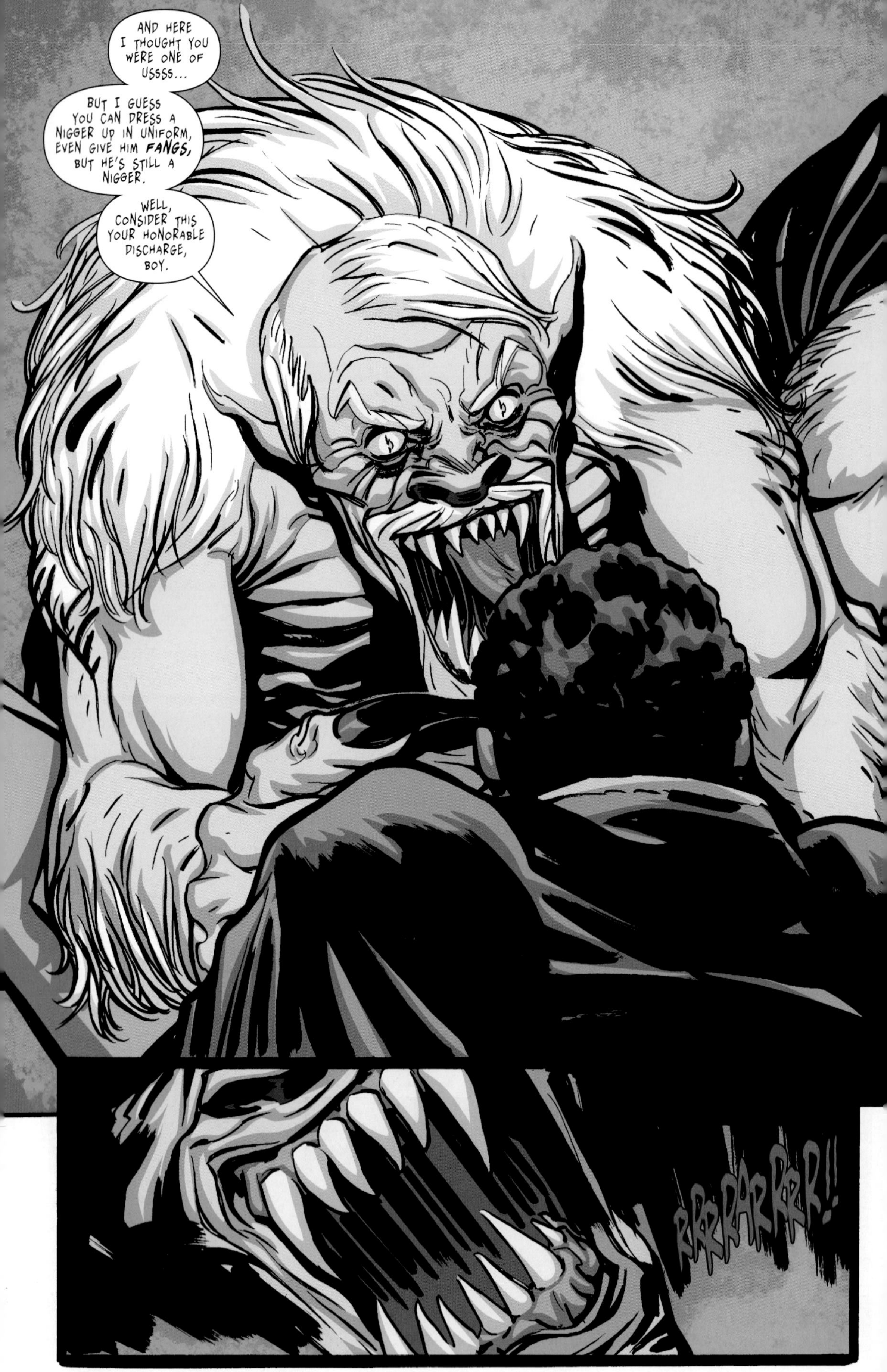
AND HERE I THOUGHT YOU WERE ONE OF USSSS...
BUT I GUESS YOU CAN DRESS A NIGGER UP IN UNIFORM, EVEN GIVE HIM FANGS, BUT HE'S STILL A NIGGER.
WELL, CONSIDER THIS YOUR HONORABLE DISCHARGE, BOY.
RRRRARRRR!!

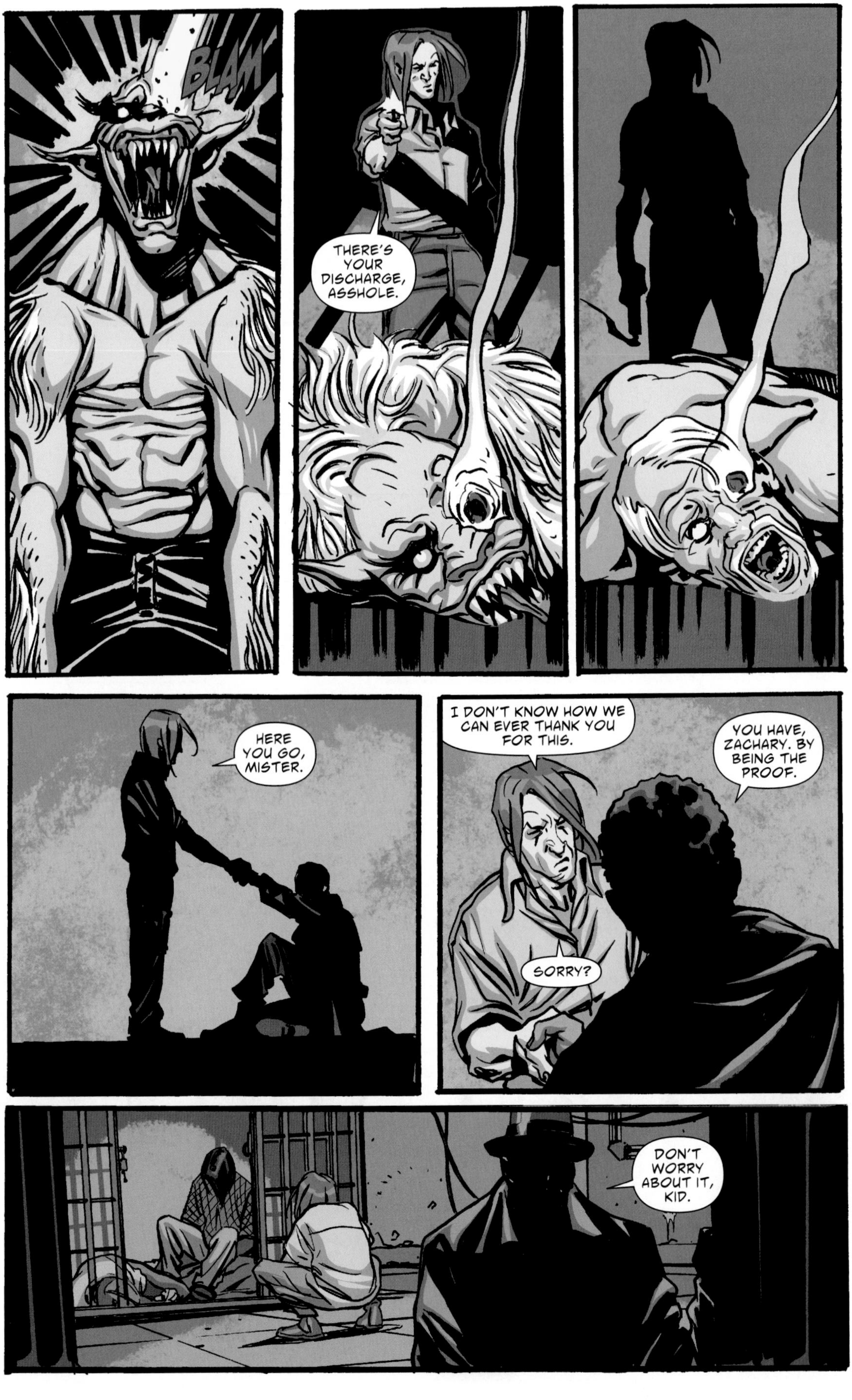
BLAM
THERE'S YOUR DISCHARGE, ASSHOLE.
HERE YOU GO, MISTER.
I DON'T KNOW HOW WE CAN EVER THANK YOU FOR THIS.
YOU HAVE, ZACHARY. BY BEING THE PROOF.
SORRY?
DON'T WORRY ABOUT IT, KID.

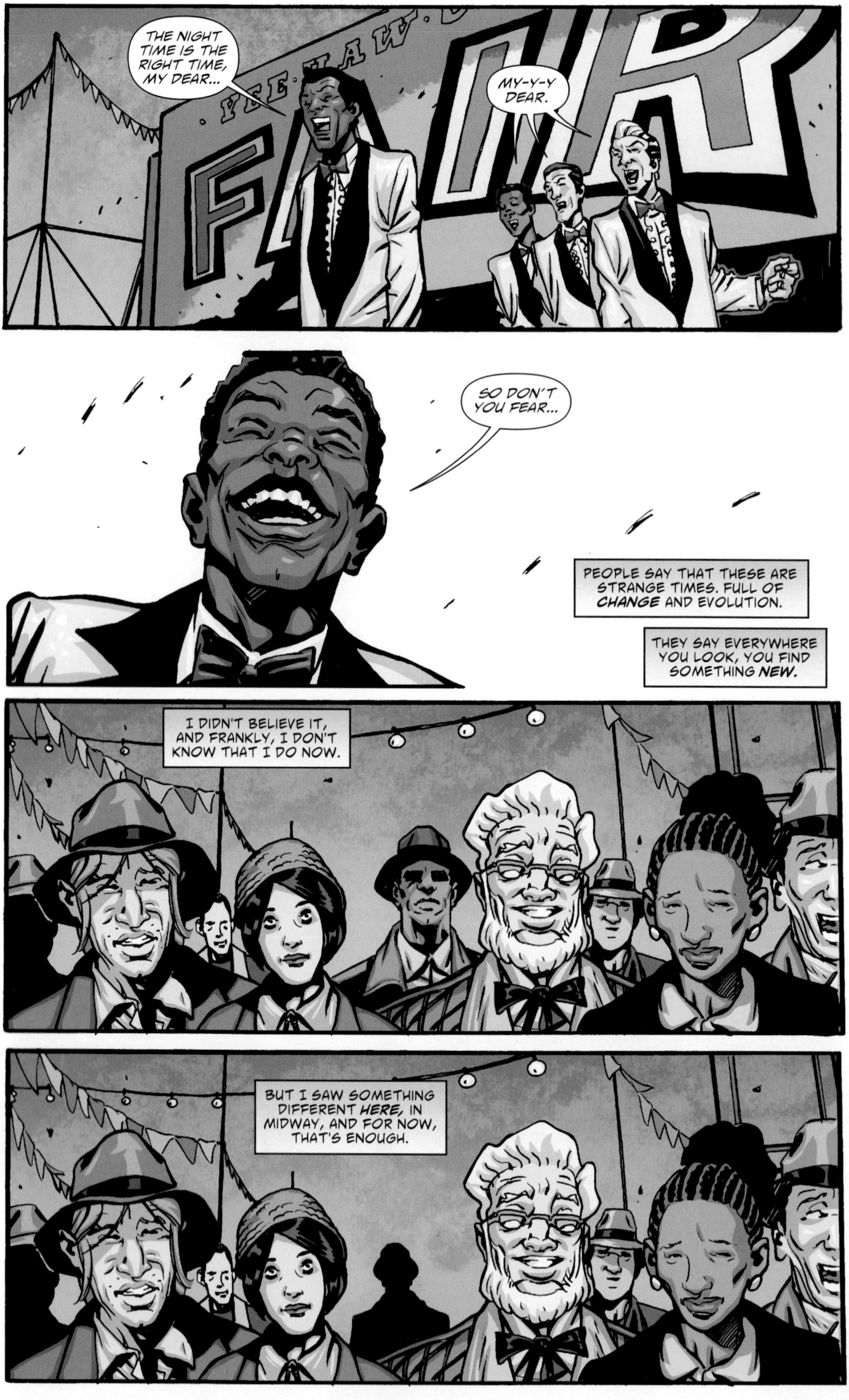
THE NIGHT TIME IS THE RIGHT TIME, MY DEAR...
MY-Y-Y DEAR.
SO DON'T YOU FEAR...
PEOPLE SAY THAT THESE ARE STRANGE TIMES. FULL OF CHANGE AND EVOLUTION.
THEY SAY EVERYWHERE YOU LOOK, YOU FIND SOMETHING NEW.
I DIDN'T BELIEVE IT, AND FRANKLY, I DON'T KNOW THAT I DO NOW.
BUT I SAW SOMETHING DIFFERENT HERE, IN MIDWAY, AND FOR NOW, THAT'S ENOUGH.

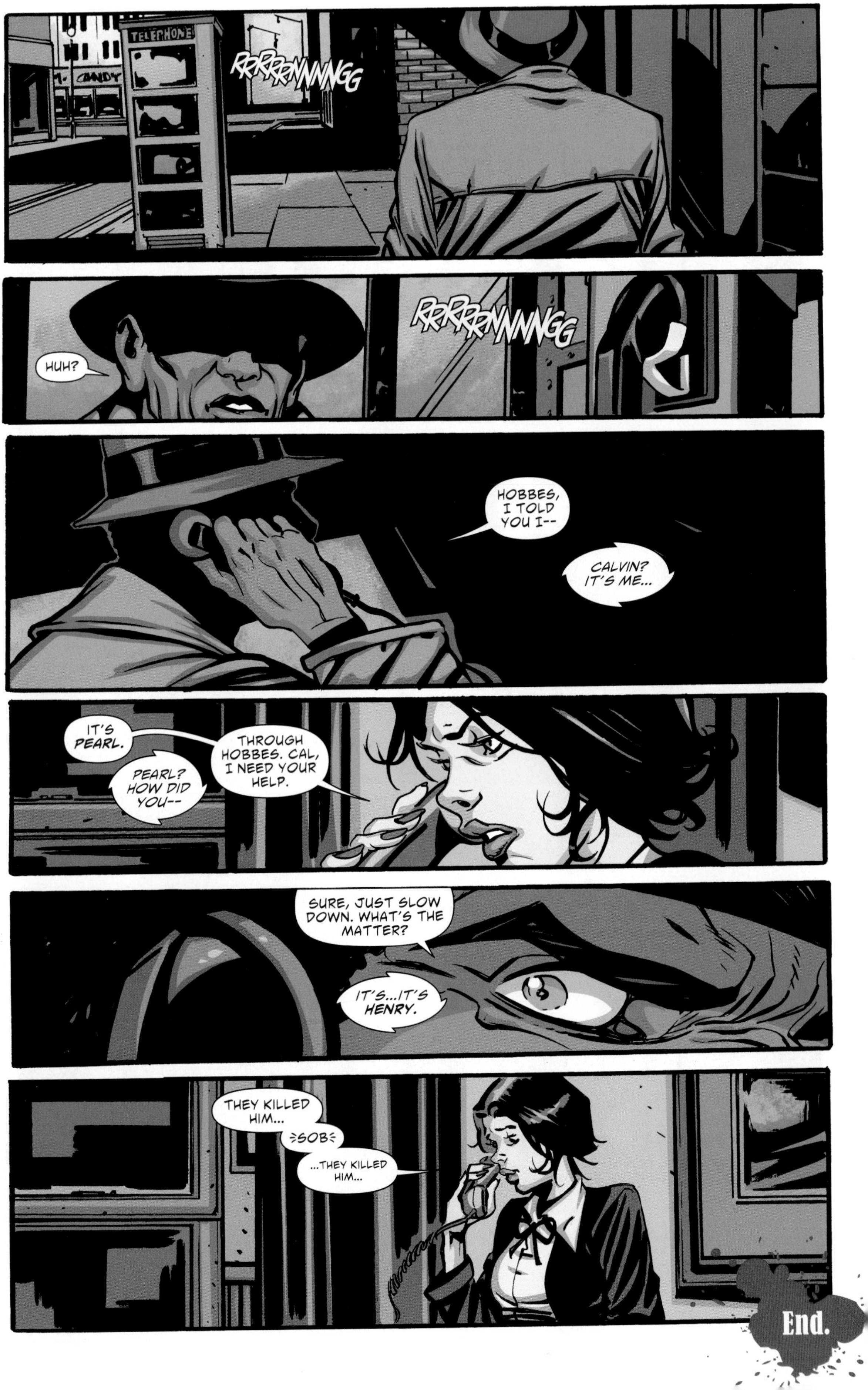
TELEPHONE
CANDY
RRRRRNNNNGG
HUH?
RRRRRNNNNGG
HOBBES, I TOLD YOU I--
CALVIN? IT'S ME...
IT'S PEARL.
PEARL? HOW DID YOU--
THROUGH HOBBES. CAL, I NEED YOUR HELP.
SURE, JUST SLOW DOWN. WHAT'S THE MATTER?
IT'S...IT'S HENRY.
THEY KILLED HIM...
SOB
...THEY KILLED HIM...
End.

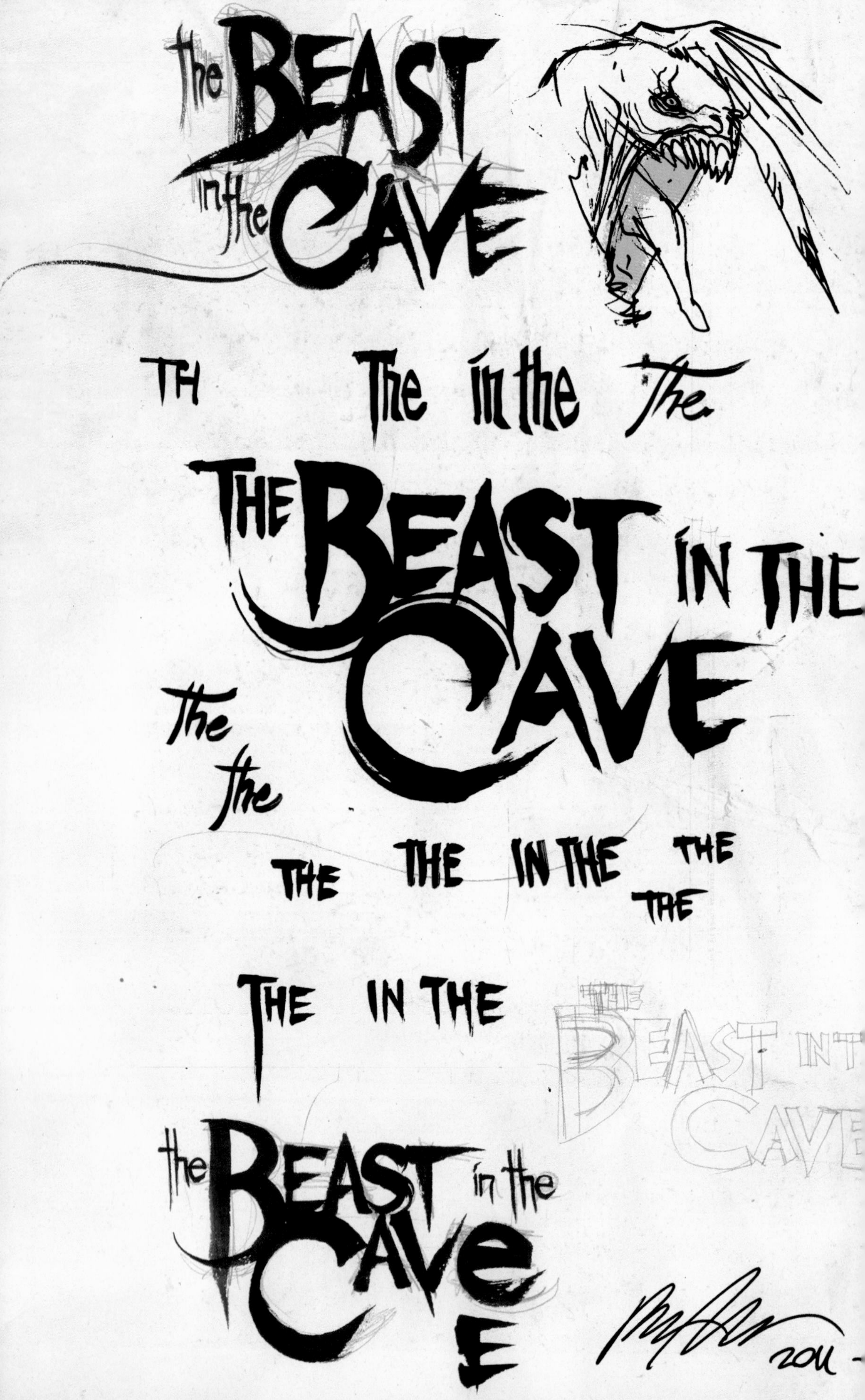
the BEAST in the CAVE
TH
The
in the
The
THE BEAST IN THE CAVE
the
the
THE
THE
IN THE
THE
THE
THE
IN THE
THE BEAST IN THE CAVE
the BEAST in the CAVE
2011

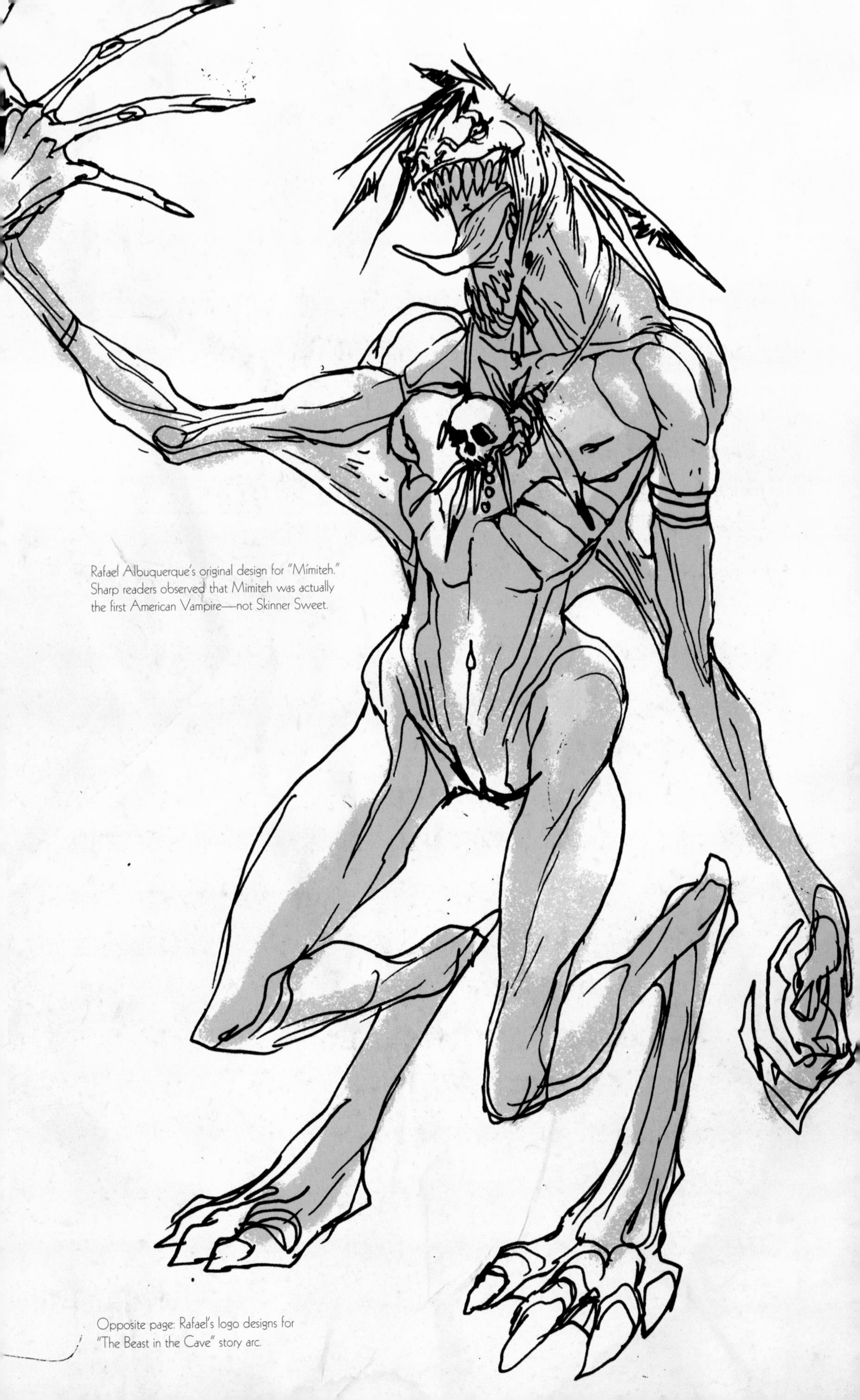

Rafael Albuquerque's original design for "Mimiteh." Sharp readers observed that Mimiteh was actually the first American Vampire—not Skinner Sweet.

Opposite page: Rafael's logo designs for "The Beast in the Cave" story arc.

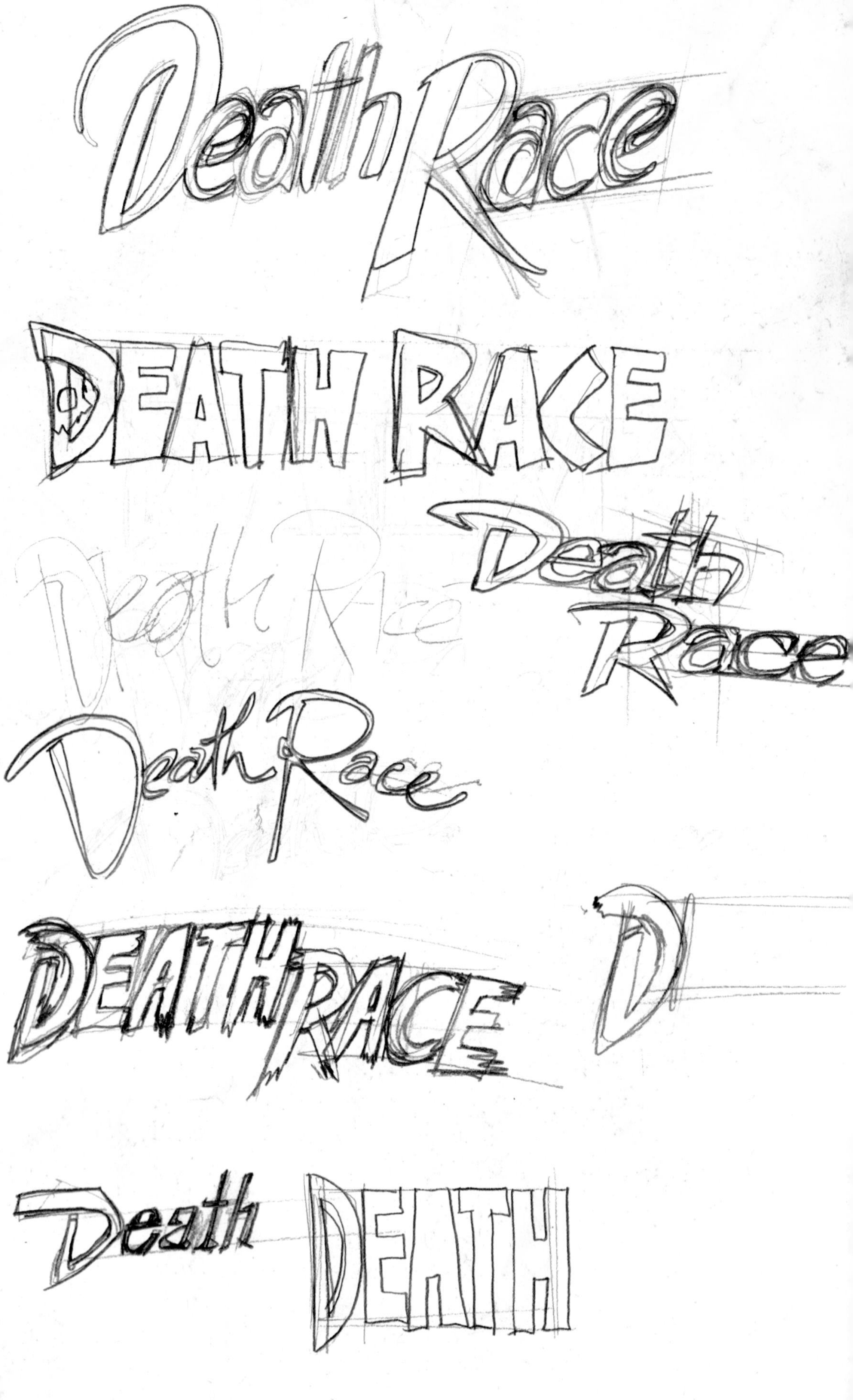
Death Race
DEATH RACE
Death Race
Death Race
Death Race
DEATH RACE
D
Death
DEATH

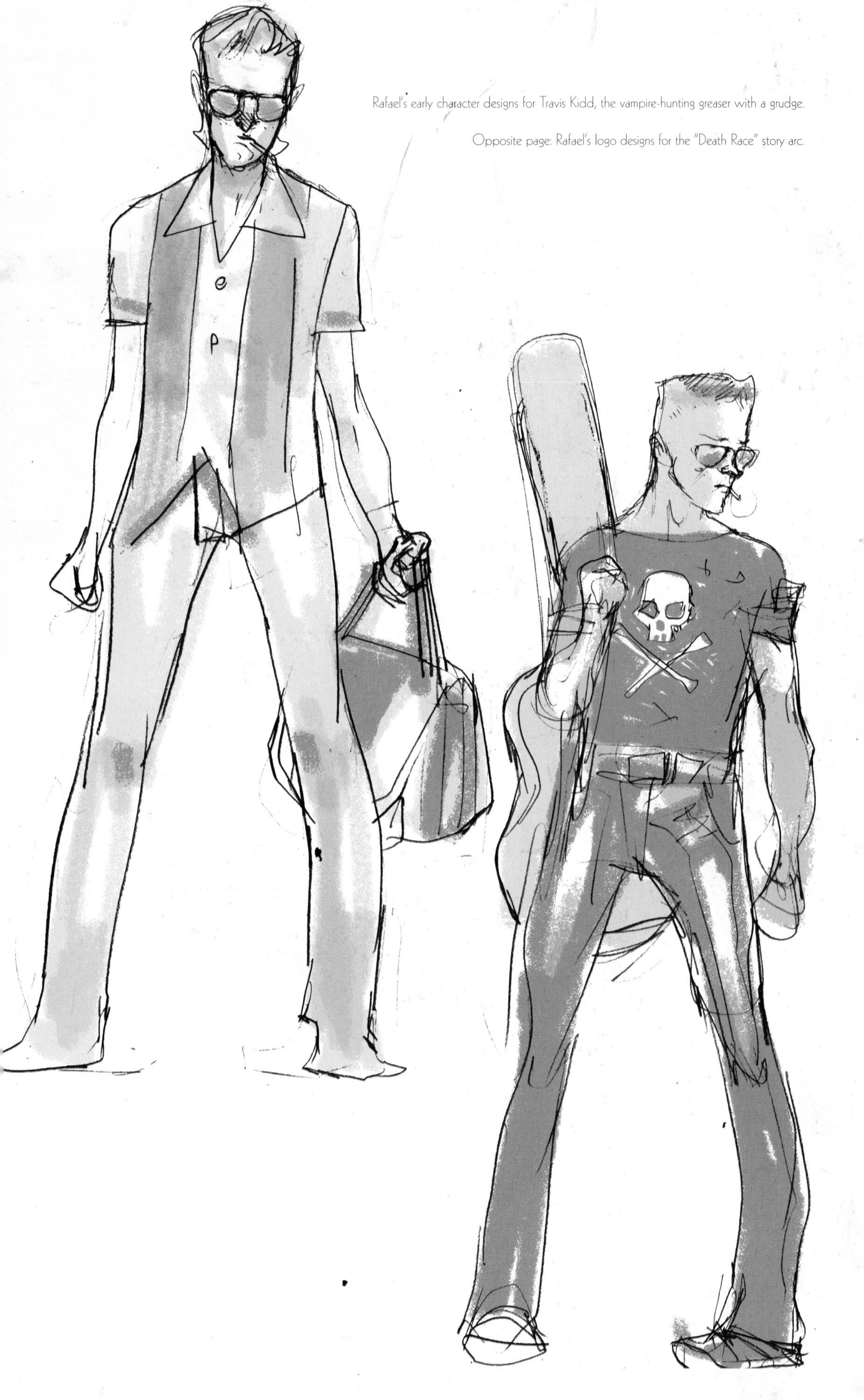

Rafael's early character designs for Travis Kidd, the vampire-hunting greaser with a grudge.

Opposite page: Rafael's logo designs for the "Death Race" story arc.

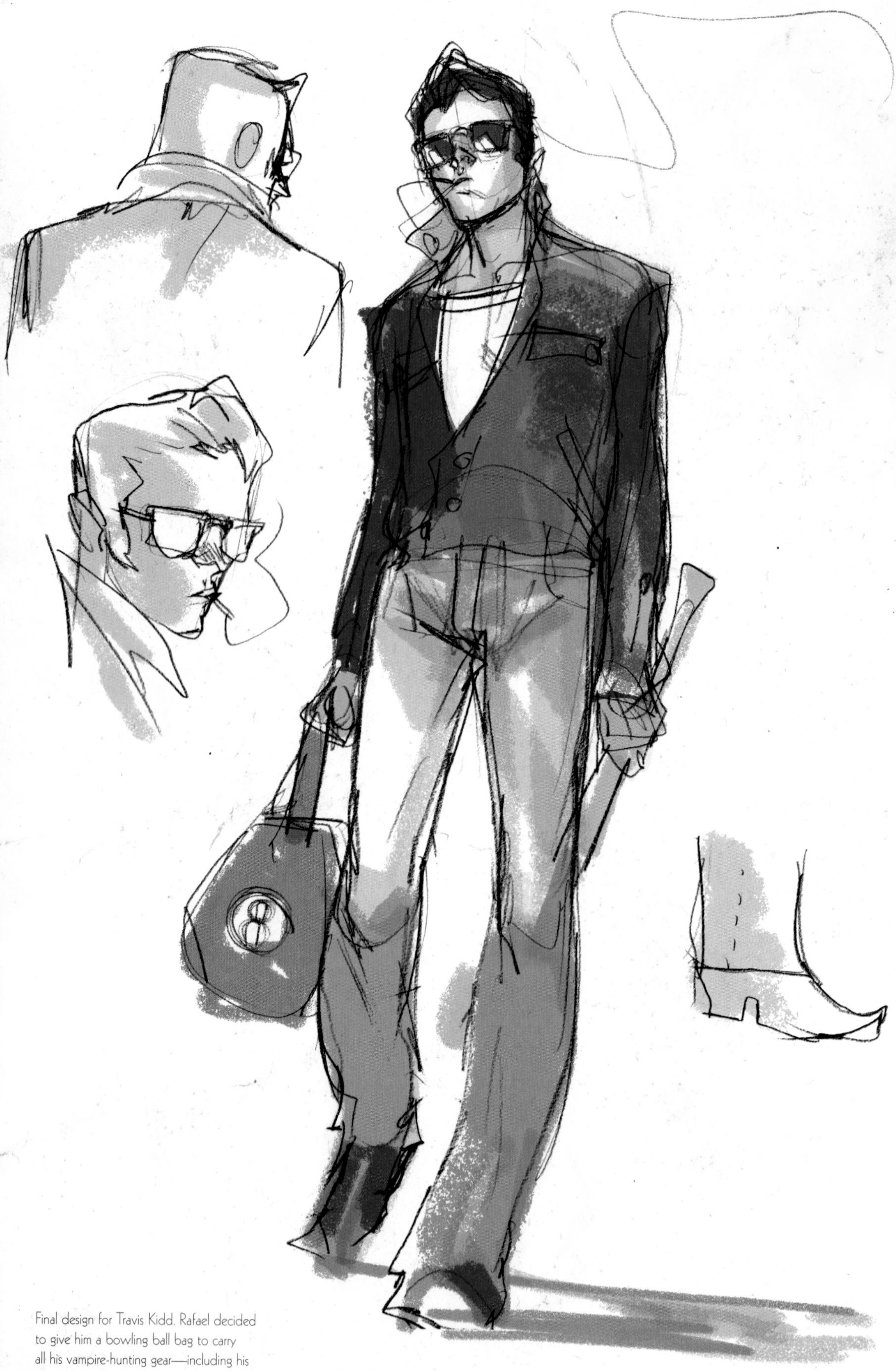

Final design for Travis Kidd. Rafael decided to give him a bowling ball bag to carry all his vampire-hunting gear—including his wooden teeth so he can "bite them back!"

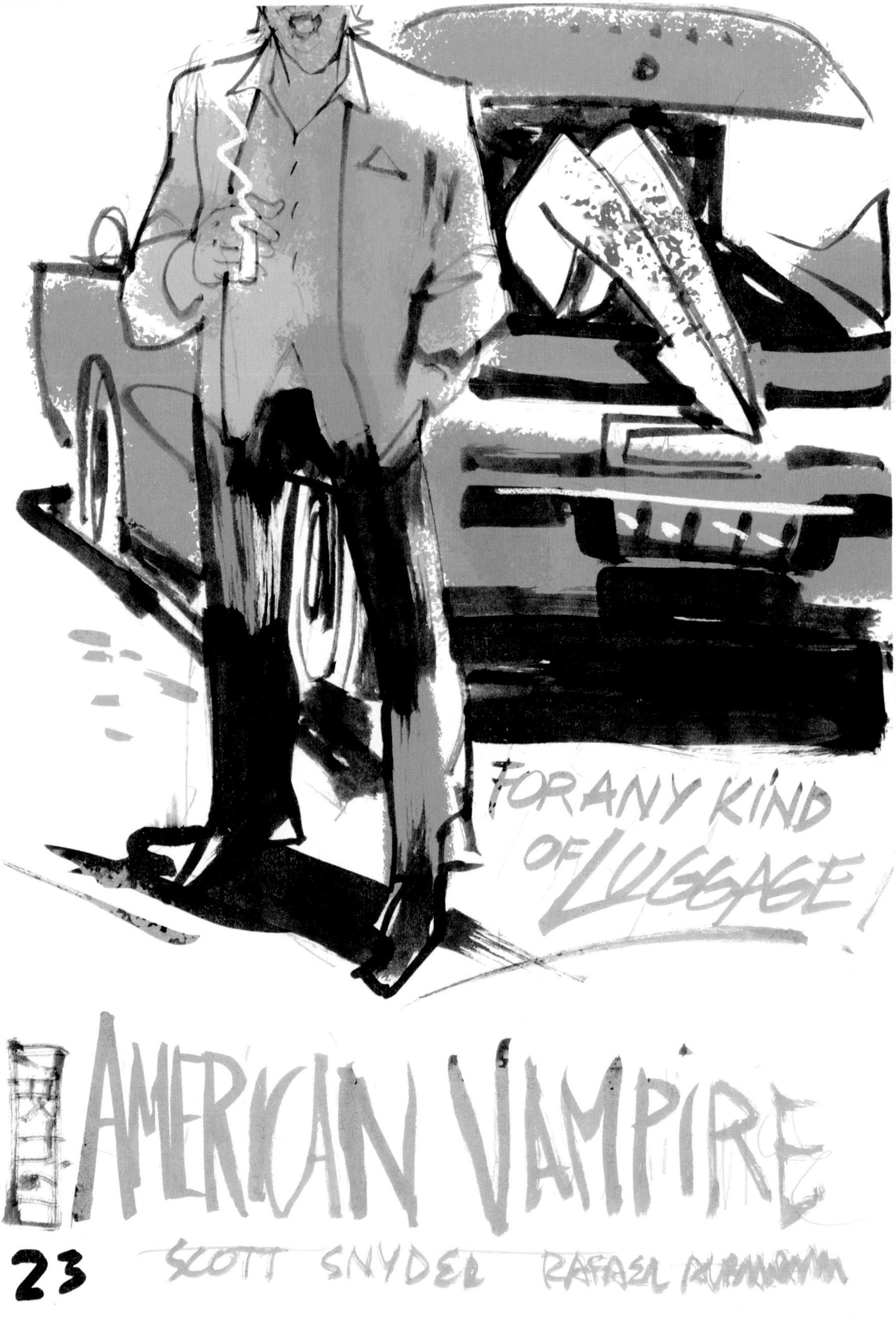
FOR ANY KIND OF LUGGAGE!
AMERICAN VAMPIRE
23
SCOTT SNYDER

For the "Death Race" arc, Rafael spoofed early 50's print ads. This is an early sketch for issue 23 cover.

At this point, we still had not revealed the identity of the vampire racing with Kidd—and Skinner was still "dead" as far as readers knew. So Rafael came up with this clever crop that hides Skinner's identity—and also makes for a great design.

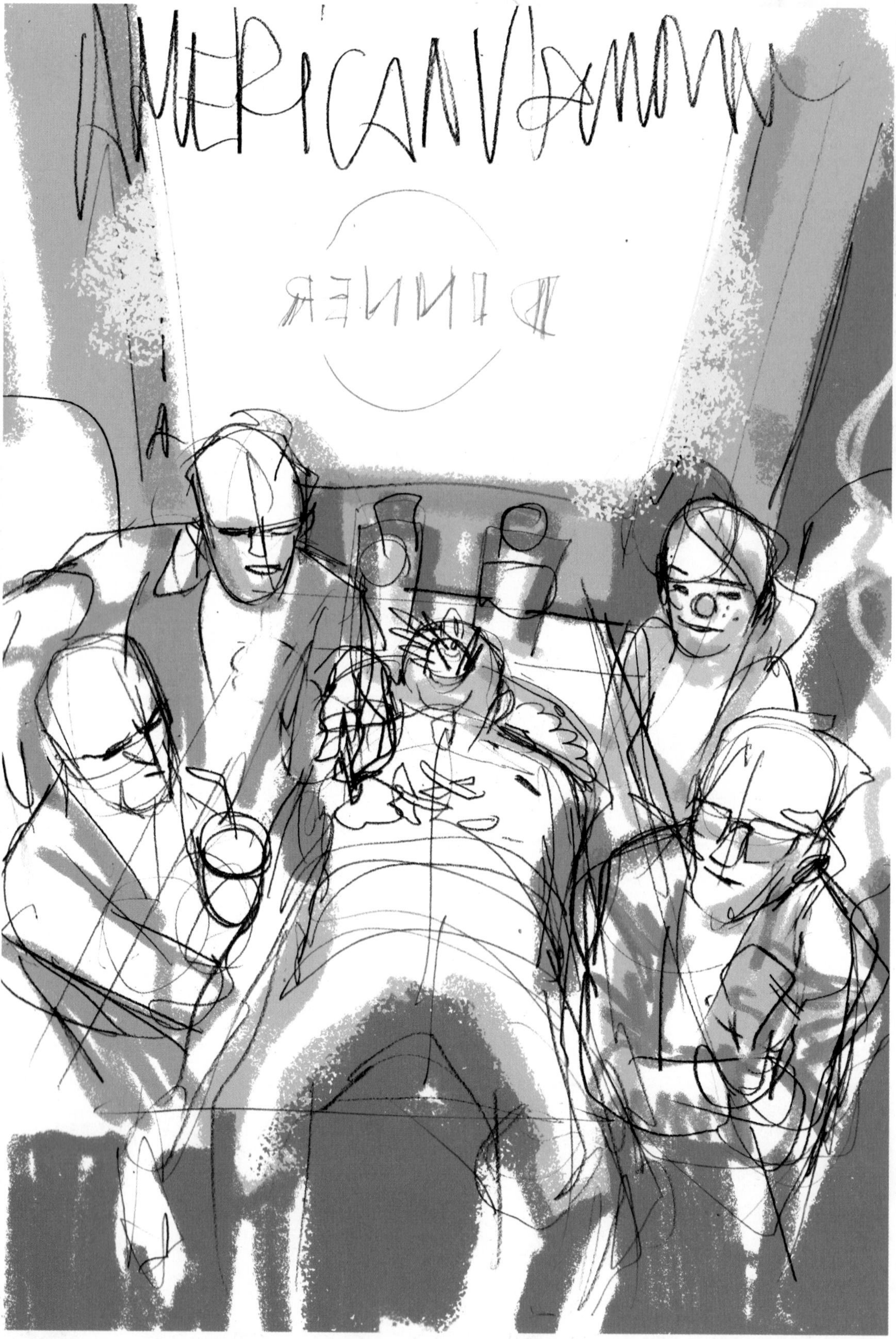

Early sketch for issue 25 cover. The concept is Hobbes, Skinner, Piper and Kidd at a diner booth—body on the table. Close, but we didn't think it worked as an ad spoof.

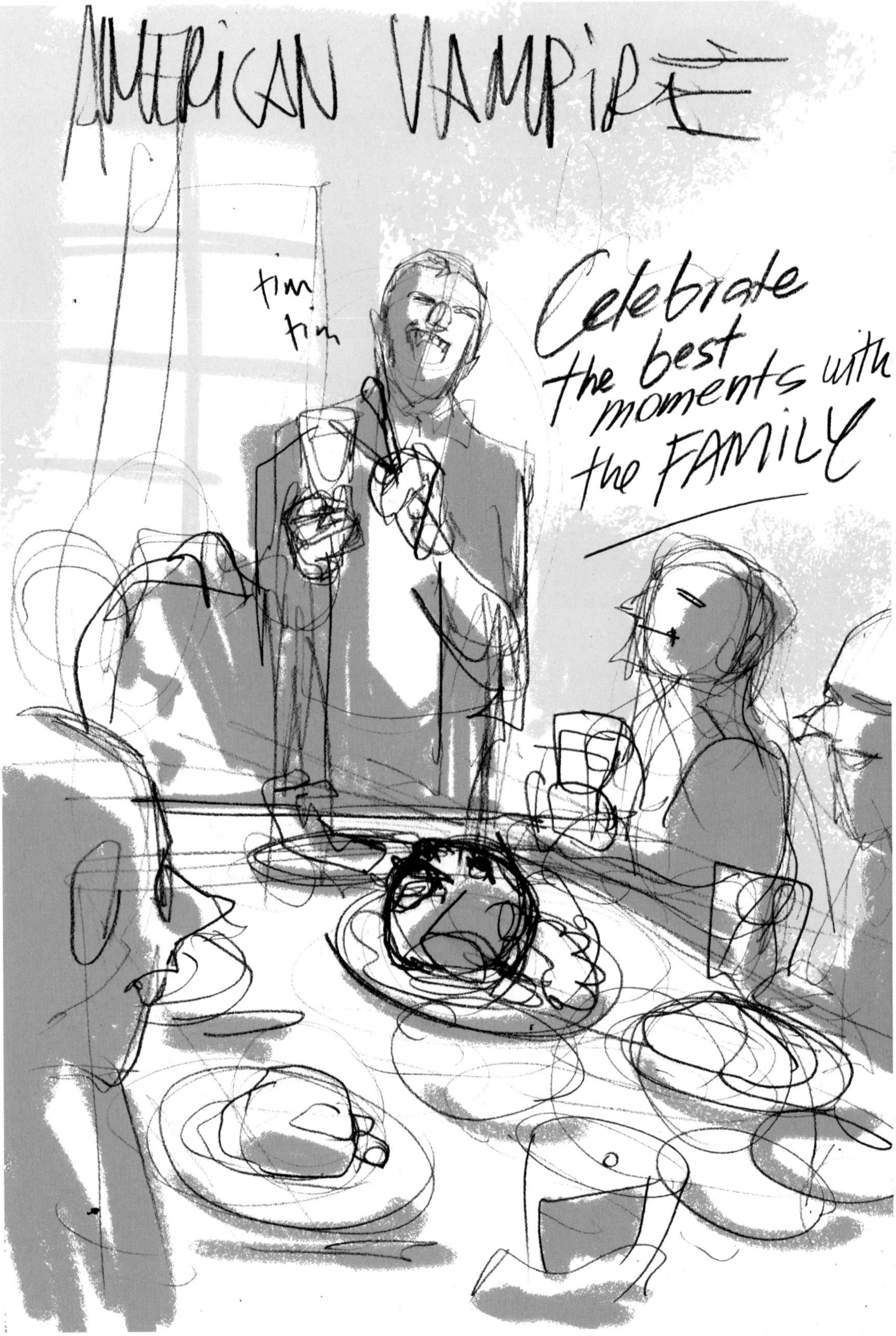
AMERICAN VAMPIRE
tim tim
Celebrate the best moments with the FAMILY

Closer to the final cover, but not perfect yet. The head on the platter evolved into the blood-soaked family in the final, and we trimmed the final line of copy to "Celebrate with family!"

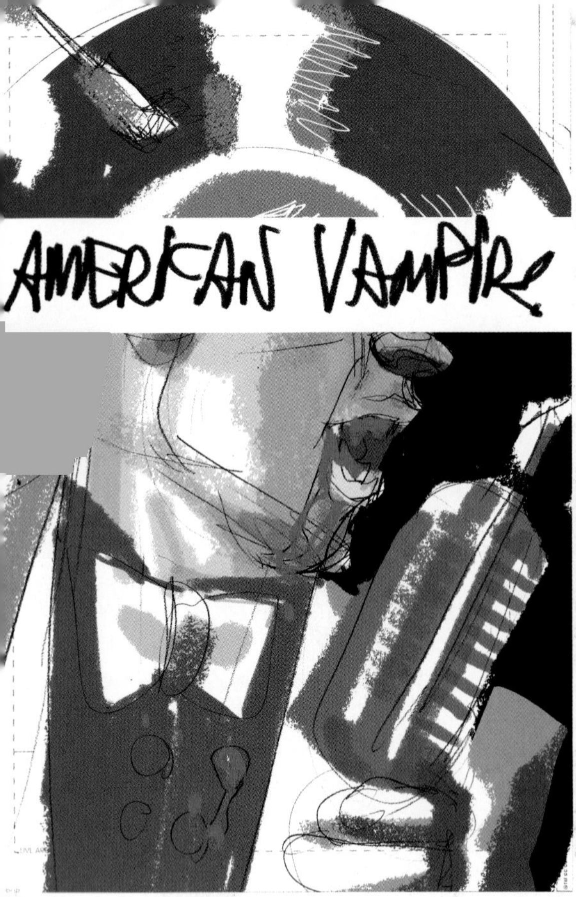
AMERICAN VAMPIRE

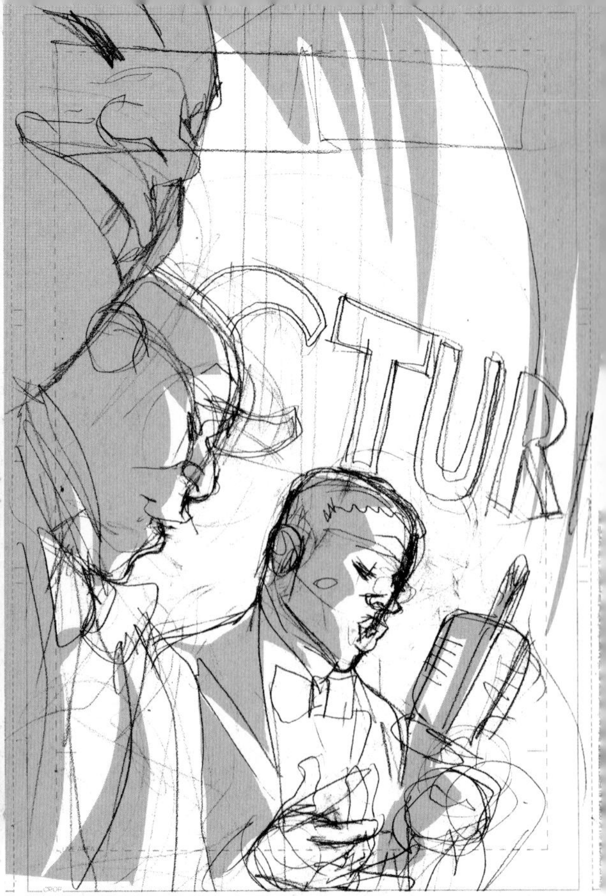

Early cover sketches for "The Nocturnes" story arc.

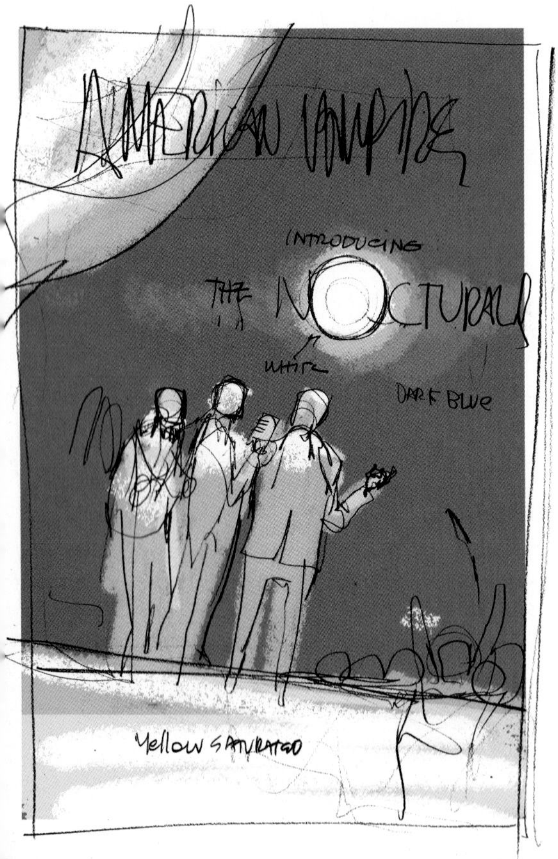
INTRODUCING
THE NOCTURNAL
WHITE
DARK BLUE
Yellow SATURATED

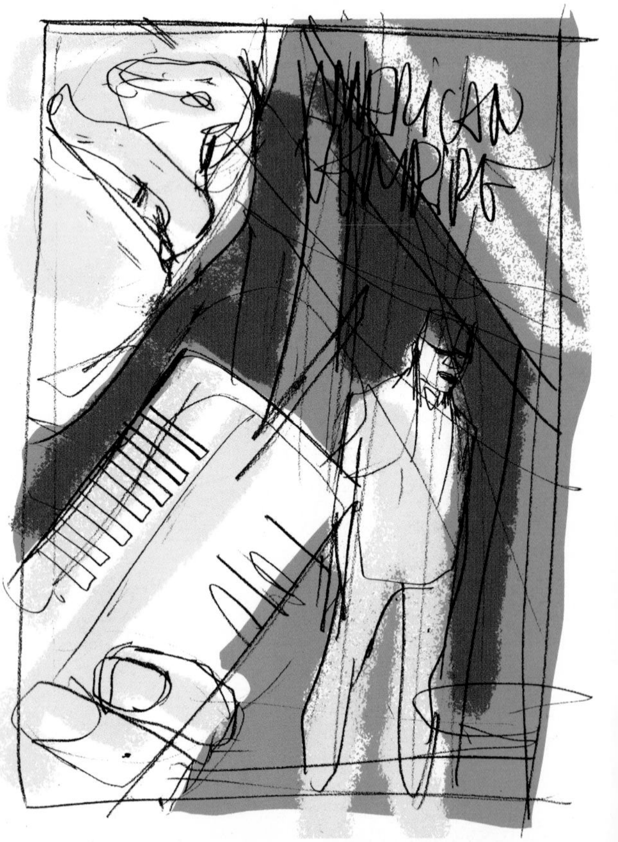
AMERICAN
VAMPIRE

In 2011, Rafael Albuquerque traveled to Avilés, Spain, for a convention where he had the honor and the privilege of meeting one of his heroes — Jordi Bernet.

"…we were talking about a lot of things. Creation process, career, friends, and not only comics but family, travels…

"It took me a while to realize that, in fact, he was not only that icon who taught me how to tell a story with images, but he was also a friend."

Scott Snyder has written comics for both DC and Marvel, including the best-selling series BATMAN and SWAMP THING, and is the author of the story collection *Voodoo Heart* (The Dial Press). He teaches writing at Sarah Lawrence College and Columbia University. He lives on Long Island with his wife Jeanie, and his sons Jack and Emmett. He is a dedicated and un-ironic fan of Elvis Presley.

Rafael Albuquerque was born in Porto Alegre, Brazil and has been working in the American comic book industry since 2005. Best known for his work on the *Savage Brothers*, BLUE BEETLE and SUPERMAN/BATMAN, he has also published the creator-owned graphic novels *Crimeland* (2007) and *Mondo Urbano* (2010).

Jordi Bernet was born in Barcelona, Spain, in 1944, and began illustrating professionally at fifteen. When his father, noted cartoonist Miguel Bernet, passed away at age 38, Jordi stepped in to draw his father's humor strip. In 1982, he took over the series *Torpedo 1936* from artist Alex Toth, following up with memorable titles *Andrax, Sarvan, Kraken, Custer* and *Tex*. In the U.S., he is best known for his work on JONAH HEX for DC Comics.